Birds of Western North America

Birds
of Western
North
America

A PHOTOGRAPHIC GUIDE

PAUL STERRY &
BRIAN E. SMALL

Princeton University Press

Princeton and Oxford

Text copyright © 2009 Paul Sterry

Photographs copyright © 2009 by the individual photographers as detailed in
the picture credits

Published by Princeton University Press
41 William Street, Princeton, New Jersey 08540

Requests for permission to reproduce material from this work should be sent
to Permissions, Princeton University Press

In the United Kingdom: Princeton University Press, 6 Oxford Street,
Woodstock, Oxfordshire OX20 1TW

Maps modified from Birds of North America Online

All Rights Reserved

Sterry, Paul.
    Birds of Western North America : a photographic guide / Paul Sterry and
Brian E. Small. — 1st ed.
        p. cm.
    Includes bibliographical references and index.
    ISBN 978-0-691-13427-7 (cloth : alk. paper)—ISBN 978-0-691-13428-4
(pbk. : alk. paper) 1. Birds—West (U.S.)—Identification. 2. Birds—West
(U.S.)—Pictorial works. I. Small, Brian E., 1959- II. Title.
    QL683.W4S74 2009
    598.0978—dc22   2009001416

British Library Cataloging-in-Publication Data is available

This book has been composed in ITC Officina Sans and Serif

Printed on acid-free paper

nathist.princeton.edu

Photograph page 1: Western Tanager
Photograph previous page: Allen's Hummingbird
Photographs opposite: Western Bluebird (top), Acorn Woodpecker (bottom
left), California Thrasher (bottom middle), Costa's Hummingbird (bottom right)

Edited and designed by D & N Publishing, Baydon, Wiltshire, UK

Printed in China by C&C Offset Printing Co.

10 9 8 7 6 5 4 3 2 1

CONTENTS

INTRODUCTION TO NORTH AMERICAN BIRDS

North America is a vast continent that embraces a huge range of climate types and habitats, from Arctic tundra and vast boreal forests in the far north, through extensive stands of temperate, deciduous forests, open grassland and wetlands galore, and superb and varied coastline, to deserts and subtropical woodland in the south. It is little wonder then that the region supports such an amazing diversity of birdlife: over 600 species are seen regularly in the region, and over 900 have been recorded in total. Man too has left his mark on the North American landscape and the history of land-use has benefited some species but been to the cost of many others.

Given the rewards on offer, it is not surprising that birding is so popular as a hobby. The enthusiastic passion for birds we see today is founded on a heritage of detailed and dedicated ornithological study dating back two centuries or more. *Birds of Western North America* builds on this cumulative wealth of knowledge, providing an instructive tool for the identification of almost any bird you are likely to encounter in our region. Furthermore, the inclusion of pertinent background information helps the reader put each species in ornithological perspective and to understand the factors influencing the status—and, in many cases, the *plight*—of North American birds today.

THE REGION COVERED BY THIS BOOK

The region covered by this book comprises the western half of the whole of mainland North America and the Arctic and sub-Arctic islands within the territories of the U.S. and Canada; it does not include Hawaii. Mexico is not covered specifically in this book; however, reference is made to the Mexican distribution of a few species whose range straddles the border. Reference is also made to Mexico and other Central and South American countries in the context of wintering ranges of certain migratory North American breeding birds. The seas that fringe the North American continent are also included in the geographical extent of this book because of their obvious significance to many of our seabirds, some of which favor offshore

Male Blue Grosbeak singing: vocalization can be extremely important in bird identification.

waters and spend much of their lives out of sight of land. They are just as much a part of our ornithological heritage as terrestrial species and, with the rise in popularity of pelagic birding trips, they are increasingly accessible to birders.

THE CHOICE OF SPECIES

This book is intended to cater for the needs of the keen birder—the sort of person whose enthusiasm is built on several years of experience—while not neglecting the needs of the beginner. All our resident species are included here, as well as seasonal visitors to the region—those that are with us in spring and summer, as well as birds that visit us during the winter months. In addition, species that occur regularly as passage migrants—birds that pass through on migration in spring and fall (mainly seabirds)—are also included. As a reflection of their importance to birding in our region, the bulk of the book is devoted to all these common, or relatively frequently occurring, species.

Accompanying the rise in popularity of birding in general, there has been an increased interest in, and knowledge of, vagrants to the region and of geographically localized rarities. To cater to this, a generous selection of out of the ordinary species is included in the book; these are featured at the back, partly as a reflection of their lesser importance in the overall scheme of things, but also to reduce the likelihood of optimistic misidentification of the more common species.

HOW TO USE THIS BOOK

This book has been designed so that the text and photographs for each species are on facing pages. A system of labeling states the identity and, if appropriate, the plumage and sex, of each photograph. The text has been written to complement the information conveyed by the photographs.

By and large, the order in which the species appear in the main section of the book roughly follows the standard systematic classification of birds, which is adopted by most contemporary field guides. However, in a few instances the standard running order has been tinkered with to allow, for example, confusingly similar species to appear on the same page, and so that, where possible, members of the same group of birds can appear side-by-side on the same page.

SPECIES DESCRIPTIONS

At the start of each species description the most commonly used and current American name is given. This is followed by the scientific name of the bird in question, which comprises the species' genus name first, followed by its specific name. In a few instances, reference is made, either in the species heading or the main body of the text, to a further subdivision—subspecies—where this is pertinent. There then follows some measure of the species' size. In most instances, the length ("L" in inches) is given, but for birds that are more commonly seen in flight, such as birds of prey, wingspan ("W" in inches) is given instead.

The text has been written in as concise a manner as possible. To avoid potential ambiguities in species descriptions, for example with regards to which age or sex is being described, the plumage in question appears in bold at the start of the relevant passage of text.

VOICE

Information is then given about the voice of the bird; in most cases this involves a phonetic description of the call and, with the majority of songbirds, the song itself is also similarly transcribed.

STATUS AND HABITAT

Details about the status of each species in the region is then given. This includes an indication of whether it is common or otherwise, and whether it is a year-round resident, or a seasonal visitor or passage migrant. A rough indication of population numbers is given in a few instances. Most birds are extremely habitat-specific and so information is provided about their preferences. Not only does this help narrow down the field for observers trying to identify a mystery bird, but it can also be used as a pointer if you want to actively seek out a particular species.

OBSERVATION TIPS

For each species, information is provided that will help birders pinpoint where to see the bird in question, or at least improve the chances of discovery or observation. In some cases, tips are provided that will help distinguish the species from any superficially similar relatives.

MAPS

The maps provide invaluable information about the distribution and occurrence of each species in the region. Three colors have been employed to assist the reader in getting the maximum information from the maps: ■ represents the range where a species is present year-round; ■ represents the range where a species is present only in summer, typically its breeding season; ■ represents the range where a species is present only in winter. The maps represent the current ranges of birds in the region in general terms. Please bear in mind that, given the size of the maps, small and isolated populations will not necessarily be featured. Furthermore, the ranges of some species changes from year to year; this is particularly true of certain winter visitors and passage migrants.

PHOTOGRAPHS

Great care has gone into the selection of photographs for this book and in many cases the images have been taken specifically for this project. Preference has been given to photographs that serve both to illustrate key identification features and to emphasize the beauty of the bird in question. Wherever possible, the rigid constraints of most previous photographic guides to birds have been avoided and contemporary approaches to design have been employed.

For each species, photographic emphasis has been given to the plumage, or plumages, most likely to be encountered in the region. However, by using inset photographs, on both the right-hand and left-hand pages, as comprehensive a range of additional plumages and poses as possible has been included.

TOPOGRAPHY

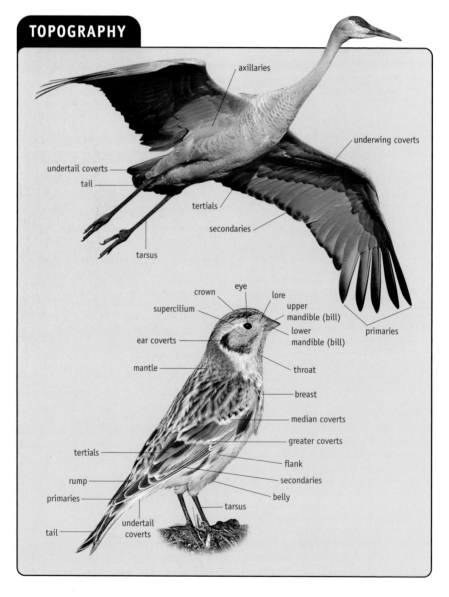

GLOSSARY

Axillaries Feathers on the part of the underwing that corresponds roughly to what we might call the "armpit."

Carpal The part of the wing that corresponds to the "wrist"; this area of feathering is contrastingly dark in several raptor species.

Cere Bare skin at the base of the bill and around the nostrils.

Eclipse The femalelike plumage acquired by many male ducks during their summer molt.

Eyestripe A stripe through the eye, from the base of the bill to the ear coverts.

1st-fall A bird in its first fall, whose plumage may be juvenile or 1st-winter, depending on when molt occurs.

1st-winter The plumage acquired after a bird's juvenile feathers have been molted.

Flight feathers The long feathers (primaries, secondaries, and tertials) on the tip and trailing half of the wing.

Immature A young bird whose plumage is not adult. Depending on the species, this stage may last months or years.

Juvenile A newly fledged bird in its first set of feathers.

Length The distance from the tip of the bill to the tip of the center of the tail.

Leucistic Atypically pale appearance of the plumage, or parts of the plumage, due to a lack of feather pigmentation.

Lore Area of feathering between the eye and the base of the upper mandible.

Malar stripe Narrow stripe of feathers that borders the throat.

Mantle Area of feathers on the upper back.

Molt The process of feather replacement in the cycle of plumage renewal.

Mustachial stripe A line of feathers running from the base of the lower mandible to the cheeks.

Orbital ring Ring of bare skin surrounding the eye.

Pelagic Favoring the open sea.

Primaries The outermost flight feathers.

Secondaries The middle flight feathers.

Species (sp.) A group of genetically similar individuals, members of which can reproduce with one another and produce viable offspring; fertile offspring cannot be produced when members of two separate species interbreed.

Speculum A glossy patch seen on the upper secondaries of some duck species.

Submustachial stripe The line of feathers (typically contrastingly pale) between the malar and mustachial stripes.

Subspecies (ssp.) A population of individuals of a given species that possess distinct plumage differences from other populations; these are often geographically separated.

Supercilium A typically pale stripe of feathers that runs much of the length of the head above the eye.

Tarsus What most people refer to as a bird's "leg," although strictly speaking it is anatomically part of the foot.

Tertials The innermost flight feathers

Tibia The visible upper part of a bird's leg.

Vagrant A bird that appears accidentally outside the species' typical range, be that breeding, nonbreeding, or migration.

Wing bar A striking bar on the wings (typically either white or dark), formed by pale or dark margins to the wing covert feathers.

Wing coverts The feathers that cloak the leading half (as seen in flight) of both surfaces of the wings.

Wingspan The distance from one wingtip to the other.

PLUMAGE

Birds are unique in many respects, but perhaps their most visible characteristic is the layer of feathers that covers their bodies. These serve a variety of functions in the day-to-day lives of birds and feathers on different parts of the body have evolved for a range of purposes. Those that cover the bulk of the body provide superb insulation against the cold and, to varying degrees, waterproofing too. And of course there are the feathers on the wing that enable flight in all its forms to take place. From the birder's point of view, feathers are there to be marveled at, but, when interpreted correctly, they can also provide a wealth of information about the bird in question. The sex of an individual can often be told at a glance and, in addition, its age and whether or not it is in breeding or nonbreeding plumage can also be discerned in many cases. Such information is interesting in its own right, but more importantly it offers clues to birdwatchers with regards to identification.

From the bird's point of view, the colors and plumage patterns are fundamentally important: during the breeding season, social responses are often dictated by appearance while at the other extreme, for birds with camouflaged plumage, the ability to blend in with the surroundings can mean the difference between life and death.

Feathers do not grow continually like mammalian hair, and once they are fully formed they are essentially dead. As a result of the wear and tear of everyday life, the feathers become abraded and over a period of time the patterns and colors fade. And it is not just a bird's appearance that can change due to wear: flight feathers can become worn and damaged to the point that the bird's ability to fly is impaired. To combat this gradual deterioration, birds molt and replace their feathers on a regular basis.

In most cases, molting occurs at specific times of the year and takes place over a comparatively brief space of time. For most birds, the main molt occurs in late summer, after the breeding season has finished; many migratory birds that breed in the region molt before they embark on their journeys in fall. Some birds, notably many passerines, have very distinct breeding and nonbreeding (or summer and winter) plumages. For some, the transformation is achieved by having a second, partial molt in the spring, but with certain groups, such as buntings and finches, comparatively dowdy plumage seen in fall and winter gives way to the bright colors of spring and early summer by abrasion of the pale tips to feathers on many parts of the body.

The ability to fly is a function that all North American birds need to retain at all costs, and so the replacement of flight feathers presents a challenge that is addressed in a variety ways by different groups of birds. Waterfowl, for example, molt all their flight feathers in one go, typically in summer. Being completely flightless for a month or more makes them vulnerable and most species undertake the process in the comparatively safe havens of inaccessible marshes or the open sea. Raptors on the other hand, which spend a far greater proportion of the lives in the air, replace their flight feathers one by one, over an extended period. As a result, they retain the ability to fly, regardless of the time of year.

Male (*top*) and female (*above*) Vermilion Flycatchers are visibly different from each other. Not all North American species show such a striking difference between the sexes.

HABITATS FOR BIRDS

A combination of geology, geography, and historical land-use has conspired to create a wealth of different habitats in North America. Although a few bird species are rather catholic in their choice of habitat, birders soon come to realize that the majority have much more specific needs. Their behavior, feeding and nesting requirements, and indeed structure, have evolved to suit special niches in particular habitats. However, although a species may be habitat-specific, it does not follow that it will be found in all examples of this habitat throughout the region. Climatic factors can have a profound effect on a species' range, influencing, for example, the ability of a bird to feed, or more profoundly, to survive extreme weather.

For some birders, studying the distinctions between our different habitats may seem like a rather esoteric pursuit, and one that lacks relevance to their everyday activities. However, it really is worth spending time familiarizing yourself with their basic characters and differences for more practical reasons. By developing an understanding of the habitat in which a bird lives, it helps us to appreciate more fully the life of the bird in question in the context of the environment as a whole. From a more practical point of view, an awareness of a given species' preferred habitat means you will save yourself a lot of time and effort when it comes to pinning down localized species. Habitat preferences are also a useful clue to the identity of many birds. The following pages detail our most characteristic and distinctive habitats.

THE COAST

North America's coastline is varied and stunningly beautiful in places. Although development mars some stretches of shoreline, much remains unspoiled and harbors some of our most charismatic birds. The rich intertidal zone, bathed twice daily by an advancing and retreating tide, and the offshore waters too, are fundamental to the diversity and abundance of birdlife around our coasts. Our coastline is extremely varied, but in all its forms, whether dramatic cliffs or expansive estuaries and salt marshes, it harbors a wonderful selection of birds.

Cliffs

For breathtaking scenery and a sense of untamed nature, coastal cliffs offer unrivaled opportunities for the birder. Man has had minimal impact on these areas and during the spring and summer months a few select locations in the northern parts of the continent are thronged with breeding seabirds. Inaccessible but stable ledges support colonies of murres and Kittiwakes and Tufted Puffins. Gulls of various species are another common feature of seabird cliffs.

TOP: **St Paul Island, Pribilofs;** ABOVE: **Tufted Puffin**

Rocky Shores

For the keen student of marine life, the intertidal zone on a rocky shore is an unbelievably rewarding place to visit. However, despite the fact that rock pools and gullies team with life, the variety of birdlife is comparatively limited. During spring and summer, you can expect to find Black Oystercatchers nesting above the high-tide line. Outside the breeding season, Black Turnstones and Surfbirds are widespread.

Sandy Shores and Dunes

Beloved of people on vacation, sandy shores are also of interest to the birder. Beneath the surface of the sand lives an abundance of marine worms, crustaceans, and mollusks whose presence would go largely undetected were it not for the feeding activities of birds and the profusion of dead shells found along the strandline.

Outside the breeding season, look for Sanderlings as they follow the line of breaking waves in search of small invertebrates; gulls of various species are seldom far away. Offshore, fish and crustaceans provide a rich supply of food for those bird species that are sufficiently well adapted to catch them. In summer, terns can be seen plunge-diving here while during the winter months grebes, loons, and sea ducks exploit this resource. On the landward side of the beach, colonizing plants establish stable dune systems where birds such as plovers and terns can nest. Sadly, however, human disturbance effectively excludes these species from many suitable areas.

ABOVE: **Surfbird**; BELOW: **Sanderling**

Estuaries and Salt Marshes

To the unenlightened eye, an estuary may seem like a vast expanse of mudflats, studded with a mosaic of bedraggled-looking vegetation and very little else. For the birder, however, this is one of the most exhilarating of all habitats to visit. Incredible numbers of marine worms and tiny mollusks thrive in the oozing mud, their numbers supported by the vast amount of organic matter deposited when river meets sea. Benefiting from all this biological richness are the shorebirds and waterfowl that feed on our estuaries in huge numbers from fall to spring.

Shorebirds are perhaps the most characteristic group to exploit this resource, each species having a bill length and feeding strategy adapted to suit a particular food source; this helps avoid undue competition between different species. Dunlins, for example, tend to feed on small surface-living animals while godwits use their long bills to probe deep for more substantial prey. Waterfowl too occur in huge numbers on many estuaries, feeding either on minute animals filtered from the mud or on plant material, depending on the species involved. Many or our larger estuaries are globally important refuges for many bird species.

Dunlin

FRESHWATER

For the birder, freshwater habitats have the same magnetic appeal as do coastal habitats. North America has a wealth of examples, from small ponds and streams to large lakes and river systems; few people have to travel far to visit one or more of these habitats.

Rivers and Streams

Flowing water has a charm all of its own and a trip to a river or stream will invariably yield sightings of interesting birds. If the margins are cloaked with vegetation, a rich variety of invertebrate life will be found there, matched, beneath the surface of the water (assuming it is clean and unpolluted), by a wealth of invertebrate and fish life, sheltering

American Dipper

among the drifts of submerged aquatic plants. In turn, this abundance of freshwater life supports a splendid array of birds, some species of which are found nowhere else.

Birdlife abounds on many rivers and streams, larger ones supporting populations of ducks and egrets in spring and summer. Martins and swallows feed overhead on flying insects in the summer months while Spotted Sandpipers forage along the margins of boulder-strewn watercourses during the breeding season. American Dippers are present year-round.

Lakes and Ponds

Bodies of standing water typically harbor a strikingly different range of plants and animals from those found in flowing water. Many seemingly natural sites are man-made, or at least man-influenced, but with maturity they can be surprisingly rich. By midsummer a rich growth of aquatic plants dominates many of our smaller ponds as well as the margins of lakes. Where they are left to their own devices, the margins are soon encroached by stands of emergent plants, and species such as the Common Reed sometimes form extensive beds around larger lakes. Evidence of the abundance of invertebrate life beneath the surface is provided by the emergence, from aquatic immature stages, of adult dragonflies and caddis flies.

American Coots and Moorhens are common on lowland lakes and ponds. If the water body in question is large enough to support a significant fish population and is relatively undisturbed then loons and grebes may nest in the summer months. In fall and winter, areas of open water become refuges for waterfowl.

ABOVE: **A classic freshwater pond fringed with emergent vegetation; INSET: American Coot**

Marshes and Bogs

The encroachment of vegetation into areas of open water leads to the creation of marshes. The term "marsh" is a rather imprecise one in ecological terms and covers wetlands found on a range of soil types. But on particularly acid soils the wetlands that form are called "bogs" and cotton grasses and *Sphagnum* mosses are typical plants. Nesting shorebirds and ducks favor these habitats during the breeding season, as do rails and specialized sparrow and wood-warbler species.

WOODS AND FORESTS

The vast tracts of virgin forest that once cloaked large areas of western North America prior to the arrival of European settlers are long since gone, felled and cleared over the centuries. However, regrowth has ensured that huge areas of wooded habitat can be found today, and birders will find they support a wealth of birdlife.

Sora

Broadleaved Forests

Woodlands of broadleaved trees are found throughout most of the region. As their name suggests, deciduous trees shed their leaves in winter and grow a new set the following spring. The seasonality seen in deciduous woodland is among the most marked and easily observed of any habitat in the region and it is reflected in the seasonal occurrence and abundance in the birdlife harbored there. Evergreen broadleaved trees are also a feature of western North American woodlands, many of them showing adaptations to seasonal drought or temperature extremes. Almost all woodland in the region has been, and still is, influenced in some way by man.

Most of our broadleaved woodlands are home to thriving populations of birds, with both residents and summer visitors breeding there. Most of our migrant visitors include insects and other invertebrates in their diet and the fact that this resource is in short supply in winter is the main reason why they are only with us during the summer months. Many residents also include insects in their diet

ABOVE: Black-headed Grosbeak;
LEFT: Pacific temperate rainforest

during the breeding season, but turn to seeds and nuts during the winter months; a few specialized birds manage to find enough invertebrates to keep them going throughout the year. Residents include species of woodpecker and chickadee while many species of flycatcher, vireo, and wood-warbler are well represented only during the summer months.

Coniferous Forests

Like evergreen broadleaved trees, conifers are, with the exception of a few species, also evergreen, and keep their leaves throughout the year. Instead of having broad, often rounded leaves, they have narrow ones, called needles. Their flowers and seeds are borne in structures known as cones, and the shape of the trees themselves is often conical in outline. Crossbills and certain nuthatch species are characteristic of mature conifer forests and several wood-warbler species are also restricted to conifers, and often associated with specific tree species. Conifer forests are often associated with upland areas in temperate regions of North America. But they are at their most extensive across the sub-Arctic where they are major components of the boreal forests (taiga) that cloak these latitudes.

PRAIRIES, GRASSLAND, FARMLAND, AND SCRUB

Little remains of the original prairies—North America's natural grasslands, dominated by wildflowers and native grasses—that once covered much of the interior. And gone with it are many populations of bird species that depend exclusively on this habitat. Fortunately, however, a few pockets of prairies still remain, typically protected to varying degrees by law, and these areas are where birders should visit in search of grouse and sparrow species that favor them exclusively. Much of the grassland that we see today is secondary habitat, colonizing and encouraged in historical terms in the wake of forest clearance, or planted subsequently. Despite its man-made or man-influenced origins, grassland can still be good for birds. Arable farmland may fall loosely under the category of grassland—crop species such as wheat, barley, and oats are grasses after all—but their interest to the birder tends to be minimal in many areas.

Formerly, populations of insects and other invertebrates would have fed hungry broods in spring and summer while weed seeds and spilt grain would have supported huge flocks of buntings and finches in fall and winter. Nowadays, however, the use of ever-more efficient insecticides and molluscicides ensures that there are precious few invertebrates for birds to feed on during the summer months. Modern herbicides

TOP: **Boreal 'Taiga' forest**; ABOVE: **Blackpoll Warbler**

White-crowned Sparrow, typical of secondary scrub habitat

ABOVE: **Prairie grassland, a wonderful habitat for birds**
LEFT: **Lesser Prairie-Chicken, a classic species of unspoiled prairies, whose decline reflects the plight of its favored habitat**
BELOW LEFT: **Western Meadowlark, a species that favors a range of grassland habitats**

ensure that "weeds" are kept to a minimum and decades of chemical use has resulted in the soil's seed bank being depleted dramatically. And the arable crops themselves are harvested extremely efficiently these days, with little left to waste.

Scrub is a transition habitat where shrubby plants, many of them associated with woodland margins, take over neglected areas of farmland and grassland. The habitat is often ignored in ecological terms but is extremely important for many birds, insects providing food in the summer months and berries and fruits in fall. Good, thick cover of impenetrable scrub provides excellent cover for nesting songbirds.

DESERTS

In North America, desert habitats are a specialty of the southwest, and in terms of scenery and wildlife they are truly amazing. A desert habitat is typically defined as an area that receives less than 10 inches of rain per year. The best examples are found in states such as California, Arizona, and New Mexico, and the finest are dominated by statuesque and impressive cacti.

BELOW: Stately cacti are iconic features of southwestern deserts.
INSET: Verdin

Mountain Chickadee

UPLANDS

The mountain ranges of western North America, in particular the Rockies, are truly impressive, offering rugged appeal on the grand scale to lovers of the great outdoors, and a wealth of birding opportunities. The lower slopes are typically forested and harbor specialized species of wood-warbler, woodpeckers, and many others. Many peaks extend well above the treeline, cloaked in dwarf, tundralike vegetation in places but barren and prone to snow cover at the highest altitudes. Soaring overhead, birds of prey such as Golden Eagles take advantage of the updrafts. The range of habitats found on many mountain slopes share similarities with more northerly habitats found at lower elevations—true Arctic tundra and boreal taiga forest in particular. Unsurprisingly, many species whose main distribution is across northern and Arctic regions of North America, extend their ranges south along mountain ranges.

TUNDRA

Northern latitudes, within the Arctic circle, are too hostile in environmental terms for trees to grow and the vegetation typically comprises low-growing shrubs, mosses, and lichens. Collectively this habitat is referred to as "tundra," and in many areas the ground itself is frozen solid for much of the year. Snow blankets the landscape in winter and, unsurprisingly, only a small number of extremely hardy, resident species are found at this time of year. But come the spring and the landscape is transformed. Insect life abounds and in turn large numbers of migratory waders and waterfowl make an appearance, nesting and feeding their young on this brief seasonal bounty.

ABOVE: **Tundra**; RIGHT: **Snow Bunting**

THE URBAN ENVIRONMENT

For many North Americans, who live in towns and cities, the urban environment is the one with which they are most familiar. It is encountered on a day-to-day basis with trips to the countryside relegated to weekend visits or vacation excursions. It would be a mistake, however, to assume that the urban environment is without its wildlife interest. Many of our birds are extremely adaptable and have

successfully colonized this seemingly unpromising habitat. In part this is because many features associated with our buildings and gardens mimic special niches in natural habitats. Mature gardens with hedgerows and shrubs, for example, recall woodland margins while buildings resemble man-made cliffs with their roof spaces doubling as artificial caves.

Visit any mature city park and you will find an array of birds more usually associated with woodland or open country. These include American Robins, Blue Jays, and even woodpeckers and chickadees in particularly leafy suburbs; European Starlings are less welcome urban residents in many areas, partly because of their sheer numbers but also for the impact they have on native bird species. A number of these park dwellers also find town gardens much to their liking—the more informal the garden the more species it is likely to attract. As a reflection of the comparatively healthy numbers of songbirds in urban and suburban districts, the Sharp-shinned Hawk population is also thriving in many towns.

RIGHT: **Bohemian Waxwings visit parks and gardens in winter to feed on berries.**
BELOW: **A typical suburban garden that is good for birds**

IDENTIFYING BIRDS

Some birds are so characteristic in appearance that, even if you have never seen one before, you will have no difficulty in identifying it correctly. In this respect, think of species like the Atlantic Puffin or Northern Cardinal. However, what about a nondescript shorebird in winter plumage, or a silent wood-warbler, or a juvenile sparrow? How should you go about making a correct identification in these cases, where plenty of alternative choices are available?

The first thing you should do is to make notes at the time of your observation; it is amazing what tricks the memory can play if you write things down later. Then you can refer to this book at your leisure. All the key information you need for a correct identification is contained within the species descriptions in *Birds of Western North America*.

Firstly, try to gauge the size of the bird in question, bearing in mind that, at a distance, absolute size is always difficult to determine: better to try and assess the size *relative* to a nearby species whose identity is known with certainty. Next, look at the shape of the bird and its proportions. For example does it have rounded or pointed wings in flight? Are its legs long and shorebird-like? What shape is the bill, and is the tail long or short?

If time permits, try to study and describe accurately the colors and patterns on the body of the bird. Bear in mind though that appearances can be deceptive: the angle of the light, for example, can have a profound influence on a bird's appearance and it is worth remembering that variations in plumage do occur, even in birds of the same species, age, and sex. You may only get a frustratingly brief, or a partial, view of a bird and consequently it can be difficult to assess all the potential characters that might be needed for identification. However, with each group of birds, there tends to one part of the body where sufficient key identification features are present to enable distinction between similar species. It might be the pattern of stripes on the head of a sparrow, for example, the presence or absence of wing bars on a warbler, or the shape and extent of white on the rump of a flying shore-bird. If you can determine which are the key areas to concentrate on for a particular bird (assuming you see it well enough to decide, for example, that it is a sparrow and not a finch), you will improve greatly your chances of making a correct identification.

Most birds found in North America are extremely habitat-specific and consequently *where* you see a mystery bird can have a profound bearing on your ability to identify it. The same is true for resident species, for migrants, and displaced vagrants. Many birds are vocal enough for their calls and songs to be used accurately in identification. Learning them with any degree of confidence is a matter of experience, but you can speed up the process by going out with an expert or listening to recordings.

A range of different features, including plumage, call, and time of year, needed to be considered before coming to the conclusion that this bird was a winter adult Short-billed Dowitcher.

MIGRATION AND MOVEMENTS

In common with other parts of the temperate Northern Hemisphere, much of North America experiences a climate that changes throughout the year. Broadly speaking, we can recognize four fairly distinct seasons—spring, summer, fall, and winter—and these have a profound influence on almost all of our birds. The seasonal responses by birds can be subtle: the diet of some species varies according to season, and hardy mountain species may be forced to descend to lower altitudes in response to bad weather. Other birds make more widespread movements, for example, birds that disperse outside the breeding season and wander nomadically in search of food within the same general area overall. Others may switch habitat altogether between the breeding and nonbreeding seasons, for example, many shorebirds, which nest on Arctic tundra but spend the rest of their lives on the coast.

In migration terms, the most conspicuous exponents of this survival strategy are those species that visit us during the summer months to breed. Many of our most familiar songbirds fall into this category and the majority of wood-warbler species, for example, are only with us for a few brief months in spring and early summer. As a general rule, summer migrant visitors that breed in our region head south in fall, many wintering in Central and South America.

Although many small birds migrate at night, and hence their migration cannot actually be witnessed, these birds have to stop off to feed during the daytime. Many concentrate along the coast—either the point of departure or the first point of arrival, depending on the direction of migration—especially if bad weather halts their progress; nocturnal migrants favor clear nights and are presumed to use the stars as navigation aids. Migration can also add a bit of spice to the life of a birder because, being influenced by the weather and hence somewhat unpredictable, you never really know what might turn up where at migration times.

RIGHT: **Black-throated Green Warblers, like many of our songbirds, are summer visitors that visit North America to breed; this species spends the winter in Central America.**
BELOW: **An evocative sight, V-formations of Snow Geese are among the most visible signs of bird migration in western North America.**

Anatidae

TUNDRA SWAN *Cygnus columbianus* L 50–60 in

A large, rather dumpy-bodied wetland bird. The proportionately long neck, short legs, and all-white adult plumage make identification relatively easy although confusion of adult birds with Trumpeter Swan is possible; juveniles are seldom seen away from company of adults. Sexes are similar. Tundra Swans feed on vegetation; terrestrial plants are "grazed" while aquatic plants are collected by submerging the long neck, and sometimes upending the body too. In flight, head and neck are held outstretched. **ADULT** Has essentially pure white plumage, although this can appear rather dirty after feeding in murky or oxide-rich waters. Legs are dark; bill is mainly dark, but note small yellow teardrop-shaped spot at base (absent in many individuals). Good views reveal bill to have a slightly concave upper profile (cf. Trumpeter Swan). **JUVENILE** Has grayish (not gleaming) white plumage, which gets whiter as winter progresses. Legs are dark and bill is dull pink, darkening with age. **VOICE** Utters a honking bark *kow-Hooo*. **STATUS AND HABITAT** Nests beside tundra lakes and pools. Resting migrants usually stop off on rivers and lakes. Winters on coastal marshes and grassland, usually in vicinity of water (favored for roosting); up to 100,000 may winter in western North America. **OBSERVATION TIPS** Pairs are typically solitary and widely dispersed while nesting and hence difficult to locate. However, birds are gregarious outside breeding season and seen in sizeable flocks in winter; this is the best time of year to look for the species. Good numbers occur in California's Central Valley. **COMMENT** Represented by ssp. *columbianus* in North America; Eurasian ssp. *bewickii* (Bewick's Swan) turns up occasionally with Tundra Swan flocks in winter; basal third of its bill is yellow.

ADULT

ssp. *bewickii*

TRUMPETER SWAN *Cygnus buccinator* L 60–70 in

Large and impressive swan; the largest of its kind in the region and a conservation icon. Appreciably bigger than Tundra Swan when seen side-by-side. Note the plump body, relatively short legs, and extremely long neck. The bill is triangular in outline and looks disproportionately large for the size of the head (looks more in proportion in Tundra Swan). The sexes are similar. Grazes on grassland, and also feeds on aquatic plants uprooted by submerging long neck. In flight, head and neck are held outstretched. **ADULT** Has essentially pure white plumage although feathers on neck and belly are sometimes stained with mud, oxides, and algae. Legs are dark and bill is mainly dark, although close inspection reveals base of lower mandible to be pale. Upper surface of bill is straight (cf. Tundra Swan) and follows slope of forehead. **JUVENILE** Has mucky gunmetal grey plumage. Bill is dirty pink. **VOICE** Utters a loud, nasal trumpeting *oh-HO*. **STATUS AND HABITAT** Nests beside forested lakes. Winters on coastal marshes and interior farmland where birds roost on freshwater lakes. **OBSERVATION TIPS** Easiest to observe in winter, with sightings at Yellowstone (the species also breeds in small numbers in the vicinity) almost guaranteed. **COMMENT** Once widespread and common, the Trumpeter Swan had been driven to the verge of extinction by the start of the 20th century due to hunting and habitat destruction. Numbers are recovering (several thousand now live in the wild), but, sadly, poisoning by lead shot (ingested when the birds feed) still kills significant numbers each year.

ADULT

JUVENILE

TUNDRA SWAN

ADULT

ADULT

TRUMPETER SWAN

JUVENILE

Anatidae

GREATER WHITE-FRONTED GOOSE
Anser albifrons L 28–30 in

Bulky goose. Adult has diagnostic white "blaze" on forehead. Juvenile lacks this feature and could be confused with feral Graylag Goose (*see* p.396). Several subspecies are recognized, but plumage variability often makes precise identification difficult. Broadly speaking, there are two extremes: pale tundra-breeding forms and darker taiga-breeding birds; they usually occur in separate populations in winter. So-called "Tule Goose" is a particularly dark taiga form. Sexes are similar. All White-fronts fly in V-formation on migration and in winter. Feed by grazing vegetation, particularly grasses in winter. **ADULT** Has gray-brown plumage, palest in tundra birds and darkest in taiga birds. All birds show variable black barring on underparts, and white vent, which extends as white line to flanks. Legs are orange and bill is pinkish orange. White on forehead is more extensive in tundra birds than taiga ones. In flight, all birds show white on upper tail. **JUVENILE** Similar to adult, but lacks white on forehead and dark markings on underparts. **VOICE** Utters musical barking calls, especially in flight. **STATUS AND HABITAT** Locally common. Breeds on tundra and taiga. Winters mainly on farmland and freshwater marshes. **OBSERVATION TIPS** Easiest to observe in winter: California's Central Valley and Texas wetlands are hotspots.

SNOW GOOSE *Chen caerulescens* L 26–33 in

Distinctive Arctic tundra goose. Confusingly, occurs in two distinct light and dark (blue) color morphs; blue morph was formerly considered a separate species, "Blue Goose." Both morphs are distinctive and confusion is only really possible with appreciably smaller Ross's Goose, or white, domesticated form of Graylag Goose (*see* p.396). Sexes are similar. Feeds by grazing vegetation. Long-distance flights usually undertaken in V-

ADULT WHITE MORPH

formation. **ADULT WHITE MORPH** Has mainly white plumage, with black primaries. Bill and legs are pink. **JUVENILE WHITE MORPH** Has whitish plumage, except for buff-brown back and dark primaries. Bill and legs are dark. **ADULT BLUE MORPH** Has mainly dark gray-brown plumage, except for white head and neck, white vent, and pale wing coverts. Bill and legs are pink. **JUVENILE BLUE MORPH** Dark buffy brown, except for white vent. Bill and legs are dark. **VOICE** utters a barking, honking *whook*. **STATUS AND HABITAT** Locally abundant. Nests on tundra and winters on farmland and wetlands. **OBSERVATION TIPS** Easiest to observe at regular wintering grounds, particularly Bosque del Apache, New Mexico.

ADULT WHITE MORPH

ROSS'S GOOSE
Chen rossii L 22–24 in

Small Arctic goose. Superficially similar to Snow Goose with which it is often observed, but appreciably smaller, with a more dainty bill. Occurs in two color forms: white morph is by far the commoner; blue morph is rare. Sexes are similar. Feeds by grazing vegetation. In flight, wingbeats are noticeably more rapid than in other, larger geese. **ADULT WHITE MORPH** Has white plumage, except for black primaries. Bill and legs are pink. **JUVENILE WHITE MORPH** Similar to adult, but with slightly dirty-looking plumage. **ADULT BLUE MORPH** Mainly dark blue-gray, except for white on face, underparts, and vent. Bill and legs are pink. **JUVENILE BLUE MORPH** Similar to adult. **VOICE** Utters a soft, squeaking *keek-keek*. **STATUS AND HABITAT** Locally common. Nests on tundra and winters on farmland and wetlands. **OBSERVATION TIPS** Good numbers winter in California's Central Valley.

ADULT BLUE MORPH

GREATER WHITE-FRONTED GOOSE

ADULT

ADULT

ADULT BLUE MORPH

ADULT WHITE MORPH

SNOW GOOSE

JUVENILE WHITE MORPH

ADULT WHITE MORPH

ROSS'S GOOSE

ADULT BLUE MORPH

Anatidae

CACKLING GOOSE *Branta hutchinsii* L 25–27 in

Recent addition to North American list—split from Canada Goose species complex. Four subspecies are recognized; plumages are all broadly comparable to Canada Goose. However, all subspecies of Cackling are small, compact birds with almost ducklike proportions; note proportionately short neck and dainty bill. Cackling also shows proportionately longer, more pointed wings in flight. Sexes are similar. Feeds by grazing vegetation. **ADULT** Has black head and neck, white cheek, and white vent. Body plumage varies according to subspecies: gray-brown in *hutchinsii* (Richardson's) and *leucoparenia* (Aleutian), and dark reddish brown in *taverneri*. **JUVENILE** Similar to adult. **VOICE** Honking *hronk*, higher pitched than Canada. **STATUS AND HABITAT** Locally common. Nests on tundra, winters on marshes and farmland. **OBSERVATION TIPS** Visit California's Central Valley in winter.

CANADA GOOSE *Branta canadensis* L 36–46 in

North America's most familiar goose. Several subspecies, separable by size and proportions, are recognized; detailed discussion of these is beyond this book's scope and only extremes are dealt with here. Confusingly, intermediates occur between Canada Goose subspecies and Cackling Goose (formerly part of Canada Goose complex), which has recently been assigned species status. Large Canada Geese are unmistakable, but smallest subspecies are similar in size to largest subspecies of Cackling Goose! Neck length is a good feature for separation: proportionately longer in Canada Goose races than in Cackling Goose. **ADULT** Has black head and neck, and white cheek. Bill and legs are black. Typical birds have gray-brown body plumage, except for white vent and pale breast. Nesters from Alaska and British Columbia ("Dusky" Canada Goose) have uniformly dark reddish brown body plumage, except for white vent. Arctic and boreal nesters are typically smaller than subspecies breeding further south. **JUVENILE** Similar to adult. **VOICE** Familiar honking *hronk*. **STATUS AND HABITAT** Abundant. Favors freshwater marshes, pasture, and farmland. **OBSERVATION TIPS** Easy to observe. Leave subspecies assignment to the experts.

BRANT *Branta bernicla* L 24–26 in

Small coastal goose. Three subspecies are recognized, separable by belly markings; they have reasonably distinct breeding and winter-

BLACK BRANT
ADULT
PALE-BELLIED BRANT
ADULT

ing grounds: *nigricans* (Black Brant) breeds in Siberia and northwestern North American Arctic and winters on Pacific coast of North America; *hrota* (Pale-bellied Brant) breeds in Greenland and eastern North American Arctic, and winters either on our Atlantic coast or in Europe; *bernicla* (Dark-bellied Brant) breeds in Russian Arctic and winters in Europe. Intermediate "Gray-bellied Brant" breeds in Canada and winters on Washington State coast. All birds feed on marine eelgrass and Sea Lettuce, sometimes also on coastal grassland. **ADULT** Has black head and neck with white "collar," dark gray upperparts, and white vent. Breast and belly are uniformly dark gray in *nigricans*; dark below, but paler on flanks in *bernicla* and Gray-bellied; uniformly pale gray in *hrota*. **JUVENILE** Similar to respective parents, but white collar is absent until late winter, and back feathers show pale edges. **VOICE** A nasal, honking *kruut*. **STATUS AND HABITAT** Breeds on tundra, winters in estuaries. Locally common. **OBSERVATION TIPS** Black Brant migrates down Pacific coast; most winter in Baja California, Mexico. Gray-bellied Brant winter in Padilla Bay, Washington.

ADULT

ADULT

CACKLING GOOSE

ADULTS

CANADA GOOSE

ADULT

BRANT

BLACK BRANT

ADULT

Anatidae

BLACK-BELLIED WHISTLING-DUCK
Dendrocygna autumnalis L 19–22 in

Colorful long-necked, long-legged duck that often adopts an upright posture, which adds to impression of it being a nervous bird; indeed, typically it is extremely wary. Note also the proportionately long wings. Often perches on branches or rocks, and nests in tree holes. Highly gregarious outside the breeding season. It feeds on aquatic plants, grass, and cereals, as well as freshwater invertebrates; typically it feeds at night. Sexes are similar. **ADULT** Has an orange-brown back, breast, and lower neck. Upper neck and head are gray, except for rufous crown. Belly is black and note the pale wing panel; in

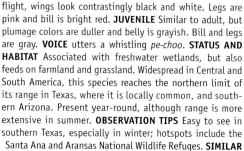

flight, wings look contrastingly black and white. Legs are pink and bill is bright red. **JUVENILE** Similar to adult, but plumage colors are duller and belly is grayish. Bill and legs are gray. **VOICE** utters a whistling *pe-choo*. **STATUS AND HABITAT** Associated with freshwater wetlands, but also feeds on farmland and grassland. Widespread in Central and South America, this species reaches the northern limit of its range in Texas, where it is locally common, and southern Arizona. Present year-round, although range is more extensive in summer. **OBSERVATION TIPS** Easy to see in southern Texas, especially in winter; hotspots include the Santa Ana and Aransas National Wildlife Refuges. **SIMILAR SPECIES Fulvous Whistling-Duck** *D. bicolor* (L 18–20 in) has similar habits and posture to Black-bellied. However, it is less colorful overall, plumage being rather uniformly orange-brown, darkest on crown, nape, and back. Bill and legs are blue-gray and wings appear uniformly dark in flight. A tropical species at the northernmost limit of its range in southern Texas. Seen only occasionally in region covered by this book, typically during post-breeding dispersal in late spring.

ADULTS

FULVOUS WHISTLING-DUCK

ADULT

WOOD DUCK *Aix sponsa* L 17–19 in

Attractive dabbling duck. Males are bizarrely colorful and instantly recognizable; even the duller females are well-marked. Flies on rapid wingbeats and is surprisingly maneuverable through forested terrain. Gregarious outside breeding season, but seldom seen in sizeable flocks. Nests in tree holes and responds well to introduction of artificial nest boxes; often perches on branches. Feeds on acorns, fruits, and invertebrates. Sexes are dissimilar. **ADULT MALE** Has shiny green-blue crown and mane, adorned with white lines. Chin and throat are white, extending onto face as white lines. Breast is maroon, flanks are buff, and back is greenish; these three areas are separated by white lines. Note red eye and red at base of bill. **ADULT FEMALE** Mainly brownish, darkest on back and head. Breast and flanks are marked with fine pale streaklike spots. Note the white spectacle around the eye and white on throat and margin of gray bill. **JUVENILE** Resembles adult female, but plumage is duller and patterns less striking. **VOICE** Mostly silent, but females utter a squealing *oo-Eeek*. **STATUS AND HABITAT** Associated with forested areas, typically flooded valleys, well-wooded swamps and the like; requires areas that are flooded during the breeding season. Overhunting and habitat destruction brought virtual extinction by end of 19th century (sadly, a familiar story). However, hunting restrictions and conservation measures have allowed population to recover to roughly 1,000,000 birds.

MALE

ADULT

JUVENILE

BLACK-BELLIED WHISTLING-DUCK

MALE

WOOD DUCK

FEMALE

Anatidae

MALLARD *Anas platyrhynchos* L 22–24 in

The most widespread and familiar duck in the region: there are few sizeable water bodies that lack their quota of resident Mallards. Feeds mainly on aquatic vegetation, and some invertebrates, by dabbling and, if necessary, upending in shallows. In flight, both sexes show a white-bordered blue speculum. Sexes are dissimilar: male has colorful elements to its plumage, while female's subdued brown coloration affords it excellent camouflage when nesting. **ADULT MALE** Has yellow bill and green, shiny head and upper neck that are separated from chestnut breast by striking white collar. Underparts are gray-brown, except for black vent and white tail. Back is gray-brown, grading to a more reddish brown. Legs and feet are orange. In eclipse plumage, male resembles an adult female, but note yellow bill color and well-defined reddish brown breast. **ADULT FEMALE** Has orange-brown bill and mottled brown plumage. Legs and feet are dull orange-yellow. **JUVENILE** Similar to adult female. **VOICE** Male utters range of whistles and nasal calls. Female utters familiar quacking calls. **STATUS AND HABITAT** Found virtually throughout the region, favoring almost every habitat where water is present, with the exception of the highest mountains and northernmost tundra. Commonest on lowland lakes, rivers, and marshes, but will also thrive on ornamental lakes in urban areas, where it often becomes tame. Most Canadian birds move south, or to the coast, in winter. **OBSERVATION TIPS** Easy to find throughout the region. Identification of the male is straightforward, except in eclipse plumage, when it resembles a female. Female could be confused with females of other larger dabbling ducks, but for much of year females seen in company of males.

MALE

GADWALL *Anas strepera* L 19–20 in

A familiar and rather understated dabbling duck. At a distance, the male's plumage simply looks gray and brown. However, at close range and in good light its beautifully intricate, vermiculate patterns become apparent. In flight, both sexes show white in the speculum, emphasized and defined by a black border; the extent of white is greatest in males, which also show chestnut on the inner wing. Sexes are dissimilar in plumage overall. **ADULT MALE** Has a buffy gray head and neck, with clear separation from the darker gray, finely patterned breast and flanks. Center of belly is white and vent is black, the latter a useful identification feature even at a distance. Note the dark bill and yellow legs. In eclipse plumage, male resembles an adult female. **ADULT FEMALE** Has mottled brown plumage with a grayish head. Note the yellow bill. White speculum can sometimes be glimpsed in feeding birds. **JUVENILE** Resembles an adult female. **VOICE** Male utters a croaking call and female utters a Mallard-like *quack*. **STATUS AND HABITAT** Gadwalls are almost invariably associated with freshwater habitats, favoring shallow water where they can dabble (and if necessary upend) for water plants. Breeds extensively across central North America, particularly in prairie pools, and winters mainly south and west of breeding range, south to Central America. Numbers have increased in recent years, due largely to conservation measures aimed at improving breeding habitat. **OBSERVATION TIPS** Easiest to find in winter months, on large lakes and freshwater marshes.

MALE

FEMALE

MALE

MALLARD

FEMALE

MALE

GADWALL

FEMALE

Anatidae

GREEN-WINGED TEAL *Anas crecca* L 14–15 in

Tiny dabbling duck. Gregarious outside breeding season. Typically nervous and takes flight—rising almost vertically from the water's surface—at slightest sign of danger. In flight, both sexes show a green speculum, highlighted by white borders. Sexes are otherwise dissimilar. Feeds on aquatic vegetation and, in summer, invertebrates too. **ADULT MALE** Has chestnut-orange head with green patch through eye, faintly bordered with yellow. Plumage is otherwise gray and finely marked, except for striking vertical white stripe on side of breast, and black-bordered yellow vent. Bill is dark gray. Eclipse male resembles adult female. **ADULT FEMALE** Has rather uniform mottled gray-brown plumage; green speculum is sometimes glimpsed in feeding birds. Bill is mainly gray, but with hint of yellow at base. **JUVENILE** Similar to adult female, but plumage is lighter buff. **VOICE** Male utters a ringing whistle, while female utters a soft *quack*. **STATUS AND HABITAT** Invariably found close to water. Nests in dense waterside vegetation beside wooded pools, lakes, and marshes, across northern North America. At other times of year, migrates south and favors more open habitats: freshwater marshes, estuaries, and mudflats. **OBSERVATION TIPS** Locally abundant in winter range. **COMMENT** *See also* European Teal (p.396).

AMERICAN WIGEON *Anas americana* L 18–21 in

Medium-sized dabbling duck. Adult male breeding plumage is distinctive, but separation of other plumages from Eurasian Wigeon is a challenge. American's white axillaries ("armpits") are useful field marks at all times (gray in Eurasian). Forms sizeable flocks outside breeding season. Feeds on aquatic plants and also grazes grassland. **ADULT MALE** Has a striking head pattern with green stripe stretching back from eye, creamy white forehead and crown, and speckled gray face and neck. Body plumage is otherwise mainly pinkish buff, except for bold black and white vent. In flight, note

MALE

striking white patch on upper surface of inner wing. **ADULT FEMALE** Has speckled gray head and neck (good for separation from female Eurasian) and otherwise orange-brown, finely marked body plumage, except for white belly. Bill and legs are gray. **JUVENILE** Similar to adult female. **VOICE** Male utters a distinctive three-noted whistle, *whi-whee-whew*. **STATUS AND HABITAT** Abundant. Nests beside tundra pools and northern marshes. Migrates south for winter, favoring open wetlands and adjacent grassland, and estuaries. **OBSERVATION TIPS** Large numbers winter in California's Central Valley.

EURASIAN WIGEON *Anas penelope* L 19–21 in

Robust duck. Male is colorful and distinctive. Gregarious outside breeding season. Feeds by dabbling and grazing terrestrial grassland. Sexes are dissimilar and females are hard to distinguish from female American Wigeon. **ADULT MALE** Has orange-red head with yellow forehead. Breast is pinkish, while rest of plumage is mainly gray and finely marked except for white belly and striking black and white vent. In flight, note striking white patch on wing. Bill is pale gray and dark-tipped. Eclipse male recalls adult female. **ADULT FEMALE** Mainly reddish brown, darkest on head and back, but with white belly and vent; lacks male's white wing patch. Bill is gray and dark-tipped. **JUVENILE** Resembles adult female. **VOICE** Male utters evocative *wheee-oo* whistling call. **STATUS AND HABITAT** A few thousand winter on Pacific coast, mainly in Washington and British Columbia.

MALE

FEMALE

MALE

FEMALE

GREEN-WINGED TEAL

FEMALE

AMERICAN WIGEON

MALE

MALE

ADULTS

EURASIAN WIGEON

FEMALE

Anatidae

NORTHERN PINTAIL *Anas acuta* L 21–26 in

An elegant duck. Feeds on aquatic plants by dabbling and upending; also feeds on land. Male is unmistakable; even rather drab female has distinctive, elongated appearance with pointed rear end. Unobtrusive during breeding season, but feeds in the open areas in flocks at other times. Looks long-winged in flight; male's gray wings and green speculum (with white trailing edge) are striking; female's white trailing edge on inner wing is obvious. Sexes are dissimilar in other respects. **ADULT MALE** Has chocolate brown head and nape, with white breast extending as stripe up side of head. Plumage is otherwise gray and finely marked, but note cream and black vent, and long, pointed tail, often held at an angle. Eclipse male resembles adult female, but retains pattern and colors on wings. **ADULT FEMALE** Has mottled buffish brown plumage. **JUVENILE** Similar to adult female, but complex feather markings are less well developed. **VOICE** Male utters a whistling call; female's call is grating and harsh. **STATUS AND HABITAT** Several million occur in North America; numbers are declining due to changes in agricultural land use during breeding season. Favors marshy edge habitat and adjacent farmland for nesting. In winter, on arable fields, marshes, and estuaries. **OBSERVATION TIPS** Easiest to observe in winter. Often upends in water to feed, revealing striking vent colors and elongated tail.

NORTHERN SHOVELER *Anas clypeata* L 17–20 in

Unmistakable, even in silhouette, due to long, flattened bill. Unobtrusive, favoring water margins with dense vegetation and moving quietly through open shallows, filtering food with bill. In flight, male shows blue forewing panel and white-bordered green speculum; female's wing pattern is similar, but blue is replaced by gray. Sexes are dissimilar in other respects. **ADULT MALE** Has shiny green head (looks dark in poor light), white breast, and chestnut on flanks and belly. Vent is black and white and back is mainly dark. Note bright yellow eye. Eclipse male resembles adult female although body is more rufous and head is grayer. **ADULT FEMALE** Has mottled buffy brown plumage and yellowish bill. **JUVENILE** Similar to adult female. **VOICE** Male utters a sharp *tuk-tuk*; female utters a soft *quack*. **STATUS AND HABITAT** Common and widespread. Nests beside shallow pools. Favors estuaries, freshwater marshes and lakes in winter. **OBSERVATION TIPS** Easiest to find in winter.

BLUE-WINGED TEAL *Anas discors* L 15–16 in

Small, distinctive duck. Feeds by dabbling in well-vegetated shallows. Male is unmistakable; female is similar to female Cinnamon Teal, which has larger bill, gently sloping forehead and uniformly brown head. Female Green-winged has smaller bill and different wing markings. In flight, all birds reveal blue panel on leading edge of upper inner wing, separated from speculum (green in male) by white wedge. **ADULT MALE** Has bluish head with diagnostic white crescent. Body is buffy brownish, marbled with dark spots; white patch contrasts with otherwise black vent. **ADULT FEMALE** Marbled brown with pale spot at base of bill, dark eyestripe, and white "eyelids." **JUVENILE** Similar to adult female, but lacks strong facial markings. **STATUS AND HABITAT** Common breeding species, particularly in prairie pothole region. Nests beside shallow pools. Most birds migrate to South America for winter; small numbers linger in the south of the region.

MALE

MALE

NORTHERN PINTAIL

ADULTS

FEMALE

MALE

NORTHERN SHOVELER

MALE

FEMALE

FEMALE

MALE

BLUE-WINGED TEAL

Anatidae

CINNAMON TEAL *Anas cyanoptera* L 15–17 in

Slim-looking dabbling duck with a proportionately long bill, recalling that of Northern Shoveler. Sexes are dissimilar: male's plumage color is unmistakable; female is superficially similar to female Blue-winged Teal, but distinguishable by bill length, uniformly brown head, and association with male. Both sexes show pale underwings in flight and upper-wing markings similar to those of Blue-winged: pale blue panel, white wedge, and greenish speculum. Not particularly gregarious. **ADULT MALE** Has mainly bright

MALE

cinnamon-red plumage, darkest on back. Note the beady reddish eye. Eclipse male recalls adult female, but plumage is redder. **ADULT FEMALE** Has buffy brown plumage. **JUVENILE** Similar to adult female. **VOICE** Male utters rattling clicks, female utters a soft *quack*. **STATUS AND HABITAT** Locally common. Widespread in breeding season, favoring marshes and shallow, weedy lakes. Outside breeding season, migrates south and west; most birds winter from Mexico southward, but small numbers remain in southwest. **OBSERVATION TIPS** Visit coastal wetlands in California in winter.

CANVASBACK *Aythya valisineria* L 20–23 in

Robust diving duck. Feeds on submerged vegetation and some invertebrates. Similar to Redhead, but separable by key plumage differences, shape of head, and structure and markings of bill: Canvasback has a long, triangular bill, uniformly dark grayish black, upperside of which follows the slope of the flat forehead; Redhead has a rounded head and comparatively dainty bill that is pale grayish blue with subterminal white band and black tip. All birds show pale underwings in flight. **ADULT MALE**

Has a reddish chestnut head, black breast and vent, and otherwise very pale gray body. Note the bright red eye, dark grayish black bill, and, in flight, whitish upper wings. **ADULT FEMALE** Has buffy brownish head and neck, pale gray-brown body with darker vent. Note the faint pale "spectacle." **JUVENILE** Similar to adult female, but more uniformly buffy gray. **VOICE** Mostly silent. **STATUS AND HABITAT** Has declined, but still locally common. Favors prairie potholes and marshes for nesting. Winters mainly on coasts, but may occur inland. **OBSERVATION TIPS** Common in San Francisco Bay area in winter.

MALE

REDHEAD *Aythya americana* L 18–21 in

Attractive diving duck that feeds on submerged plants and some invertebrates. Superficially similar to Canvasback, but *see* that species' description for differences. In particular, note the Redhead's rounded head shape. In flight all birds show pale underwings. Sexes are dissimilar in other respects. **ADULT MALE** Has a reddish orange head and upper neck, clearly demarcated from the black lower neck and breast. Vent is black and

body is otherwise gray. In flight, gray upper wing coverts contrast with paler flight feathers. Note the bright yellowish eye. **ADULT FEMALE** Has mainly buffy brownish plumage, with a faint pale "spectacle" and whitish throat. **JUVENILE** Similar to adult female. **VOICE** Mostly silent. **STATUS AND HABITAT** Favors prairie pothole habitats for nesting. Winters mainly on Gulf of Mexico, specifically Laguna Madre, Texas and Laguna Madre, Tamaulipas, Mexico. Small numbers winter in southern states' wetlands. **OBSERVATION TIPS** Relatively easy to find, within range, at start of breeding season. Otherwise, visit coastal wetlands in winter. **COMMENT** Occasional nest parasite of other Redheads and other ducks.

MALE

CINNAMON TEAL

FEMALE

MALE

CANVASBACK

FEMALE

MALE

REDHEAD

FEMALE

MALE

Anatidae

RING-NECKED DUCK *Aythya collaris* L 15–18 in

Distinctive diving duck that feeds on submerged seeds, roots, and
invertebrates. Male in particular is strikingly marked, but both sexes
can be recognized by peaked crown and tricolored bill: dark gray with a
subterminal white band and black tip. In flight, all birds show whitish underwings and pale gray flight feathers, contrasting with darker upper wing
coverts. **ADULT MALE** Has light gray belly and flanks, the leading edge of
which is pale and appears as a vertical white line in swimming birds. The
plumage is otherwise mainly black, although in good light note the purple sheen
to the head and neck. Note also the white border defining base of bill. **ADULT**
FEMALE Has a grayish head with a white patch at base of bill, and a white "spectacle" around eye.

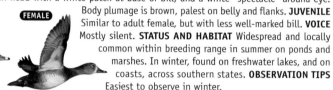

Body plumage is brown, palest on belly and flanks. **JUVENILE**
Similar to adult female, but with less well-marked bill. **VOICE**
Mostly silent. **STATUS AND HABITAT** Widespread and locally
common within breeding range in summer on ponds and
marshes. In winter, found on freshwater lakes, and on
coasts, across southern states. **OBSERVATION TIPS**
Easiest to observe in winter.

GREATER SCAUP *Aythya marila* L 17–19 in

Bulky, robust diving duck. Feeds on submerged roots, seeds, and
invertebrates. Superficially similar to slightly smaller Lesser Scaup,
but size is not always a useful means of field identification. Head shape is
generally reliable in relaxed birds: rounded in Greater, but
distinctly peaked in Lesser. In flight, more of the upper-
wing flight feathers appear whitish in Greater than in
Lesser. At close range, black tip to otherwise dark gray bill
is more extensive in Greater than Lesser (hard to judge in
field). **ADULT MALE** Has green-glossed head and dark breast;
both can look black in poor light. Belly and flanks are white and back is pale gray,
palest toward front. Vent is black; note bright yellow eye. Eclipse plumage pattern
recalls adult male, but pale elements are buffy gray. **ADULT FEMALE** Has mainly brown plumage, palest
and grayest on flanks and back; white belly is seen in flight. Note striking white patch at base of bill.
JUVENILE Similar to adult female. **VOICE** Mostly silent. **STATUS AND HABITAT** Locally common. Nests
on tundra marshes and pools, winters mainly on coasts or large lakes. **OBSERVATION TIPS** Easiest to
observe in winter. **COMMENT** Coastal winter scaup flocks are likely to be Greaters.

LESSER SCAUP *Aythya affinis* L 16–17 in

Familiar diving duck. Similar to Greater Scaup counterparts—*see* that
species' account for details, but peaked crown is reliable diagnostic
feature as is upper wing pattern in flight—only inner flight feathers are
whitish. **ADULT MALE** Has black head and neck, former appears shiny purple
in good light (green in male Greater). Belly and flanks are white and back
is gray, palest towards front.
Vent is black; note beady yellow eye. Eclipse plumage pattern
recalls adult male, but pale ele-
ments are buffy. **ADULT FEMALE** Mainly brown, palest and
grayest on back and flanks. White belly is seen in flight.
JUVENILE Similar to adult female. **VOICE** Mostly silent.
STATUS AND HABITAT Abundant and widespread, nesting
beside marshes and prairie potholes and wintering in
pools and lakes further south. **OBSERVATION TIPS** Easiest to observe in winter. **COMMENT** Scaup flocks on inland
freshwater are likely to be Lessers.

FEMALE

RING-NECKED DUCK

MALE

FEMALE

GREATER SCAUP

MALE

FEMALE

LESSER SCAUP

MALE

Anatidae

BLACK SCOTER *Melanitta nigra* L 18–20 in

Rather uniformly dark diving duck. Male is only duck in the region with all-black plumage and female's nearly all-dark plumage is relieved only by her contrasting pale cheeks. Relatively long tail is sometimes elevated when swimming. Outside breeding season, Black Scoters are highly gregarious. In flight, all birds look mainly dark, although in good light paler flight feathers can sometimes be discerned. **ADULT MALE** Has uniformly black plumage. Otherwise-dark bill has a striking bulbous yellow knob at base.

First-winter male is similar to adult although plumage is browner and bill color is duller. **ADULT FEMALE** Has mainly dark brown plumage, but with well-defined pale buff cheeks and throat. **JUVENILE** Resembles an adult female. **VOICE** Displaying males utter whistling calls. **STATUS AND HABITAT** Locally common. Nests beside tundra pools. Outside breeding season, almost entirely marine and quite at home in rough seas. Winters on Pacific coast, south to California. **OBSERVATION TIPS** In winter, flying Black Scoters are seen in trailing lines snaking along horizon. During migration, small flocks may be observed.

WHITE-WINGED SCOTER
Melanitta fusca L 20–22 in

Bulky duck that dives frequently and for long periods. Similar to, but larger than, Black Scoter with which it sometimes consorts in winter. Both sexes have white inner flight feathers, striking and obvious in flight, but often visible, albeit only partially, in swimming birds too. White markings on head of male enable easy identification while female's facial markings are useful features to look for. **ADULT MALE** Has mainly black plumage (dark brown on flanks), which emphasizes striking white horizontal comma-shaped patch seen below pale eye, and glimpsed patch of white on closed wings of swimming birds. Bill is mostly pinkish, but more blackish near the base. First-winter male is browner overall than adult and lacks white under eye. **ADULT FEMALE** Has mainly dark sooty brown plumage, but note pale cheek

patch and pale patch at base of dark bill. **VOICE** Mostly silent, but ccasionally quacks and breeding males whistle. **STATUS AND HABITAT** Locally common. Nests beside inland tundra pools in Alaska and western Canada. Outside breeding season, almost exclusively coastal, favoring bays and estuaries with sandy seabeds. **OBSERVATION TIPS** Easiest to find in winter—scan a sheltered bay from an elevated vantage point and look for the diagnostic white highlights on otherwise dark-looking birds.

SURF SCOTER *Melanitta perspicillata* L 19–20 in

Sea duck with large, triangular bill. Dives often and for long periods, after marine invertebrates. In flight, all birds show uniformly dark wings. Male is distinctive, white head markings and colorful bill contrasting with otherwise black plumage. Female could be confused with females of other scoter species: head markings and bill size allow separation from Black; uniformly dark wings distinguish it from White-winged. **ADULT MALE** Has mainly black plumage, but note prominent white patches on nape and forehead. Bill is orange-yellow on top and to the tip, with a white basal patch encompassing a large black spot; at close range

note the whitish eye. First-winter male has brownish plumage, but a hint of adult's bill pattern. **ADULT FEMALE** Has mainly dark gray-brown plumage with white patch at base of bill, and one behind eye. **VOICE** Mostly silent, but sometimes croaks, and breeding males whistle. **STATUS AND HABITAT** Common. Nests beside northern lakes and winters on coasts. **OBSERVATION TIPS** Often feeds close to shore.

BLACK SCOTER

FEMALE

MALE

WHITE-WINGED SCOTER

FEMALE

MALE

SURF SCOTER

FEMALE

MALE

Anatidae

HARLEQUIN DUCK
Histrionicus histrionicus L 16–18 in

Plump-bodied diving duck. Feeds on submerged aquatic inverte-brates. Male is stunningly marked and unmistakable. Female's plumage recalls that of female scaups and scoters; note, however, small bill (cf. other diving ducks) and more rounded head shape (shared with male). Not especially gregarious, even outside breeding season. **ADULT MALE** Has mainly dark blue body plumage and red on flanks. Head is adorned with white markings: crescent at base of bill, spot, and streak behind eye. Note also the white half collar and white stripes on flanks and back. Eclipse male is sooty brown, but with hint of adult markings. **ADULT FEMALE** Brown, palest on belly, with a white spot on side of head. **JUVENILE** Similar to adult female. **VOICE** Mostly silent, but sometimes quacks or whistles. **STATUS AND HABITAT** Very locally common. During breeding season, found on fast-flowing rivers. Outside breeding season, mostly coastal, favoring exposed rocky shores; several hundred thousand may be present in winter range. **OBSERVATION TIPS** Hike alongside a mountain river in spring and you should see the occasional pair. Most birds are found on coasts between August and March.

MALE

LONG-TAILED DUCK *Clangula hyemalis* L 16–22 in

Attractive diving duck associated with open seas in winter and in its element even among tempestuous waves. Dives frequently, in search of bottom-dwelling invertebrates. Gregarious outside breeding season. In flight, note dark wings and mainly white underparts. Sexes are dissimilar and plumage of both varies considerably throughout year. Only male sports a long tail. **ADULT MALE** In winter and spring looks mainly black, gray, and white, with buffish patch around eye and pink band on bill. In summer and in eclipse has mainly brown and black plumage, with white on belly and flanks and pale buff patch around eye. **ADULT FEMALE** In winter has mainly brown and white plumage; face is white except for dark cheek patch and crown. In summer, similar, but face is mainly brown, with pale patch around eye. **JUVENILE** Similar to an adult female in summer, but more brown overall. **VOICE** Male utters characteristic nasal *ow–owlee*. **STATUS AND HABITAT** Common, but possibly in decline. Found on tundra marshes and pools during breeding season. At other times, mainly coastal. **OBSERVATION TIPS** Cliff-top vantage points overlooking, wide, sandy bays, often provide the best chances of seeing the species well, other than in flight.

MALE, SUMMER MOLTING

BUFFLEHEAD *Bucephala albeola* L 13–14 in

Small, distinctive diving duck with a dainty bill. Feeds on aquatic invertebrates. Male is unmistakable and female is easy to identify when plumage and size are considered fully. In flight, all birds show white inner flight feathers and take off almost vertically from water when alarmed. **ADULT MALE** Has rather large, rounded head that looks black and white in poor light; good light reveals an iridescent purple sheen to black elements. Body plumage otherwise white, except for black back. Eclipse and first-winter males recall adult female. **ADULT FEMALE** Has dark brown back and head, except for striking white oval patch on cheek. White on wing can be glimpsed in swimming birds. Neck and underparts grayish white. **JUVENILE** Similar to adult female. **VOICE** Mostly silent. **STATUS AND HABITAT** Fairly common. Found on wooded lakes in breeding season, nesting in tree holes. In winter, on sheltered coastal bays and inland lakes.

FEMALE

FEMALE

MALE

HARLEQUIN DUCK

MALE

FEMALE, WINTER

LONG-TAILED DUCK

MALE, WINTER
DISPLAYING

BUFFLEHEAD

MALE

Anatidae

BARROW'S GOLDENEYE
Bucephala islandica L 17–19 in

Compact diving duck that feeds on aquatic invertebrates. Similar
to Common Goldeneye, but note Barrow's steeper forehead and smaller bill.
Adult male's crescent-shaped (not oval) white face patch is diagnostic and
greater extent of black on back is a useful distinguishing feature. In flight,
white on inner upper wing is less extensive than in Common Goldeneye.
ADULT MALE Has proportionately large, rounded, iridescent purple head with
a very steep forehead and vertical white crescent marking just behind base of bill. Ladder of white
markings can be seen on otherwise black back; black extends forward as prominent "spur" shape in
swimming birds. Vent is black, but neck and underparts are otherwise white. Note beady yellow eye.
First-winter plumage has colors of adult female, but hint of adult's facial crescent. **ADULT FEMALE** Has
dark brown head separated from gray-brown body plumage by pale neck. Bill is mostly dull orange-
yellow (color confined to tip in female Common), but a bit darker in summer. **JUVENILE** Similar to
adult female, but bill and eye are dark. **VOICE** Mostly silent. **STATUS AND HABITAT** Locally common.
In summer, found on upland lakes, nesting in tree holes. Most move to sheltered coasts in winter, but
also occurs inland on ice-free lakes. **OBSERVATION TIPS** Easy to find in Puget Sound in winter.

COMMON GOLDENEYE
Bucephala clangula L 17–19 in

Robust diving duck. Both sexes are similar to their Barrow's counterparts—*see* that species' description for differences. In flight, white on
inner upper wings is more extensive in male than female. **ADULT MALE** Has
mainly black and white plumage. Rounded, peaked head appears dark in

MALE

poor light, but iridescent green in
sunshine. Note beady yellow eye and
striking white oval patch at base of bill.
Eclipse male resembles an adult female,
but retains his more striking white wing pattern. **ADULT FEMALE**
Has gray-brown body plumage separated from dark brown head
by pale neck. Note beady yellow eye. **JUVENILE** Similar to adult
female, but with dark eye. **VOICE** Displaying male utters squeaky
calls. Otherwise silent. **STATUS AND HABITAT** Common and widespread. In summer, found on wooded lakes, nesting in tree holes.
In winter, commonest on coasts, although also found on ice-free
inland lakes across region.

RUDDY DUCK *Oxyura jamaicensis* L 14–16 in

Small diving duck that feeds on aquatic invertebrates and submerged
roots and seeds. Both sexes regularly cock their spiky-looking
tails. Breeding male is unmistakable. In winter, all birds could perhaps be
confused with a small grebe, but Ruddy Duck's proportionately large bill easily dispels confusion. **ADULT MALE** In breeding plumage has orange-chest-
nut body plumage, white cheeks, black cap and nape, and bright blue bill.
Note also the small, white vent. Outside breeding season, body plumage is

MALE, NONBREEDING

gray-brown and bill is more dull grayish. **ADULT FEMALE** Has gray-brown
plumage, with paler cheeks that are broken by dark line from
base of bill; bill is dull blue-gray, similar to that seen in winter
male. **VOICE** Mostly silent. **STATUS AND HABITAT** In summer,
favors freshwater marshes and lakes with well-vegetated margins,
nesting among emergent vegetation. In winter, moves south of
breeding range and found on sheltered estuaries and bays on the
coast, and ice-free lakes and ponds inland. **COMMENT** Males
engage in "bubbling," chest-beating courtship displays in spring.

FEMALE

BARROW'S GOLDENEYE

MALE

FEMALE

COMMON GOLDENEYE

MALE

FEMALE

RUDDY DUCK

MALE

Anatidae

HOODED MERGANSER
Lophodytes cucullatus L 17–19 in

Small, bizarrely shaped diving duck with slender bill and large head.
Dives frequently in search of small fish and invertebrates. Male is unmistakable; size, proportions, and color in female are a good means of identification. **ADULT MALE** Has a large crest that can be flattened or fanned out, presenting a large, gleaming white patch on otherwise dark head. Bill is dark and note beady yellow eye. Back is mainly dark and breast is white, marked with two black lines on sides, separating breast from otherwise orange-brown flanks. Eclipse male is similar to adult female, but with duller colors; retains bright eye. **ADULT FEMALE** Has orange-buff head with long, shaggy crest. Plumage is otherwise mainly gray-brown, darkest on back; belly is white. Eye is dark. **JUVENILE** Similar to adult female. **VOICE** Mostly silent. **STATUS AND HABITAT** In summer, found in forested wetlands; nests in tree holes. Outside breeding season, most birds move to coastal wetlands, favoring freshwater sites. **OBSERVATION TIPS** Typically shy during breeding season; easier to observe in winter, although still has retiring habits.

COMMON MERGANSER
Mergus merganser L 24–26 in

Large, slender-bodied, and elegant diving duck that swims with a stately posture. Dives frequently for fish and invertebrates. In flight, upper surface of male's inner wing is white, except for narrow black line; in female, white is restricted to trailing edge. **ADULT MALE** Unmistakable, with bright red-orange bill, glossy-green head (looks dark in poor light), white body, and black back. Close view reveals pink wash on white breast and underparts. Eclipse male resembles adult female, although white wing pattern is retained. **ADULT FEMALE** Has orange-red head and neck with shaggy crest and well-defined white throat. Body plumage is grayish, palest on breast. Note the reddish orange bill. **JUVENILE** Resembles adult female, but with duller colors. **VOICE** Male utters ringing display calls. Otherwise silent.

MALES AND FEMALE

STATUS AND HABITAT Widespread and common. In summer, favors wooded lakes and rivers; nests in tree holes. Outside breeding season, moves south to ice-free freshwater lakes across region; occasionally found on coasts. **OBSERVATION TIPS** Ice-bound lake margins often serve to concentrate birds in winter.

RED-BREASTED MERGANSER
Mergus serrator L 22–24 in

Slim diving duck. Recalls Common Merganser, but smaller; both sexes have shaggy, spiky crest rather than a sleek head. Dives frequently in search of fish and invertebrates. In flight, both sexes show white on upper inner wing; extent is greatest in males, the white divided by two black lines. **ADULT MALE** Has narrow reddish bill, a green head (looks dark in poor light), white neck, and streaked orange-red breast. Flanks are gray and back is black. Eclipse male is similar to adult female, but retains wing pattern. **ADULT FEMALE** Has reddish bill, dirty orange head and nape, but a paler throat; body plumage is otherwise grayish buff.

MALE

JUVENILE Resembles adult female. **VOICE** Males utter soft, grunting display calls. Otherwise silent. **STATUS AND HABITAT** Common. In summer, found on tundra and boreal forest lakes. Outside breeding season, most birds move to coasts, although some may occur on large, ice-free freshwater lakes. **OBSERVATION TIPS** Easiest to find in winter: search estuaries and large, sheltered bays.

FEMALE

MALE

HOODED MERGANSER

FEMALE

COMMON MERGANSER

MALE

FEMALE

RED-BREASTED MERGANSER

MALE

Anatidae

COMMON EIDER *Somateria mollissima* L 23–25 in

Bulky sea duck that dives frequently and for long periods. Distinctive even in silhouette, on account of its large wedge-shaped bill,
which forms an almost continuous line with slope of forehead. Highly gregarious for most of year. In summer, several females may band together,
accompanied by "creche" of youngsters. In flight, males look black and
white, while females can look uniformly dark in poor light. Except during
summer molt, sexes have strikingly dissimilar plumages. Four subspecies occur in North America, but
only ssp. *v-nigrum* (so-called "Pacific Eider") is common in west. **ADULT MALE** ssp. *v-nigrum* has mainly
black underparts and white upperparts, except for black cap, lime green nape, and pinkish flush on
breast. Bill is orange. Jaw line is defined by narrow black line; when head is raised this appears as a
V-marking. In eclipse plumage, male is mainly a mixture of brown and black, although some white
feathering is always visible on back. Adult males of other subspecies (from eastern North America)
have yellow or lime green bills. **ADULT FEMALE** Brown with darker barring, plumage affording superb
camouflage when bird is nesting. Bill is dark gray. **JUVENILE** Similar to adult female, but typically
shows a pale stripe above eye. **VOICE** Male utters a characteristic, and rather endearing, cooing *ah-
Whooo*. While doing so, head is thrown back in a distinctive manner. **STATUS AND HABITAT** Mainly
coastal; nests on seashore, feeds in inshore seas diving mainly for mollusks. Locally common breeding species in coastal Alaska and northern Canada. In winter, most move to Bering Sea and Aleutian
Islands. **OBSERVATION TIPS** Easy to see on Arctic shores of Alaska and Canada in summer. **COMMENT**
See also Spectacled Eider and Steller's Eider (*see* p.396).

FEMALE

KING EIDER *Somateria spectabilis* L 21–23 in

A distinctive sea duck that dives regularly and for extended periods in search of marine invertebrates. Adult male in summer is
unmistakable, but female could be confused with female Common Eider:
note King Eider's smaller size, more dainty bill and smaller head, and more
prominent pale line running back from eye and pale eye surround. Extremely gregarious during migration and in winter. **ADULT MALE** Spectacular, the
rather oversized-looking blue head bearing a red bill and large orange basal
knob. Black lines demarcate areas of color on head. Breast is pinkish orange
and rest of body is mainly black, with a white patch on side of vent, and a horizontal white line on flanks. Raised, sail-like scapulars can be discerned at close range. In flight, note
the white wing coverts, above and below. **ADULT FEMALE** Has warm brown, marbled plumage and dark
gray bill. In flight, note the pale underwing coverts. **STATUS AND HABITAT** Locally common, but
declining. Nests beside coastal tundra pools. Most migrate to coastal seas off south Alaska for winter:
500,000+ may be present at this time. **OBSERVATION TIPS** Spring migration (May) off Alaskan coast
is spectacular, as are winter concentrations.

MALE

COMMON EIDER

MALE

KING EIDER

FEMALE

Phasianidae and Cracidae

CHUKAR *Alectoris chukar* L 13.5–14 in

Well-marked, secretive partridge. Sometimes seen in small groups
(coveys) outside breeding season. Seldom takes to the air willingly,
but, if flushed, rises noisily on whirring wingbeats and glides away. Sexes
are similar. **ADULT** Has red bill, creamy white throat and lower face, defined
by black border that runs through eye. Crown, nape, and breast are blue-gray,
grading to buffy brown on back; note pale supercilium behind eye. Belly is
buff and flanks are marked with striking black and white lines. **JUVENILE**
Has scaly brown plumage with a hint of adult's head and flank markings; adult
plumage acquired by fall. **VOICE** Male utters repetitive *chuk-ar chuk-ar* calls.
STATUS AND HABITAT Native range is the Middle East eastward. Introduced for hunting and now locally
common; introductions continue to occur. Favors dry, stony slopes and desert canyons with scrubby
cover. **OBSERVATION TIPS** Typically, views are brief, birds being glimpsed as they scuttle from one patch
of vegetation to another. Easier to hear than to see in spring, when males are calling.

GRAY PARTRIDGE *Perdix perdix* L 12–13 in

Subtly attractive and nonnative partridge. Usually wary due to hunting. Typically seen in small groups (coveys) that prefer to run from
danger rather than fly. Sexes are separable with care. **ADULT MALE** Has
orange-buff face and finely marked blue-gray nape, neck, and breast. Note the
striking maroon horseshoe marking on mostly white belly. Body plumage is
otherwise brown, but with intricate markings, fine streaks on back, and
reddish brown stripes on flanks. **ADULT FEMALE** Similar to male, but marking
on belly is indistinct or absent and plumage is duller overall. **JUVENILE** Gray-
buff, but with a suggestion of adult's dark markings. **VOICE** Male utters a choked
and harsh *kierr-ikk* call. **STATUS AND HABITAT** Native of Eurasia. Introduced for hunting and now local,
but scarce and possibly declining. Favors open grassland and arable farmland. **OBSERVATION TIPS**
Easiest to observe outside breeding season when small groups can be observed feeding in open fields.

RING-NECKED PHEASANT *Phasianus colchicus*
L 26–35 in (male) 21–30 in (female)

Male is colorful and unmistakable; adult female is also difficult to
confuse. Takes to the air noisily and explosively when flushed. Sexes are
strikingly dissimilar. **ADULT MALE** Has orange-brown body plumage, blue-
green sheen on head, striking red wattle, and long, orange and barred tail;
white collar is absent in some birds. Captive-bred violet-blue forms are sometimes released and can be confused with male Japanese Green Pheasant
P. versicolor. **ADULT FEMALE** Mottled buffy brown, with a shorter tail than male.
JUVENILE Resembles a small, short-tailed and dowdy female. **VOICE** Territorial
male utters a loud, shrieking call, followed by bout of vigorous wing beating. In alarm, utters a loud *ke-
tuk, ke-tuk, ke-tuk* as bird flies away. **STATUS AND HABITAT** Native to Asia and introduced for hunting.
Now locally common and populations are boosted each fall by release of captive-bred birds for hunting.
Favors mixed agricultural landscapes with scattered woodland and brushy borders. **OBSERVATION TIPS**
Male's territorial call is a distinctive sound in spring and displaying birds are entertaining to watch.

PLAIN CHACHALACA *Ortalis vetula* L 21–22in

Long-tailed, rather secretive southern Texas specialty. Best located
by listening for call. Typically found in social groups. Sexes are
similar. **ADULT** Has gray-brown head and neck, grading to warm brown
on back and wings, and warm buff on underparts. Tail is relatively long,
mostly dark, but with striking white feather tips. Bare throat skin becomes
reddish in breeding male. **JUVENILE** Similar to adult but duller, with pale
feather margins. **VOICE** A loud and harsh *cha-chalac*. **STATUS AND HABITAT**
Local woodland resident in southern Texas; range extends into Central America.
OBSERVATION TIPS Listen for the distinctive call.

PARTRIDGES, PHEASANTS, and CHACHALACAS

CHUKAR

ADULT

MALE

GRAY PARTRIDGE

FEMALE

PLAIN CHACHALACA

ADULT

FEMALE

RING-NECKED PHEASANT

MALE

Phasianidae

WILD TURKEY *Meleagris gallopavo*
L 45–46 in (male) 36–37 in (female)

Unmistakable and iconic native bird, and the largest of its kind in the region. Male appears particularly impressive when displaying, with puffed-up body feathers and fanned tail. The sexes are dissimilar both in terms of size and colors. Feeds mainly on seeds, fruits, nuts, and invertebrates. **ADULT MALE** Essentially has dark brown plumage, but with a bronzy, greenish sheen on the back, neck, and underparts. Tail is reddish brown and proportionally long, with whitish tips to tail feathers, upper tail coverts, and rump feathers; these appear as bold concentric rings in fanned tail. Note the tuft of feathers on the breast. Head and upper neck are bare, bristly, and mainly blue, but red on the throat. **ADULT FEMALE** Smaller and duller than male and lacks the tuft of feathers on the breast. **JUVENILE** Similar to adult female. **VOICE** Displaying male utters familiar gobbling call in spring. Otherwise,

MALE, SOUTHWESTERN

all birds utter subdued clucking calls at other times. **STATUS AND HABITAT** Hunted to local extinction in many places by the start of 20th century. Now locally common thanks to hunting regulations and breeding for release programs. **OBSERVATION TIPS** Easiest to find in spring, when males engage in noisy display. **COMMENT** Eastern race has brownish feather tips on tail. In the past, this race was inadvertently and occasionally used for restocking in the west and it persists in parts of the region. Note also that domesticated turkeys are sometimes encountered in the wild, having been released and become feral; typically they are appreciably larger and plumper, and more tame, than their wild counterparts.

RUFFED GROUSE *Bonasa umbellus* L 17–18 in

A plump grouse whose understated colors and beautifully intricate plumage patterns afford it superb camouflage on the woodland floor. Gray and reddish brown color forms occur throughout the region, but birds from the west typically are darkest and brownest, while those from the east are palest and grayest. Sexes are superficially similar, given the variation in colors. All adult birds show a striking subterminal black band on the otherwise brown or gray tail, most noticeable when seen in flight. Feeds mainly on buds, shoots, and fruits, but occasionally invertebrates too. **ADULT MALE** Has either gray or brown plumage, darker above than below, with pale streaks on upperparts and dark barring on underparts. Dark tail feather bars appear as concentric rings on fanned tail. Black feathers on neck form a ruff when displaying; otherwise they are hard to see. **ADULT FEMALE** Similar to adult male, but smaller, with a proportionately shorter tail. **JUVENILE** Similar to adult female, but duller; the dark subterminal

ADULT, RUFOUS

tail band is absent. **VOICE** Utters various squeaks. Male's drumming display is created by rapid wingbeats. **STATUS AND HABITAT** Locally common in deciduous woodland, especially where Aspen *Populus tremuloides* is common (buds and shoots feature in the diet). **OBSERVATION TIPS** The wonderfully cryptic camouflage makes this a difficult species to spot. Often it is first noticed when it "explodes" into flight at your feet. In spring, listen carefully for the male's drumming, which carries a long distance on still days. If you are lucky enough to find the bird in question, note the ruffed-up neck feathers, raised crest, and fanned tail.

MALE, DISPLAYING

WILD TURKEY

RUFFED GROUSE

MALE

ADULT, GRAY

Phasianidae

SPRUCE GROUSE
Falcipennis canadensis L 16–16.5 in

Beautifully marked, well-camouflaged grouse. Two forms exist (may be separate species): ssp. *franklinii* (Franklin's Grouse) from Cascades and Rockies; taiga forms (comprising several subspecies) across rest of species' range. Franklin's and taiga forms separable by differences in male's tail markings and display flights. Sexes are dissimilar. Feeds on conifer shoots and needles, and berries. **ADULT MALE** Has mainly dark brown plumage; white feather edges create scaly appearance, particularly on belly and flanks.

FRANKLIN'S GROUSE

MALE, DISPLAYING

Breast and neck are mainly black; black throat is defined by white border. Red wattles above both eyes are striking in display. Franklin's has uniformly dark tail, with white tips to upper tail coverts; in taiga grouse, dark tail has terminal rufous margin. **ADULT FEMALE** Either mainly gray or brown, with dark scaling above and white spots on belly. **JUVENILE** Similar to brown-morph female. **VOICE** Mostly silent. Wing claps form part of display of male Franklin's. **STATUS AND HABITAT** Fairly common in dense, young conifer forests. **OBSERVATION TIPS** Tame, but unobtrusive habits make it hard to spot initially. **COMMENT** Displaying males perform strutting displays with fanned tails, culminating in bout of rapid wingbeats. All males also perform display flights; that of Franklin's ends in loud wing claps.

DUSKY GROUSE *Dendragapus obscurus* L 17–20 in

Plump-bodied grouse with long tail and neck. Male's otherwise rather unremarkable plumage is transformed during display by broadly fanned tail, puffed-up body feathers and colorful, inflated neck sac fringed by white feathers. Feeds on shoots, leaves, and berries in summer; winter diet is mostly conifer needles. Sexes are dissimilar. **ADULT MALE** Has lilac-gray underparts and gray-brown upperparts with white spots and streaks on wings and flanks. Orange-yellow wattle above eye, and reddish orange neck sac, are prominent only in display. Tail is dark with faint pale terminal band. **ADULT FEMALE** Similar to, but smaller than, male and with more mottled and marbled plumage. Wattle and neck sac are absent. **JUVENILE** Similar to adult female, but has more extensive pale streaking on back. **VOICE** Both sexes utter low growls. Displaying males hoot. **STATUS AND HABITAT** Generally common, but found at low densities. In mixed woodland for much of year, but favors conifer forests in winter. **OBSERVATION TIPS** Usually solitary. Not unduly wary, but unobtrusive and hence often hard to locate. A displaying male is a fantastic sight.

SOOTY GROUSE *Dendragapus fuliginosus* L 17–20 in

Coastal counterpart of Dusky Grouse, the two formerly treated as conspecific. Plumage is darker overall than Dusky but habits are similar. **ADULT MALE** Has dark lilac-gray underparts and gray-brown upperparts. Orange-yellow wattle above eye and yellowish neck sac are seen in display. Tail is dark above with broad, terminal pale band. **ADULT FEMALE** Similar to, but smaller than, male and with more mottled and marbled plumage. Wattle and neck sac are absent. **JUVENILE** Similar to adult female, but has more extensive pale streaking on back. **VOICE** Both sexes utter low growls. Displaying males hoot. **STATUS AND HABITAT** Found at low densities in mixed woodland for much of year, but favors conifer forests in winter. **OBSERVATION TIPS** Unobtrusive and easy to overlook.

FEMALE

MALE, TAIGA

SPRUCE GROUSE

FEMALE

MALE DISPLAYING

DUSKY GROUSE

FEMALE

SOOTY GROUSE

MALE

Phasianidae

ROCK PTARMIGAN *Lagopus mutus* L 13–15 in

Hardy northern grouse. Despite size and indifference to people, hard to spot: feeds unobtrusively among rocks and seasonal plumage variation provides good camouflage at all times of the

MALE, WINTER

year. In flight, both sexes always reveal striking white wings and prominent black tail feathers. Forms small flocks outside breeding season. **ADULT MALE** Pure white in winter except for dark eye, lores, and bill; upper tail coverts often conceal black tail feathers. In spring, acquires marbled grayish buff upperparts; extent of white on back decreases gradually. Belly and legs remain white and note striking red wattle. **ADULT FEMALE** In winter is mainly white; only eye, bill, and tail are black. In spring and summer, has barred yellowish buff and gray upperparts; extent of white on back diminishes with time. **JUVENILE** Similar to summer female. **VOICE** Utters a rattling *kur-kurrrr* call. **STATUS AND HABITAT** Common on rocky tundra and mountain slopes. Mostly sedentary, but may move down slopes in winter. **OBSERVATION TIPS** Easiest to see when unseasonal winter thaw or summer snowfall renders camouflage inappropriate.

WILLOW PTARMIGAN *Lagopus lagopus* L 14–16 in

The largest ptarmigan. Similar to Rock—both have white wings at all times. Like Rock, has black tail feathers, but these are often concealed by white upper tail coverts. Willow's larger bill is not easy to discern; call differences are obvious, however. In summer, Willow has reddish plumage tone overall (gray-buff in Rock). Separation in winter is problematic: pure white plumage including lores, plus dark eye and bill is common to both sexes of Willow, and to female Rock. Not unduly wary, but if alarmed takes flight explosively: bouts of rapid wingbeats are then interspersed with long glides on bowed wings. **ADULT MALE** In winter has pure white plumage except for black tail, bill, and eye; hint of red wattle is sometimes seen. Acquires summer plumage through gradual spring molt; finally appears mainly reddish brown, but with white wings, legs, and belly. Note red wattle above eye. **ADULT FEMALE** Has paler, more buffy red and marbled plumage than male; well camouflaged when nesting. **JUVENILE** Resembles summer female. **VOICE** Call is a distinctive, nasal *go-back, go-back, go-back*. **STATUS AND HABITAT** Usually common, but numbers fluctuate. Favors willow scrub (shoots and buds feature in diet). Mainly sedentary, but some move south in winter. **OBSERVATION TIPS** In spring, territorial males sometimes tolerate close observation.

WHITE-TAILED PTARMIGAN
Lagopus leucurus L 12–13 in

Hardy, plump-bodied ptarmigan; the smallest of its kind in North America. White tail is diagnostic at all times (Rock and Willow have black tail feathers). Usually solitary during breeding season, but forms small flocks at other times. Feeds on seeds, shoots, and stems. **ADULT MALE** In winter, has pure white plumage with black eye and dainty bill. In summer, has barred and marbled brown and yellow-buff upperparts with black feathering on flanks and breast. Underparts are mainly white. **ADULT FEMALE** In winter is pure white and similar to male. In summer, similar to male, but with less white on underparts. **JUVENILE** Similar to summer female. **VOICE** Utters a *kik kik kik ki-KEEa* call. **STATUS AND HABITAT** Locally common, but numbers fluctuate. Favors rocky mountain slopes and willow scrub above treeline. **OBSERVATION TIPS** A real effort is required to find this species; consider yourself lucky if you succeed.

ROCK PTARMIGAN

FEMALE, SUMMER

MALE, SUMMER

FEMALE, SUMMER

MALE, SUMMER

WILLOW PTARMIGAN

MALE, SPRING

ADULT, WINTER

FEMALE, SUMMER

MOLTING MALE, SPRING

WHITE-TAILED PTARMIGAN

ADULT, WINTER

Phasianidae

GREATER PRAIRIE-CHICKEN
Tympanunchus cupido L 16–18 in

Plump-bodied bird. Male's rather understated plumage (for much of the time) is transformed in display by inflated orange neck sacs, yellow wattles above eyes, and raised head feathers that look almost like a hare's ears. In spring, birds gather at communal leks where males perform foot-stamping and booming displays, accompanied by tail fanning at start and end of performance. Comprises three subspecies: *pinnatus* is still widespread; *attwateri* (Attwater's Prairie-chicken) is close to extinction; *cupido* (Heath Hen) is now extinct. Following descriptions relate to *pinnatus*; *attwateri* is similar, but smaller and darker. **ADULT MALE** Warm buffish gray overall with extensive dark barring, including on belly. When not displaying, note pale throat, dark stripe through eye, and dark elongated feathers on side of neck—the "hare's ears" feathers that are raised in display. **ADULT FEMALE** Similar to male, but paler with less distinct dark barring. **JUVENILE** Similar to adult female. **VOICE** All birds utter clucking calls. Displaying male's deep, far-carrying booming note recalls sound made by blowing across the top of empty bottle. **STATUS AND HABITAT** Local and generally uncommon. Restricted to native prairies, typically in wetter sites, with lusher grass growth, than Lesser prefers. Range and numbers have declined catastrophically over last 200 years due to hunting and prairie habitat destruction (for agriculture). Some *pinnatus* populations are stable at local level, but habitat degradation (e.g. by grazing farm animals) and fragmentation continue to pose threats, given species' essentially sedentary nature. Population of *pinnatus* exceeds 600,000; *attwateri* numbers around 60 at two sites in southeastern Texas. **OBSERVATION TIPS** Easiest to see in spring when males display at communal leks; typically these are on raised hillocks. At other times of year, leads a rather unobtrusive life. **COMMENT** A pragmatic way of separating the two prairie-chicken species is on geographical range and habitat, neither of which overlap.

LESSER PRAIRIE-CHICKEN
Tympanunchus pallidicinctus L 15–17 in

Superficially similar to Greater, but displaying males in particular are separable with care: inflated neck sacs are reddish, calls are higher pitched and more frantic, and tail is fanned only at start of performance. Lesser's smaller size is not a useful identification feature in the field, especially since you are most unlikely to encounter both species side-by-side. Compared to Greater, Lesser has paler barring, which creates grayer plumage overall, and a less distinct pale throat. **ADULT MALE** Appears gray-buff overall, but close inspection reveals dark buff barring, least striking on belly. Note dark stripe through eye, pale throat, and dark feathers on side of neck; appearance of head is transformed in display by raised "hare's ears" feathers and inflated reddish neck sac. **ADULT FEMALE** Similar to male, but with less distinct dark markings. **JUVENILE** Similar to adult female. **VOICE** All birds utter clucking calls. Displaying male's calls are higher pitched than Greater's. **STATUS AND HABITAT** Uncommon and local, restricted to arid native prairie habitats where short bluegrass and sagebrush predominate. Has suffered catastrophic decline (population now around 20,000); current problems mirror those faced by Greater. **OBSERVATION TIPS** Easiest to see in spring when males display at communal leks, usually on slightly raised ground. Unobtrusive at other times of year.

MALE DISPLAYING

GREATER
PRAIRIE-CHICKEN

FEMALE

MALE

FEMALE

MALE

LESSER
PRAIRIE-CHICKEN

Phasianidae

SHARP-TAILED GROUSE
Tympanunchus phasianellus L 15–18 in

Plump-bodied grouse. Closely related to prairie-chickens, but note the pointed or wedge-shaped (not broad and rounded) tail. Plumage is beautifully patterned, dark feather borders creating a scaly effect, particularly on underparts (prairie-chickens, particularly Greater, look barred below). Feeds on shoots, buds, fruits, and seeds, with some invertebrates. Unobtrusive outside breeding season, but in spring, males display loudly at communal leks. Ritual involves birds bending low with head and neck extended, wings drooped, and yellow neck sacs and wattles above eye inflated; tail is held erect and shaken vigorously, accompanied by foot-stamping. **ADULT MALE** Has brown plumage with

MALE DISPLAYING

white spots on back and wings and scaly pattern on neck and underparts. Tail is yellowish buff above, fringed with barred feathers. When not displaying, note dark stripe through eye, bordered with white above and behind eye and below and in front. **ADULT FEMALE** Similar to male, but smaller and with less striking markings; neck sacs and wattles are absent. **JUVENILE** Similar to adult female. **VOICE** Displaying male utters hoots and clucks. **STATUS AND HABITAT** Has declined markedly due to habitat destruction and degradation, but still locally common. Associated with sagebrush habitat and grassland at moderate altitudes. **OBSERVATION TIPS** Easily overlooked except in breeding season. Displaying birds can be seen and heard from a distance.

GREATER SAGE-GROUSE
Centrocercus urophasianus
L 28–29 in (male); L 22–23 in (female)

Large and impressive grouse. Males are particularly stunning when displaying. Ritual involves a strutting display with spiky tail feathers raised and fanned, head feathers held erect, and ruff of white neck feathers puffed up. Accompanied by wing swishing sounds and two loud pops caused by yellow air sacs on the neck being inflated and deflated (normally not visible). At other times, adopts a horizontal posture, emphasized by proportionately long tail. Typically gregarious throughout the year. Mostly sedentary although some food-related dispersal may occur during harsh winter weather. Feeds primarily on sagebrush, but also takes invertebrates in summer. **ADULT MALE** Has finely marked, dark brown upperparts, white on breast and side of neck, and black belly; latter is striking in flight, as are white underwings. Note white-bordered black throat and yellow wattles above eye, expanded during display. **ADULT FEMALE** Similar to male, but paler overall, with less distinct head markings and shorter tail. **JUVENILE** Similar to adult female. **VOICE** Male produces popping sounds during display, audible over a considerable distance. **STATUS AND HABI-**

GUNNISON SAGE-GROUSE

MALE

TAT Has declined markedly over the last 200 years due to habitat destruction and degradation (for agriculture), exacerbated by hunting. Favors sagebrush habitats and still very locally common; total population exceeds 100,000. **OBSERVATION TIPS** Easiest to find, and most rewarding to observe, in spring (mainly Mar–May) when displaying. **SIMILAR SPECIES Gunnison Sage-Grouse** *Centrocercus minimus* is similar to Greater, but appreciably smaller (L 22 in (male); 18 in (female)). Restricted to small areas in eastern Utah and western Colorado and population numbers just a few thousand. Similar habitat requirements and appearance to Greater; upper side of male's tail feathers are white-barred.

SHARP-TAILED GROUSE

MALE

GREATER SAGE-GROUSE

FEMALE

MALE

Odontophoridae

SCALED QUAIL *Callipepla squamata* L 10 in

Plump-bodied quail with scaly-looking neck and breast, and a distinct, pale-tipped crest. Hard to flush, preferring to run from danger rather than fly. Gregarious outside breeding season, forming coveys often numbering several dozen birds. Feeds on seeds, shoots, and invertebrates. Sexes are similar. **ADULT** Has a grayish lilac neck and breast, with dark feather margins that create a scaly appearance. Note pale streaks on flanks and buff belly, variably flushed with chestnut according to subspecies; this forms a distinct dark patch in *castanogastris* from southern Texas. Head is buffy, with chestnut brown ear coverts and subterminal band on pale-tipped crest feathers. Back and wings are plain buffy brown. **JUVENILE** Similar to adult, but with streaks on back and almost unmarked crest. **VOICE** Utters a *chip-cherr* contact call. **STATUS AND HABITAT** Locally fairly common in arid grassland, but has declined markedly in recent decades, due to habitat loss and degradation, and hunting. **OBSERVATION TIPS** Look for coveys in the winter, particularly in the vicinity of waterholes.

GAMBEL'S QUAIL *Callipepla gambelii* L 10–10.5 in

Attractive quail. Males are particularly well-marked and have an evocative call. Both sexes are adorned with a forward-curving, "comma-shaped" head plume, a feature shared with superficially similar California Quail; subtle plumage differences, habitat preferences, and geographical range (little overlap) aid separation from that species. Gregarious outside breeding season. Sexes are dissimilar. **ADULT MALE** Has mainly gray upperparts, with scaly feathering on nape. Head markings comprise chestnut crown and black face and throat, colors defined by white lines. Neck is blue-gray and underparts are otherwise mainly buffy yellow, but note dark belly patch and chestnut flanks adorned with pale streaks. **ADULT FEMALE** Similar to male, but duller; male's head markings are absent. **JUVENILE** Similar to adult female, but with less distinct markings. **VOICE** Male utters *kup-werr-kip* or *kup-keWerr-kip* calls. **STATUS AND HABITAT** Common in deserts with dense scrub cover, often in the vicinity of waterholes. **OBSERVATION TIPS** Easiest to find in winter.

CALIFORNIA QUAIL
Callipepla californica L 10–10.5 in

Well-marked quail, similar to Gambel's, but separable with care: California male has mainly scaly belly and pale brown (not black) forehead. Note the distinctive curved head plume shared by both sexes of both species. Highly gregarious outside the breeding season. Feeds on seeds, shoots,

MALE

and invertebrates. Sexes are dissimilar. **ADULT MALE** Has mainly gray-brown upperparts, the nape finely marked with black and white, and a dull brown crown. Black on face and throat is defined by white and separated from crown by white line above the eye. Breast is lilac-gray, belly appears scaled due to dark feather margins, and flanks are brown with pale streaks. **ADULT FEMALE** Similar to male, but duller overall and lacks striking head markings. **JUVENILE** Similar to adult female, but duller still, and more mottled. **VOICE** Male utters an insistent *whe-kee-go* call. **STATUS AND HABITAT** Locally common in open woodland and scrub (including urban fringes), usually in vicinity of water. **OBSERVATION TIPS** Easiest to find in winter, early in the morning.

SCALED QUAIL

ADULT

GAMBEL'S QUAIL

FEMALE

MALE

FEMALE

CALIFORNIA QUAIL

MALE

Odontophoridae

MOUNTAIN QUAIL *Oreortyx pictus* L 10.5–11 in

Attractive and distinctive quail. Combination of chestnut throat, elegant straight head plume, and bold white bars on flanks is unique and diagnostic. Rather shy and male's distinctive call is heard more often than bird is seen. Sometimes seen in family groups, but otherwise not especially gregarious. Feeds on seeds, berries, acorns, and bulbs. Sexes are similar. **ADULT** Has brown upperparts and chestnut belly and flanks, the latter adorned with striking white bars (which "glow" in poor light). Breast is bluish lilac and throat is chestnut, defined by a white border. Note very long and straight head plume, which can be raised or lowered. **JUVENILE** Similar to adult, but white bars on flanks are indistinct and plumage is otherwise duller and marbled; head plume is shorter. **VOICE** Male utters a shrill *Quee-aark* call. **STATUS AND HABITAT** Rather uncommon and possibly declining, probably due to habitat destruction and degradation. Favors montane scrub and chaparral, to altitudes of up to 10,000ft. **OBSERVATION TIPS** Try to pinpoint a calling male, although this is easier said than done.

NORTHERN BOBWHITE
Colinus virginianus L 9–10 in

North America's most familiar quail, although range is more extensive in east than west. Male's white throat and stripe above the eye are distinctive and diagnostic in almost all birds; plumage otherwise shows considerable regional variation, particularly in the extent of rufous. So-called "Masked Bobwhite" (ssp. *ridgwayi*) is strikingly different, with mainly rufous-orange body plumage and largely black face and throat. Distinctive call is common to males of all subspecies. Omnivorous diet includes seeds, fruits, bulbs, and invertebrates. Gregarious outside the breeding season and seen in coveys. Sexes are dissimilar. **ADULT MALE** Has striking head pattern: white throat and stripe above eye are constant, but dark elements of pattern vary from almost black to rufous, according to geographical region; lower margin of white throat is defined by black "necklace." Body plumage is brown overall, but with pale barring on underparts and streaking on flanks. **ADULT FEMALE** Rufous brown overall, palest below, with streaked flanks and marbled upperparts. Shows hint of male's head pattern, but pale elements of this are buffy yellow. **JUVENILE** Similar to adult female, but duller and with less striking markings. **VOICE** Male utters a strident *bob-White* call. **STATUS AND HABITAT** Has declined markedly in recent years, but still locally common in open woodland and scrub within its limited range in west. Masked Bobwhite is a bird of desert grassland. Following extinction in southern Arizona (probably as a result of cattle ranching), it has been reintroduced using Mexican birds, e.g. at Buenos Aires National Wildlife Reserve. **OBSERVATION TIPS** Typically wary in areas where hunting pressure is extreme. Elsewhere, family parties can be relatively confiding. **SIMILAR SPECIES Montezuma Quail** *Cyrtonyx montezumae* (L 8–9 in) is a tiny, beautifully marked quail, with a rather spherical body shape (seemingly no tail) and a proportionately large head (as if it is wearing a cap). The male has brown, streaked upperparts, chestnut underparts, and black flanks marked with striking white spots. The head is adorned with bold black and white markings. The female is more uniformly brown than the male. A secretive species of arid, wooded canyons with grassy ground vegetation. South Arizona, New Mexico, and Texas.

MONTEZUMA QUAIL

MALE

FEMALE

MOUNTAIN QUAIL

ADULT

NORTHERN BOBWHITE

FEMALE

MALE

Gaviidae

COMMON LOON *Gavia immer* L 32–33 in

Elegant waterbird. Long, pointed bill held horizontally or only
slightly elevated. In flight, head and neck held outstretched, with
feet and legs trailing behind (true of all loons). Dives for fish. Sexes are similar. **ADULT** In summer has iridescent greenish black head and neck; note two
rows of white stripes on neck. Blackish upperparts have checkerboardlike
pattern of white spots on mantle and smaller white spots elsewhere. Underparts are gleaming white and bill is dark. In winter, has dark gray upperparts
and whitish underparts; note dark half
collar on neck. Pale gray bill has notice-

ADULT, WINTER

YELLOW-BILLED LOON

ADULT, SUMMER

ably dark culmen. **JUVENILE** Similar to winter adult, but upperparts
brownish gray while underparts are off-white. **VOICE** Utters evocative, wailing cry and eerie yodeling sound on breeding grounds.
STATUS AND HABITAT Fairly common on large lakes in breeding
season. In winter, mainly on rocky coasts. **OBSERVATION TIPS** Most
lakes rich in fish within breeding range support a pair in summer.
SIMILAR SPECIES Yellow-billed Loon *G. adamsii* (L 34–35 in)
has similar summer plumage. Pale yellow bill is straight (convex
in Common), with a paler culmen; bill and angular head are held
tilted upward. In winter, bill is uniformly pale (dark culmen in Common); eye surround is pale. Juvenile recalls winter adult with "scaly"
back. High Arctic breeder. Scarce in winter on Pacific coast.

PACIFIC LOON *Gavia pacifica* L 24–25 in

Buoyant waterbird. Relatively small, daggerlike bill is held horizontally. Sexes are similar. **ADULT** In summer, has gray nape and head;
throat is black and sides of neck are adorned with black and white lines.
Black back has checkerboardlike pattern of white spots, while underparts are
white. In winter, has mainly gray-brown upperparts (darker on back than on
neck) and whitish underparts. Demarcation between brown and white on neck

1ST-WINTER

ARCTIC LOON

ADULT, SUMMER

is well defined, more so than in Common. Most birds show a narrow, dark
"chinstrap." **JUVENILE** Similar to winter
adult, but back looks "scaly." **VOICE** On breeding territory, utters
croaking and grunting calls. **STATUS AND HABITAT** Locally common
breeder on large northern lakes. Outside breeding season, mainly
coastal; rare on inland lakes. **OBSERVATION TIPS** Easiest to find in
winter. **SIMILAR SPECIES Arctic Loon** *G. arctica* (L 26–27 in) has
larger bill and more angular head. In summer, similar to Pacific,
but gray on head and neck is darker. In winter, dark elements of
plumage are darker than in Pacific (especially neck); patch of white
feathering usually visible at water level towards stern. Rare breeder in western Alaska; very rare in winter on Pacific coasts.

RED-THROATED LOON *Gavia stellata* L 24–25 in

Elegant loon that holds head and daggerlike bill tilted upward. Sexes
are similar. **ADULT** In summer, has blue-gray on face and sides of
neck, red throat, and black and white lines on back of neck, and, lower down,
on sides of neck too. Upperparts are otherwise gray-brown while underparts
are whitish. In winter, has gray upperparts, spangled with small white spots.
Underparts are white. **JUVENILE** Similar to winter adult, but upperparts
are browner and more streaked, and underparts appear off-white. **VOICE**
Utters a gooselike *kaa-kaa-kaa* in flight. **STATUS AND HABITAT** Nests beside
small pools and fairly common within range. Outside breeding season, found in
shallow coastal seas. **OBSERVATION TIPS** Easiest to find in winter.

ADULT, SUMMER

COMMON LOON

1ST-WINTER

ADULT AND CHICK

ADULT, SUMMER

PACIFIC LOON

1ST-WINTER

ADULT, SUMMER

RED-THROATED LOON

ADULT, WINTER

ADULT, SUMMER

Podicipedidae

WESTERN GREBE
Aechmophorus occidentalis L 23–26 in

Elegant waterbird with a slender neck and long, narrow bill. Dives well and for extended periods after fish. Sexes are similar and all birds can be confused with Clark's Grebe. Extent of black cap is a good feature in breeding season: extends below beady red eye in Western, but not in Clark's; less obvious in winter. Bill color is more reliable year-round: yellowish green with a darker culmen in Western, but uniformly bright yellow in Clark's. Somewhat gregarious outside breeding season. **ADULT** In summer, has blackish upperparts and white underparts; demarcation between these is most striking on head and neck. In winter, retains black and white appearance overall, but plumage surrounding eye is gray not black. **JUVENILE** Similar to winter adult, but dark elements of plumage are paler and eye is duller. **VOICE** Utters a harsh, squealing *kreeh kreet*. **STATUS AND HABITAT** Locally common, found on reed-fringed freshwater lakes in breeding season, but mainly coastal in winter. Suffers from marine oil spills. **OBSERVATION TIPS** Conspicuous at start of breeding season when pairs perform elaborate displays that involve presenting each other with aquatic plants and ritual courtship "dances."

CLARK'S GREBE *Aechmophorus clarkii* L 22–25 in

Superficially very similar to Western Grebe and once considered conspecific. Subtle differences in bill color and extent of black cap enable separation: *see* description of Western for specific differences. Somewhat gregarious outside breeding season and sometimes consorts with Western. Sexes are similar. **ADULT** In summer, has dark gray upperparts (slightly paler than Western) and white underparts; demarcation between these is most striking on head and neck. Black cap does not encompass beady red eye, which is surrounded by white. In winter, plumage is similarly black and white overall, but black cap extends to eye-level behind eye; lores are whitish (very dark gray in Western). **JUVENILE** Similar to winter adult, but duller and paler overall. **VOICE** Utters a slurred, shrieking *kree-eet*. **STATUS AND HABITAT** Locally fairly common, but generally less numerous than Western. Found on freshwater lakes in summer, but mainly on Pacific coast in winter. **OBSERVATION TIPS** Courtship display is fascinating to watch. Scan flocks of Western Grebes in winter to find the occasional Clark's.

RED-NECKED GREBE
Podiceps grisegena L 18–20 in

Appreciably smaller and more stocky than Western and Clark's grebes. Swims buoyantly and dives frequently for fish. Note well-defined white panels on wings (cf. broad white wing bar seen in Western and Clark's). Sexes are similar. **ADULT** In summer, has dark gray-brown upperparts, including nape. Neck and upperparts are brick-red, cheeks are pale gray bordered with white, and cap is dark with a hint of a crest. Underparts are otherwise whitish, with gray streaking on flanks. Bill is stocky and yellow with a dark culmen. In winter, neck colors are lost, but often retains a

ADULT, WINTER

hint of reddish collar. Cheek pattern is less well defined and ear coverts are grubby-looking. **JUVENILE** Recalls winter adult, but shows more extensive red on neck; note striking dark stripes on cheeks. **VOICE** Utters subdued wails during breeding season. **STATUS AND HABITAT** Fairly common, breeding on shallow, northern freshwater lakes; winters mainly on sheltered inshore seas.

WESTERN GREBE

ADULT, WINTER

ADULT, SUMMER

CLARK'S GREBE

ADULT, WINTER

ADULT, SUMMER

RED-NECKED GREBE

ADULT, SUMMER

Podicipedidae

HORNED GREBE *Podiceps auritus* L 12–14 in
Elegant waterbird that swims buoyantly and dives frequently in search
of small fish and aquatic invertebrates. All birds have a bright red eye.
Flattish crown and bill shape (both mandibles are curved) allow separation
from similar Eared Grebe at all times; note also whitish tip to bill. In flight,
wings show white patches on both leading and trailing edges. Sexes are
similar. **ADULT** In summer, has reddish orange neck and flanks. Back is black
and black head is adorned with golden yellow plumes. In winter, has mainly
black upperparts and white underparts. Note clear demarcation between black
cap and white cheeks. **JUVENILE** Similar to winter adult. **VOICE** Utters territorial calls, including various rattling trills and squeals. **STATUS AND HABITAT** Locally common. In breeding season, favors ponds and shallow lakes with abundant emergent vegetation. In winter, mainly
coastal, but also on ice-free freshwater lakes in south. **OBSERVATION TIPS** In winter, search sheltered
stretches of coast on calm days. Unobtrusive in breeding season, except when displaying in spring.

EARED GREBE *Podiceps nigricollis* L 11–13 in
Distinguished from Horned by slightly upturned bill and steeper
forehead. All birds have a bright red eye. In flight, note white patch
on trailing edge of wing. Dives for aquatic invertebrates. Sexes are similar.
ADULT In summer, has blackish head, neck, and back; face is adorned with
golden yellow tufts. Flanks are chestnut. In winter, has mainly blackish
upperparts and white underparts; separable from similar Horned Grebe by
greater extent of dark coloration on cheeks, as well as head shape. **JUVENILE**
Similar to winter adult, but white elements of plumage are buffy. **VOICE** Calls
include various whistles and squeaks. **STATUS AND HABITAT** Common. Favors
shallow, well-vegetated inland lakes and ponds in breeding season. In winter, moves south to ice-
free freshwater and brackish lakes. **OBSERVATION TIPS** Breeding birds have stunning plumage and are
an impressive sight: easiest to find in spring when displaying. For a spectacle of numbers, visit Mono
Lake, California in fall: thousands congregate on migration.

PIED-BILLED GREBE
Polilymbus podiceps L 11–13 in
Stocky, plump-bodied grebe. Note the pale "powderpuff" of fluffy
feathers at rear end. Bill is proportionately large and thick; black band is
absent during winter months. Dives frequently for small fish and aquatic
invertebrates. Sexes are similar. **ADULT** In summer, has gray-brown plumage,
palest on flanks and neck. Bill is pale gray with a striking black band. In
winter, plumage is more orange-buff, particularly on neck. Throat is pale and
bill is uniformly yellowish gray. **JUVENILE** Has head stripes at first, but after
molt acquires plumage
like winter adult. **VOICE** Utters various clucking
and chattering calls. **STATUS AND HABITAT**
Widespread and common. Breeds on well-
vegetated ponds and lakes and in winter moves
south to ice-free similar freshwater habitats.
OBSERVATION TIPS Usually indifferent to
observers, but seldom remains at water surface for long. **SIMILAR SPECIES Least Grebe**
Tachybaptus dominicus (L 9–10 in) recalls a tiny
version of Pied-billed, but note the darker
plumage overall in summer, beady yellow eye
(dark in Pied-billed), and daintier bill. Locally
common only in southern Texas, on well-
vegetated ponds and lakes.

LEAST GREBE

ADULT, BREEDING

ADULT, WINTER

HORNED GREBE

ADULT, SUMMER

ADULT, WINTER

EARED GREBE

ADULT, SUMMER

ADULT, WINTER

PIED-BILLED GREBE

ADULT, SUMMER

BLACK-FOOTED ALBATROSS
Phoebastria nigripes W 80–84 in

A huge seabird, unmistakably an albatross on account of its size, proportionately very long wings, large bill, and flight pattern. The mainly all-dark plumage separates it from Laysan Albatross, which has a white head, neck, and underparts, and is the only other of its kind to occur regularly off Pacific coasts. Flies in typical albatross fashion: the wings are held stiff and outstretched and seldom flapped, as the bird glides and banks effortlessly. Sexes are not separable in the field, but aging differences are discernible with care. **ADULT** Has mainly dark brown plumage, but tail is noticeably darker than back and most birds show variable amounts of white at base of bill and on undertail coverts. Typically, the extent of white in both these areas increases with age and some birds appear very pale-headed. Bill is dark pink in all birds. **JUVENILE** Similar to adult, but usually the pale elements of adult's plumage are absent. **VOICE** Mostly silent. **STATUS AND HABITAT** Breeds on remote islands off Japan and Hawaii. Occurs year-round off North American Pacific coasts as a feeding visitor; most widespread and numerous outside the breeding season, from fall to spring. **OBSERVATION TIPS** Easiest to see on pelagic trips. **COMMENT** Like other albatross species, suffers mortality from long-line fishing. **SIMILAR SPECIES Laysan Albatross** *P. immutabilis* (W 78–80 in) has blackish brown upper wings, back, and tail. Plumage is otherwise mainly white, but, seen from below, note the dark primaries and dark margins to the wings; wing coverts are also variably dark. At close range, note the grayish cheeks and dark "eyebrow." Bill is pink with a dark tip in all birds. Breeds on Kauai and remote islands off Hawaii. Occurs off Pacific North American coasts as a wandering, feeding visitor. Easiest to see on pelagic trips.

LAYSAN ALBATROSS

ADULT

ADULT

NORTHERN FULMAR *Fulmarus glacialis* W 40–42 in

A medium-sized seabird and a superficially gull-like relative of shearwaters and petrels. Easily distinguished from gulls at close range by its long, tubular nostrils and, in flight, by its more stiffly held wings and effortless gliding action. Exceptionally buoyant, rides very high in the water, and often gathers in groups where feeding is good, for example, around fishing boats. Generally sociable and nests in loose colonies on sea cliffs. Typically indifferent to human observers, although capable of regurgitating oily and smelly crop contents in a projectile fashion if alarmed by an intruder. Sexes are similar, but birds occur at different color morphs. **ADULT** Pale morph has pale gray upper wings, back, and tail. Head and underparts are white. Note dark smudge around eye. Dark morph is variably dark blue-gray or brownish, uniform in color, except for paler primaries. **JUVENILE** Similar to adult, once chick's fluffy white down has been lost. **VOICE** Utters various gurgling cackles and grunts at colonies, but otherwise silent. **STATUS AND HABITAT** Common and found year-round in sub-Arctic waters of Pacific Northwest. Nests on ledges on sea cliffs and locally forms sizeable colonies along shores of Arctic Alaska. In winter, range extends south to most of Pacific coast, but numbers vary annually. **OBSERVATION TIPS** Frequently seen on pelagic trips, but also occasionally from headlands, especially during onshore gales. Although not tied to land, sub-Arctic birds often linger in vicinity of nesting colonies throughout year.

ADULT

ADULT

BLACK-FOOTED ALBATROSS

DARK MORPH

PALE MORPH

NORTHERN FULMAR

Procellariidae

ADULT

FLESH-FOOTED
SHEARWATER

ADULT

SOOTY SHEARWATER
Puffinus griseus W 40–41 in

Medium-sized shearwater. Relatively long, stiffly held wings allow it to bank and glide effortlessly; particularly impressive in strong winds. Angle and intensity of light affects appearance allowing for confusion with similar Short-tailed. **ALL BIRDS** Can appear all-dark at a distance, but at close range, and in good light, note sooty brown plumage and silvery white underwing coverts that form a striking bar, palest and broadest toward wingtip. Bill is slender, rather long, and narrowest in middle, with a hooked tip and tubular nostrils. **VOICE** Silent at sea. **STATUS AND HABITAT** Breeds in Southern Hemisphere. Nonbreeding visitor to North Pacific and common in inshore seas May–Aug. **OBSERVATION TIPS** Easy to see from pelagic trips and occasionally congregates in large numbers close to shore in Jul–Aug if feeding is good. **SIMILAR SPECIES Flesh-footed Shearwater** *P. carneipes* (W 40–41 in) is closest, structurally, to Pink-footed (*see* below), but uniformly dark brown plumage allows for confusion with Sooty. Note, however, the broader wings, uniformly dark underwing coverts, thicker, longer neck and the relatively large, dark-tipped pale bill. Nests in Southern Hemisphere and a nonbreeding visitor, in small numbers, to Pacific coast of North America. Feeds alongside other shearwaters, but rare.

SHORT-TAILED SHEARWATER
Puffinus tenuirostris W 38–39 in

Medium-sized shearwater that glides on stiffly held wings, flapping only occasionally in short bursts. Very similar to Sooty and poor views may not allow specific identification. Good views do, however, permit separation by studying key features. Has similarly dark sooty brown plumage, but wings are relatively shorter and pale underwing coverts are palest and broadest toward the body (broadest toward wingtip in Sooty). Note also Short-tailed's shorter, smaller bill, more rounded head, and generally shorter neck, creating an impression overall of a more compact, less cigar-shaped body. **ALL BIRDS** Can appear all-dark at a distance, but in good light plumage is mainly sooty brown. Pale underwing coverts create a striking, narrow bar in some individuals. Some birds have a pale throat. Bill is dark and relatively short and an even thickness (cf. Sooty). **VOICE** Silent at sea. **STATUS AND HABITAT** Nests in Southern Hemisphere and a nonbreeding visitor to north Pacific, mainly May–Sep. Occurs alongside Sooty, but usually the scarcer of the two. **OBSERVATION TIPS** Easy to see on pelagic trips.

PINK-FOOTED SHEARWATER
Puffinus creatopus W 42–43 in

Large, plump-bodied, relatively broad-winged shearwater. Has a proportionately long, thick neck, large head, and elongated tail end. Flight is impressive and effortless in strong winds, but labored on calm days. Underwing markings are useful in identification. **ALL BIRDS** Have uniformly dark brown upperparts, but mainly pale underparts: throat and belly are white and underwing coverts are often mainly pale, but with variable dark mottling. Bill is large, thick, pink, and dark-tipped. **VOICE** Silent at sea. **STATUS AND HABITAT** Nests in Southern Hemisphere; nonbreeding visitor to North Pacific, common May–Aug. **OBSERVATION TIPS** Favors offshore waters; easiest to see on pelagic trips, hard to observe from land. **SIMILAR SPECIES Buller's Shearwater** *P. bulleri* (W 39–40 in) has gleaming white underparts and gray upperparts boldly marked by black bar on wing coverts. Nonbreeding visitor to North Pacific and locally common May–Aug.

SOOTY SHEARWATER

ADULT

SHORT-TAILED
SHEARWATER

ADULT

ADULT

PINK-FOOTED
SHEARWATER

BULLER'S SHEARWATER

ADULT

ADULT

Procellariidae and Fregatidae

BLACK STORM-PETREL

ADULT

ASHY STORM-PETREL

ADULT

LEACH'S STORM-PETREL
Oceanodroma leucorhoa
W 18–20 in

Tiny by seabird standards, but with relatively long wings and a deeply forked tail. Flight direction and pattern are ever-changing, often bounding with deep, powerful wing-beats, but occasionally gliding in an almost shearwater-like fashion. Combination of forked tail and white, wedge-shaped rump (divided down middle by gray line) is diagnostic in those birds that have these features. However, some southern birds have uniformly dark rumps, while others are intermediate between the extremes; these can be confused with Ashy and Black Storm-petrels. Sexes are similar. **ALL BIRDS** Sooty gray, but can look all-dark at a distance, except for pale panel on upper wing coverts. Note that tail's fork is not always easy to discern and pale gray line that divides rump is discernible only at very close range. Underwings are all-dark. **VOICE** Silent at sea, but at breeding colonies birds utter a bizarre-sounding gurgling rattle. **STATUS AND HABITAT** Oceanic, seldom approaching land except during breeding season at night (nests on remote islands), or when driven onshore by storm. **OBSERVATION TIPS** Tricky to observe since it shuns land and typically does not follow boats. Chance encounters from pelagic trips offer the best opportunities. **SIMILAR SPECIES Black Storm-petrel** *O. melania* (W 19–22 in) has relatively longer tail and wings than dark-rumped form of Leach's. Feet project beyond tail (hard to see), but flight pattern is a useful feature: direct, powerful, and ternlike, or gliding and shearwater-like. **Ashy Storm-petrel** *O. homochroa* (W 17–18 in) is smaller than dark-rumped form of Leach's, with silvery underwings and fluttering flight.

FORK-TAILED STORM-PETREL
Oceanodroma furcata W 18–19 in
Mainly gray plumage makes this storm-petrel unmistakable within our region. Tail is deeply forked and wings are relatively broad by storm-petrel standards. Flight is powerful, but relaxed, with occasional glides. Sexes are similar. **ALL BIRDS** Mainly pale gray, but note dark and white pattern on upper wing coverts that creates a striking "V." Seen from below, note the dark underwing coverts. At close range, dark eye patch can be discerned. **VOICE** Silent at sea, but utters rasping calls at breeding colonies. **STATUS AND HABITAT** Nests on remote islands, but otherwise seen at sea. Fairly common northward from latitude of central California, but seldom seen from land. **OBSERVATION TIPS** Easiest to see on pelagic trips.

MAGNIFICENT FRIGATEBIRD
Fregata magnificens W 87–90 in
Huge and unmistakable seabird with long, pointed, and angular-looking wings, long and deeply forked tail, and long, hook-tipped bill. Aerial mastery is aided by excellent weight : wing area ratio (feathers weigh more than bones): soars and glides effortlessly, but capable of amazing speed and agility when in pursuit of food or when parasitizing other feeding birds. Sexes are dissimilar. **ADULT MALE** Mostly all-dark, but purple sheen is seen in good light. Bright red throat sac is inflated in display. **ADULT FEMALE** Lacks male's throat sac and has white on belly. **JUVENILE** Mainly dark, but note the white head, neck, and belly patch, and brown upper wing coverts. **VOICE** Mainly silent. **STATUS AND HABITAT** Breeds in mangrove swamps on Mexican coast; scarce, but regular visitor to southern California coast in summer and fall. **OBSERVATION TIPS** Most regular after hurricane-force winds.

LEACH'S STORM-PETREL

ADULT

ADULT

FEMALE

FORK-TAILED STORM-PETREL

ADULT

JUVENILE

MAGNIFICENT FRIGATEBIRD

JUVENILE

MALE

Pelicanidae

AMERICAN WHITE PELICAN
Pelecanus erythrorhynchos L 61–63 in

Huge and unmistakable waterbird with the typical pelican form: plump body, proportionately long neck, and extremely long, hooked-tip bill with expandable gular pouch. Essentially white plumage, seen in standing and swimming bird, is transformed when bird takes to the air revealing contrasting black flight feathers. Wingspan is immense (108 in), allowing bird to soar and glide with ease; note the distinctive wing pattern, proportionately short tail, and forward-projecting bill. Swims with ease, by means of large, webbed feet. Feeds on fish by engulfing shoals in huge, yellow gular pouch; often feeds collectively. Sexes are similar. **ADULT** Appears mainly white, but in breeding season breast is flushed faintly with yellow-buff and crown sometimes appears grubby-looking. Black flight feathers are mostly hidden in swimming and standing birds. Legs are reddish orange; bill and bare skin surrounding eye are reddish orange in breeding season, but more yellowish in winter. **JUVENILE** Similar to adult, but with faint graying feathering on neck and upper wing coverts, and duller bill colors. **VOICE** Mostly silent, although soft grunts are uttered by nesting birds. **STATUS AND HABITAT** Locally common breeding species, nesting colonially on large lakes with abundant fish, mainly in Midwest prairie states. Outside breeding season, moves south to southern U.S. states and Mexico, favoring large freshwater lakes, coastal lagoons, and estuaries. **OBSERVATION TIPS** Large enough not to be missed easily, and usually tolerant of people to allow good views, especially during winter months. Soaring flocks are an amazing sight, as are groups engaged in collective feeding.

BROWN PELICAN *Pelecanus occidentalis* L 48–51 in

Huge and impressive waterbird. Unmistakably a pelican, given the body shape, huge bill, and expandable gular pouch; mainly dark plumage allows easy separation from American White Pelican. Swims effortlessly and with grace, using large, webbed feet. Also extremely impressive in flight and capable of sustained gliding and soaring. Feeds in a spectacular manner: dives from a considerable height, pulling back the wings at the last second and engulfing fish in expanded gular pouch when submerged. Sexes are similar. **ADULT** Has streaked, silvery gray upperparts and pale-streaked, brown underparts. Pacific bird has whitish head and neck in winter, variably flushed with orange on crown and forehead, with yellowish pink bill and gray-brown gular pouch; breeding bird is similar, but has dark brown on rear of neck and mainly red gular pouch. Atlantic bird is similar to Pacific and shows similar seasonal variation, but gular pouch is dark brown at all times. **JUVENILE** Has mainly brown plumage, but with a whitish belly; seen from below in flight, note the pale

ADULT, WINTER

margin to underwing coverts that forms a subtle stripe. **VOICE** Mostly silent. **STATUS AND HABITAT** Locally fairly common in southern California and south Texas. Mainly coastal, feeding in both sheltered bays and relatively exposed seas. Often seen perched on boat moorings and posts. Seldom seen on inland freshwater lakes. **OBSERVATION TIPS** Usually easy to see in suitable coastal locations and typically not bothered by the presence of people, allowing superb views. Fishing birds provide a wonderful spectacle and the activities of one diving bird usually quickly attracts a small gathering of feeding pelicans.

JUVENILE

ADULT

AMERICAN WHITE PELICAN

ADULT

JUVENILE

BROWN PELICAN

ADULT

Phalacrocoracidae

DOUBLE-CRESTED CORMORANT
Phalacrocorax auritus L 32–33 in

Robust waterbird with relatively long neck and stout, hook-tipped
bill and long tail. Gular pouch is orange; rear margin is square-ended or rounded (cf. Neotropic). Swims low in water, diving frequently for fish. Flies with
head and neck outstretched; often perches with wings outstretched. Our most
widespread cormorant and the one most likely to be seen near freshwater.
Sexes are similar. **ADULT** Has mainly dark plumage, but pale feather centers on
back and upper wings create a scaly appearance. Acquires whitish head plumes
in breeding season. Note orange gular pouch,
base to lower mandible, and skin in front of eye; color is most
intense in breeding birds. **JUVENILE** Has gray-buff plumage, darkest
on back and usually palest on breast and throat. Bill, eye surround,
and gular pouch are yellowish orange; note truncated rear margin.
Acquires darker adult plumage over 3-year period. **VOICE** Mostly
silent. **STATUS AND HABITAT** Locally common on coasts, freshwater
marshes, and lakes. Present year-round on coast, but summer visitor
to many interior freshwater habitats. **OBSERVATION TIPS** Easy to find
on a wide range of wetland habitats. Often perches on posts and
moorings, allowing scrutiny of facial markings. **SIMILAR SPECIES**
Neotropic Cormorant *P. brasilianus* (L 25–26 in) is smaller, more
slender-bodied, and longer-tailed. Adult has dark plumage with gray
feather centers on back and upper wings. Bill and gular pouch are
yellowish; margin is pointed and has white border. Juvenile has buffy
brown plumage and is best distinguished from juvenile Double-crested
by angled rear margin to gular pouch. Extreme southeast only.

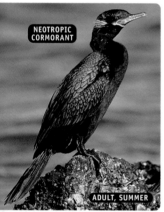

NEOTROPIC CORMORANT

ADULT, SUMMER

BRANDT'S CORMORANT
Phalacrocorax penicillatus L 34–35 in

Mainly dark seabird. Swims low in water, its slender neck raised high. Flies with head
and neck outstretched. Gregarious at all times. Note rounded head outline. Sexes are similar. **ADULT** Has blackish plumage; sheen to feather centers on back and upper wings seen
only at close range. Bill is dark and throat is yellowish buff. Acquires bluish throat and white
streaks on side of neck in breeding season. **JUVENILE** Has brown plumage, palest on breast;
note pale, yellowish throat. Darker, adult plumage is acquired over 3-year period. **VOICE** Mostly silent. **STATUS AND HABITAT** Locally common on coast, both inshore and offshore. **OBSER-
VATION TIPS** Widespread on Pacific coast. **SIMILAR SPECIES** **Pelagic Cormorant** *P. pelagicus*
(L 28–29 in) is slimmer-bodied, with relatively long neck and tail, and daintier bill. Note dark throat
and angular head profile, pronounced in breeding adult, which has a tufted crown and crest. Breeding
bird also has white rear flanks and dull red skin at base of bill and around eye; face is dark at other times.
Juvenile is uniformly dark brown. Locally common on inshore rocky coasts; usually solitary.

ADULT, SUMMER

PELAGIC CORMORANT

ADULT, SUMMER

ADULT

ADULT

ADULT, WINTER

ADULT, WINTER

DOUBLE-CRESTED
CORMORANT

ADULT, SUMMER

BRANDT'S
CORMORANT

ADULT, WINTER

Threskiornithidae and Ardeidae

WHITE-FACED IBIS *Plegadis chihi* L 23–24 in

Distinctive waterbird with long legs and neck, bulbous head, and long, downcurved bill. In good light, plumage looks richly colorful with metallic sheen to wing coverts. Feeds by probing for aquatic inverte-brates. In flight, neck and head are held outstretched, with legs trailing.

ADULT

Sexes are similar. **ADULT** Has mainly deep maroon plumage. Darker feathers on wing coverts and lower back have green sheen in bright light (most intense in breeding season). Bill is grayish yellow and beady red eye and red facial skin have a white border. Legs are pinkish red. In flight, wings look all dark. **JUVENILE** Similar to adult, but with duller plumage, leg and bill colors; facial markings are absent until following spring. **VOICE** Utters a *huerr-huerr-huerr* call. **STATUS AND HABITAT** Locally common in freshwater and brackish habitats. Found on inland, interior lakes and marshes during breeding season. Moves south in fall, wintering mainly in coastal districts. **OBSERVATION TIPS** Unusual profile and deliberate feeding pattern make identification easy. East of Texas, can be confused with eastern counterpart, Glossy Ibis *P. falcinellus* (L 22–24 in), which lacks red and white face markings.

LEAST BITTERN *Ixobrychus exilis* L 13–14 in

A tiny heron. Unobtrusive habits and largely inaccessible favored habitats make it fairly hard to observe. Sometimes climbs up tall cat-tail stem or more typically seen briefly in flight, low over marsh vegetation. If alarmed, "freezes" with body, neck, and head elongated and pointing verti-cally. Sexes are dissimilar. **ADULT MALE** Mainly yellow-buff, palest on under-parts, which have buff stripes on throat and breast. Cap and back are blackish, latter contrasting with pale buff panel on wings (striking in flight when dark flight feathers are obvious). **ADULT FEMALE** Similar to male, but black elements of plumage are dark brown. **JUVENILE** Similar to female, but cap and back are gray-buff. **VOICE** Utters a quacking alarm call. Singing male utters a short succession of cooing notes. **STATUS AND HABITAT** Locally common summer visitor, but easily overlooked in favored cattail swamps. Most migrate south of region for winter, but a few linger in the south. **OBSERVATION TIPS** Presence easiest to detect by recognizing male's song. Patient observation may yield a brief view, perhaps of a flying bird.

AMERICAN BITTERN *Botaurus lentiginosus* L 28–29 in

Distinctive wetland bird. Despite size, cryptic plumage makes it very hard to spot and behavior enhances the effect: moves at a slow, stealthy pace and alarmed birds "skypoint," swaying with same motion as surrounding wetland vegetation. Flies with deep, powerful wingbeats, head and neck held hunched; dark flight feathers contrast with otherwise brown plumage. Feeds on amphibians, fish, and aquatic invertebrates. Sexes are similar. **ADULT** Has beautifully patterned brown plumage. Neck and breast have chestnut stripes on paler background and feathers on back and upper wing are marbled and finely marked. Note the white throat and supercilium, and black malar stripe.

ADULT

Daggerlike bill is yellow and legs are greenish. **JUVENILE** Similar to adult, but facial markings are less striking. **VOICE** Territorial birds utter a far-carrying, booming *BOonk-aLOonk*. **STATUS AND HABITAT** Widespread, but seldom common. Asso-ciated with well-vegetated freshwater marshes. Moves south and west in winter. **OBSERVATION TIPS** Presence often detected by song.

ADULT, WINTER

ADULT, BREEDING

WHITE-FACED IBIS

MALE

LEAST BITTERN

ADULT

AMERICAN BITTERN

FEMALE

ADULT

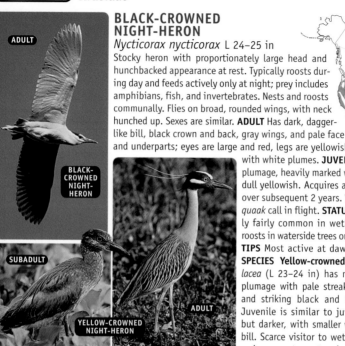

BLACK-CROWNED NIGHT-HERON

Nycticorax nycticorax L 24–25 in

Stocky heron with proportionately large head and hunchbacked appearance at rest. Typically roosts during day and feeds actively only at night; prey includes amphibians, fish, and invertebrates. Nests and roosts communally. Flies on broad, rounded wings, with neck hunched up. Sexes are similar. **ADULT** Has dark, dagger-like bill, black crown and back, gray wings, and pale face and underparts; eyes are large and red, legs are yellowish, and head is adorned with white plumes. **JUVENILE** Has mainly brown plumage, heavily marked with white spots; bill is dull yellowish. Acquires adult plumage gradually over subsequent 2 years. **VOICE** Utters a barking *quaak* call in flight. **STATUS AND HABITAT** Locally fairly common in wetland habitats; usually roosts in waterside trees or bushes. **OBSERVATION TIPS** Most active at dawn and dusk. **SIMILAR SPECIES Yellow-crowned Night-Heron** *N. violacea* (L 23–24 in) has mainly blue-gray adult plumage with pale streaks on back and wings, and striking black and white face markings. Juvenile is similar to juvenile Black-crowned, but darker, with smaller white spots and a dark bill. Scarce visitor to wetlands and coasts from main range, to east and south.

GREEN HERON *Butorides virescens* L 17–18 in

Small, compact heron. Colorful adult blends in well with dappled waterside vegetation. Often perches on branches overhanging water, remaining motionless for minutes on end while waiting for prey such as fish and amphibians. Bill is proportionately long and daggerlike. Sexes are similar. **ADULT** Has dark green crown, rufous maroon face and neck, and white running from throat down center of neck and breast to whitish belly. Upperparts are otherwise greenish gray; wing feathers have pale margins. **JUVENILE** Mainly brown, tinged rufous on face and with rufous streaks on otherwise paler throat, neck, and breast. **VOICE** Utters a sharp *skeeow* call in flight. **STATUS AND HABITAT** Locally common wetland bird. Summer migrant to north and interior parts of range; moves south and to coastal districts outside breeding season. **OBSERVATION TIPS** Unobtrusive, but not unduly wary.

GREAT BLUE HERON *Ardea herodias* L 45–47 in

Huge and unmistakable heron with long legs and neck, and huge, daggerlike bill. Highly variable diet includes fish, amphibians, and crustaceans, and even mammals and birds on occasion. Flies with deep, powerful wingbeats, with neck hunched up and legs trailing. Sexes are similar. **ADULT** Appears blue-gray overall, but neck is tinged pinkish and adorned with black and white streaks down center. Note the mainly white face and crown, separated by broad black stripe that ends in short plumes. Lower breast feathers form shaggy plumes; note also the reddish "pants." Lores are blue at height of breeding season. In flight, seen from above, note the dark flight feathers; from below, wings look uniformly dark gray, except for reddish leading edge to inner wing. **JUVENILE** Similar to adult overall, but less strikingly marked, particularly on head: crown is dark and head plumes are absent. **VOICE** Utters a hoarse *fraarnk* call in flight; otherwise mostly silent. **STATUS AND HABITAT** Locally common wetland bird. Range shifts south and to coasts in winter. **OBSERVATION TIPS** Easy to see.

ADULT

BLACK-CROWNED NIGHT-HERON

GREEN HERON

JUVENILE

ADULT

JUVENILE

ADULT

GREAT BLUE HERON

ADULT

Ardeidae

SNOWY EGRET *Egretta thula* L 24 in

Pure white heronlike bird. Superficially similar to Cattle and Great
egrets, but adult Snowy Egret's bright yellow feet, contrasting with
otherwise black legs, and its black bill, are diagnostic. Long periods of time
are spent roosting and preening. Sometimes adopts a patient, wait-and-see
approach to feeding, but also employs more energetic tactics in pursuit of
fish, amphibians, and crustaceans. Sexes are similar, but immatures and adults
can be separated with care. Beware confusion with immature Little Blue
Heron, which is all white, but has yellowish legs as well as feet, and a two-
toned bill. **ADULT** Has pure white plumage with elegant plumes evident during
breeding season. Legs are black and feet are yellow (orange tinged at height of breeding season).
Daggerlike bill is dark and lores are yellow for much of the time, but flushed red in breeding season.
IMMATURE Similar to adult, but backs of legs are yellow. **VOICE** Mostly silent. **STATUS AND HABITAT**
Associated with wetland habitats, ranging from sheltered coasts and brackish lagoons to freshwater lakes
and rivers. Present year-round on coasts, but summer breeding range extends inland. **OBSERVATION
TIPS** Easy to see in suitable habitats.

CATTLE EGRET *Bubulcus ibis* L 20 in

Stocky, mainly white heronlike bird with a proportionately large
head and bulbous throat. Gregarious and often associates with grazing livestock, chasing after insects and other prey disturbed by feeding animals. Sexes are similar, but breeding adults are more colorful than nonbreeding
and immatures. **ADULT** Has pure white plumage for much of year, but at
height of breeding season it becomes flushed yellowish buff on crown, breast,

ADULT

and back. Bill is yellow for most of
year, turning orange-red in breeding season; legs are dark for most
of year, but turn orange-yellow during breeding season.
IMMATURE Similar to nonbreeding adult. **VOICE** Mainly
silent. **STATUS AND HABITAT** Originates from Old World and
is a relatively recent arrival to our region; first noted in
South America (presumably from Africa) and reached Florida in mid 20th century. Now resident in southwest, favoring grassland and wetlands; from spring to fall, also occurs
inland and in winter it is more widespread in coastal California. **OBSERVATION TIPS** Usually found in drier habitats
than other egret species.

GREAT EGRET *Ardea alba* L 39 in

A stately, pure white, heronlike bird, appreciably larger than Snowy
Egret; size and color alone are often enough to allow certain identification. Great Egrets use their daggerlike bills to good effect when capturing
prey, which includes fish and the occasional aquatic mammal or bird. Sexes are
similar and outside breeding season adults and immatures are not easily separable. **ADULT** Has pure white plumage; during breeding season, long
back plumes trail beyond tail. At all times, legs are dark and bill is yellow.
Lores are yellow for much of year, but turn bluish green in breeding season.
IMMATURE Similar to nonbreeding adult. **VOICE** Mainly silent. **STATUS AND
HABITAT** Much reduced (by persecution and habitat loss) compared to, say, a century ago. Nevertheless,
still relatively common in wetland habitats (mainly freshwater and brackish). Resident year-round in
some coastal districts; more widespread on coasts in winter when numbers are boosted by birds aban-
doning inland sites occupied from spring to fall. **OBSERVATION TIPS** So large and conspicuous that you
should have no difficulty finding it.

SNOWY EGRET

ADULT

ADULT, BREEDING

CATTLE EGRET

ADULT, BREEDING

ADULT, SPRING

ADULT

GREAT EGRET

ADULT

Cathartidae and Accipitridae

TURKEY VULTURE *Cathartes aura* W 67–69 in

The larger and more widespread of our two vulture species. Soars and glides with consummate ease with wings held in a shallow "V";

JUVENILE

active flight is labored. Confusingly, referred to as a "Buzzard" by many nonbirders. Bald head helps reduce feather contamination when feeding on carrion; this is located by both sight and smell. Often perches with wings spread. Sexes are similar. **ADULT** Appears mainly blackish in harsh light, but brownish plumage tone is revealed at close range. Bald head is reddish and bill is pale. In flight, seen from below, silvery gray flight feathers contrast with otherwise dark plumage; note the proportionately long tail. **JUVENILE** Similar to adult, but with browner plumage and dark head and bill. **VOICE** Mostly silent. **STATUS AND HABITAT** Fairly common summer visitor throughout U.S. and into southern Canada. Range contracts southward in fall, many birds migrating to Central America. Found mainly in open and lightly wooded country. **OBSERVATION TIPS** Easiest to see on sunny mornings before too many thermals have been generated.

BLACK VULTURE
Coragyps atratus W 57–59 in

Compact vulture with all-dark plumage. In flight, note the broad wings and silvery white tips (primary feathers), most striking when seen from below; tail is proportionately short. Soars and glides with wings almost level. Gregarious when feeding on carrion, and when roosting. Often perches with wings outstretched. Sexes are similar. **ADULT** Has blackish plumage, except for silvery white primaries. Bald head and upper neck are gray with a wrinkled texture. Bill is relatively slender and pale-tipped. **JUVENILE** Similar to adult, but with dark head, neck, and bill. **VOICE** Mostly silent. **STATUS AND HABITAT** In west, restricted mainly to southern desert states and present there year-round. **OBSERVATION TIPS** Relatively easy to find in southern Arizona and southwestern Texas.

OSPREY *Pandion haliaetus* W 60–65 in

The classic fish-eating raptor, invariably seen near water. In soaring flight, with its rather long, narrow wings, it can look rather gull-like. However, fishing technique is unmistakable: typically hovers and then plunges, talons first, into water. **ADULT** Has mainly brown upperparts, except for the pale crown; underparts generally look pale; body is mostly unmarked except for streaked chest band (most obvious in females). In flight, seen from below inner wing coverts are pale except for dark carpal patch, while flight feathers have dark brown barring; note the dark terminal band on the barred tail. **JUVENILE** Similar to adult, but dark elements of plumage are paler, back and upper

ADULT WITH NEST MATERIAL

wing covert feathers have pale margins, and nape and chest are often flushed orange-buff. **VOICE** Utters various whistling calls. **STATUS AND HABITAT** Fairly common summer visitor to northern half of the region. Associated with fish-rich lakes, rivers, and coasts. Most migrate south to Central and South America for winter, but a few remain in southern states of U.S. **OBSERVATION TIPS** Usually easy to find on suitable wetland habitats. Note, Ospreys spend long periods perched, often on a dead tree, and so careful scrutiny of waterside trees may be required. In some areas, they are bold enough to build their twiggy nests on man-made structures such as powerline poles and towers, and deliberately built nesting platforms.

TURKEY VULTURE

ADULT

ADULT

BLACK VULTURE

ADULT

ADULT

OSPREY

ADULT

Accipitridae

WHITE-TAILED KITE *Elanus leucurus* W 39–42 in

Attractive and distinctive raptor. In flight, often looks all-white, but close view reveals distinctive pattern of gray and black on upperparts. Frequently hovers, while searching for prey, but also glides with wings held in a "V"; also perches on roadside posts. Sexes are similar. **ADULT** Has mainly pale gray back and upper wings, except for black "shoulders" (inner upper wing coverts). Head is paler whitish, but note the large, red eye with black surrounding patch. Tail is pure white when seen from below, but gray-centered seen from above. Underparts are mainly white, but seen from below in flight, note the dark wingtips and carpal patch. Legs and feet are yellow. **JUVENILE** Similar to adult, but breast, nape, and crown are flushed and streaked orange-buff, and back feathers have pale margins. **VOICE** Utters whistling calls. **STATUS AND HABITAT** Local resident of grassland habitats with scattered trees; seldom numerous. **OBSERVATION TIPS** Often active at dawn and dusk, when white plumage shows up particularly well.

MISSISSIPPI KITE
Ictinia mississippiensis W 30–35 in

A small raptor, superficially similar to larger White-tailed Kite, but plumage is much darker overall and note the all-dark tail. Flight is buoyant and it soars and glides on flat wings in a falconlike manner, but note the proportionately long tail that is often fanned. Feeds primarily on insects, often caught on the wing. Sexes are dissimilar. **ADULT MALE** Has mainly plain gray plumage, dark on the tail, back, upper wing coverts, and primaries, and palest on the head (note the dark patch surrounding the red eye) and white upper surface of secondaries. Close view reveals chestnut shafts on upper surface of primaries. **ADULT FEMALE** Similar, but has darker head and paler undertail coverts. **JUVENILE** Recalls adult, but underparts and underwing coverts are streaked and mottled chestnut, and tail is barred. **VOICE** Utters whistling calls. **STATUS AND HABITAT** Locally common migrant visitor (mainly Apr–Aug) to open country, including farmland, with scattered woods. Nests colonially. Winters in South America. **OBSERVATION TIPS** Concentrates where feeding is good.

NORTHERN HARRIER *Circus cyaneus* W 40–46 in

Long-winged, long-tailed raptor, typically seen gliding at slow speeds, low over the ground with almost effortless ease and seldom

FEMALE

JUVENILE

a wingbeat. Feeds mainly on small mammals and birds, located in part by hearing. In direct flight, wing-beats are deep and powerful. Sexes are dissimilar, males being smaller than females. **ADULT MALE** Has pale blue-gray head and upperparts and a striking white rump (only obvious in flight); underparts are mainly pale, but note the reddish streaks, most intense on chest. In flight, dark trailing edge to wings and black wingtips are most striking when seen from below, when faintly barred tail can also be discerned. **ADULT FEMALE** Brown, with darker barring on wings and tail, streaking on body underparts, and narrow white rump; white head markings create an owl-like facial disc. **JUVENILE** Similar to adult female, but plumage is tinged reddish orange, particularly underparts. **VOICE** Mostly silent. **STATUS AND HABITAT** Fairly common, although seldom seen in any numbers, except when gathering at communal winter roosts. Favors grassland and open country. **OBSERVATION TIPS** Easiest to find in winter.

SUBADULT

JUVENILE

ADULT

ADULT

WHITE-TAILED KITE

JUVENILE

MALE

MISSISSIPPI KITE

MALE

NORTHERN HARRIER

MALE

MALE

MALE

Accipitridae

BALD EAGLE *Haliaeetus leucocephalus* W 75–90 in

A huge, iconic bird of prey and national symbol of the U.S. Adult is unmistakable. Immature birds, which lack adult's white head and tail, could possibly be confused with a Golden Eagle. However, note Bald Eagle's distinctive flight silhouette with much broader wings and proportionately shorter tail than its cousin; thicker neck and larger head and bill are also useful pointers. Fish are important in the diet and are snatched from water with surprising agility for a bird of this size. Carrion is eaten, mainly in winter when fish are less active at water's surface and sometimes protected from predation by ice. **ADULT** Has a white head, neck, and tail, contrasting with dark brown upperparts and belly. Powerful bill and feet are yellow. **JUVENILE** Mainly uniformly dark brown although underparts, including underwings and undertail, are rather irregularly marked with white; bill and cere are dark (latter feature is yellowish in juvenile Golden Eagle) while legs and feet are yellow.

JUVENILE

SUBADULT Gradually acquires adult plumage through successive molts over several years. **VOICE** A variety of hoarse and rather plaintive whistling calls. **STATUS AND HABITAT** Usually seen near water, except occasionally on migration; occurs both on coasts and beside fish-rich rivers and freshwater lakes. Once widespread, but suffered badly in the past from pesticide accumulation and habitat destruction in many parts. Numbers are now recovering and before long it may no longer be classed as threatened. Mainly a summer visitor to north of its range although often occurs year-round in coastal districts; northwest is a particular stronghold. Most northern breeders migrate south in fall and are widespread, but generally scarce in winter across U.S., some joining resident populations. **OBSERVATION TIPS** Bald Eagles are easiest to observe in the Pacific Northwest and their calls are an evocative sound associated with wooded coves and inlets. Wonderful views of feeding birds can often be obtained beside salmon rivers, for example, the Chilkat River near Haines, Alaska, where up to 4,000 eagles gather, but for the most spectacular observations, visit one of the winter feeding stations on the Alaskan coast.

GOLDEN EAGLE *Aquila chrysaetos* W 80–90 in

A large and majestic raptor. Seen distantly, it could be confused with certain soaring, *Buteo* raptors. However, even in silhouette, a closer view reveals Golden Eagle's proportionately long wings (which narrow toward base) and relatively long tail. An active predator, it catches live prey typically the size of hares and ptarmigan; also feeds on carrion, especially in winter. Sexes are similar, but adults, juveniles, and immature subadults are separable with care. **ADULT** Has mainly dark brown plumage, with paler margins to feathers on back, and golden brown feathers on head and neck. Tail is dark-tipped and barred, but, in flight and against the sky, it can look uniformly dark. **JUVENILE** Similar to adult, but note striking white patches at base of outer flight feathers; tail is white with a broad, dark tip. **SUBADULT** Gradually loses white elements of juvenile plumage by successive molts over several years. **VOICE** Mainly silent. **STATUS AND HABITAT** Favors mountains and hilly terrain, typically soaring over hilltops and hunting over bare slopes and open plains; often at lower altitudes in winter. Widespread resident in west, numbers boosted in winter by migrants from the north. **OBSERVATION TIPS** Spend a few days driving around hilly areas and uplands in western U.S. and you will be unlucky not to see this species. Most sightings will be distant.

2ND-YEAR

ADULT

ADULT

JUVENILE

BALD EAGLE

ADULT

ADULT

GOLDEN EAGLE

JUVENILE

Accipitridae

SHARP-SHINNED HAWK
Accipiter striatus W 20–25 in

Our smallest *Accipiter*. Employs rapid, agile, low-level flight to catch small songbirds in surprise attacks. Similar plumage, but different proportions to larger Cooper's: in flight, note Sharp-shinned's relatively short, broad and rounded wings, shorter square-ended, barred tail, and short neck. Soars with wings angled forward and active flight involves stiff-winged, flapping

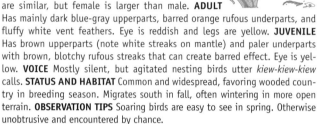

wing action. Seen perched, note relatively small head, steep forehead, and rather dainty bill. Sexes are similar, but female is larger than male. **ADULT** Has mainly dark blue-gray upperparts, barred orange rufous underparts, and fluffy white vent feathers. Eye is reddish and legs are yellow. **JUVENILE** Has brown upperparts (note white streaks on mantle) and paler underparts with brown, blotchy rufous streaks that can create barred effect. Eye is yellow. **VOICE** Mostly silent, but agitated nesting birds utter *kiew-kiew-kiew* calls. **STATUS AND HABITAT** Common and widespread, favoring wooded country in breeding season. Migrates south in fall, often wintering in more open terrain. **OBSERVATION TIPS** Soaring birds are easy to see in spring. Otherwise unobtrusive and encountered by chance.

COOPER'S HAWK *Accipiter cooperii* W 30–34 in

Medium-sized *Accipiter*. Catches larger prey than does Sharp-shinned. Compared to that species, note relatively longer wings, longer and rounded (not square-ended) tail, and appreciable neck. Plumage differences are little use in flying birds, but note Cooper's more fluid wing action in

active flight, and wings held out straighter (not angled forward) when soaring. Seen perched, gentle slope of forehead is more continuous with line of thick bill (steeper forehead in Sharp-shinned). Sexes are similar; female is larger than male. **ADULT** Has dark blue-gray upperparts, darkest on crown and palest on nape (creating capped effect). Underparts are paler and barred orange-rufous. **JUVENILE** Has brown upperparts and pale underparts with bold dark brown streaks. **VOICE** Utters *kiek-kiek-kiek* call at nest; otherwise silent. **STATUS AND HABITAT** Widespread and common in wooded country. Northern populations move south in fall. **OBSERVATION TIPS** Seen mainly by chance. **COMMENTS** Tolerate hunting by both Cooper's and Sharp-shinned at bird feeders: they are just as much a part of the natural environment as the songbirds they catch.

NORTHERN GOSHAWK *Accipiter gentilis* W 40–44 in

Our largest *Accipiter* (*Buteo*-sized). Feeds on medium-sized birds and mammals, caught in agile surprise attacks. In flight, broad, rounded wings and relatively long, broad, and barred tail

are noticeable. Soaring birds often fan their tails, which then appear rounded, with striking white, fluffy undertail coverts. Close view of perched bird (an unusual event) reveals differences from appreciably smaller Cooper's: large head and striking pale supercilium, and pale gray (not rufous) underparts. Sexes are similar; female is larger than male. **ADULT** Has mainly gray-brown upperparts; pale underparts are finely barred with gray. Legs are yellow and eye is orange. **JUVENILE** Has brown upperparts; buffy underparts are marked with dark, teardrop-shaped spots. Eye is yellow and supercilium is pale. **VOICE** Utters a harsh *kie-kie-kie* at nest; otherwise silent. **STATUS AND HABITAT** Widespread but scarce forest species. **OBSERVATION TIPS** Look for displaying birds in spring.

ADULT

ADULT

JUVENILE

COOPER'S HAWK

SHARP-SHINNED HAWK

ADULT

ADULT

NORTHERN GOSHAWK

FEMALE

MALE

Accipitridae

RED-SHOULDERED HAWK
Buteo lineatus W 38–41 in

Familiar and well-marked hawk. Subtle plumage variations exist among the several recognized subspecies that occur across its wide range, but all adults show striking reddish orange "shoulders." Adopts an upright posture when perched and mostly employs a sit-and-wait hunting approach, scanning ground from an unobtrusive woodland perch (typically a branch); feeds on small mammals, amphibians, reptiles, and large insects. In flight, note broad, rounded wings and rounded tail, which is often fanned. Sexes are similar, but geographical variation is discernible with care. **ADULT** From California (ssp. *elegans*), has barred reddish orange underparts, including vent. Head is reddish and faintly streaked, and feathers on upperparts are boldly marked with black, white, and brown; note the reddish "shoulders." In flight, seen from below, body and wing coverts are barred reddish orange, while flight feathers and tail are barred black and white; note pale bases to primaries, which form a narrow band. From above, red-

ADULT

dish inner wing coverts (the "shoulders") and head contrast with otherwise dark plumage, but note the strongly barred tail. Eastern adult is similar, but reddish orange elements of plumage (except for "shoulders") are less intense and vent feathers are white. **JUVENILE** From California, is similar to adult, but reddish elements of plumage (including "shoulders") are darker brown. Eastern juvenile is dark brown above, but pale below, heavily streaked on breast; looks pale-winged in flight, with dark-tipped primaries and evenly barred tail. **VOICE** Breeding birds utter a shrill, repeated *Kee-yur* call. **STATUS AND HABITAT** Common in riverside and swamp woodland. Mostly resident. **OBSERVATION TIPS** Easiest to see in spring when birds are displaying.

BROAD-WINGED HAWK
Buteo platypterus W 33–35 in

The smallest *Buteo* hawk in the West. Not unduly shy, but unobtrusive habits (often perches for long periods in woodland cover) mean it is easy to overlook. In flight, note broad and rather pointed wings and medium-length tail. Sexes are similar, but rare dark morph exists. **ADULT** Light morph has brown upperparts including head; throat is pale (defined by dark malar stripe), breast is reddish brown, and otherwise pale underparts are marked with broad, reddish brown bars. In flight, seen from below, note mainly pale wings with dark tips and trailing edge, barred brown body and inner

ADULT, DARK MORPH

wing coverts, pale vent, and striking, broad white band on otherwise dark tail (indistinct, narrow second band sometimes discernible near base of tail feathers). Adult dark morph is uniformly dark brown when perched, except for pale band on tail; in flight, flight feathers are pale, but with dark trailing edge and primary tips. **JUVENILE** Similar to light morph adult, but underparts are usually paler, with less extensive brown barring; in flight, from below, looks pale except for gray trailing edge and wingtips, and gray-barred tail. **VOICE** Utters a shrill, almost electronic-sounding, *tuee-ee-ee-ee-ee-ee* call. **STATUS AND HABITAT** Common summer visitor (much more widespread in east) that favors forests for nesting. Winters in South America. Migrants avoid crossing water and in fall funnel through southern Texas before following Central American land chain south; spring migrants follow reverse route. **OBSERVATION TIPS** Migrates in spectacular numbers, and sizeable groups, known as "kettles," utilize thermal updrafts to gain lift. Well-known migration watchpoints are easy to find on the web.

ADULT

JUVENILE

RED-SHOULDERED HAWK

ADULT

BROAD-WINGED HAWK

JUVENILE

ADULT

RED-TAILED HAWK *Buteo jamaicensis* W 48–51 in

North America's most widespread *Buteo*. Detailed discussion of extensive plumage variation is beyond this book's scope. Nevertheless, adults of all subspecies and morphs (except Harlan's) have diagnostic reddish tail, above and below (adult Ferruginous's tail is tinged reddish above, toward tip, but is whitish below). Juvenile shares characteristics with juveniles of other *Buteo* species. Sexes are similar. **ADULT** (except Harlan's) Has brown head, back, and upper wings, and reddish tail. Light morph has underparts flushed rufous buff and variably streaked dark brown, mainly on belly; in flight, from below, pale flight feathers have dark trailing edge and tips and plumage is otherwise pale buff, with diagnostic dark leading edge to inner wing. Perched dark morph looks uniformly dark brown, except for red tail; in flight, from below, pale flight feathers contrast with otherwise dark brown body plumage. Intermediate morphs have a reddish buff chest band. Adult Harlan's (ssp. *harlani*) occurs as both light and dark morphs; similar to previously described morphs, but tail is gray, not red. Krider's (ssp. *krideri*) has whitish underparts,

ADULT, LIGHT MORPH

with red flush restricted to outer margins of tail (cf. light morph Ferruginous p.102). **JUVENILE** Similar to adult counterparts, but reddish elements of plumage are replaced by whitish; tail has fine, even barring. Light morph is similar to Rough-legged, but note that species' pale leading edge to inner wing and dark carpal patch; Rough-legged has dark subterminal band or barring on otherwise white tail, and juvenile and adult female have striking dark belly. **VOICE** Utters various whistles and screams. **STATUS AND HABITAT** Common in a range of habitats; range contracts south in winter. Harlan's breeds in Alaska and winters in southern Great Plains. Krider's is a scarce Great Plains subspecies. **OBSERVATION TIPS** Easy to observe and often rather bold.

SWAINSON'S HAWK *Buteo swainsoni* W 50–52 in

Large, well-marked raptor with variable plumage. Rather long-winged: wings often extend beyond tail in perched birds; often hovers. Sexes are similar. **ADULT** Light morph has mainly dark brown upperparts. Head is mainly dark, except for white forehead, chin, and throat. Has rufous brown breast band, but underparts are otherwise gleaming white. In flight, from below shows rufous brown head and chest (except for white throat), otherwise white body plumage and wing coverts, and gray flight feathers and finely barred tail. Adult dark morph is mainly uniformly dark brown, except for rufous "pants" and vent. In flight, seen from below can look all-dark, but rufous wing coverts seen in good light. Adult intermediate has dark upperparts, white "face," dark breast, and mainly barred rufous underparts, except for pale vent. **JUVENILE** Similar to their adult morph counterparts except that rufous elements of plumage are replaced by streaked brown on otherwise pale

2ND-YEAR JUVENILE

feathering. Light morph juvenile has a very pale head, hence very similar to Rough-legged; note differences in tail and underwing pattern, especially absence in Swainson's of contrastingly dark carpal patches. **VOICE** Utters high-pitched whistles and screams. **STATUS AND HABITAT** Widespread and locally common in open prairie country. Long-distance migrant that summers in western North America, but winters in southern South America. **OBSERVATION TIPS** Migrates in large flocks in fall.

ADULT, DARK MORPH

ADULT, RUFOUS MORPH

ADULT, HARLAN'S

RED-TAILED HAWK

ADULT

ADULT, RUFOUS MORPH

ADULT, DARK MORPH

ADULT, INTERMEDIATE

ADULT, LIGHT MORPH

SWAINSON'S HAWK

ADULT, LIGHT MORPH

ADULT, DARK MORPH

Accipitridae

ROUGH-LEGGED HAWK *Buteo lagopus* W 52–55 in

Large, rather long-winged raptor with feathered legs and dainty (by *Buteo* standards) bill. Hunts at low level for rodents and small birds, and often hovers. Perches for long periods and then looks plump-bodied, with wings roughly same length as tail. Plumage is variable, but in all light morphs white upper tail contrasts with otherwise dark upperparts. Sexes are dissimilar. **ADULT MALE** Light morph has gray-brown upperparts and pale head. Underparts are pale, but streaked heavily dark brown on breast, with dark feathers on flanks. In flight, from below, wings look pale except for dark carpal patch, tips, and trailing edge, while tail is white with broad, dark subterminal band; from above, tail is white with dark barring toward tip. Dark morph looks uniformly dark when perched; in flight, looks all dark from above, but from below note whitish flight feathers (except for wingtips and trailing edge) and whitish tail with dark subterminal band. **ADULT FEMALE** Light morph

JUVENILE

ADULT

COMMON BLACK-HAWK

ADULT

is similar to male, but note dark belly patch and (in flight) more contrasting black and white pattern on tail and on underwings (except for streaked brown underwing coverts); from above, tail is white with broad black terminal band. Dark morph is similar to dark-morph male, but plumage is browner; underwing coverts are noticeably paler than dark carpal patches. **JUVENILE** Light morph is similar to adult female, but in flight note cleaner, paler underwing coverts and gray (not black) subterminal band on tail seen from below; from above, wing coverts and inner primaries are paler than rest of upper wing. Dark morph is similar to dark-morph female, but with paler subterminal band on tail underside. **VOICE** Mostly silent except at nest. **STATUS AND HABITAT** Breeds across Arctic North America and winters from southern Canada southward. Favors open country, including farmland in winter; prefers marshes and open tundra. **OBSERVATION TIPS** Widespread in winter but seldom numerous. A hovering *Buteo* in winter, with a pale upper tail, is a contender for this species.

ZONE-TAILED HAWK
Buteo albonotatus
W 50–52 in

Large, dark raptor. Rather long tail is banded black and white in adult birds. Wings are long and an even width; in all birds flight feathers are paler than rest of body and soaring birds (wings held stiffly in a shallow "V") could be confused with Turkey Vulture (*see* p.88). Note, however, Zone-tailed's banded (adult) or barred (juvenile) tail (uniformly grayish in Turkey Vulture) and thicker neck. Sexes are similar. **ADULT** Has uniformly blackish plumage except for tail, which is banded above and below. Legs, feet, and cere are yellow. **JUVENILE** Similar to adult, but tail is gray with narrow, darker barring. **VOICE** Mostly silent. **STATUS AND HABITAT** Rather scarce summer visitor to dry, wooded valleys and riparian woodland in southern states; winters in Central America. **OBSERVATION TIPS** Search for soaring birds riding morning thermals, but beware confusion with Turkey Vulture. **SIMILAR SPECIES Common Black-Hawk** *Buteogallus anthracinus* (W 44–47 in) has similar adult plumage when perched, but entirely different outline in flight: wings are extremely broad and rounded and tail is very short and typically widely fanned. Adult is blackish, except for single broad white band on upper tail (above and below). Juvenile is brown and streaked; tail has many narrow and wavy dark bands. Scarce summer visitor to southern Utah and Texas wetlands.

FEMALE

MALE

MALE

ROUGH-LEGGED HAWK

FEMALE

ADULT

ADULT

ZONE-TAILED HAWK

ADULT

JUVENILE

Accipitridae

FERRUGINOUS HAWK *Buteo regalis* W 54–56 in

The largest western *Buteo*; has a powerful bill and feathered legs.
In flight, note long, broad-based, but rather pointed wings.
Plumage is variable, but, in flight, all birds show white base to upperside
of primaries and pale tail. Perches on posts and employs active, low flights
when hunting small mammals and birds. Sexes are similar. **ADULT** Light
morph has a rufous back, pale head streaked gray on nape and cheeks, and
pale underparts with rufous streaks on flanks and "pants." In flight, from
below looks pale with rufous on wing coverts and flanks; from above note
rufous back and inner wing coverts and pale tail flushed rufous toward tip.
Dark morph is dark brown with rufous on upper inner wing coverts, breast, and vent, and pale gray tail.
In flight, from below the dark body and wing coverts contrast with pale wings and tail (wings have

gray trailing edge and tips); from above, pale tail and primary
bases contrast with otherwise dark plumage. **JUVENILE**
Light morph is similar to adult, but rufous elements of
plumage are gray-brown; looks very pale from below in
flight. Dark morph is similar to adult, but pale carpal crescent
on underwing is more striking. **VOICE** Utters a harsh whistling
call at nest, but otherwise silent. **STATUS AND HABITAT** Widespread, but scarce. Favors arid, open country including farmland. Range contracts southward in winter. **OBSERVATION
TIPS** Perched birds often give prolonged views. **SIMILAR
SPECIES White-tailed Hawk** *B. albicaudatus* (W 51–52 in)
is confined to grassland in southern Texas and so range does
not overlap. Adult has gray head and back, rufous "shoulders"
(inner wing coverts), dark wings, and white underparts; tail
is white with a broad, black subterminal band. Juvenile is
mainly dark, with white breast and vent; tail is buffy gray
with a pale base. Acquires adult plumage over 3-year period.

HARRIS'S HAWK *Parabuteo unicinctus* W 42–44 in

Well-marked and distinctive raptor. Combination of rufous wing coverts (above
and below), dark body, and broad, black subterminal band on otherwise white
tail make identification easy. In flight, wings are broad and rounded, while tail
is relatively long. Hunts cooperatively for desert animals; has a complex social
structure involving related birds. Sexes are similar. **ADULT** Has mainly dark brown
head, back, underparts, and wings, darkest on wingtips. Perched birds show rufous

"shoulders" and "pants," white vent, and black and white tail.
Cere and relatively long legs are yellow. **JUVENILE** Similar to
adult, but dark elements of plumage have pale streaks and tail
markings are less striking. **VOICE** Utters a harsh, almost corvid-
like *kaar-kaar-kaar* in alarm. **STATUS AND HABITAT** Fairly common resident of desert regions of southern U.S. **OBSERVATION
TIPS** Where you see one Harris's Hawk you are likely to see several. Often rather indifferent to people, but note that a tame,
lone individual outside main range could be an escaped fal-
coner's bird. **SIMILAR SPECIES Crested Caracara** *Caracara
cheriway* Falconidae (W 49–51 in) is unmistakable, with long
legs, neck, wings, and tail, and large, flat-crowned head, with
a massive bill. Adult's dark crown and red cere contrast with
otherwise whitish neck and barred white breast. Back, underparts, and wings are dark brown, except for barred pale base
to primaries, and barred, pale tail with a dark terminal band.
Juvenile has pale spots on back and wings. Southern Texas and
Arizona deserts only.

ADULT, LIGHT MORPH

FERRUGINOUS HAWK

ADULT

JUVENILE

ADULT, DARK MORPH

JUVENILE

HARRIS'S HAWK

ADULT

ADULT

Falconidae

AMERICAN KESTREL *Falco sparverius* W 21–23 in

A familiar raptor, our smallest falcon and the one most likely to be seen hovering above a field along the roadside. Feeds on small mammals and insects. In flight, note typical falcon outline with relatively narrow, pointed wings and proportionately long tail; latter is fanned when hovering or soaring, but otherwise straight. Sexes are dissimilar and males are well marked and colorful. **ADULT MALE** Has dark-spotted rufous back and blue-gray wing coverts; striking head pattern includes blue-gray cap with central rufous spot, brown nape with twin dark spots, and two vertical black lines running down from eye-line and framing white cheek. Underparts are pale buff with dark spots on belly. Tail is rufous with black subterminal band and white tip. In flight, from above, rufous back and tail contrast with blue-gray and black pattern on wings; from below, underwings are barred gray and well-patterned tail is most striking feature. **ADULT FEMALE** Has mainly dark-spotted rufous brown upperparts, except for dark primaries; head pattern is similar to male's, but duller. Underparts are pale, with lines of rufous spots on breast and belly. In flight, looks mainly rufous brown above and pale buff below. **JUVENILE** Similar to adult counterparts, but male is more streaked below and less colorful overall. **VOICE** Utters a screaming *killy-killy-killy* or rapid *kee-kee-kee*. **STATUS AND HABITAT** Widespread and common in open country, including farmland. Mainly a summer migrant to Canada, birds moving south in fall boosting resident numbers in southern U.S. **OBSERVATION TIPS** Easy to find in open country, perched on poles or overhead wires, or hovering while scanning ground for prey. **SIMILAR SPECIES Aplomado Falcon** *F. femoralis* (W 32–36 in) is much larger, but with rather similar head pattern, except for dark crown and eyestripe, and pale supercilium. Upperparts are blue-gray, while underparts are buff on belly and "pants," and dark on sides of breast; throat and chest are white in male, streaked buff in female. A Central and South American species, formerly extinct, but very locally reintroduced to U.S. in New Mexico.

APLOMADO FALCON

MALE

MERLIN *Falco columbarius* W 22–24 in

Small falcon, often seen flying low over ground in dashing hunting flight while pursuing small bird prey. Perches for extended periods on lookout, using fenceposts or rocky outcrops. Soaring Merlin could perhaps be confused in silhouette for a small Peregrine, but its low, dashing flight is vaguely reminiscent of Sharp-shinned Hawk. Sexes are dissimilar and northern birds (Taiga Merlin, ssp. *columbarius*) are smaller and darker than birds breeding further south (Prairie Merlin, ssp. *richardsoni*); Pacific Northwest residents (Black Merlin, ssp. *suckleyi*) are darker still overall. Following descriptions apply to ssp. *columbarius*. **ADULT MALE** Has blue-gray upperparts and buffy, streaked and spotted underparts. In flight, and from above, blue-gray back, inner wings and tail contrast with dark wingtips and dark terminal band on tail. **ADULT FEMALE** Has brown upperparts and pale underparts with large, brown spots. In flight, from above, upperparts are rather uniform brown with numerous faint bars on wings and tail; from below, body is streaked, while tail is distinctly barred. **JUVENILE** Recalls adult female. **VOICE** Mainly silent although a shrill *kee-kee-kee* is uttered in alarm. **STATUS AND HABITAT** Widespread and fairly common in open country. **OBSERVATION TIPS** Easiest to find in winter.

JUVENILE

MALE

AMERICAN KESTREL

MALE

FEMALE

MALE

FEMALE

MERLIN

Falconidae

PRAIRIE FALCON *Falco mexicanus* W 38–41 in

Large, stocky falcon. Confusion with juvenile Peregrine is possible, but Prairie is paler overall, with less contrast on head; note pale behind eye. In flight, from below, Prairie looks very pale (especially tail), except for dark bar on outer coverts and axillaries (juvenile Peregrine is uniformly barred and streaked gray below, palest on throat and vent). Typically hunts at low levels for small mammals and birds (Peregrine usually dives from a great height). Sexes are similar. **ADULT** Has sandy brown upperparts, including nape and crown. Head has pale supercilium, cheek, and throat, with dark eyestripe and "mustache." Underparts are pale, with dark streak on breast and belly, particularly intense on flanks. **JUVENILE** Similar to adult, but darker and more heavily patterned. **VOICE** Utters a loud *kek-kek-kek...* call. **STATUS AND HABITAT** Widespread, but scarce in open, grassy habitats. Mostly resident, but some dispersal in winter. **OBSERVATION TIPS** Least tricky to find in winter.

PEREGRINE FALCON *Falco peregrinus* W 39–42 in

Robust and stocky falcon. Soars on broad, bowed wings, but stoops at phenomenal speed with wings swept back after prey such as pigeons. Striking head pattern and contrast between dark upperparts and paler, well-marked underparts are useful in identification. However, geographical variation confuses matters. Sexes are similar. **ADULT** Tundra race has dark blue-gray upperparts and pale, barred underparts. Note dark facial mask (dark "mustache" extends well behind eye and borders white cheek) and powerful, yellow legs and feet. In flight, from above, looks rather uniform; from below,

JUVENILE

pale underparts are barred and contrast between pale cheeks and throat, and dark "mustache" is usually striking. Pacific race is similar, but pale elements of underparts are flushed buff, and dark on head is more extensive (white on cheek is reduced). **JUVENILE** Similar to adult, but upperparts are brownish, while paler underparts are suffused with buff. **VOICE** Utters a loud *kek-kek-kek...* call. **STATUS AND HABITAT** Once widespread on open habitats, pesticides decimated interior populations in 1960s by thinning eggshells. Reintroduction program is aiding recovery here. Tundra populations, less affected by pollution (except in winter), remain stable and these birds winter further south. Pacific birds are mainly resident. **OBSERVATION TIPS** Panic attacks in winter flocks of waders and ducks may mean a hunting Peregrine is nearby.

GYRFALCON *Falco rusticolus* W 47–53 in

Huge and impressive falcon, *Buteo*-sized, but note typical falcon shape with long, pointed wings and long tail. White morph (the real prize for birders) is unmistakable. Dark and gray morphs could perhaps be confused with Peregrine, but note Gyrfalcon's much larger size, more bulky body, and broader, less pointed wings. Hunts up to goose-sized prey. Sexes are similar, although female is appreciably larger than male. **ADULT** Pale morph has mainly white head and underparts; upperparts including upper tail are white with dark barring. Gray morph has gray head and upperparts; underparts are pale with dark barring. Dark morph has dark brown head and upperparts, with heavily streaked underparts. **JUVENILE** Similar to adult counterparts. **VOICE** Mostly silent. **STATUS AND HABITAT** Widespread, but scarce Arctic breeder. Moves south in winter, but still usually remains in snowbound areas. **OBSERVATION TIPS** Seen mainly by chance.

FALCONS

PRAIRIE FALCON

ADULT

JUVENILE

ADULT

PEREGRINE FALCON

JUVENILE

ADULT

GYRFALCON

ADULT, GRAY MORPH

ADULT, GRAY MORPH

JUVENILE, PALE MORPH

Rallidae

CLAPPER RAIL *Rallus longirostris* L 14–15 in

Long-billed, short-tailed wetland bird. Laterally compressed body
form allows it to pass through dense vegetation with ease. Like other
Rallus species, legs appear set far back on body (note very long toes) and
flanks are barred. Shy and retiring: heard more than seen. Seldom seen in
flight. Feeds mainly on invertebrates. Confusion is possible with Virginia
Rail and (in southern Texas only) with King Rail. Calls and habitat choice
are useful in identification. Several subspecies exist; western birds are more
colorful than those from southern Texas. Sexes are similar. **ADULT** From southwest, has mainly orange-buff head, neck, and breast, darkest on crown.
Flanks are gray-brown with white vertical stripes, and back is brown with dark-centered feathers. Tail
and pale, gray-barred undertail coverts are often cocked. Bill is pinkish orange. Gulf Coast birds are duller
overall, with paler, grayer cheeks and gray breast. **JUVENILE** Similar to adult, but orange-buff elements of plumage are drab gray-buff and bill is dull. **VOICE** Utters a distinctive clattering call, and birds'
responses to playback of taped calls is an important way of monitoring the species. **STATUS AND HABI-
TAT** Scarce and only very locally common. California birds are resident in coastal salt marshes (San Francisco Bay is the stronghold), while interior southwestern birds favor dense freshwater marshes. Gulf coast
birds occur in coastal brackish marshes. **OBSERVATION TIPS** If you hear a calling bird, sit quietly and

KING RAIL

ADULT

eventually it may venture out of cover
to feed. Views are often brief as birds
quickly scuttle back into vegetation. High
tides sometimes force birds to swim from
inundated vegetation to drier ground.
SIMILAR SPECIES King Rail *R. elegans* (L
15–16 in) has blackish (male) or dark,
rich brown (female) flanks and undertail,
marked with striking white stripes;
orange on underparts is richer than on
Gulf coast Clapper, and King favors freshwater, not brackish, marshes. Call of
King is similar to, but deeper than, that
of Clapper. Confusion is only possible
where ranges overlap, on Gulf coast.

VIRGINIA RAIL *Rallus limicola* L 9–11 in

Small rail (body size of Sora), but with the proportions of Clapper
and King Rails. Shy and retiring, and heard more often than it is
seen. Laterally compressed body allows it to pass with ease through dense
cattail stems and other emergent wetland vegetation. Long toes enable it
to walk on yielding mud and uses its long bill to probe for invertebrate prey.
Sexes are similar. **ADULT** Has orange-buff throat, neck, and breast, contrasting with black and white stripes on flanks and gray cheeks and dark
brown crown. Upperparts are orange-brown with dark feather centers. Bill is
long, slightly decurved and reddish, and legs are reddish pink; note the beady
red eye. **JUVENILE** Similar to adult, but orange elements of plumage are gray or dark brown, and bill
is dark. **VOICE** Utters a distinctive *wik-wiDik-wiDik* in breeding season; piglike squeals heard year-round.
STATUS AND HABITAT Common summer visitor to freshwater marshes. Winters in southwestern U.S.
and Mexico, when it favors both brackish and freshwater marshes. **OBSERVATION TIPS** Patience is the
key to viewing this species and lengthy periods of motionless observation are often needed in order
to see a bird that you know, from its calls, to be present nearby. Scan wetland margins where emergent
vegetation meets open mud for the best chances of observation.

ADULT, GULF COAST

CLAPPER RAIL

ADULT, CALIFORNIA

VIRGINIA RAIL

ADULT

ADULT

Rallidae

SORA *Porzana carolina* L 8–9 in

Dumpy and rather secretive waterbird. Heard more often than it is seen. Typically skulks along marsh margins, its long toes allowing it to walk over soft mud or floating plants. Walks with a bobbing action and occasionally swims short distances. Feeds mainly on aquatic invertebrates. In flight (typically brief and low), note white trailing edge to inner wing (above and below) and white leading edge to underside of inner wing. Sexes are separable with care in summer. **ADULT MALE** In breeding season has blue-gray face, neck, and breast, but note black between base of bill and eye, continuing as line down to center of chest. Belly is pale and flanks are barred brown, black, and white. Upperparts are brown, spangled with white on back; undertail is creamy white. Bill is yellow and legs are yellowish green. Nonbreeding bird is similar, but with duller bill and leg colors, and less extensive black on face. **ADULT FEMALE** Similar to nonbreeding male. **JUVENILE** Recalls adult female, but blue-gray elements of plumage are buff and bill is darker. **VOICE** Utters a whinnying squeal, and a loud *keek* in alarm. **STATUS AND HABITAT** Widespread and common summer visitor to freshwater marshes. Migrates south in fall and winters from southern U.S. to northern South America. Migrant and winter birds favor similar habitats, but also turn up in coastal wetlands. **OBSERVATION TIPS** Learn to recognize a Sora's call and you are soon likely to detect its presence in your local wetland. Seeing one is a different matter, but with great patience it should emerge from cover sooner or later. Typically, a feeding Sora will follow a circuit around its territory, appearing in the same spot every hour or so.

YELLOW RAIL *Coturnicops noveboracensis* L 6–7 in

Tiny wetland bird. Habits are so secretive, and favored habitat so impenetrable, that few people ever see this enigmatic species well. Most satisfy themselves with hearing the call or catching a glimpse of a flushed bird in brief flight (note white secondaries and underwing coverts). Sexes are similar. **ADULT** In breeding season, has buffy yellow plumage overall, palest on throat, with darker feathering on crown, through eye, and on flanks; back feathers have dark centers. Back and flanks are spangled with fine white bars. Bill is yellow and legs are dull pink. Nonbreeding adult is similar, but with dull bill. **JUVENILE** Similar to adult, but head, neck, and breast are darker overall, but with more extensive white spangling. **VOICE** Utters a rhythmic clicking *tic-tic-tic-tic*; imitate this by tapping two stones together. **STATUS AND HABITAT** Threatened and declining as a result of wetland habitat destruction. Endemic to North America and entire world population may number just a few tens of thousands of birds. In breeding season, favors freshwater marshes with abundant, emergent grasses and sedges. Winters on Gulf and South Atlantic coasts of U.S., favoring grassy wetlands and rice fields. **OBSERVATION TIPS** Tricky to observe, so consider yourself lucky if you succeed. Perhaps least difficult to see in winter in flooded agricultural fields. **SIMILAR SPECIES Black Rail** *Laterallus jamaicensis* (L 4–6 in) is smaller still and also seldom seen. Has mainly dark blue-gray underparts, dark crown and face, rufous collar, and white-spangled dark brown back and wings. Presence usually detected by its diagnostic *kee-kee-drrr* call. Favors brackish and freshwater marshes or very damp areas with dense grass; California birds are mostly resident.

MALE

BLACK RAIL

FEMALE

MALE

SORA

ADULT,
WINTER

ADULT,
WINTER

YELLOW RAIL

ADULT

Rallidae and Gruidae

COMMON MOORHEN
Gallinula chloropus L 13–14 in

Dark-looking wetland bird that swims with jerky movements and flicks
its tail constantly. Flight looks labored with dangling legs. Very long toes
allow it to walk on soft mud and on floating plant debris. Feeds on aquatic
invertebrates and plants. Sexes are similar. **ADULT** Can look all-dark, but has
dark blue-gray head, neck, and underparts, and brownish back, wings, and tail.
Note yellow-tipped red bill, red frontal shield on forehead, and yellowish
legs and toes. Sides of undertail are white; note white line on flanks. **JUVENILE**
Grayish brown, but with white on throat, sides of undertail coverts, and on flanks.
VOICE Utters a far-carrying *kurrrk*. **STATUS AND HABITAT** Local resident in southwest (more widespread
in eastern North America), in well-vegetated freshwater (sometimes brackish) wetlands. **OBSERVATION
TIPS** Not unduly shy and easy to see.

AMERICAN COOT *Fulica americana* L 14–16 in

Dumpy waterbird with long, lobed toes that facilitate swimming.
Feeds by upending or by making shallow dives, but also grazes waterside vegetation. In breeding season, constructs large mound nests of water-
plants. Outside breeding season, often forms large flocks. When taking off
from water, typically runs along surface, splashing its feet before finally
getting airborne. Sexes are similar. **ADULT** Has essentially all-dark plumage,

darkest on head and neck; note
white on outer undertail coverts.
Bill and frontal shield are mainly
white, except for dark subterminal band on bill and red
patch on forehead shield; note the beady red eye. Legs
are greenish yellow. In flight, note white trailing edge to
otherwise dark, rounded wings. **JUVENILE** Has dark grayish brown upperparts and white on throat and front of
neck. Bill is dull pink. Recalls an oversized, winter
plumage Pied-billed Grebe (*see* p.70). Acquires adultlike
plumage by first winter, but bill is pure white and red
on forehead is absent. **VOICE** Utters a loud *kwoot* call.
STATUS AND HABITAT Widespread and common on freshwater wetlands; range contracts southward in winter.
OBSERVATION TIPS Easy to observe.

SANDHILL CRANE *Grus canadensis* L 40–46 in

Large and almost unmistakable bird with a stately posture and gait.
Confusion with Great Blue Heron (*see* p.84) is possible, but note
differences in plumage, structure, and head markings. Outside breeding season, Sandhill is invariably seen in large flocks, whereas Great Blue is usually
solitary. In flight, Sandhill holds head and neck outstretched, while Great
Blue has neck hunched and "S"-shaped. Seen from below in flight, note
mainly pale flight feathers. Arctic nesters are appreciably smaller and short-
er-billed than birds from south of breeding range. Sexes are similar. **ADULT**
Has mainly blue-gray plumage, palest on face. Note red crown and variable
rufous feathering on wings. Legs and daggerlike bill are dark. **JUVENILE** Has variably blue-gray and
rufous plumage, but typically rufous predominates on head, neck, and back. Bill is dull pink and red
crown is absent. **VOICE** Utters evocative, rattling, bugling calls. **STATUS AND HABITAT** Very locally
common. Nests in remote tundra or expansive wetlands and winters in wetland areas with adjacent
farmland. **OBSERVATION TIPS** At traditional migration staging areas and winter roosts, the massive
numbers of Sandhill Cranes provide one of North America's greatest wildlife spectacles. Probably the
best site is Bosque del Apache NWR in New Mexico.

JUVENILE

COMMON MOORHEN

ADULT

ADULT

AMERICAN COOT

ADULT

ADULT

SANDHILL CRANE

ADULT

Charadriidae

SNOWY PLOVER *Charadrius alexandrinus* L 6.25–6.5 in

Dumpy little plover that looks mostly very pale. Typically feeds near water's edge, running at great speed then pausing momentarily to pick invertebrates from surface of sand. Sexes are separable with care. **ADULT MALE** In summer, has pale sandy brown upperparts and white underparts. Note black patches at front of sandy crown, behind eye, and on the side of breast. Legs and bill are black. In winter, resembles adult female.

ADULT FEMALE In summer is similar to male, but black elements of plumage are a paler dark brown. In winter, plumage shows even less contrast. **JUVENILE** Resembles winter female. **VOICE** Utters a soft *bruip* call. **STATUS AND HABITAT** Scarce and threatened species associated with wide-open sandy habitats or mudflats. Occurs year-round on coastal beaches; in summer, also found on expansive sand-flats inland. Human disturbance badly affects breeding success and seldom thrives unless nests are specifically protected. **OBSERVATION TIPS** Heat haze and harsh sunlight make it difficult to spot, so easiest to see on dull days.

PIPING PLOVER *Charadrius melodus* L 7–7.5 in

Another pale and endangered plover. Easily told from Snowy by orange (not blackish) legs and orange base to bill in breeding adults (otherwise dark, and similar to Snowy). Runs in short bursts at great speed; hard to locate when it stops because it blends so well with favored sandy habitats. Sexes are separable with care. **ADULT MALE** In summer, has mainly pale sandy upperparts and white underparts. Note narrow black collar and (usually incom-

plete) breast band, and black band on forehead. Legs are orange and dainty orange bill is black-tipped. In winter, black elements of plumage are brown and bill is dark. **ADULT FEMALE** In summer is similar to male, but black elements of plumage are brown. In winter, resembles winter male. **JUVENILE** Similar to winter adult. **VOICE** Utters a piping *peep-lo*. **STATUS AND HABITAT** Scarce and endangered. In summer, favors drying margins of Great Plains lakes; breeding success badly affected by disturbance from humans and their dogs and cats. In winter, moves to Gulf coast sandy beaches. **OBSERVATION TIPS** As with Snowy, easiest to detect first of all when it runs. To minimize disturbance, probably best looked for in winter.

SEMIPALMATED PLOVER
Charadrius semipalmatus L 7–7.5 in

Small, dumpy wader typically seen near water. Runs at speed (as if powered by clockwork) and then stands still for a few seconds before picking a food item from ground. Webbing between outer toes is hard to discern, except in very close views. Sexes are separable with care. **ADULT MALE** Has mainly sandy brown upperparts and white underparts, with a continuous

black breast band and collar. Note distinctive black patch through eye and on forecrown, defining white patch in front of eye. Legs are orange-yellow and bill is orange with a dark tip. In winter, black elements of plumage on head are mainly brown, especially on forecrown; bill is mainly dark, but with dull orange at base of lower mandible. **ADULT FEMALE** Similar to male, but black elements of plumage on head are brown. **JUVENILE** Recalls winter adult with broken breast band. **VOICE** Utters a soft *tchu-eep*. **STATUS AND HABITAT** Common; nests besides freshwater; winters on coasts. **OBSERVATION TIPS** Easy to find in winter.

ADULT, WINTER

MALE, SUMMER

SNOWY PLOVER

PIPING PLOVER

ADULT, SUMMER

ADULT, WINTER

ADULT, WINTER

ADULT, SUMMER

SEMIPALMATED PLOVER

Charadriidae

KILLDEER *Charadrius vociferus* L 10–11 in

Boldly marked, long-legged and noisy plover. The two black breast
bands are striking and diagnostic. Long wings and tail give standing
bird a more elongated appearance. Feeds in characteristic plover manner:
runs at speed for short distances, then pauses to pick invertebrate prey from
ground. In flight, long wings with bold white wing stripe, and long, wedge-
shaped tail with orange rump are striking features. Sexes are similar. **ADULT**
Has mainly brown upperparts and white underparts, but note two black breast
bands (upper one continues as a narrow collar) and striking black and white
markings on face (black forecrown, and white forehead and supercilium). Bill
is slender and dark and legs are pale. Tail darkens toward tip, but note terminal white margin. **JUVENILE**
Similar to adult, but black elements of plumage are brown or dark brown. **VOICE** Utters a shrill, piping
kiu-dee or *tee-dee-dee*. **STATUS AND HABITAT** Common and widespread in summer across much of the
region south of the Arctic, favoring short grassy areas, including urban sites such as roadside verges,
golf courses, parks, and playing fields. Migrates south in fall and winters in southern half of region.
Seen in the vicinity of water far less frequently than most shorebird family members. **OBSERVATION
TIPS** Easy to see and identify. **COMMENTS** Breeding birds, with eggs or chicks, are famous for feigning
injury, with a broken wing display, to distract the attentions of predators away from the nest.

MOUNTAIN PLOVER
Charadrius montanus L 8.75–9 in

Sandy-colored plover that blends in well with its surroundings.
Despite its understated plumage, it has an iconic conservation status because
of its vulnerability to habitat loss. In flight, dark upper wingtips and dark subterminal patch on upper tail are useful in identification. Feeds on invertebrates. Sexes are similar. **ADULT** In summer has mainly sandy brown upperparts
and white underparts. Note, however, black loral line from eye to base of bill,
black forecrown, and white on forehead extending as superciliary stripe above
eye. Bill is dark and legs are relatively long and pale buff-gray. In winter, black
elements of head plumage are sandy brown and neck and breast can look grubby buff. **JUVENILE** Similar to winter adult, but pale feather edges on back create a scaly appearance. **VOICE** Utters a harsh *krrrt*.
STATUS AND HABITAT Endangered and declining. Breeds on Midwest High Plains and nesting require-

JUVENILE

ments are specific: needs naturally
grazed, shortgrass prairies, such as
those found in the vicinity of prairie-
dog "towns"; sadly of course, these
too are in decline as a result of habitat loss and degradation from agriculture. Gregarious outside the breeding
season. From Nov–Feb, found in arid
southern regions from California to
Texas. **OBSERVATION TIPS** An enigmatic species that you are unlikely to
encounter by chance. Probably easiest to find in winter and flocks can
sometimes be discovered by scanning
bare, plowed fields or short grassland
in arid parts of southern California;
the general vicinity of Salton Sea
would be a good starting point. Mid-
day heat haze hampers observation,
so early mornings are best. Note that
birds are surprisingly difficult to spot
until they move, so persistent observation is usually needed.

JUVENILE

ADULT

KILLDEER

ADULT

MOUNTAIN PLOVER

ADULT, WINTER

ADULT, SUMMER

Charadriidae

BLACK-BELLIED PLOVER
Pluvialis squatarola L 11.25–11.5 in

Plump-bodied, well-marked plover. In flight, all birds reveal striking black "armpits" (axillaries) on otherwise white underwings, white upper tail, and white wing stripe. Mostly solitary outside breeding season. Sexes are separable with care in summer plumage. **ADULT MALE** In summer, has striking black underparts, separated from spangled gray upperparts by broad white band. In winter, looks gray overall. Close view reveals spangled black and white upperparts and whitish underparts. Legs and bill are dark. **ADULT**

ADULT, WINTER

FEMALE Similar to male, but black on underparts is variably mottled. In winter, similar to male. **JUVENILE** Resembles winter adult, but has pale buffy wash, hence potential for confusion with golden-plovers. **VOICE** Utters a diagnostic *pee-oo-ee* call, like a human wolf-whistle. **STATUS AND HABITAT** Breeds on high Arctic tundra. In winter, almost exclusively coastal, on salt marshes and estuaries. On migration, occasionally stages on lake margins in interior. **OBSERVATION TIPS** Easiest to observe in winter and hence mostly seen in nonbreeding plumage. However, breeding plumage is often retained briefly by birds in fall newly arrived on wintering grounds and acquired, prior to departure, in spring.

AMERICAN GOLDEN-PLOVER
Pluvialis dominica L 10–10.5 in

Beautifully marked plover and renowned long-distance migrant. Almost unmistakable in breeding plumage, when entirely black underparts allow separation from Pacific. In other plumages, grayer, less golden-spangled upperparts are a pointer, but greater wing projection beyond tail and relatively shorter tertials are most reliable guides for separation from Pacific. Compared to larger Black-bellied, looks slim-bodied and long-legged with pronounced wing projection (wings roughly same length as tail in Black-bellied), gray underwings (black "armpits" in Black-bellied), dark rump, and only faint wing stripe. Often gregarious outside breeding season. Feeds on invertebrates and berries in summer. Sexes are separable with care in summer. **ADULT MALE** In summer, has striking black underparts, separated

MALE, SUMMER

PACIFIC GOLDEN-PLOVER

ADULT, WINTER

from golden-spangled upperparts by broad white band running from forehead to sides of neck. In winter, looks gray overall, with dark crown, and pale supercilium. **ADULT FEMALE** In summer is similar to male, but black elements of plumage are mottled. In winter, similar to winter male. **JUVENILE** Similar to winter adult, but with a hint of golden spangling on crown and back. **VOICE** Utters a mournful *quee-dle*. **STATUS AND HABITAT** Fairly common breeding species in western Arctic, favoring dry tundra. Winters in southern South America, favoring dry grassland. Typically flies nonstop from Arctic to northeastern South America, then nonstop to southern South America. Fall sightings often involve juveniles. Flocks of returning migrants are sometimes seen in spring, typically in grassland and agricultural fields. **OBSERVATION TIPS** Most reliably found by visiting Arctic breeding grounds in summer. **SIMILAR SPECIES Pacific Golden-Plover** *P. fulva* (L 9.75–10 in) has a shorter wing projection, but longer tertials than American, and longer bill and legs. In summer, black on underparts is marbled white on flanks and under tail. In other plumages, especially juvenile, looks golden spangled on back and crown, with yellow flush to face and chest. Main breeding range is Arctic Asia, but also nests in western Alaska. Most winter in southern Pacific, but small numbers winter on western coast of North America, mainly southern California.

ADULT, WINTER

BLACK-BELLIED PLOVER

MALE, SUMMER

JUVENILE

ADULT, WINTER

MALE, SUMMER

ADULT, WINTER

AMERICAN GOLDEN-PLOVER

BLACK OYSTERCATCHER
Haematopus bachmani L 17–18 in

Robust and stocky shorebird. Entirely black plumage and bright red bill make it almost unmistakable. Feeds on intertidal invertebrates, using chisel-like bill to hammer mollusks from rocks and break their shells. Somewhat gregarious outside the breeding season. Sexes are similar. **ADULT** Has all-dark plumage, but in good light, brown wash can be dis-

AMERICAN OYSTERCATCHER

ADULT, SUMMER

cerned on back. Bill is red, legs are dull pink, and eye is yellow with a red surround. **JUVENILE** Similar to adult, but bill is dark-tipped and back feathers have pale margins. **VOICE** Utters are shrill, piping *kweep*. **STATUS AND HABITAT** Found on rocky shores and often nests on shingle beaches. However, human disturbance excludes it from many potentially suitable areas in breeding season. **OBSERVATION TIPS** Easy to find in suitable habitats. **SIMILAR SPECIES American Oystercatcher** *H. palliatus* (L 17–19 in) occurs on Gulf coast and rarely in southern California. Has pied plumage and favors mudflats as well as rocky shores.

AMERICAN AVOCET
Recurvirostra americana L 18 in

Elegant wading bird. Despite seasonal differences in plumage, unmistakable with black and white plumage overall, extremely long pale bluish legs, and slender, upcurved bill. Long, thin bill is swept from side to side in shallow water, collecting tiny invertebrate prey. Looks striking in flight: seen from above, black wingtips, outer wing coverts, and scapular stripes contrast with otherwise white plumage. Sexes are similar, but male's bill is straighter than female's. **ADULT** In summer, has orange-buff flush to head and neck. Underparts are white and upperparts are black with white on scapulars and upper back. In winter, buffy elements of plumage become whitish. **JUVENILE** Similar to dull summer adult with washed out orange-buff coloration and pale edges to back feathers. **VOICE** Utters a sharp *kweet*. **STATUS AND HABITAT** Locally common, favoring shallow lakes, ponds, and marshes in breeding season. In winter, mainly coastal, found on pools and mudflats; occasionally inland too, e.g. at Salton Sea. **OBSERVATION TIPS** Easy to observe and identify.

BLACK-NECKED STILT
Himantopus mexicanus L 13–14 in

Unmistakable, elegant wading bird, with ridiculously long, red legs, striking black and white plumage, and a long, straight, and very thin bill. Long legs allow it to feed in deep water, but also forages in shallows, picking small invertebrates from surface with precision. In flight, uniformly black wings and long, trailing legs make identification straightforward. Sexes are separable with care. **ADULT MALE** Has mainly black upperparts and white

MALE

underparts; sometimes acquires pinkish flush to underparts in breeding season. Throat and front of neck is white and note white patch above eye on otherwise black face. **ADULT FEMALE** Similar to male, but back is brownish, not jet-black. **JUVENILE** Similar to adult, but with less extensive black on neck, and pale feather edges on back. **VOICE** Utters an insistent *kleet*. **STATUS AND HABITAT** Locally fairly common in shallow ponds, lake margins, and marshes. Summer range contracts south and west in fall and mainly coastal in winter, often favoring brackish lagoons. **OBSERVATION TIPS** Easy to observe and identify if suitable habitats are visited.

BLACK OYSTERCATCHER

ADULT

ADULT

ADULT

AMERICAN AVOCET

FEMALE

BLACK-NECKED STILT

MALE

Scolopacidae

GREATER YELLOWLEGS
Tringa melanoleuca L 13–14 in

Robust, elegant wading bird. Extremely long, orange-yellow legs and long, relatively thick and slightly upturned bill make identification easy. However, confusion is possible with Lesser Yellowlegs, which is smaller and an altogether more dainty bird (*see* that species' description for further distinctions). Feeds primarily in shallow water, catching aquatic invertebrates and small fish, but equally at home on open mudflats. Often chases wildly, like a thing possessed, after prey. Seen from above in flight, all birds have mainly dark upperparts, with contrasting white rump and pale-barred tail. Typically rather wary and nervous. Sexes are similar. **ADULT** In summer plumage, has beautifully patterned brown, black, and white feather markings on back and upper wings. Head, neck, and breast are streaked with brown, and underparts are mainly white, but with brown spots and barring on flanks. Bill is usually all-dark. In winter, looks more pale with gray-brown feathers overall on back and upper wings marked with marginal white spots and scallops. Bill is pale-based. **JUVENILE** Similar to winter adult, but feathers on back have buffy marginal spots and breast has obvious dark streaking. Bill is paler at base. **VOICE** Utters a stri-

JUVENILE

dent *tiu-tiu-tiu* in flight; song is a yodeling *twee-ooo*. **STATUS AND HABITAT** Widespread and common breeding species in open, boggy, boreal forests. Long-distance migrant that winters from southern U.S. to South America. Usually found on coast (mudflats and lagoons) outside breeding season, but, during migration, sometimes stages on lakes. **OBSERVATION TIPS** Distant birds can sometimes be identified with reasonable certainty because of their frenetic feeding habits. Close views allow separation from Lesser Yellowlegs: concentrate on relative body sizes, and bill size and shape.

LESSER YELLOWLEGS *Tringa flavipes* L 10–11 in

Elegant wading bird with long, orange-yellow legs. Bill is thin, long and straight. It only just exceeds head length whereas Greater's bill is much longer than head length. Note also that Lesser's bill is always all dark, whereas Greater's is pale-based in juveniles and winter adults. Feeds in a more precise manner than Greater (which runs around wildly) and generally much less wary. In flight, dark upperparts contrast with white rump and pale-barred tail. Sexes are similar. **ADULT** In summer, has back feathers beautifully patterned with brown, black, and white. Head and neck are heavily streaked brown and underparts are mainly white (Greater's flanks have dark barring). In winter, looks much paler grayish overall. Head, neck, and upperparts are pale gray-brown, feathers on

JUVENILE

back being marked with pale marginal spots and scallops. Underparts are white. **JUVENILE** Similar to winter adult, but with more streaking on neck and breast, and buffy marginal spots and scallops on back feathers. **VOICE** Utters a sharp *tew* or *tew-tew* in flight; song is a yodeling *tweedle-ee*. **STATUS AND HABITAT** Common breeding species in taiga or lightly wooded tundra habitats. Watchful nesting birds sometimes perch on stunted trees. Long-distance migrant, wintering as far south as southern South America. Widespread on migration throughout North America and winters in smaller numbers than Greater on Gulf coast and in southern California. **OBSERVATION TIPS** Bill length and more controlled feeding habits are pointers allowing separation from Greater.

GREATER YELLOWLEGS

JUVENILE

ADULT, SUMMER

LESSER YELLOWLEGS

JUVENILE

Scolopacidae

SOLITARY SANDPIPER *Tringa solitaria* L 8–8.5 in

Compact, medium-sized sandpiper. As its common name suggests, it has typically solitary habits and usually feeds unobtrusively around muddy pool margins or in shallow marshes. Characteristically bobs body up and down as it walks. Flight is rapid and often rises steeply if flushed: note wings are dark above and below and tail has dark center and white margins, barred toward tip. Sexes are similar. **ADULT** In summer plumage, has dark brown upperparts, feathers on back finely marked with pale marginal spots. Head and neck are streaked brown; crown is darkest and note white eyering. Underparts are white, with faint barring on flanks. Legs are dull yellowish green and relatively long bill is dull pinkish gray, darkening toward tip. Winter adult is similar, but is duller overall with less intense pale spots on back, and only faint streaking. **JUVENILE** Similar to winter adult, but has more striking white spots on back and upper wings, but only very faint streaking on otherwise uniformly buffy brown head and neck. **VOICE** Utters a shrill *peet-wheet* or *peet-wheet-wheet* when flushed; song includes elements of call-like notes. **STATUS AND HABITAT** Widespread in breeding season in taiga marshes and bogs. Nests in abandoned songbird nests in trees. Winters almost exclusively in South America (only very rarely in southern U.S.), but widespread across region during migration, often stopping off at surprisingly small pools for a few hours or days. **OBSERVATION TIPS** Displaying or watchful breeders will sometimes perch on dead branch. Migrants are easiest to find on southbound journey, mainly late Jul–Sep; juvenile migration follows that of adults.

SPOTTED SANDPIPER *Actitis macularius* L 7–8 in

Widespread and familiar sandpiper with distinctive habits and unique and diagnostic summer plumage. Typically seen feeding on the margins of pools, streams, and lakes; as it walks, constantly bobs its body up and down. Usually flies low over water on bowed wings and shallow, rapid wingbeats; tail looks rather long and indeed, at rest, it extends well beyond wings. Feeds on aquatic invertebrates and is usually solitary. Sexes are similar. **ADULT** In summer plumage, has rich brown upperparts marked with dark spots and streaks on back. Underparts are whitish, but boldly marked with dark spots; these are particularly intense on throat and chest. Note the dark eyestripe and pale white supercilium. Bill is pale pinkish orange and legs are more pinkish yellow. In winter plumage, upperparts are uniform gray-brown. Head is mainly buffy brown, but note pale supercilium and throat.

JUVENILE

Chest is buffy brown and note clear demarcation from otherwise white underparts. Bill is pale and legs are pale pink. **JUVENILE** Similar to winter adult, but note the black and buff barring on wing coverts. **VOICE** Utters a sharp *weet* or *peet-weet-weet*...; display song comprises whistling notes. **STATUS AND HABITAT** Widespread and common in breeding season, typically found along stony or gravelly shores and steep banks of streams and lakes. Winters mainly in Central and South America, but some linger in southern U.S., particularly on coasts. Migrants turn up on inland pools and lakes, and on coastal lagoons and estuaries. **OBSERVATION TIPS** Almost any unpolluted, relatively undisturbed stream or lake within summer range is likely to accommodate the species.

SOLITARY SANDPIPER

ADULT, SUMMER

ADULT, SUMMER

SPOTTED SANDPIPER

1ST-WINTER

Scolopacidae

MARBLED GODWIT *Limosa fedoa* L 18–19 in

Large and subtly patterned shorebird. Bill is extremely long and nearly straight (distal half is slightly upturned), allowing easy separation
from similarly sized Long-billed Curlew (has downcurved bill); bill is used to
probe mud and soft sand for invertebrates. In flight, wings are mainly uniformly orange-buff with dark carpal patch on upper wings. Typically tolerant
of observers. Sexes are similar. **ADULT** Looks pale buffy orange overall, darkest on back and wings. In summer plumage, close inspection reveals intricate dark marbling on back and upper wings and subtle barring on underparts.
Bill is mostly pink with a dark tip. Legs are dark. In winter, plumage looks paler
overall, and pink on bill is more extensive. **JUVENILE** Similar to winter adult. **VOICE** Utters a loud *ker-Wik* in flight. **STATUS AND HABITAT** Fairly common, breeding in wet grassland and marshes. Winters
on coasts, mainly south of our region, but common on migration. **OBSERVATION TIPS** Easiest to see
in spring and fall on coasts.

WILLET *Tringa semipalmata* L 14.5–15 in

Plump-bodied shorebird with a stout, straight, pale-based bill and
longish blue-gray legs. Plumage appears undistinguished when feeding, but transforms in flight to striking black and white markings on
wings. Typically tolerant of observers. Sexes are similar. **ADULT** In breeding
season, is gray-brown overall, but heavily streaked on head and neck, and
with dark scallops on lower neck, chest, and flanks. In winter, looks rather
uniformly pale gray-brown. **JUVENILE** Similar to winter adult, but back and
upper wing coverts are washed and spotted yellow-buff. **VOICE** Utters a sharp
klip in alarm; song is a ringing *peel-will-willet*. **STATUS AND HABITAT** Locally
common, nesting beside marshes and wintering on coastal beaches. Represented in
western North America by ssp. *inornatus*, paler than eastern counterpart. **OBSERVATION TIPS** Easy to
find on coasts in winter.

WANDERING TATTLER
Tringa incana L 10–11 in

Plump-bodied shorebird, with a slender, straight bill and stout yellow legs. Plumage appears rather undistinguished, but close inspection
reveals subtly attractive markings in breeding season. In flight, note uniformly dark wings. Unobtrusive habits (often feeds where waves are breaking on rocky shores) make it easy to overlook. Sexes are similar. **ADULT** In
breeding season, has dark gray upperparts and paler underparts heavily
marked with dark barring; note pale supercilium. In winter, has uniformly gray
upperparts and
underparts with white belly. **JUVENILE**
Similar to winter adult, but note subtle
pale fringes to feathers on back and
upper wing coverts. **VOICE** Utters a
whistling *tui-tui-tui*. **STATUS AND
HABITAT** Fairly common, nesting in
Alaska and northwestern Canada beside
mountain streams above timberline.
Long-distance migrant, some birds wintering in Australia. Some remain in
southern California; widespread and
fairly common on Pacific rocky coasts
on migration. **OBSERVATION TIPS** Fairly easy to find on rocky coasts in spring
and fall; presence often first detected
by hearing call.

ADULT, WINTER

GODWITS, WILLET, and TATTLERS

MARBLED GODWIT

ADULT

ADULT, SUMMER

ADULT, WINTER

WILLET

ADULT, WINTER

ADULT, WINTER

ADULT, SUMMER

ADULT, SUMMER

JUVENILE

WANDERING TATTLER

ADULT, SUMMER

Scolopacidae

LONG-BILLED CURLEW
Numenius americanus L 21–23 in

A large shorebird, with an immensely long, downcurved bill, used to probe for mud-dwelling invertebrates in winter, and grassland insects etc. in summer. Its onomatopoeic call is evocative of lonely, upland grasslands in spring and summer, and estuaries and coastal grassland at other times of the year. In flight, all birds reveal rather uniform upperparts, darkest on outer half of wing. Sexes are similar, although males have shorter bills than females. **ADULT** Has mainly warm buff plumage, flushed orange-brown on back, belly, and breast, and particularly noticeable on underwings in flight. Plumage is streaked and spotted on the neck and underparts, and wing and back feathers have dark centers and bars, creating scalloped effect. **JUVENILE** Similar to adult, but it looks paler overall, particularly on neck, and has appreciably shorter bill. **VOICE** Utters a characteristic *curlee* call and also delivers whistling song on breeding grounds. **STATUS AND HABITAT** Breeds in dry prairie and upland grassland in Great Plains area. Favored habitat has suffered substantial loss and continues to suffer degradation due to farming practices. Consequently, species is vulnerable and declining. On migration, found on arable fields and grassland and in winter mainly associated with mudflats and estuaries, but also coastal freshwater wetlands. **OBSERVATION TIPS** Easiest to see in winter, on coasts, where it feeds in the open and roosts in sizeable flocks.

ADULT

WHIMBREL *Numenius phaeopus* L 17–18 in

Smaller cousin to Long-billed Curlew with an appreciably shorter, but still obviously downcurved bill; this is used to probe mud and soil for invertebrates. Head markings are striking and call is a reasonably distinctive means of identification. In flight, could be confused with Long-billed Curlew, but appears much grayer overall, with darker outer wings and noticeably shorter bill. Sexes are similar. **ADULT** Has gray-brown plumage overall with fine, dark streaking on neck and breast. Back and wing feathers have small, pale marginal spots. Head pattern comprises two broad, dark lateral stripes on otherwise pale crown, and dark stripe through eye. Legs are bluish gray. **JUVENILE** Similar to adult, but feathers of wing and back have larger pale spots. **VOICE** Call typically comprises 5–7 whistling notes delivered at same pitch. **STATUS AND HABITAT** Locally fairly common breeding species on tundra, mainly in Alaska and Hudson Bay areas. Long-distance migrant; many birds winter in South America, but fairly common outside breeding season on California and Gulf coast beaches and rocky shorelines. **OBSERVATION TIPS** Easiest to find outside breeding season on coasts, mudflats, and coastal wetlands. **SIMILAR SPECIES Bristle-thighed Curlew** *N. tahitiensis* (L 17–18 in) is much warmer buff with bolder head markings, proportionately longer tail, larger and more obvious pale spots on wing and back feathers, and striking orange-buff rump seen in flight. Extremely rare Alaskan breeding species that typically flies nonstop to oceanic island wintering grounds in Pacific.

BRISTLE-THIGHED CURLEW

ADULT

LONG-BILLED CURLEW

ADULT

WHIMBREL

ADULT

ADULT

Scolopacidae

RUDDY TURNSTONE *Arenaria interpres* L 9–10 in

Robust and pugnacious shorebird. Short, triangular bill is used to turn stones and tide-line debris in search of seashore invertebrates. Unobtrusive when feeding among seaweed and rocks. All birds have reddish

orange legs and striking black and white pattern in flight. Sexes are similar. **ADULT** In summer plumage, has bold patches of orange-red on back, white underparts, and bold black and white markings on head. Male has brighter back colors than female and more distinct black head markings. In winter, has mainly gray-brown upperparts, including head and neck. Blackish, rounded breast band shows clear demarcation from white underparts. **JUVENILE** Similar to winter adult, but upperparts are paler and back feathers have pale fringes. **VOICE** Utters a rolling *tuk-ut-ut* in flight. **STATUS AND HABITAT** Locally common high Arctic tundra breeder. Outside breeding season, found on range of coastal habitats; rocky shores with extensive strandline are ideal. **OBSERVATION TIPS** Easy to see on coasts Aug–Apr; early arrivals and late departures sometimes seen in summer plumage.

BLACK TURNSTONE
Arenaria melanocephala L 9–10 in

Structurally similar to Ruddy Turnstone, but separable by plumage details when feeding. In flight, striking black and white wing pattern is similar to Ruddy's, cre-

ating potential for confusion, especially in poor light. All birds have narrow triangular bill. In winter, often associates with Surfbird, with which it can be confused. Note that species' stubby (not pointed bill), yellowish (not dull reddish brown) legs, and streaked white underparts (clean white in Black Turnstone). Sexes are similar. **ADULT** In winter, has dark blackish brown upperparts with clear horizontal demarcation from white underparts; median coverts are long and black, overhanging white greater coverts and wing edge. Breeding adult acquires white lores, supercilium and small white spots on dark upperparts. **JUVENILE** Similar to winter adult, but with paler legs and shorter median coverts. **VOICE** Utters a rattling *urkt-ut-ut* call in flight. **STATUS AND HABITAT** Very locally common with a limited coastal breeding range in western Alaska. Winters along Pacific rocky coasts. **OBSERVATION TIPS** Usually easy to find on rocky breakwaters in winter.

SURFBIRD *Aphriza virgata* L 10–10.5 in

Robust, plump-bodied shorebird associated with rocky shores and undaunted by breaking waves. Feeds in small groups outside breeding season and associates with Black Turnstone. All birds have a rather short, slender, and stubby bill, orange-yellow legs, and, in flight, striking white pattern on wings and tail (but not on back, as in turnstones). Sexes are similar. **ADULT** In breeding season, has heavily streaked head, neck, and mantle; scapulars are marked with orange-brown and wings are otherwise dark. Underparts are white, but boldly marked with dark arrowhead spots. In winter, upperparts are mainly dark gray-brown, but note white throat and wing stripe; underparts are white with gray-brown spots. **JUVENILE** Similar to winter adult, but feathers on back and wings have pale margins. **VOICE** Mostly silent. **STATUS AND HABITAT** Locally common breeding species on rocky ridges among upland tundra. In winter, found on rocky shores along Pacific coast. **OBSERVATION TIPS** Usually easy to find on rocky breakwaters in winter.

RUDDY TURNSTONE

MALE, SUMMER

ADULT, WINTER

ADULT, SUMMER

ADULT, WINTER

BLACK TURNSTONE

SURFBIRD

ADULT, SUMMER

ADULT, WINTER

ADULT, WINTER

Scolopacidae

ROCK SANDPIPER *Calidris ptilocnemis* L 9–9.5 in

Plump-bodied shorebird that feeds on rocky shores, often among breaking waves. All birds have a slender, downcurved bill. In flight, uniformly dark upperparts reveal only faint pale wing stripe. In summer plumage recalls breeding Dunlin, but note dark patch on chest (not belly). Sexes are similar. **ADULT SUMMER** Has chestnut-brown crown and feather margins on back; face and neck are streaked and note dark ear coverts. Underparts are mainly white with dark patch on breast. **ADULT WINTER** Has dark blue-gray upperparts including head, neck, and chest; underparts are whitish, with faint spots on flanks. Legs are dull orange-yellow. **JUVENILE** Has streaked buffy brown upperparts with distinct pectoral transition on chest from white underparts. **VOICE** Utters a sharp *kwiit* in flight. **STATUS AND HABITAT** Locally fairly common. Breeds on coastal tundra in western Alaska. Winters on rocky shores on Pacific coast. **OBSERVATION TIPS** Easiest to find in winter on rocky coasts. Usually tolerant of observers, but unobtrusive and rather easy to overlook.

STILT SANDPIPER *Calidris himantopus* L 8–9 in

Elegant shorebird with long, yellowish legs; long bill is downcurved towards tip. In flight, note long, trailing legs and white rump and upper tail. Usually feeds in deep water, probing mud in deliberate manner. Sexes are similar. **ADULT SUMMER** Beautifully marked with chestnut on crown and ear coverts, broad pale supercilium, and otherwise dark-streaked face and neck. Underparts have distinct dark bars; feathers on back have dark centers. **ADULT WINTER** Has mainly gray upperparts and white underparts; note pale supercilium. **JUVENILE** Similar to winter adult, but feathers on back have cleaner-looking pale margins. **VOICE** Mostly silent. **STATUS AND HABITAT** Very locally common high Arctic breeding species, from north Alaska to Hudson Bay. Winters mainly in Central and South America, but small numbers remain in southern U.S. **OBSERVATION TIPS** In winter, regular only at Salton Sea, California and on Gulf coast. Migrants are occasional on inland wetlands; breeding birds are easiest to see at Churchill, Manitoba.

ADULT

RED KNOT *Calidris canutus* L 10–11 in

Dumpy and robust shorebird with short and stout legs and bill. In winter, forms large flocks, which fly in tight formation. Faint white wing stripe is visible in flight, but otherwise lacks distinctive features in winter plumage. Sexes are similar. **ADULT SUMMER** Has orange-red on face, neck, and underparts; many back feathers have black and orange-red centers and gray fringes. Legs and bill are dark. **ADULT WINTER** Has uniform gray-brown upperparts and white underparts. Bill is dark and legs are dull yellowish green. **JUVENILE** Similar to winter adult, but back feathers have pale fringes and dark submarginal bands, creating a scaly look. Usually has buff tinge to plumage, particularly on breast. **VOICE** Utters a sharp *kwet* call. **STATUS AND HABITAT** Locally fairly common. Breeds on high Arctic tundra. Migration is mainly coastal, but typically uses regular staging posts away from which only lone individuals are seen. Winters on sandy beaches and estuaries from southern U.S. southward to South America. **OBSERVATION TIPS** Significant wintering grounds are few and far between on Pacific coasts; Point Pinole, California is probably the best.

ADULTS, WINTER

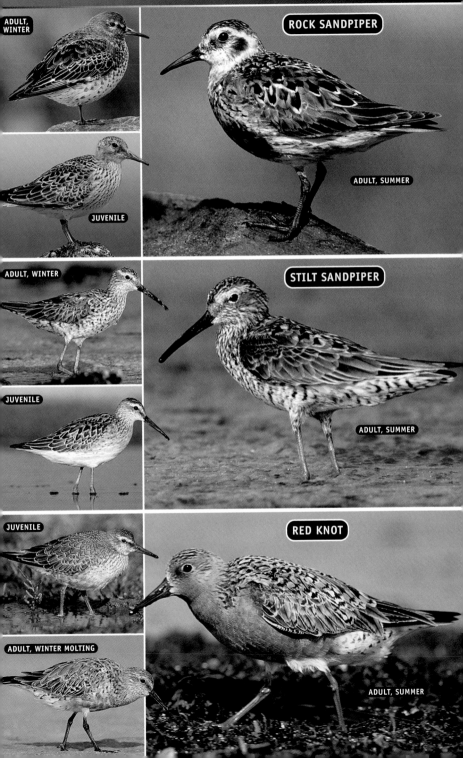

ADULT, WINTER

ROCK SANDPIPER

JUVENILE

ADULT, SUMMER

ADULT, WINTER

STILT SANDPIPER

JUVENILE

ADULT, SUMMER

JUVENILE

RED KNOT

ADULT, WINTER MOLTING

ADULT, SUMMER

Scolopacidae

DUNLIN *Calidris alpina* L 8–9 in

The archetypal small, coastal wader in winter. Represented globally by several races, each with subtly different bill lengths; ssp. *pacifica* is commonest in western North America. Forms flocks outside breeding season. Sexes are subtly different in summer, but separation is tricky. **ADULT SUMMER** Has a reddish brown back and cap, whitish underparts with bold black belly, and streaking on neck. Males are more boldly marked than females, but considerable variation exists within sexes. Bill and legs are dark. **ADULT WINTER** Has uniform dull brownish gray upperparts, mostly dingy white underparts, and dark legs and bill. **JUVENILE** Has pale-fringed reddish brown

ADULT, WINTER

and black feathers on back; some align so pale fringes form "V" patterns. Underparts are whitish, but with black streak-like spots on breast and (diagnostically for juvenile shorebird) on flanks too; head and neck are brown and streaked. **VOICE** Utters a *preeit* call; display flight "song" comprises series of whistles. **STATUS AND HABITAT** Locally very common. Nests on Arctic tundra marshes. In winter favors estuaries and mudflats. Occasional at inland wetlands on migration. **OBSERVATION TIPS** Easy to find on coasts in winter. Get to know it in summer and winter plumages—it is the yardstick by which other small waders can be judged.

SANDERLING *Calidris alba* L 7.5–8 in

Characteristic shorebird of sandy beaches, seen in small flocks running at speed, and feeding, along edges of breaking waves. Striking

ADULT, WINTER

white wing stripe, seen in flight, and dark legs and bill are seen at all times. Sexes are similar. **ADULT WINTER** Has uniform dull gray upperparts and white underparts. **ADULT SUMMER** (seen in late spring or sometimes early fall) Flushed red on head and neck and has scattering of dark-centered feathers on back; underparts are white. **JUVENILE** Similar to winter adult, but many back feathers are dark-centered. **VOICE** Utters a sharp *plit* call. **STATUS AND HABITAT** Common winter visitor (mainly Sep–Apr) to coastal sandy beaches. Breeds on high Arctic tundra. Occasional on inland wetlands during migration. **OBSERVATION TIPS** Easy to see in winter.

LEAST SANDPIPER *Calidris minutilla* L 5.75–6 in

The world's smallest shorebird, smaller even than Semipalmated and Western sandpipers (*see* p.136); distinguished from them at all times by yellow (not dark) legs; collectively, these three birds are known as "peeps." Needlelike bill is dark at all times. All birds show faint white wing stripe and white sides to tail in flight. Sexes are similar. **ADULT SUMMER** Has streaked brown head and neck, with reasonably clear demarcation from mostly white underparts; note pale, but not very prominent supercilium. Upperparts are brownish overall, with many feathers dark centered and with buff or white margins. **ADULT WINTER** Has gray-brown head and upperparts and streaked gray-brown chest and breast showing clear demarcation from white throat and underparts; note pale supercilium. **JUVENILE** Similar to summer adult, but upperparts are warmer brown, feather margins are cleanly defined, and pale margins to mantle feathers create a striking "V." **VOICE** Utters a thin *kreet* call. **STATUS AND HABITAT** Common. Nests on tundra wetlands and open marshes in boreal forest. Winters on coasts and beside freshwater from southern U.S. southward. **OBSERVATION TIPS** Easy to find outside breeding season; commonest during fall migration.

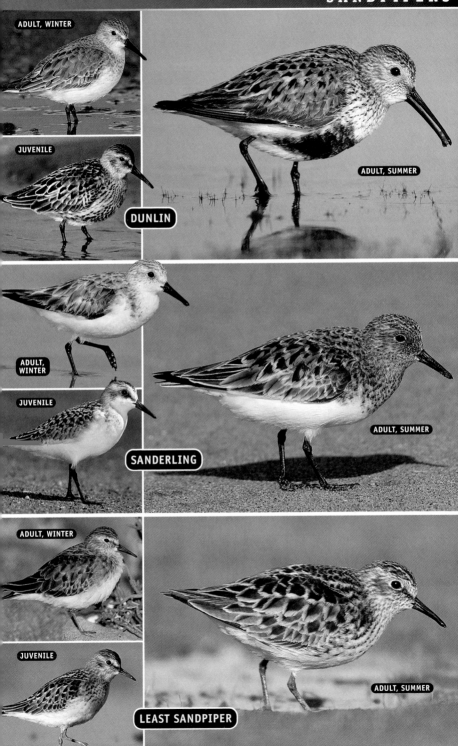

ADULT, WINTER

JUVENILE

DUNLIN

ADULT, SUMMER

ADULT, WINTER

JUVENILE

SANDERLING

ADULT, SUMMER

ADULT, WINTER

JUVENILE

LEAST SANDPIPER

ADULT, SUMMER

Scolopacidae

SEMIPALMATED SANDPIPER
Calidris pusilla L 6–6.5 in

Tiny shorebird with dark legs; webbing between toes only seen at
very close range. Short, dark bill appears "blob-tipped" (longer and tapering
in Western). **ADULT SUMMER** Has streaked brown
upperparts, neck, and chest, and otherwise white
underparts. Many back feathers are dark-centered, with rufous margins; has hint of rufous on
crown, but never as striking as Western. **ADULT
WINTER** Has gray-brown upperparts and white under-
parts. **JUVENILE** Has brown upperparts and white underparts overall; note
long, bold supercilium (meets at front of head), rather dark crown and ear
coverts, and more scaly-looking back. **VOICE** A clipped *tchrrp* call. **STATUS
AND HABITAT** Common high Arctic tundra breeder. Most migrate across
plains to southeastern U.S. before flying directly to South America, so
scarce on migration in west; essentially absent in winter. **OBSERVATION
TIPS** Migrants sometimes seen at inland freshwater; mostly juveniles in Sep.

ADULT,
WINTER

WESTERN SANDPIPER *Calidris mauri* L 6.25–6.5 in

The common "peep" in the west. Has relatively long, dark legs and
rather long, tapering dark bill. **ADULT SUMMER** Has striking rufous
crown and ear coverts, and dark-centered rufous back feathers. Underparts
are white with streaking on neck and chest, and arrowhead streaks on breast
and flanks. **ADULT WINTER** Has gray-brown upperparts and white underparts.
JUVENILE Recalls summer adult, but lacks streaking on breast and flanks,
and has only hint of rufous on crown and ear coverts. **VOICE** A shrill *jeet*
call. **STATUS AND HABITAT** Common. Nests on tundra from Alaska to Siberia,
migrates across region and winters from west and south coasts to South America. **OBSERVATION TIPS** Large migrant concentrations found in San Francisco Bay area.

WHITE-RUMPED SANDPIPER
Calidris fuscicollis L 7–7.5 in

Wings extend beyond tail at rest. White rump is seen in flight.
Slightly downcurved bill is mainly dark, but with orange base to lower
mandible. **ADULT SUMMER** Has rufous on back and bold streaking on crown,
neck, and chest, arrowheaded on breast and flanks. Underparts are otherwise white. **ADULT WINTER** Grayish above and white below. **JUVENILE**
Has dark-centered and rufous back feathers with pale margins, some of which
align to create a white "V." Dark brown crown and ear coverts contrast with
otherwise pale face and long, pale supercilium. **VOICE** A thin *tseet* call. **STA-
TUS AND HABITAT** Common Arctic breeder. Migrates across plains in spring, and mainly down Atlantic
seaboard in fall, hence rare in much of west. **OBSERVATION TIPS** Hard to find in west, but occasional
spring migrants are seen at inland pools.

BAIRD'S SANDPIPER *Calidris bairdii* L 7.5–7.75 in

Long-distance migrant whose wings extend beyond tail at rest. Bill
is tapering and straight. **ADULT SUMMER** Has gray-brown, almost
silvery looking, upperparts with dark centers to some back feathers. Neck and
chest are streaked, but underparts are otherwise white. **ADULT WINTER** Has
grayish upperparts and white underparts. **JUVENILE** Has scaly-looking back
(feathers have dark centers and pale margins) and buffy wash to face, neck,
and chest. Indistinct pale supercilium is most obvious in front of eye. **VOICE**
A trilling *prrrp*. **STATUS AND HABITAT** Common dry tundra nester. Most migrate
inland across plains, pausing only briefly before flying to South America; hence
migrants are tricky to find. **OBSERVATION TIPS** Migrants often favor dry, short grassland and mudflats.

SEMIPALMATED SANDPIPER

ADULT, WINTER

JUVENILE

ADULT, SUMMER

JUVENILE

WESTERN SANDPIPER

ADULT, WINTER

JUVENILE

ADULT, SUMMER

ADULT, SUMMER

ADULT, WINTER

WHITE-RUMPED SANDPIPER

ADULT, SUMMER

JUVENILE

BAIRD'S SANDPIPER

JUVENILE

JUVENILE

ADULT

Scolopacidae

PECTORAL SANDPIPER *Calidris melanotos* L 8–9 in

Well-marked shorebird. At all times has yellowish legs, gently down-curved, mainly dark bill with a dull orange base, and strongly streaked throat and breast, showing clear pectoral demarcation from otherwise white underparts. Male is larger than female with darker throat and breast markings. **ADULT SUMMER** Has brown upperparts overall, back feathers with dark centers and buff margins. Crown is rufous and contrasts with white supercilium. **ADULT WINTER** Similar, but markings are less intense and less colorful. **JUVENILE** Similar to breeding adult, but with brighter upperparts, feathers of back having buff, rufous, or white margins (latter align on mantle and scapular feathers). **VOICE** A trilling *krrrk* call and hooting song. **STATUS AND HABITAT** Common Arctic breeder. Fairly common on migration through Midwest, usually beside freshwater or on grassy mudflats; seen west of Rocky Mountains only in fall. **OBSERVATION TIPS** Easy to find on high Arctic breeding grounds. Otherwise, look for fall migrants beside inland pools or (more rarely) on coast.

ADULT

TERRITORIAL ADULT

UPLAND SANDPIPER
Bartramia longicauda
L 11.5–12 in

Distinctive, curlew-colored, dry grassland shorebird with long neck, short, straight bill, and long-bodied appearance (due to long wings and very long tail). Legs are yellow in all birds and note large, dark eye on otherwise rather pale face. Perches on fenceposts on breeding grounds. In flight, wingtips are noticeably darker than rest of wings, but with white outer primary shaft. Sexes are similar. **ADULT** Has gray-brown upperparts, feathers on back with dark centers creating barred effect. Underparts are mainly whitish, but with streaking on neck and chevron-shaped markings on breast and flanks. **JUVENILE** Similar to adult, but plumage is subtly flushed buffy brown. **VOICE** Utters a "wolf whistle" call on breeding grounds, bubbling *quilip-ip-ip* at other times. **STATUS AND HABITAT** Formerly much more abundant. Still widespread, but much declined (hunting and habitat loss). Nests in tall grassland (prairies and seminatural habitats). On migration, favors shorter grassland. Winters mainly on Argentinian pampas. **OBSERVATION TIPS** Easy to find within range and in suitable habitat in breeding season. Scarce on migration.

BUFF-BREASTED SANDPIPER
Tryngites subruficollis L 8–8.5 in

Charming and usually tame shorebird, associated with grassland not water. Plumage is pale buff overall. Dark eye is emphasized by dark cap and otherwise pale buffy face. At all times, note rather short, dark bill and relatively long yellow legs. In flight and display, reveals mainly whitish underwings (dark primary coverts appear as contrasting dark crescent). Sexes are similar. **ADULT** Has streaked crown, nape, and back, and dark centers to otherwise buff feathers on wings. Underparts are buffy and mainly unmarked. **JUVENILE** Similar to adult, but rather uniformly dark-centered, buff-margined feathers on back and wings create a rather scaly appearance to upperparts. **VOICE** Mostly silent. **STATUS AND HABITAT** Once abundant, but decimated (literally) by hunting, mainly during 19th century; still a fairly common breeding species on high Arctic tundra. Long-distance migrant that winters in pampas grassland of southern South America. Migrants pass over Great Plains and occasionally stop off to feed, favoring short, drier grassland; scarce away from this migration route. **OBSERVATION TIPS** Search short grassland, e.g. airfields and golf courses in September for migrant juveniles.

JUVENILE

ADULT

UPLAND
SANDPIPER

PECTORAL SANDPIPER

JUVENILE

ADULT

ADULT

ADULT, DISPLAYING

BUFF-BREASTED
SANDPIPER

JUVENILE

Scolopacidae

WILSON'S PHALAROPE
Phalaropus tricolor L 9.5 in

Elegant shorebird with needlelike bill. Like all phalaropes, has lobed feet used for swimming (often spins) and exhibits sex role reversal: more colorful female courts male who incubates eggs. **ADULT BREEDING** Female is stunning, with black and maroon stripe on side of neck and peachy orange throat and chest. Back is gray and maroon, underparts are mostly white. Breeding male is similar, but darker overall and less colorful. **ADULT WINTER** Has pale gray upperparts and whitish underparts. **JUVENILE** Recalls winter adult, but upperparts are brownish, back feathers with pale margins. **VOICE** Utters soft croaking calls. **STATUS AND HABITAT** Widespread and common, nesting beside muddy ponds, shallow lakes, and reservoirs. Winters in South America, but migrants gather in large numbers on saline lakes to molt prior to migration. **OBSERVATION TIPS** Easy to see, and enchanting to watch, during nesting season on suitable pools within breeding range. Visit Mono Lake, California, for spectacular post-breeding concentrations (mainly Jun–Jul) involving 100,000+ birds.

RED-NECKED PHALAROPE
Phalaropus lobatus L 7–8 in

Delightful and confiding little shorebird. Uses all-dark, needlelike bill to pick small invertebrates from water's surface, typically while swimming. Shows role reversal at nest and breeding females are brighter than males. **ADULT BREEDING** Female has brown upperparts (many back feathers have yellow-buff margins), white throat, dark cap, and reddish orange neck; gray breast and mottled flanks grade into white underparts. Breeding male is similar, but colors are duller. **ADULT WINTER** Has mainly gray upperparts and white underparts, with grayish

JUVENILE

hindcrown and nape and black patch through eye. **JUVENILE** Recalls winter adult, but has brown upperparts with pale buff fringes to back feathers; gradually acquires gray back feathers in fall. **VOICE** Utters a sharp *kip* call. **STATUS AND HABITAT** Widespread and common nesting species beside tundra pools. Winters at sea off South America. Migration is mainly at sea, but good numbers take overland route down west coast, pausing briefly on freshwater pools. **OBSERVATION TIPS** Easy to see, mid-May–Jul, in Arctic; otherwise seen on pelagic boat trips during migration, from coasts during onshore gales in fall, or at Mono Lake in May and August.

RED PHALAROPE *Phalaropus fulicarius* L 8–8.5 in

Charming little shorebird, typically seen swimming, often spinning rapidly. Most individuals are oblivious to human observers. Bill is shorter and stouter than that of Red-necked, and is yellow with dark tip. Breeding female is more colorful than male. **ADULT BREEDING** Female has orange-red plumage on neck and underparts, dark crown and white facial patch, and buff-fringed dark feathers on back. Breeding male is similar, but duller. **ADULT WINTER** Has gray upperparts, white underparts, dark cap and nape, and black "panda" patch through eye. **JUVENILE** Loosely recalls winter adult, but breast, neck, and back are tinged buff, and back feathers are dark with buff fringes. **VOICE** Utters a sharp *pit* call. **STATUS AND HABITAT** Common breeding species (Jun–Jul) beside high Arctic tundra pools. Winters at sea off South America and migration is mainly pelagic. **OBSERVATION TIPS** Visit high Arctic for guaranteed sightings. Otherwise pelagic boat trips offer best chances during migration. Lone migrants sometimes found on coastal pools after gales in fall. Rarely observed inland.

JUVENILE

FEMALE, BREEDING

WILSON'S PHALAROPE

MALE, BREEDING

MALE, BREEDING

FEMALE, BREEDING

RED-NECKED PHALAROPE

RED PHALAROPE

ADULT, WINTER

FEMALE, BREEDING

ADULT, WINTER

Scolopacidae

SHORT-BILLED DOWITCHER
Limnodromus griseus L 11–11.5 in

Stout-bodied shorebird with long, straight, grayish bill. Very similar
to Long-billed and specific identification is often not possible with poor
views, and even close views of some individuals. All birds have yellowish green
legs and pale supercilium; white rump and lower back is revealed in flight.
Feeds by probing mud in deliberate, sewing machinelike manner. Forms flocks
outside breeding season. Sexes are sim-

ADULT,
WINTER

ilar. **ADULT SUMMER** Has most feathers
on back beautifully patterned with dark
centers and orange margins, although some appear uniform gray.
Underparts are flushed orange on neck and breast, grading to white
on belly and toward vent; intensity and extent of color, and of dark
barring, varies between subspecies, but typical western birds (*caurinus*) are well marked. **ADULT WINTER** Has gray upperparts, neck,
and breast, and otherwise white underparts. **JUVENILE** Has back
feathers with dark centers and orange margins; diagnostically, tertials have dark internal bars and stripes on otherwise
paler background. Neck and breast are flushed orange-
buff; underparts are otherwise whitish. **VOICE** Utters
a rattling *tu-dlu* call. **STATUS AND HABITAT** Common;
nests on northern marshes and in boreal forest clearings. Migration is coastal and ssp. *caurinus* (typical
western subspecies, which breeds in Alaska)
winters on Pacific coast from U.S. to Peru.
OBSERVATION TIPS Outside breeding season, dow-
itchers are common on Pacific estuaries and coastal
lagoons. Short-billed is commoner than Long-billed
during migration. Specific identification may not be
possible with some individuals.

JUVENILE

LONG-BILLED DOWITCHER
Limnodromus scolpaceus L 11–11.5 in

Very similar to Short-billed. Bill length is not useful in identification
due to variation within, and overlap between, the two species. However, a
bird with a strikingly long bill is likely to be a female Long-billed. Subtle
plumage differences (tertial markings in juveniles; extent of orange in
breeding birds; gradation from gray to white on underparts in winter birds)
and distinctly different calls are most useful diagnostic features. Habits and
behavior are similar to Short-billed. Sexes are similar. **ADULT SUMMER** Has
beautifully marked upperparts, back feathers with dark centers and orange or
white margins. Cap is dark and underparts are flushed orange, more extensively than in Short-billed,
and with more extensive dark barring on neck and breast. **ADULT WINTER** Has gray upperparts, neck,
and breast, grading less abruptly into otherwise white underparts than in Short-billed. **JUVENILE** Similar
to juvenile Short-billed, but note uniformly dark-cen-
tered tertials, lacking internal barring seen in juvenile
Short-billed. **VOICE** Utters a shrill *kyeep* call. **STATUS
AND HABITAT** Common; nests on tundra. Migration is
coastal and winters on Pacific and Gulf coasts, south
to Central America, favoring mudflats and estuaries.
OBSERVATION TIPS Easy to see on coasts outside
breeding season. Less numerous than Short-billed
during migration, but commoner in winter.

ADULT, WINTER

ADULT, SUMMER

SHORT-BILLED DOWITCHER

ADULT, WINTER

ADULT, SUMMER

ADULT, SUMMER

LONG-BILLED DOWITCHER

ADULT, WINTER

JUVENILE

Scolopacidae and Laridae

WILSON'S SNIPE
Gallinago delicata L 10.5–11 in

Plump-bodied shorebird with long, pale-based bill, used to probe soft
ground in sewing machinelike manner. Flight is rapid and zigzagging when
flushed. Sexes are similar. **ALL BIRDS** Have brown upperparts and dark-
barred paler underparts overall. Note beauti-
ful pattern on back and wing feathers, pale
margins forming white stripes, and bold dark
and white stripes on head. **VOICE** Utters a
sneezing *ske-erch* call in alarm. Bleating, whistle-
like sound heard as outer tail feathers vibrate in display flight. **STATUS AND
HABITAT** Common wetland species, most breeding birds moving south in
winter. **OBSERVATION TIPS** Well camouflaged among dead wetland plants
and easily overlooked. **SIMILAR SPECIES American Woodcock** *Scolopax
minor* (L 11–11.5 in) is plumper, with larger, paler head (except for dark
crown), beautifully patterned brown upperparts, and unbarred orange-
flushed underparts (include underwing coverts). Woodland bird whose
range just extends into west.

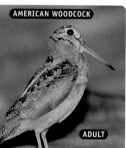

AMERICAN WOODCOCK

ADULT

SOUTH POLAR SKUA
Stercorarius maccormicki L 21–22 in

Powerfully built pelagic seabird. Recalls large, immature gull, but has
thickset, cigar-shaped body, thick neck, and relatively broad, short tail and
wings that are dark brown, except for bold, white "blaze" at base of primaries.
Note dark legs and dark, hook-tipped bill. Scavenges, kills smaller birds, and
harasses large ones into regurgitating previous meal. Sexes are similar, but
adults occur in two extreme morphs and intermediate forms. **ADULT** Dark morph
has subtly streaked dark brown plumage, apart from white wing "blazes," and
paler nape. Pale morph has dark wings and tail, but contrastingly pale buff head,
neck, and body. Some morphs are intermediate between these two extremes. **JUVENILE** Similar to
dark-morph adult, but with dark-tipped pale bill, paler legs, and absence of streaking on body. **VOICE**
Silent in our region. **STATUS AND HABITAT** Nests in Antarctic and nonbreeding species to Pacific coast,
mainly Jul–Oct. Mainly pelagic and offshore. **OBSERVATION TIPS** Easy to see, at right time of year,
from pelagic boat trips. Seen from land only occasionally, usually during or just after severe gales.

POMARINE JAEGER *Stercorarius pomarinus* L 18–23 in

Powerful, stocky seabird with broad, long wings, strong and direct
flight, and diagnostic twisted, spoon-shaped extensions to central tail
feathers in adults. Latter feature, and larger size, allows separation from rather
daintier Parasitic Jaeger. Harasses other seabirds into regurgitating previous
meal, and sometimes kills smaller birds. Sexes are similar, but adults occur in
two color morphs. **ADULT** Pale morph has dark wings (except for white "blaze"
at base of primaries) and tail. Head has dark hood, neck is variably flushed with
yellow, especially on nape, and other-
wise whitish underparts have variable dark
breast brand, most striking in females. Dark morph is uniformly
dark brown, except for white wing "blazes." **JUVENILE** Has brown
upper wings, barred brown underparts and barred gray underwings
except for white "blaze" at base of primaries. Note stubby central
tail extensions and subtly paler rump. **VOICE** Silent away from
breeding grounds. **STATUS AND HABITAT** Nests on high Arctic tundra. Pelagic at other times, migrating down Pacific coast, where it
is common Jul–Oct; winters in small numbers. **OBSERVATION TIPS**
Easy to see from pelagic boat trips; occasional sighting from land,
primarily during strong onshore gales.

ADULT

WILSON'S SNIPE

ADULT

ADULT

ADULT

ADULT

SOUTH POLAR SKUA

ADULT, PALE MORPH

POMARINE JAEGER

JUVENILE, DARK MORPH

ADULT

Laridae

PARASITIC JAEGER
Stercorarius parasiticus L 16–20 in

Elegant seabird with buoyant and graceful flight. Deep, powerful
wingbeats and narrow, pointed wings can give it an almost falconlike appearance, especially when aerobatically chasing seabirds such as Arctic Terns and
Kittiwakes, which it harasses into relinquishing their last meal. All birds
have a white patch near tip of wing (most noticeable on underwing), but
only adults have pointed tail streamers that extend beyond wedge-shaped
tail. Female is larger than male, but both occur in two color phases and take 2
years to acquire full adult plumage. **ADULT** Pale phase has a whitish neck, breast,

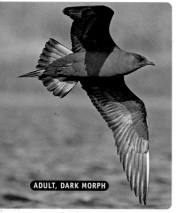

ADULT, DARK MORPH

and belly, with variable yellow flush on cheeks and neck; has a dark
cap and plumage is otherwise uniform dark gray-brown. Dark
phase is uniformly dark gray-brown, darkest on cap. **JUVENILE**
Variably rufous brown, palest and distinctly barred on belly, throat,
and underwings. Compared to juvenile Pomarine, note rather dainty, dark-tipped pale bill and wedge-shaped tail that bears tiny,
pointed central projections. Juvenile Long-tailed has longer, blunter
tail projections. **VOICE** Utters nasal calls near nest. **STATUS AND
HABITAT** Widespread and common breeding species in marshy
tundra and coastal wetlands across North American Arctic. Common passage migrant in spring and fall down Pacific seaboard and
sometimes seen in coastal waters; very occasionally inland too.
Winters at sea, mainly south of equator, but some remain as far
north as southern California. **OBSERVATION TIPS** Easy to see on
Arctic breeding grounds and on pelagic trips during migration. The
most likely skua or jaeger species to be seen from land during
migration, often harassing terns and other small seabirds.

LONG-TAILED JAEGER
Stercorarius longicaudus L 15–23 in (+5–6 in tail)

Elegant and distinctive seabird. Shares some characters with Parasitic, but relatively easy to identify, even distantly. In flight, has rather long,
pointed wings that lack white patch seen on Parasitic's outer wing. Adult has
extremely long central tail streamers. At close range, note dainty bill. Sexes
are similar. **ADULT** Uniform gray-brown on back and upperside of inner wing,
contrasting with dark outer half of wing and trailing margin of inner wing.
Cap is dark and neck and underparts are whitish, with faint yellow flush on
cheeks seen at close range. **JUVENILE** Variably gray-brown, with some individuals being rather dark. Note relatively long and rather wedge-shaped tail; pale-morph juvenile has pale

ADULT

belly and nape with a hint of a darker breast band.
Compared to juvenile Parasitic, bill is stubbier,
outer half being darker than inner half (dark tipped
in juvenile Parasitic); pale-morph juvenile is grayer
overall than juvenile Parasitic, and pale "wedge" is
often obvious on nape. **VOICE** Utters harsh anxiety
calls on breeding grounds, but otherwise silent. **STA-
TUS AND HABITAT** Common and widespread Arctic
tundra breeding species. Otherwise, exclusively
pelagic and mostly offshore, even during migration.
Winters at sea, mainly south of equator. **OBSERVA-
TION TIPS** Easy to see on Arctic breeding grounds.
Pelagic boats, typically venturing beyond sight of
land, are required to see migrants (commonest May
and Aug–Sep). Only very rarely seen from land or
inland during migration, usually after severe gales.

JUVENILE

ADULT, PALE MORPH

PARASITIC JAEGER

JUVENILE

LONG-TAILED JAEGER

ADULT

Laridae

HEERMANN'S GULL *Larus heermanni* L 19–20 in

Striking and distinctive, long-bodied and long-winged gull. Adult has unique combination (for a gull) of dark body and white head; takes 4 years to acquire adult plumage. Juvenile and first-year birds are dark brown and could be confused with immature jaegers or skuas; note, however, Heermann's lack of pale crescent at base of primaries, seen in those species. Sexes are similar. **ADULT SUMMER** Has dark gray upperparts and paler gray underparts including neck. Head is white, bill is proportionately long and red with dark tip, and legs are dark. In flight, note white trailing edge to otherwise dark wings (above and below), and white-tipped, dark tail feathers that contrast with pale rump. **ADULT WINTER** Similar, but head and neck are streaked and grubby-looking. **JUVENILE** Juvenile and first-winter birds are dark brown with dark legs and dark-tipped, dull pink bill. Adult plumage is acquired gradually by successive molts over subsequent 3 years. **VOICE** Utters a harsh *krrrh* call. **STATUS AND HABITAT** Breeds off western coast of Mexico (Feb–May); vast majority nest on Isla Raza in Gulf of California. Post-breeding birds move north along Pacific coast, and are common as far north as Vancouver Island Jul–Oct; thereafter range contracts south in fall and southern California is northernmost limit of winter range. Outside breeding season, favors sandy beaches, sometimes congregating in vicinity of river mouths. **OBSERVATION TIPS** Easy to see on many sandy beaches in California, Jul–Feb.

ADULT, SUMMER

BONAPARTE'S GULL *Larus philadelphia* L 13–14 in

Dainty little gull and the smallest of its kind to be seen regularly in west. Flight is buoyant and often dips to surface of water in ternlike manner to snatch food items. Confusion is only really possible with marginally larger Franklin's Gull (*see* p.150), adults of which also have dark hoods when breeding, but wing patterns of adults are entirely different: white leading edge and dark trailing margin to primaries in Bonaparte's, but black tip and white trailing edge to otherwise dark gray upper wings in Franklin's. Bonaparte's form loose flocks outside breeding season. Sexes are similar. **ADULT SUMMER** Has pale gray back and upper wings, white underparts and neck, and blackish hood. Bill is dark and legs are red. **ADULT WINTER** Similar, but dark hood is lost and dark ear coverts contrast with otherwise white head. **JUVENILE** Mainly mottled brown, but acquires first-winter plumage in early fall: similar to winter adult, but with dark trailing edge to entire wing (not just primaries), less striking pale leading edge (some dark feathering), and dark bar on inner upper wing; legs are pale pink. **VOICE** Call is ternlike, nasal, and higher pitched than that of other gulls. **STATUS AND HABITAT** Common breeding species; forms loose colonies in marshes and around lakes in boreal forests; nests in trees. Outside the breeding season, mainly coastal in west and commonest Oct–Mar; favors fairly sheltered shores and beaches, but often ones affected by strong currents. **OBSERVATION TIPS** Easy to see during breeding season in Alaska and across large parts of western Canada. Outside breeding season, common, but rather local on western coast. Concentrations often found near sewage outfalls and river mouths.

1ST-WINTER

2ND-WINTER

HEERMANN'S GULL

ADULT, SUMMER

BONAPARTE'S GULL

ADULT, SUMMER

ADULT, WINTER

1ST-WINTER

ADULT, WINTER

Laridae

FRANKLIN'S GULL *Larus pipixcan* L 14–15 in

Small, elegant gull. Superficially similar to larger Laughing, but separable on basis of daintier proportions, particularly legs and bill; latter is straight (slightly downcurved in Laughing). Adult has distinctive markings on wingtips: pattern of white-black-white (wingtip of Laughing is uniformly black). In winter, adult retains more extensive dark markings on head than winter Laughing. First-winter has narrower dark tail band than similar age Laughing. Breeds colonially and often migrates in flocks. Sexes are similar. **ADULT SUMMER** Has mainly dark gray back and upper wings, with white trailing edge and black and white tips to wings; underparts, including neck, are white, sometimes flushed pink on breast and belly. Note dark hood and striking white "eyelids," and red legs and bill. **ADULT WINTER** Similar, but dark hood is much reduced and absent altogether on forecrown. **JUVENILE** Resembles brownish version of winter adult, but molts in fall to first-winter plumage: gray back, gray inner upper wing marbled with brown feathering, and mainly dark flight feathers. Legs and bill are dark, and note narrow dark tail band that does not reach outer margins. **VOICE** Utters clipped, yelping calls. Colonies sound like an audience's hysterical laughter. **STATUS AND HABITAT** Locally common breeding species, restricted to prairie marshes. Post-breeding birds wander south, Aug–Nov, before migrating to coasts of South America for winter. **OBSERVATION TIPS** Relatively easy to see if you visit suitable habitats within breeding range, May–Aug. Migrants and post-breeding wanderers are sometimes seen at freshwater sites south of breeding range, but species seldom reaches western coast.

LAUGHING GULL *Larus atricilla* L 16–17 in

Medium-sized, but powerfully built gull with proportionately long wings (extend well beyond tail at rest). Alert birds often look rather long-necked, and note dark red legs and rather long and slightly downcurved bill. In areas where common (mainly southeastern North America) it is a bold and opportunistic feeder, happily rubbing shoulders with people. **ADULT SUMMER** Has dark gray back and upper wings, except for white trailing edge and dark tips to wings. Underwings show contrast between mainly dark flight feathers and white wing coverts (Franklin's underwings are more uniformly pale). Underparts and neck are white, and note dark hood and white "eyelids." Bill is reddish. **ADULT WINTER** Similar, but dark hood is lost except for dark streaking on nape; bill is dark. **JUVENILE** Mainly brown, but molts to first-winter plumage in fall: gray back, gray and brown inner upper wing coverts, and dark outer wing and flight feathers. Plumage is otherwise mainly grubby white with broad, dark tail band (extends across entire width of tail), and streaking and gray feathering on breast and neck (particularly striking on nape). Bill is dark. **VOICE** Utters laughing, gull-like calls. **STATUS AND HABITAT** Breeds on rocky coasts and mainly coastal in winter. Common on Gulf coast, especially outside breeding season (mainly Aug–Mar), but rare on western coast at all times. **OBSERVATION TIPS** For guaranteed sightings, visit the Gulf coast. Otherwise the species is most regular in west at Salton Sea, California, mainly Jun–Oct. For separation from smaller Franklin's, concentrate on bill size and shape, upper wing markings, and proportions overall.

ADULT, SUMMER

ADULT, WINTER

FRANKLIN'S GULL

ADULT, SUMMER

ADULT, SUMMER

1ST-WINTER

LAUGHING GULL

ADULT, SUMMER

ADULT, WINTER

1ST-WINTER

Laridae

RING-BILLED GULL *Larus delawarensis* L 17–20 in

Medium-sized gull and the most familiar of its kind in our region. Often bold and approachable, and an opportunistic feeder, quick to capitalize on man-made sources of food and seasonal natural bounties. Takes 2 years to reach adult plumage. Sexes are similar. **ADULT SUMMER** Has pale gray back and upper wing, except for white-spotted black wingtips and pale gray trailing edge. Plumage, including tail, is otherwise white. Bill is yellow with dark subterminal band, and iris and legs are yellow. **ADULT WINTER** Similar, but head and neck are streaked brown and leg and bill colors are duller. **JUVENILE** Has mottled gray and brown plumage, palest on head; note also, pinkish legs and dark bill and eye. First-winter plumage (acquired in fall) is similar, but back is gray, bill is pink, but dark-tipped, iris is pale, and tail has dark terminal band. By second winter, plumage approaches that of winter adult, but retains faint, narrow dark band on tail. **VOICE** Utters a mewing *kyow* call, higher pitched than that of larger, similar gulls. **STATUS AND HABITAT** Widespread and generally common across much of central and southern North America, although range changes seasonally: breeds colonially beside lakes in Canada and northern U.S.; outside breeding season, northern populations move south, and in winter found along coasts, and near freshwater and food sources inland. **OBSERVATION TIPS** Easy to see on most coasts, including populated beaches and seafronts, outside breeding season. Some individuals actively seek out people as potential providers of food and are a common sight in littered parking lots and at garbage heaps.

ADULT, SUMMER

MEW GULL *Larus canus* L 16–17 in

Relatively small gull with a rather dainty bill, dark eye, and rounded head that has a "gentle" expression, akin to that of Black-legged Kittiwake (*see* p.158), but note that species' short black legs and almost entirely black wingtips with only tiny white markings. Told from Ring-billed by smaller size, smaller bill (lacking a dark subterminal band), and dark eyes (pale iris in all but juvenile Ring-billed). Forms flocks outside the breeding season. Takes 2 years to reach adult plumage. Sexes are similar. **ADULT SUMMER** Has blue-gray back and upper wings except for white trailing edge and black wingtips with white "windows" (largest on outer two primaries). Plumage is otherwise white, including tail. Bill and legs are yellow. **ADULT WINTER** Similar, but head and neck are streaked and mottled brown, bill is dull and dark-tipped, and leg color is duller. **JUVENILE** Has grayish back and upper wing with darker feather centers creating scaly appearance; plumage is otherwise white, streaked with brown; note the mainly dark tail. Legs are pink and bill is pinkish and dark-tipped. Acquires first-winter plumage in fall: similar, but back is gray and note mainly dark tail. Second-winter is similar to winter adult, but retains faint dark band on tail. **VOICE** Utters a mewing, high-pitched *kyaa* call. **STATUS AND HABITAT** Widespread and locally common tundra breeding species, usually nesting colonially in the vicinity of lakes and marshes. Outside breeding season, almost exclusively coastal, favoring estuaries, river mouths, and coastal pools. **OBSERVATION TIPS** Easy to see on coasts in winter and separation from Ring-billed is straightforward: study size overall, bill size and markings, and eye color.

ADULT, SUMMER

ADULT, SUMMER

RING-BILLED GULL

ADULT, WINTER

ADULT, WINTER

1ST-WINTER

ADULT, SUMMER

MEW GULL

ADULT, WINTER

1ST-WINTER

Laridae

HERRING GULL *Larus argentatus* L 22–26 in

Large, robust gull with relatively deep body, large head, and thick bill. Wings are proportionately broader and shorter than California, and note Herring's pink legs at all times. Adults are best separated on proportions overall and leg color: California is slimmer, longer winged and longer billed than Herring, and adults have yellow legs. Immatures are best separated by studying overall proportions and subtle differences in upper wing patterns. Takes 3 years to reach adult plumage. Represented in west mainly by ssp. *smithsonianus* (aka American Herring Gull). Sexes are similar. **ADULT SUMMER** Has pale blue-gray back and upper wings, except for white trailing edge and dark wingtips with white "windows." Plumage is otherwise white. Bill is yellow with orange spot on gonys, and eye has yellow iris and orange eyering. **ADULT WINTER** Similar, but head and neck are streaked brown; leg, bill, and eyering colors are duller. **JUVENILE** Juvenile and first-winter birds have mottled brown plumage, dark tail, and dull pink legs. Initially bill is dark, but becomes dark-tipped pink by first winter. Note pale inner primaries create pale panel on upper wing (flight feathers more uniformly dark in similar age California) and otherwise uniformly brown upper wings (two dark bars seen on similar age California). Adult plumage acquired through successive molts: becomes more uniform gray on back and

ADULT, WINTER

upper wings and whiter elsewhere. Retains dark band on tail and some brown feathering on upper wings into third winter. **VOICE** Utters distinctive *kyaoo* and anxious *ga-ka-ka*. **STATUS AND HABITAT** Widespread and common, nesting on islands in northern lakes, and on coasts. Winter range is mainly coastal. **OBSERVATION TIPS** Easy to find on coasts outside breeding season. Become familiar with proportions of known adult California and Herring Gulls (easily separated on leg color). Then apply what you have learned, especially about bill size and shape, and wing length, to any immatures you happen to come across.

CALIFORNIA GULL *Larus californicus* L 21–22 in

Medium-sized gull. Compared to Herring, has slimmer body, long wings and legs, and longer, more even-width bill; appreciably larger than Ring-billed (*see* p.152), with much longer bill and dark (not yellow) iris in adult birds. Legs are yellow in adults, but pinkish in younger birds. Eye is dark at all times. Takes 3 years to reach adult plumage. Sexes are similar.

ADULT SUMMER Has gray back and upper wings with white trailing edge and black wingtips with small white "windows." Bill is yellow with small red spot on gonys and dark

ADULT, WINTER

subterminal band; note red orbital ring. **ADULT WINTER** Similar, but has brown streaking on head and nape, mainly on nape (dark streaking is more extensive on similar age Herring, and extends to throat and chest). **JUVENILE** Juvenile and first-winter birds have mottled brown plumage, with uniformly dark wingtips and two dark bands on inner upper wing. Bill is dark at first, but dark-tipped pink by first winter. Acquires adult plumage through several successive molts, back and upper wing becoming more uniformly gray. Retains some brown feathers on upper wing coverts, and faint dark band on tail, into third winter. **VOICE** Utters *kyaoo* calls, higher pitched than Herring. **STATUS AND HABITAT** Locally common. Nests colonially, mainly on islands in inland lakes. Mainly coastal outside breeding season, often congregating near regular food sources. **OBSERVATION TIPS** Easy to see along coast in winter months.

1ST-WINTER

HERRING GULL

ADULT, SUMMER

CALIFORNIA GULL

ADULT, WINTER

2ND-WINTER

ADULT, SUMMER

Laridae

GLAUCOUS GULL *Larus hyperboreus* L 23–29 in

Large, bulky, and pale gull. All birds have pale wings, pink legs, large head, and massive bill. Juvenile acquires adult plumage over 3-year period. Sexes are similar. **ADULT SUMMER** Has very pale gray back and upper wings with white trailing edge and wingtips. Plumage is otherwise white. Bill is yellowish with orange spot on gonys, and iris is pale yellow with orange orbital ring. **ADULT WINTER** Similar, but head and neck are streaked grubby brown; bill and eye colors are duller. **JUVENILE** Pale mottled brown, but first-winter plumage is whitish overall, with

ADULT, SUMMER

pale buff marbling on back and upper wing coverts, and pale buff barring on tail; plumage becomes paler as winter progresses. Bill is dark-tipped pink and eye is dark. Second-winter is paler still, variably pale gray on back and upper wing, with buff barring on tail; iris is usually pale. Third-winter resembles winter adult, but retains faint buff barring on tail. **VOICE** Utters deep *kyaoo* and *ga-ka-ka* calls. **STATUS AND HABITAT** Common breeder on Arctic coastal tundra. Outside breeding season, mainly coastal. **OBSERVATION TIPS** Easy to see within winter range, typically within harbors or at garbage dumps.

GLAUCOUS-WINGED GULL *Larus glaucescens* L 25–26 in

Large, bulky gull. Similar to Glaucous, but marginally darker overall in all plumages, with appreciably darker wingtips. Takes 3 years to acquire adult plumage. Legs are pink at all times. Sexes are similar. **ADULT SUMMER** Has pale blue-gray back and upper wings with white trailing edge and white "windows" on primaries, which are marginally darker than mantle (charcoal gray rather than blue-gray). Bill is yellow with orange spot on gonys; eyes are dark with pink orbital ring. **ADULT WINTER** Similar, but has brown streaks and bars on head and upper neck; bill and leg colors often duller. **JUVENILE** Juvenile and first-winter are mottled pale gray-brown overall with dark bill. Second-winter is similar, but paler overall, with rather uniform pale gray back; dark bill often has pale base. Third-winter recalls winter adult, but bill is dark-tipped dull pink. **VOICE** Utters a loud *kwaaw* call. **STATUS AND HABITAT** Common on rocky coasts. Winter range extends south to California. **OBSERVATION TIPS** Easy to find on most suitable coasts. Hybridizes with Western Gull. Hybrids have darker wing tips.

ADULT, WINTER

THAYER'S GULL *Larus thayeri* L 22–24 in

Medium-sized pale gull; western counterpart of Iceland Gull. Compared to larger species, has relatively short legs (pink at all times), rounded head, and smaller bill. Takes 3 years to acquire adult plumage. Sexes are similar. **ADULT SUMMER** Has pale gray back and upper wings with white trailing edge and black primaries with long white "windows." Underwings are pale with black tips to primaries. Bill is dull greenish yellow with red spot on gonys. Eye is usually dark with red orbital ring. **ADULT WINTER** Similar, but head and neck have extensive brown mottling. **JUVENILE** Juvenile and first-winter are pale marbled brown with darker primaries and dark bill. Second-winter is much paler with gray back, but dark primaries and dark-tipped tail; bill is dark-tipped pale pink. Third-winter is similar to winter adult, but retains faint dark markings on tail and mantle. **VOICE** Utters a high-pitched *kyaaa* call. **STATUS AND HABITAT** Nests on high Arctic tundra and winters mainly on Pacific coast; sometimes inland at garbage dumps and large gull roosts. **OBSERVATION TIPS** Regular in winter, but seldom numerous.

ADULT

1ST-WINTER

ADULT, WINTER

1ST-WINTER

GLAUCOUS GULL

ADULT, WINTER

ADULT, SUMMER

GLAUCOUS-WINGED GULL

THAYER'S GULL

1ST-WINTER

2ND-WINTER

GLAUCOUS-WINGED GULL

THAYER'S GULL

ADULT, SUMMER

1ST-WINTER

JUVENILE

2ND-WINTER

WESTERN GULL
Larus occidentalis L 24–26 in

Bulky, large-billed gull. All birds have pink legs. Two subspecies recognized: southern *wymani* has darker upperparts and paler eyes than northern *occidentalis*. Sexes are similar. **ADULT** Has dark gray back and upper wings, except for white trailing edge and black wingtips with white "window" on outer primary and white tips to others. Plumage is otherwise white. Bill is yellow with red spot on gonys, and eye has yellow orbital ring. **JUVENILE** Juvenile and first-winter are mottled brown overall with dark primaries and dark tail, and pink-based dark bill. By second winter, has mainly dark gray back, although wing coverts remain mottled brown; plumage is otherwise white, except for dark tail. Third-winter resembles adult, but with some dark feathering on tail and upper wing coverts, and little or no white on otherwise dark wingtips. **VOICE** Utters a *kyaah* call. **STATUS AND HABITAT** Common resident on Pacific coast and seldom found inland. Nests colonially on islands and at other times seen on beaches, rocky coasts, or feeding at sea. **OBSERVATION TIPS** Easy to see within its coastal range.

SABINE'S GULL *Xema sabini* L 13–14 in

Graceful gull with readily diagnostic wing pattern, forked tail, and buoyant flight. Sexes are similar. **ADULT SUMMER** Has gray back and upper inner wing coverts, and mainly white body plumage, except for dark gray hood. Unmistakable in flight: gray on upper wings contrasts with triangle of white on inner wing and triangle of black on leading edge of primaries. Legs are black, bill is dark with yellow tip; orbital ring is red. **ADULT WINTER** Similar, but head is mainly white except for hint of dark hood; seldom seen here, but molting birds (part way to winter plumage) are encountered. **JUVENILE** Has pale-edged tawny gray feathers on back and inner upper wing coverts, creating scaly appearance. Plumage is otherwise mainly white, except for gray-buff markings on crown and nape, black wingtips, and black tip to tail. In flight, has similar upper wing pattern to adult (three contrasting triangles of color), but gray is replaced by tawny gray. Legs are pink and bill is dark. **VOICE** Silent in our region. **STATUS AND HABITAT** Nests on coastal tundra. Migrates and winters (in southern oceans) at sea. **OBSERVATION TIPS** Seldom seen from land, or inland, except in severe weather, but found on pelagic trips, mainly May and Aug–Sep.

BLACK-LEGGED KITTIWAKE
Rissa tridactyla L 17–18 in

Elegant, marine gull with buoyant flight and short black legs. Juvenile recalls juvenile Sabine's Gull. Sexes are similar. **ADULT SUMMER** Has pale gray back and upper wings, except for white trailing edge and well-defined black wingtips. Plumage is otherwise white and bill is yellow. **ADULT WINTER** Similar, but has gray nape and blackish on rear of crown. **JUVENILE** Has gray back and inner upper wing with black line running across coverts and along leading edge of primaries; these two colors contrast with white triangle on trailing half of wing. Note black half collar, black tip to tail, and black bill. **VOICE** Utters diagnostic *kitti-wake* call at colonies. **STATUS AND HABITAT** Locally common, nesting colonially on sea cliffs. **OBSERVATION TIPS** Easy to see at seabird colonies within breeding range, mainly May–Aug, and commonly seen from land on outer coast of Washington. Otherwise, seen from land only during severe gales. Seen regularly on pelagic trips south of breeding range from fall to spring. *See also* Red-legged Kittiwake (p.400).

GULLS

ADULT, WINTER

ADULT, SUMMER

1ST-WINTER

WESTERN GULL

ADULT, SUMMER

ADULT, SUMMER

JUVENILE

JUVENILE

SABINE'S GULL

ADULT, SUMMER

ADULT, SUMMER

JUVENILE

BLACK-LEGGED KITTIWAKE

ADULT, WINTER

ADULT, SUMMER

Laridae

BLACK TERN *Chlidonias niger* L 9–10 in

Elegant wetland bird whose plumage varies markedly according to time of year and age. Breeding adults are stunning but seldom remain in pristine plumage for long. Buoyant and aerobatic flight is used to good effect when hawking insects or picking food items from water's surface. Sexes are similar. **ADULT SUMMER** Has mainly gray upperparts but head and neck, along with breast and belly, are black; note white vent and undertail coverts, and slightly forked

ADULT, WINTER

tail, and gray upperparts. Bill is black and legs are dark red. **ADULT WINTER** (this plumage is acquired gradually Jul–Sep) Has gray upperparts, entirely white underparts; black on head is restricted to cap, nape, and ear coverts. Birds in intermediate stages of molt can look a bit "moth-eaten." Bill is black and legs are dull red. **JUVENILE** Similar to winter adult but back is brownish gray and scaly-looking due to pale feather margins. First-summer birds resemble winter adults but with irregular dark spots on underparts. **VOICE** Utters a harsh *scherr*. **STATUS AND HABITAT** Locally common in summer months but declining due to habitat destruction and degradation. Favors marshes and other freshwater habitats and breeds colonially, building nests on floating vegetation. Migrates mainly overland, sometimes in flocks, and winters on coasts and at sea from Central to South America. **OBSERVATION TIPS** Easy to see at breeding colonies in summer months although sometimes abandons previously used sites if water levels are not suitable. Turns up during migration (Apr–May and Aug–Sep) at inland freshwater sites south of breeding range but often only pauses to feed for a day or so, sometimes just a matter of hours.

LEAST TERN *Sternula antillarum* L 8–9 in

Our smallest tern. Flight is rapid and buoyant and it frequently hovers before plunge-diving into shallow water for small fish and shrimp. Sexes are similar. **ADULT SUMMER** Has gray back and upper wings and mainly black cap, although forehead is white; plumage is otherwise pure white. Note the black-tipped yellow bill and yellow-orange legs. In flight, outer two primaries are noticeably dark (show as black wingtips at rest). **ADULT WINTER** (acquires this plumage from late summer onward) Similar, but white on forehead is more extensive, and leg and bill colors are duller; upper wing is more uniformly pale. **JUVENILE** Similar to winter adult, but back appears scaly, and outer 4–5 primaries and leading edge of inner wing are dark. Most first-summer birds resemble

ADULT, SUMMER

winter adult but with dark leading edge to inner wing and dark outer primaries. **VOICE** Utters a raucous *kree-ick* call. **STATUS AND HABITAT** Declining but still very locally common. Nests colonially on sandy and pebbly beaches, both on coasts and at inland freshwater sites. Badly and directly affected by man's actions, specifically disturbance, or exclusion from, beach nest sites, as well as habitat destruction and degradation. Ground predators compound the problem. California populations do best on beaches that are Navy and Marine Corps bases, protected from standard human disturbance. Migrates along coasts and river courses and winters on coasts and at sea off Central and South America. **OBSERVATION TIPS** Easy to see at locations where nesting colonies are protected (search the web for sites and access details). If you come across nesting birds elsewhere, keep your distance and avoid disturbing this vulnerable species.

ADULT, SUMMER

BLACK TERN

ADULT, SUMMER

ADULT, SUMMER

LEAST TERN

JUVENILE

Laridae

COMMON TERN *Sterna hirundo* L 11–12 in

Elegant tern that plunge-dives for fish and hawks insects. Sexes are similar. **ADULT SUMMER** Has gray upperparts, black cap, and whitish gray underparts. Compared to Arctic, note black-tipped orange-red bill, longer red legs, and paler underparts. In flight from below, only inner primaries look translucent and wings have diffuse dark tips; from above, outer primaries have dark tips and shafts, inner ones are dark and appear as "wedge." **ADULT WINTER** Similar, but has white forehead and dark carpal bar; bill and legs are dark. **JUVENILE** Has white underparts, incomplete dark cap, and scaly gray upperparts; leading and trailing edges of inner upper wing are darker. **VOICE** Utters a harsh *kreeear* call. **STATUS AND HABITAT** Locally common, but declining overall. In west, breeds beside boreal forest lakes, mainly in Canada; present mainly May–Sep. Winters on coasts of Central and South America. Migrants are seen on Pacific coast in small numbers, mainly in fall; overland migrants occasionally pause to feed at inland freshwater. **OBSERVATION TIPS** Easy to see at suitable habitats in Canada in summer, and locally in Alberta and Montana.

ARCTIC TERN *Sterna paradisaea* L 12–13 in

Renowned long-distance migrant. Compared to Common, adult has smaller blood-red (not black-tipped orange-red) bill, different upper wing pattern (inner primaries pale gray in Arctic, seen as dark "wedge" in Common), longer outside tail feathers, shorter legs, and darker belly. **ADULT SUMMER** Has gray upperparts, with black cap; underparts are palest on throat and cheeks and darkest on belly. In flight from below, flight feathers look translucent, with narrow, dark trailing edge to primaries; from above, wings look rather uniformly gray. **ADULT WINTER** Not seen here. **JUVENILE** Has white underparts, incomplete dark cap, and scaly gray upper-

1ST-SUMMER

parts. In flight, note dark leading edge and white trailing edge to inner upper wing (leading *and* trailing edges dark in juvenile Common). Legs are dull red and bill is completely or mostly dark. **VOICE** A harsh *krt-krt-krt*. **STATUS AND HABITAT** Locally common, nesting on tundra and coasts. Migrates at sea (seldom seen from land) and winters in Antarctic. **OBSERVATION TIPS** Easy to see in Alaska and northern Canada, May–Aug. Migrants seen on pelagic trips. *See also* Aleutian Tern (p.400).

FORSTER'S TERN *Sterna forsteri* L 13–14 in

Similar to Common, but paler overall with longer, more deeply forked tail, longer legs, and different upper wing pattern. Much less pelagic than Arctic and, of the three, the only one likely to be seen in winter in U.S. Sexes are similar. **ADULT SUMMER** Has mainly pale gray back and upper wings, black cap, and otherwise white plumage. Legs are orange-red and bill is orange-red with black tip. In flight, note dark trailing edge to otherwise white primaries (lack dark "wedge" on Common's inner upper pri-

ADULT, WINTER

maries). **ADULT WINTER** Looks pale overall, except for dark "mask" through eye, black bill, and darker primaries (especially margins). **JUVENILE** Similar to winter adult, but with buffy feathers on back, upper wing, and crown, pale-based bill and shorter outside tail feathers; first-winter is similar to winter adult, but with shorter outside tail feathers. **VOICE** A harsh *kree-err* call. **STATUS AND HABITAT** Nests beside freshwater marshes; other times commonest near coasts. **OBSERVATION TIPS** Easy to see at suitable inland sites in summer or on coasts in winter.

1ST-SUMMER

COMMON TERN

ADULT, SUMMER

ADULT, SUMMER

ADULT

ARCTIC TERN

ADULT

ADULT, WINTER

ADULT, SUMMER

FORSTER'S TERN

ADULT, SUMMER

GULL-BILLED TERN *Gelochelidon nilotica* L 13–14 in

Robust, pale tern with controlled flight and relatively deep bill. Does not plunge-dive like other terns and habits are more terrestrial, often hawking insects and picking prey from surface of ground. Sexes are similar. **ADULT SUMMER** Has pale gray upperparts, black crown and nape, and white underparts. In flight, wings appear almost uniformly white except for dark edges to underside of primaries. Bill and legs are black. **ADULT WINTER** Similar, but head is white except for gray streak from behind eye to nape. **JUVENILE** Similar to winter adult, but back, upper wings, and crown have faint brown feathering. Legs and bill are dark reddish. **VOICE** Utters a *kerr-wick* call. **STATUS AND HABITAT** Rare breeding species in west (200 or so pairs), mainly near Salton Sea, California. More numerous in eastern U.S., and seen regularly during migration on Gulf coast, wintering from there southward. **OBSERVATION TIPS** Visit Salton Sea (mainly Apr–Jul) for a chance of seeing this species. **SIMILAR SPECIES Sandwich Tern** *S. sandvicensis* (L 14–15 in), an east coast species, is similar, but with a slender, yellow-tipped black bill. It winters from the Gulf coast southward.

ADULT, SUMMER

ADULT, WINTER

SANDWICH TERN

ADULT, SUMMER

ROYAL TERN *Thalasseus maximus* L 18–21 in

Large, robust tern with buoyant, direct flight. Plunge-dives after fish. Bill is stout and orange (noticeably thicker than Elegant) and legs are black and long (relatively longer than in Elegant). Tail is deeply forked. Sexes are similar. **ADULT SUMMER** Pale gray above and whitish below, palest on head and neck. Has a black cap and, in flight, note dark upper surface to outer primaries and dark-edged wingtips seen from below. **ADULT WINTER** Similar, but shows only remnant of dark cap on nape. **JUVENILE** Juvenile and first-winter are similar to winter adult, but with dark spots on back, upper wings, and upper tail, and yellowish legs and bill. **VOICE** Utters a coarse, low-pitched *kree-eh*. **STATUS AND HABITAT** Very locally common breeding species in southern California; common on east coast, so common on Gulf coast year-round. Nests on islands and feeds in shallow seas. Disperses outside breeding season and many winter south of our region. **OBSERVATION TIPS** Relatively easy to see on coasts. Congregates and mixes with other terns where feeding is good.

ELEGANT TERN *Thalasseus elegans* L 14–16 in

Similar to Royal, but separable (especially if seen side-by-side) by smaller size, more slender bill, shorter legs, and markedly more shaggy crest. Flight is buoyant and graceful. Sexes are similar. **ADULT SUMMER** Has pale gray upperparts, black, crested crown and whitish underparts, palest on head and neck. In flight, upper surface of outer primaries is dark; from below, wingtips have dark margins. **ADULT WINTER** Similar, but forecrown becomes speckled white. **JUVENILE** Similar to winter adult, but upperparts are darker overall, particularly on flight feathers, and speckled brown on back, wing coverts, and upper tail. **VOICE** Utters a harsh *kree-err* call. **STATUS AND HABITAT** Entire world breeding population restricted to just five sites on islands in Gulf of California and on south Californian coast; U.S. population is therefore of global significance. Feeds in shallow seas. Disperses along the coast outside breeding season and winters on Pacific coasts of Central and South America. **OBSERVATION TIPS** Easy to see at Bolsa Chica, southern California, mainly Apr–Jul.

ADULT, SUMMER

GULL-BILLED TERN

ADULT, SUMMER

ADULT, SUMMER

ADULT, SUMMER

ADULT, WINTER

ADULT, SUMMER

ROYAL TERN

ADULT, WINTER

ADULT, SUMMER

1ST-WINTER

ELEGANT TERN

ADULT, SUMMER

Laridae

CASPIAN TERN *Hydroprogne caspia* L 20–22 in

A giant among terns, and the largest of its kind in the world. Most distinctive and diagnostic feature is huge, daggerlike bill, which is dark red with dark subterminal band and small pale tip. Body is plump and robust, with gull-like proportions. Tail is forked, but outer feathers are not particularly long. Flight is powerful, direct, and gull-like. Plunge-dives after fish. Sexes are similar. **ADULT SUMMER** Has pale gray back and upper wing and mainly white underparts. In flight, however, note that upper surface of primaries is marginally darker than rest of upper wing, and trailing margin of primaries is darker still; from below, primaries are blackish. Legs are black and cap is uniformly black. **ADULT WINTER** Similar, but cap is streaked black and white, darkest below eye, rather than uniformly dark. **JUVENILE** Similar to winter adult, but with paler bill and subtle scaling effect on back and upper tail. **VOICE** Utters a harsh, slightly menacing *kraa-aar* call. **STATUS AND**

ADULT, SUMMER

HABITAT Very locally common breeding species (mainly May–Jul), nesting in colonies on gravel or sand islands and bars in or near freshwater lakes and rivers rich with fish, and coastal estuaries and lagoons. Coastal birds seldom feed far from shore. Disperses and moves south outside breeding season, wintering on coasts of southern U.S., Central and northern South America. **OBSERVATION TIPS** Typically rather thinly scattered, but usually easy to see at any freshwater or coastal sites where medium-sized fish are plentiful. Size of bill and stature overall make this species unmistakable.

BLACK SKIMMER *Rynchops niger* L 17–18 in

Extremely distinctive, ternlike waterbird with wonderfully bizarre and laterally flattened diagnostic bill. Lower mandible is appreciably longer than upper one and used in characteristic fashion when fishing: feeds in flight (mostly after dark), skimming low over water, bill open, then snapping at prey that comes into contact with lower mandible as it is dragged through the water surface. Tail is slightly forked. Often seen in flocks. Sexes are similar. **ADULT SUMMER** Has mainly black upper wing and back, continuous with black cap and back of neck; forecrown and underparts are white. In flight, note dark center to otherwise white upper tail, dark gray primaries and white trailing edge to dark upper wing. Legs are short and red and bill is red-based and dark-tipped. **ADULT WINTER** Similar, but black cap and nape are separated from black back by streaked white hindneck. **JUVENILE** Similar to winter adult, but with paler gray-buff margins to feathers of otherwise dark

ADULT, SUMMER, FEEDING

elements of upperparts. These are molted gradually through first winter. **VOICE** Utters a nasal *kwuup* call. **STATUS AND HABITAT** Local and generally scarce in southwestern U.S., but common and much more widespread on Gulf coast. Nests on sandy beaches, mainly on coasts, but also inland at Salton Sea, California. Extremely vulnerable to changing water levels, but more so to human disturbance, both directly and by the presence of dogs. Outside breeding season, entirely coastal and range extends south to northern South America. **OBSERVATION TIPS** Can be seen at Salton Sea in breeding season (mainly May–Aug) and at other times on both Pacific and Gulf coasts.

ADULT, WINTER

CASPIAN TERN

ADULT, SUMMER

ADULT, WINTER

BLACK SKIMMER

ADULT, SUMMER

Alcidae

THICK-BILLED MURRE *Uria lomvia* L 17–18 in

Similar to, but marginally smaller than, Common Murre. Recognized at all times by shorter, thicker bill (almost gull-like) with striking white stripe along gape. Neck is thicker than Common, and plumage darker overall, although latter feature is often hard to discern in poor light. Adopts upright posture when resting on cliff. Swims well, dives frequently, and flies on whirring wingbeats. Sexes are similar. **ADULT SUMMER** Has blackish head, neck, and upperparts, with clean demarcation on chest from white underparts. **ADULT WINTER** Similar, but throat becomes white (lacks white cheeks seen in winter Common). White gape stripe is less striking. **JUVENILE** Similar to winter adult. **VOICE** Utters rumbling *har-rrrhr* calls at breeding colonies. Otherwise silent. **STATUS AND HABITAT** Restricted mainly to cold northern and Arctic seas. Nests colonially on precipitous sea-cliff ledges and very locally abundant; often found alongside Common Murre. Entirely pelagic outside breeding season, some birds remaining in Arctic waters, but many drifting southward. **OBSERVATION TIPS** More than 2 million Thick-billeds breed in Alaska. Easy to see at colonies where easy access is possible, such as on St. Paul Island in the Pribilof Islands. Suffers badly from oil pollution, chronic marine pollution, and the fishing industry (overfishing and being caught in nets).

ADULT, WINTER

COMMON MURRE *Uria aalge* L 17–18 in

Stoutly built seabird and the largest member of the alcid family. Best known for its large and densely packed breeding colonies, found on sea cliffs. Adopts upright posture when standing on cliff ledge. When not nesting, spends its entire life at sea; swims well and dives frequently. Flies on whirring wingbeats; its relatively narrow wings are also used when swimming—essentially it "flies" underwater. Sexes are similar. **ADULT SUMMER** Has dark chocolate brown head and upperparts, including upper wings (darker in northern birds than southern ones), and white underparts. Bill is dark, daggerlike and straight in all birds. **ADULT WINTER** Similar, but with more white on head, specifically white cheeks and throat separated by black line running back from eye. **JUVENILE** Similar to winter adult, but with more extensive dark streaking on head and neck. **VOICE** Utters nasal, growling *har-rrrhr* calls at breeding colonies. **STATUS AND HABITAT** Locally numerous member of selected seabird colonies. Precipitous cliff ledges are favored and where requirements are met, hundreds, sometimes thousands, of birds stand side-by-side. During breeding season, off-duty birds often feed and swim in inshore seas adjacent to colony. At other times, moves further offshore. Suffers badly during oil spills and the subject of restoration projects, e.g. at Devil's Slide Rock in California. Also significantly affected by overfishing and chronic marine pollution. **OBSERVATION TIPS** Easy to see, May–Jul, at selected breeding colonies (search the web for details). Most numerous on suitable northern and Arctic sea cliffs.

THICK-BILLED
MURRE

ADULT, SUMMER

ADULT, SUMMER

COMMON MURRE

ADULT, WINTER

COMMON MURRE

ADULT, SUMMER

PIGEON GUILLEMOT
Cepphus columba L 13–14 in

Plump-bodied seabird. Strikingly pied plumage is contrastingly different in summer and winter. Swims well, dives frequently, and flies on whirring wingbeats low over water. All birds have dark under wings, red legs, and red inside of mouth (obvious when bird is calling). Sexes are similar. **ADULT SUMMER** Has mainly blackish plumage with striking white patch on wing, part-dissected by black wedge. **ADULT WINTER** Has white underparts and mainly white neck with dark streaks down nape. Head is dark-streaked (especially through eye) and has dark-centered gray back feathers and black flight feathers; retains white wing patch. **JUVENILE** Similar to winter adult, but with more dark streaking on face, neck, and underparts. **VOICE** Utters high-pitched whistles at breeding colonies. **STATUS AND HABITAT** Locally common year-round on rocky coasts. Range extends south in winter. **OBSERVATION TIPS** Easy to see on suitable coasts, sometimes in harbors. **SIMILAR SPECIES Black Guillemot** *C. grylle* (L 13–14 in) has white underwings and oval (not squarish), unbroken white wing patch. In west, found only on northern Alaska coast.

MARBLED MURRELET
Brachyramphus marmoratus L 9.5–10 in

Compact alcid. Swims buoyantly with tail cocked up; flies on whirring wingbeats. Upper margin of bill follows line of sloping forehead. Sexes are similar. **ADULT SUMMER** Has rufous brown upperparts and paler marbled brown underparts. **ADULT WINTER** Has black back, wings, cap, and narrow dark line down nape, with otherwise whitish plumage. Note white scapular feathers and white spot in front of eye. **JUVENILE** Similar to winter adult, but white elements of plumage have faint brown marbling. **VOICE** Utters piercing squeals near nest. **STATUS AND HABITAT** Locally common, but declining due to forest destruction and fishing activities. Nests in old-growth forest, often well inland. At other times, always found at sea. **OBSERVATION TIPS** Hard to observe, other than at sea. **SIMILAR SPECIES Kittlitz's Murrelet** *B. brevirostris* (L 9–10 in), an Alaskan specialty, is smaller; in summer, belly is white; in winter largely white face contrasts with narrow black crown. *See also* Long-billed Murrelet (p.400).

ANCIENT MURRELET *Synthliboramphus antiquus* L 9.5–10 in
Strikingly marked, plump-bodied alcid. Swims well (note short-necked appearance) and dives frequently. Sexes are similar. **ADULT SUMMER** Has mainly gray back and upper wings, with black flight feathers. Nape, crown, throat, and upper breast are black; underparts are otherwise white. Note white "eyelids," white plumelike crown feathers, and yellow bill. In flight, white underwing coverts contrast with dark flight feathers. **ADULT WINTER** Similar, but black on throat and chest is less extensive and white "plumes" on crown are absent. **JUVENILE** Similar to winter adult, but throat and chest are mainly white. **VOICE** Utters loud chirping calls. **STATUS AND HABITAT** Locally common, but declining. Breeds in burrows on islands and vulnerable to introduced ground predators. At other times, found at sea. **OBSERVATION TIPS** Seen on sea in vicinity of breeding colonies, but most colonies are themselves hard to access. Occasional in inshore waters in winter. **SIMILAR SPECIES Xantus's Murrelet** *S. hypoleucus* (L 9.5–10 in) has black upperparts and white underparts, including throat; breeds on islands off California and Mexico and otherwise found at sea.

ADULT, SUMMER

ADULT, SUMMER

PIGEON GUILLEMOT

1ST-WINTER

ADULT, WINTER

ADULT, SUMMER

MARBLED MURRELET

ADULT, WINTER

ANCIENT MURRELET

ADULT, TRANSITIONAL PLUMAGE

Alcidae

CASSIN'S AUKLET
Ptychoramphus aleuticus L 9–9.5 in

Dumpy seabird. Looks short-necked when swimming. Often dives or paddles away (rather than flies) from boats. Sexes are similar. **ADULT** Has smoky blue-gray plumage overall, darkest on head, back, and upper wings, and palest below (white belly is seen in flight). Eye has pale, yellowish iris and white "eyelids." Bill is relatively narrow and pointed, mostly dark, but with a pale base.

ADULT

JUVENILE Similar to adult, but with darker, duller eye color. **VOICE** Vocal, after dark, uttering hissing screeches. **STATUS AND HABITAT** Very locally common, breeding on isolated islands. Nests in burrows and under boulders, with activity at colonies taking place after dark. Suffers badly from introduced ground predators, but local extinction of these is helping redress balance. **OBSERVATION TIPS** Hard to observe except at sea because of nocturnal habits at breeding colonies (which are themselves hard to access) and pelagic, offshore life outside breeding season.

PARAKEET AUKLET *Aethia psittacula* L 9.5–10 in

Distinctive alcid with diagnostic bill in breeding season (vaguely parakeetlike); when calling, strongly upcurved lower mandible is revealed. Swims well and dives frequently. Adopts upright posture when perched on rocks, when body looks dumpy and neck relatively long. Sexes are similar. **ADULT SUMMER** Has blackish upperparts, including throat (and sometimes neck and chest too), and otherwise white underparts. Bill is bright red, eye has white iris, and note slender white plumes behind eye. **ADULT WINTER** Similar in plumage terms overall, but throat becomes white, head plumes are less obvious, and bill is duller. **JUVENILE** Similar to winter adult, but eye and bill are dark. **VOICE** Utters high-pitched squeals when alarmed. **STATUS AND HABITAT** Very locally common in Bering Sea area, breeding colonially on Alaskan islands; nests under boulders and in rock crevices on sea cliffs. Moves to offshore waters outside breeding season. **OBSERVATION TIPS** Easy to see at breeding colonies, e.g. St. Paul Island, in the Pribilof Islands; off-duty birds often sit around on rocks. At other times, seen only rarely from land, but occasionally observed from boats.

LEAST AUKLET *Aethia pusilla* L 6–7 in

Tiny, dumpy alcid. Flight sometimes seems "out of control", with direction veering from side-to-side. Adopts upright posture when perched on rock and often looks rather long-necked. Sexes are similar. **ADULT SUMMER** Has mainly brown upperparts (note pale wing bars and scapulars) and paler underparts, variably mottled brown (some birds are mainly white below, others are almost entirely marbled brown, except for white throat). Iris is white; bill is stubby, dark, and red-tipped, with "knob" on upper surface; note also subtle white streaks on forecrown and lores. **ADULT WINTER** Similar, but underparts are entirely white, white streaking on head is indistinct, and bill lacks "knob." **JUVENILE** Similar to winter adult, but elements of upperparts are dark brown, not black. **VOICE** Utters high-pitched squeals at colonies. **STATUS AND HABITAT** Very locally common, breeding on Alaskan islands in Bering Sea. Nests colonially, under boulders and in rock crevices. Otherwise found at sea. **OBSERVATION TIPS** Easy to see if you visit a breeding colony, e.g. St. Paul Island, in the Pribilof Islands; off-duty birds often sit around on rocks.

CASSIN'S AUKLET

ADULT

ADULT, SUMMER

PARAKEET AUKLET

ADULT, SUMMER

LEAST AUKLET

ADULT, SUMMER

ADULT, SUMMER

Alcidae

CRESTED AUKLET *Aethia cristatella* L 9–11 in

Plump-bodied and distinctive alcid with mostly all-dark plumage, but bizarrely ornamented head in breeding season. Adopts upright posture when sitting on rocks; swims well and dives frequently. Sexes are similar. **ADULT SUMMER** Has sooty black plumage that is darker above than below. Bill is bright orange-red and similar in shape overall to that of Parakeet Auklet. Iris is white and note forward-curling tuft on forecrown and white plumes behind eye. **ADULT WINTER** Similar in plumage terms overall, but forecrown plumes are much shorter and bill is duller and smaller (breeding season plates are

shed). **JUVENILE** Similar to winter adult, but bill is duller still, forecrown plumes are even shorter, and eye is darker. **VOICE** Utters peculiar yapping and hooting calls at breeding colonies. **STATUS AND HABITAT** Very locally common, breeding colonially on islands in Bering Sea; nests in crevices on sea cliffs. Otherwise seen only at sea, winter range typically determined by extent of pack ice. **OBSERVATION TIPS** Easy to see only if you visit a breeding colony; those on St. Paul Island in Pribilof Islands provide good opportunities. **SIMILAR SPECIES Whiskered Auklet** *A. pygmaea* (L 7.5–8 in) is smaller and darker, with white belly (dark in Crested) and stubbier red bill. In breeding season has similar forecrown plumes to Crested, but additional two white "whiskers" arising from base of bill; in winter, head ornamentation is reduced and bill is duller. An Aleutian Island specialty, hard to see anywhere else.

WHISKERED AUKLET

ADULT, SUMMER

RHINOCEROS AUKLET *Cerorhinca monocerata* L 15–16 in

Relatively large and bulky alcid. Breeding season bill ornamentation is distinctive and diagnostic, even in silhouette. Swims buoyantly and often seen in flocks. Sexes are similar. **ADULT SUMMER** Has gray-brown upperparts, darkest on crown, nape, back, and wings; neck and chest are also gray-brown, but underparts are otherwise whitish. Has shaggy white plumes running back from eye and from base of bill. Bill is orange-yellow, relatively large (like a scaled-down puffin bill) and with a forward-projecting, pale hornlike plate after which species

is named. Iris is white. **ADULT WINTER** Similar, but white plumes are much-reduced and bill is smaller, duller, and lacks the projecting "horn." **JUVENILE** Similar to winter adult, but bill is smaller and duller still, and iris is darker. **VOICE** Utters groaning calls, after dark, at colonies. Otherwise silent. **STATUS AND HABITAT** Widespread and locally common, breeding colonially on islands and nesting in burrows; activity at colonies is mainly nocturnal. Suffers badly on islands where ground predators have been introduced. Otherwise seen at sea, range extending south in winter to Baja California. **OBSERVATION TIPS** As auklets go, one of the easier species to see, partly because of wide-ranging distribution, but also because it often feeds in inshore seas, even outside breeding season, making it easier to observe from land. You are most unlikely to see the species *on* land, however, unless you visit a colony after dark.

ADULT, WINTER

ADULT, SUMMER

CRESTED AUKLET

ADULT, SUMMER

RHINOCEROS AUKLET

ADULT, SUMMER

Alcidae

HORNED PUFFIN *Fratercula corniculata* L 15–15.5 in

Bizarre-looking and distinctive alcid that is unmistakable within its western range. In breeding season, laterally flattened bill is disproportionately huge and colorful. Swims buoyantly, dives frequently after small fish, and flight is speedy. Adopts upright posture when standing on rocks. Sexes are similar. **ADULT SUMMER** Has black neck, back and wings, dark gray crown, and otherwise white plumage that includes striking white face. Bill is mainly yellow with orange-red tip and notably swollen orange base of gape. Eye is surrounded by orange-red orbital ring and dark eyeline and vertical "horn" above eye are highlighted as if by mascara. **ADULT WINTER** Similar, but has darker, duller, and smaller bill plates, bill being "pinched in" at base. Face is much darker and eye lacks ornamentation. **JUVENILE** Recalls winter adult in plumage terms, but dark bill is much shallower (almost gull-like). **VOICE** Sitting birds

ADULT, NONBREEDING

sometimes utter grumbling calls from within rock-crevice nesting sites; otherwise silent. **STATUS AND HABITAT** A mainly Alaskan specialty in breeding season, and locally common there, nesting colonially in crevices on sea cliffs. Off-duty breeders are often seen swimming in waters close to breeding colonies. In winter, range extends south and species is entirely pelagic and typically lives in offshore waters, well away from land. **OBSERVATION TIPS** Easy to see if you visit an Alaskan breeding colony in summer and relatively easy to see in inshore Alaskan seas at this time of year. Outside breeding season, most sightings comprise chance oceanic encounters from boats.

TUFTED PUFFIN *Fratercula cirrhata* L 15–16 in

Large, plump-bodied and unmistakable alcid, particularly so in breeding season when its head adornments and bill colors lend it an almost comical appearance. Swims sedately and dives frequently after fish. In flight, which is direct and powerful, bright orange-red feet and legs are obvious; webbed feet are proportionately large. Adopts upright posture when standing on rock. Sexes are similar. **ADULT SUMMER** Has very dark brown plumage that in most situations appears almost jet-black. Note, however, contrasting gleaming white face. Eye has white iris and red orbital ring, and shaggy golden-yellow tufted plumes arise from behind eye. Laterally flattened bill is massive and horny-looking. Lower mandible is orange-red while upper mandible has orange-red outer half and yellow inner half; note swollen orange base of gape. **ADULT WINTER** Has entirely dark sooty brown plumage. Eye has pale iris and dull red orbital ring. Bill has smaller plates than in summer and is mainly dull orange, but grubby yellow toward base of upper mandible. **JUVENILE** Similar to winter adult in plumage terms, but has much smaller, shallower, and stubbier bill. **VOICE** Mainly silent although incubating birds utter grumbling calls from within burrows. **STATUS AND HABITAT** Widespread breeding species on Pacific coast, from California (where it is scarce and very local) to Alaska (where it is locally abundant). In breeding season, often seen swimming in inshore seas in vicinity of colonies. Nests in burrows on islands. Outside breeding season, more widespread, but mainly pelagic and offshore. **OBSERVATION TIPS** Easy to see in breeding season if you visit a colony. Otherwise, sightings relate to chance encounters at sea.

HORNED PUFFIN

ADULT, SUMMER

ADULT, SUMMER

TUFTED PUFFIN

ADULT, SUMMER

ADULT, SUMMER

ADULT, SUMMER

Columbidae

BAND-TAILED PIGEON
Patagioenas fasciata L 14–15 in
Plump-bodied, rather dark-looking pigeon. Seen in flocks, especially
outside breeding season, and typically most evident on woodland margins
or in clearings where food (berries, fruits, nuts, and seeds) is plentiful;
usually feeds in trees. Sexes are similar. **ADULT** Has blue-gray back, upper wing
coverts, and rump, palest (and forming pale bar) on greater coverts. Flight
feathers are dark and bases of otherwise gray tail feathers are dark, forming a
band. Head, throat, and breast are mainly reddish purple with white half-collar
bordering band of iridescent feathers on nape. Feet and iris are yellow, and bill
is dark-tipped yellow. **JUVENILE** Similar, but less colorful and lacking nape markings. **VOICE** Utters
a repetitive series of upslurred cooing *whaOOO* calls. Note clattering wing-clapping, heard on takeoff.
STATUS AND HABITAT Locally fairly common in mixed and conifer woodland; often in mountainous
terrain, especially in south of range. Roosts in large, dense conifers. **OBSERVATION TIPS** Easy to see in
suitable habitat, and presence often detected by sound of wing-clapping or call.

ROCK PIGEON *Columba livia* L 12–13 in
Our most familiar pigeon, especially in towns and cities. Typically
utterly fearless and many depend to large extent on "hand-outs" or

the carelessly discarded refuse of people. Forms flocks and usually feeds on
ground. Nowadays, most birds are free-
living, but centuries of domestication
have produced spectrum of color vari-
eties. Hence hard to discern sex differences within species' variation overall.
ADULT Ancestral form has blue-gray plumage overall, palest on
upper wings and back, and flushed pinkish maroon on breast. Has
two dark wing bars and dark-tipped tail. In flight, note small white
rump patch; upper wings have dark trailing edge and narrow wing
bar, while underwings are white. Pure white, reddish brown, and
marbled and mottled color forms are all common too. **JUVENILE**
Similar, but duller. **VOICE** Utters various cooing calls. **STATUS AND
HABITAT** Old World species, introduced by original European settlers and now common and widespread. Favors urban settings
where food is available, but also seen on farmland. **OBSERVATION
TIPS** Hard to miss. A positive benefit to urban Peregrine Falcons.

MOURNING DOVE *Zenaida macroura* L 11–12 in
Slim-bodied, long-tailed dove. Feeds on ground (mainly on seeds)
and walks with jerky, but rapid manner on short legs. Forms flocks
outside breeding season. Sexes are separable with care. **ADULT** Male has
pinkish buff plumage overall. Upper wings, back, and rump are buffy brown
with black spots on tertials and wing coverts. Head, neck, and breast are paler
buff, flushed pink on breast and with iridescent bluish feathers on nape. Note
dark crescent on lower margin of ear coverts, dark bill, and pinkish red legs.
Adult female is similar, but less colorful on neck and breast. **JUVENILE** Similar
to adult female, but has spotted and barred appearance to back, neck, and breast,
and pale face with dark line through eye. **VOICE** Utters a series of mournful, hooting calls. **STATUS AND
HABITAT** Common in open terrain, including arable farmland, parks, suburbs, and roadsides. Northern
populations are mostly migratory, present Mar–Sep and wintering south to Mexico. Birds from further
south of range are often rather sedentary and at best locally nomadic in winter in search of food.
OBSERVATION TIPS Easy to see.

ADULT

ADULT

BAND-TAILED PIGEON

ADULT

MOURNING DOVE

ADULT

ADULT

ROCK PIGEON

ADULT

ADULT

MOURNING DOVE

JUVENILE

Columbidae

WHITE-WINGED DOVE *Zenaida asiatica* L 11 in

Compact and proportionately plump, arid-country dove. Forms flocks, especially outside breeding season; easily recognized in flight by white, crescent-shaped mark on upperwings; white tip to tail is most obvious when fanned, on takeoff and landing. Sexes are similar. **ADULT** Gray-brown overall with a pinkish flush most evident on neck and breast. Bill is dark, legs are reddish, and note black crescent below eye, which has red iris and blue orbital skin. In flight, white outer margins to upper wing coverts contrast with blackish outer wing. **JUVENILE** Similar, but with less striking wing markings and subdued colors and markings on head. **VOICE** Series of owl-like cooing calls is sometimes rendered "who cooks for you." **STATUS AND HABITAT** Mainly Central American species with toehold in southwestern U.S., favoring deserts, arid scrub, and adjacent farmland. Locally common summer visitor, resident only in south of region. **OBSERVATION TIPS** Easy to see in suitable desert habitats, e.g. near Phoenix, Arizona.

ADULT

COMMON GROUND-DOVE
Columbina passerina L 6–7 in

Charming and dainty dove with compact body, relatively short tail and proportionately large head. Feeds unobtrusively, mainly on ground. In flight, chestnut and black pattern on outer wing is striking, above and below. Sexes are dissimilar. **ADULT** Male has buffy brown back and gray-buff wing coverts adorned with black spots. Crown and nape are iridescent bluish and face, neck, and underparts are pinkish with dark scaly-looking barring. Face looks particularly pale and shows off beady red eye. Bill is dainty, pale reddish pink, and dark-tipped. Adult female is similar, but nape and crown are brownish (and lack iridescence) and face and underparts are less colorful. **JUVENILE** Similar to adult female, but browner and with fewer, or no, black spots. **VOICE** Utters monotonously repeated, upslurred *whoo-errp* calls. **STATUS AND HABITAT** Mainly Central American species that is a locally common resident in southwestern U.S., commonest near Mexican border. Favors dry, open, bushy terrain with sandy ground. Often found in disturbed and urban sites such as farms and city parks. **OBSERVATION TIPS** Surprisingly easy to overlook when feeding on ground in dappled shade.

INCA DOVE *Columbina inca* L 8–9 in

Small, plump-bodied and long-tailed ground-feeding dove. Most distinctive and diagnostic feature is "scaly" appearance to feathers on back, wing coverts, and underparts. In flight, note white sides on long tail and striking chestnut pattern on outer flight feathers, above and below; chestnut is also visible on closed wing. Sexes are similar, although seen side-by-side, male is brighter than female. **ADULT** Has mainly gray-brown upperparts and pinkish gray underparts, palest on belly. Note that all parts of body, but especially back and belly, have black feather margins creating "scaly" look. Bill is dark, legs are pinkish, and eye has red iris and hint of blue orbital skin. **JUVENILE** Similar, but duller and less well patterned. **VOICE** Utters subdued, chuckling and cooing calls including *coo-coo* and *kup-kup-kup ker-rWhoo*. **STATUS AND HABITAT** A mainly Central American species whose range extends to southwestern U.S., where it is locally common. Favors arid ground and often associated with disturbed land, often around human dwellings, on lawns, and in gardens. **OBSERVATION TIPS** Easy to see in southwestern U.S., and typically indifferent to human observers.

JUVENILE

ADULT

WHITE-WINGED DOVE

FEMALE

MALE

COMMON GROUND-DOVE

INCA DOVE

ADULT

ADULT

Columbidae and Cuculidae

EURASIAN COLLARED-DOVE
Streptopelia decaocto L 12–13 in

Superficially similar to Mourning Dove, but with shorter tail, unmarked upperparts, and diagnostic dark half collar on nape. Distinctive call is well known in urban areas, as is gliding display flight performed on bowed, outstretched wings. Sexes are similar. **ADULT** Has mainly sandy brown plumage with pinkish flush to head and underparts. Black wingtips and white outer

tail feathers are most noticeable in flight. Bill is dark and legs are reddish. **JUVENILE** Similar, but has duller color and black half collar is absent. **VOICE** Utters repetitive (some would say mildly irritating) song that comprises much-repeated *oo-oo-oo* phrase. **STATUS AND HABITAT** Introduced to Bahamas in 1970s, and has since spread across much of U.S.; range expansion mirrors that seen in western Europe since 1950s. Often found in urban areas and gardens, but also in vicinity of farm buildings and grain spills. **OBSERVATION TIPS** Easy to see within range, which is expected to expand further.

YELLOW-BILLED CUCKOO
Coccyzus americanus L 12–13 in

Unobtrusive, long-tailed bird associated with wooded habitats. Presence often easiest to detect by first hearing its distinctive call. Feeds on caterpillars, including hairy ones. Sexes are similar. **ADULT** Has dark gray-brown upperparts, least colorful on crown and darkest through eye. Rufous flight feathers are most obvious in flight, above and below. Underparts are otherwise whitish. Tail is long and wedge-shaped when spread; from above, central upper tail is reddish, while rest of tail is black, all feathers having striking white tips; from below, note striking, large white spots (feather tips) to otherwise black tail feathers. Bill is downcurved with yellow base to lower mandible. Note yellow orbital ring. **JUVENILE** Similar to adult, but less colorful and with less contrasting undertail pattern. **VOICE** Utters a rapid *ke-ke-ke-ke-keeooa-keeooa-keeooa*. **STATUS AND HABITAT** Local, scarce, and declining summer visitor (much commoner in eastern North America), mainly May–Sep; winters in northern and central South America. Favors dense scrub and woodland, typically alongside rivers. Builds its own nest (many cuckoo species elsewhere in World are obligate nest parasites), but occasionally lays eggs in nest of other species, notably that of Black-billed Cuckoo. **OBSERVATION TIPS** Easiest to see and hear shortly after arrival from migration in late spring.

BLACK-BILLED CUCKOO
Coccyzus erythropthalmus L 11–12 in

Unobtrusive woodland bird. Similar to Yellow-billed, but separable by studying bill and orbital ring colors, and tail patterns, and by noting calls. Feeds on hairy caterpillars. Sexes are similar. **ADULT** Has gray-brown upperparts (crown is concolorous with back) and whitish underparts. Flight feathers are buffy brown (not rufous), and note uniformly dark bill and reddish orbital ring. Tail is long and wedge-shaped when fanned; upperside is brown with small pale tips to feathers; underside is gray-brown with small white spots (feather tips), defined by subterminal black bands. **JUVENILE** Similar to adult, but duller overall, with grubby-looking underparts and indistinct pattern on undertail. **VOICE** Utters a subdued piping *cu-cu, cu-cu, cu-cu-cu...* . **STATUS AND HABITAT** Scarce summer visitor (more widespread in east), mainly May–Sep; winters in northern South America. Favors dense deciduous woodland. **OBSERVATION TIPS** Easiest to see upon arrival from migration in spring.

EURASIAN COLLARED-DOVE

ADULT

YELLOW-BILLED CUCKOO

ADULT

ADULT

BLACK-BILLED CUCKOO

ADULT

Cuculidae

GROOVE-BILLED ANI
Crotophaga sulcirostris L 13–14 in

Engaging and distinctive, long-tailed, all-dark bird with a proportionately large bill. Gregarious and typically seen in groups of 5–10 birds. Usually nests communally and social groups engage in cooperative breeding behavior. Flight is weak and characteristic, involving interspersed glides on rounded wings and brief bouts of flapping; in flight, tail appears to have a mind of its own. Usually adopts an upright posture when perched, with dangling tail. Feeds mainly on insects, caught on ground or while foraging among leaves. Sexes are similar. **ADULT** Appears uniformly black, although oily blue-green iridescence can be seen in good light. Nape and throat appear shaggy. Bill is large, dark, and laterally flattened; curved upper margin continues profile of crown. Close inspection of bill reveals obvious horizontal grooves on upper mandible. **JUVENILE** Similar to adult, but bill lacks grooves. **VOICE** Utters a distinctive, repeated, piping *tee-wuup, tee-wuup*. **STATUS AND HABITAT** A mainly Central and South American species, with a foothold in southern Texas, where it is present mainly May–Sep. Usually associated with dense scrub and woodland beside river courses, but sometimes feeds in more open, grassy situations. **OBSERVATION TIPS** Easiest to find when fledged young have joined feeding groups, in late summer.

GREATER ROADRUNNER
Geococcyx californianus L 23–24 in

Large, distinctive, and unmistakable ground-dwelling bird whose status among desert species is iconic. It is related to cuckoos. Prefers to run rather than fly from danger, or when chasing prey, and powerful feet and legs reflect this preference. Bill is large and powerful and used to good effect in catching and dispatching prey such as lizards, insects, small mammals, and birds. In flight (seldom observed), pale primary bases appear as a white crescent on wings. Sexes are similar. **ADULT** Has mainly brown plumage, palest and least marked on belly; feathers on rest of body have pale, buff margins or are adorned with buff streaks and spots, creating rather mottled appearance overall. Crest is bushy and can be raised or lowered at will. Tail is long, mainly dark brown, but with pale tips to feathers. **JUVENILE** Similar to adult. **VOICE** "Song" comprises a series of dovelike cooing notes that descend in pitch from start to finish. Utters bill-snapping sounds in alarm. **STATUS AND HABITAT** Strongly territorial and hence never numerous. Nevertheless reasonably easy to find in arid habitats in southwestern U.S. Favors desert with light scrub and open chaparral habitat. **OBSERVATION TIPS** Most encounters are by chance, for example, when a bird runs speedily across a desert track or road. Surprisingly hard to spot when standing in dappled shade of a desert bush. Some individuals are inquisitive about human intruders into their territories. Often sunbathes in early morning hours, allowing more prolonged views from a distance.

ADULT

GROOVE-BILLED ANI

ADULT

ADULT

GREATER ROADRUNNER

ADULT

Tytonidae and Strigidae

BARN OWL *Tyto alba* L 16–17 in

Beautiful owl that looks ghostly white when caught in car headlights. Flight is leisurely and slow on broad wings. Sexes are often separable although considerable variation and overlap exists. **ADULT MALE** Has orange-buff upperparts that are speckled with tiny black and white dots. Underparts are whitish overall, but adorned with numerous black spots. White facial disc is heart-shaped and bill is yellowish. In flight, underwings are pure white. **ADULT FEMALE** Similar, but underparts (including underwings) are variably

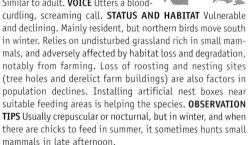

flushed with orange-buff. **JUVENILE** Similar to adult. **VOICE** Utters a blood-curdling, screaming call. **STATUS AND HABITAT** Vulnerable and declining. Mainly resident, but northern birds move south in winter. Relies on undisturbed grassland rich in small mammals, and adversely affected by habitat loss and degradation, notably from farming. Loss of roosting and nesting sites (tree holes and derelict farm buildings) are also factors in population declines. Installing artificial nest boxes near suitable feeding areas is helping the species. **OBSERVATION TIPS** Usually crepuscular or nocturnal, but in winter, and when there are chicks to feed in summer, it sometimes hunts small mammals in late afternoon.

ADULT

SHORT-EARED OWL *Asio flammeus* L 14–15 in

Medium-sized, well-marked owl that often hunts in daylight, mainly for small mammals. Flight is leisurely and slow: glides frequently, and flies holding its long, narrow, and round-tipped wings rather stiffly. Usually quarters ground at low level, but displaying birds sometimes rise to considerable heights. Often sits on fence posts or grassland tussocks. Sexes are similar, although female is larger and often darker than male. **ADULT AND JUVENILE** Buffy brown plumage overall, but heavily spotted and streaked on upperparts, including neck; underparts are paler overall, but heavily streaked. Facial disc is round; note staring yellow eyes and short "ear" tufts. **VOICE** Displaying birds sometimes utter deep hoots. **STATUS AND HABITAT** Declining, but still fairly common, especially in Alaska and northern Canada during breeding season. Favors open habitats—tundra, undisturbed grassland and prairie. Northern birds move south in fall. **OBSERVATION TIPS** Partly diurnal habits mean it is relatively easy to see in suitable open habitats.

ADULT

LONG-EARED OWL *Asio otus* L 15–16 in

Nocturnal and secretive owl. When alarmed, sometimes adopts elongated posture with "ear" tufts raised. In flight, could be mistaken for Short-eared, but has orange-buff underwing color overall (whitish in Short-eared) and more extensive, but barred, dark wingtip. Orange-buff upper wing patch is more striking than on Short-eared. Sexes are similar. **ADULT AND JUVENILE** Have dark brown upperparts and paler underparts; however, whole body is heavily streaked. At close range, note rounded, orange-buff facial disc and staring orange eyes. "Ear" tufts are appreciably longer than those of Short-eared. **VOICE** Mostly silent, but series of deep hoots is sometimes heard in spring. **STATUS AND HABITAT** Nests in dense woodland and scrub thickets, usually in vicinity of open country for hunting. Outside breeding season, birds disperse and northern populations migrate south. In winter, roosts communally in dense thickets. **OBSERVATION TIPS** Hard to observe in daytime; most people's experience will be a partial view of a bird at a daytime winter roost.

BARN OWL

ADULT

SHORT-EARED OWL

ADULT

LONG-EARED OWL

ADULT

ADULT

Strigidae

GREAT HORNED OWL *Bubo virginianus* L 22–23 in

Huge and impressive owl with a bulky body, proportionally large head, and striking "ear" tufts that may be raised or flattened. Active mainly at dusk and after dark; has a broad diet, but prefers tackling prey the size of rabbits and hares. Typically scans for prey from lookout perch, then glides down on broad wings, grabbing and killing victim with powerful talons. Several subspecies exist: coastal birds typically are smaller and darker than ones from interior; palest of all is ssp. *subarcticus* that occurs across Arctic and sub-Arctic North America. Within subspecies, sexes are similar, although female is larger than male. **ADULT** Has mostly brown plumage overall, beautifully patterned on upperparts and resembling tree bark; underparts are strongly barred. Head has rounded, orange-brown facial disc and yellow eyes. **JUVENILE** Has fluffy down at first, but by fall acquires adultlike plumage. **VOICE** Territorial "song" (heard in midwinter) comprises a series of tremulous hoots; male's hoot is deeper than female's. **STATUS AND HABITAT** Common, but strongly territorial, hence thinly spread. Tolerates a wide range of habitats from forests in north of range to deserts in south. Sometimes also in surprisingly urban settings. **OBSERVATION TIPS** Nests extremely early in season (eggs typically laid Jan–Mar depending on geographical location), so incubating birds are sometimes obvious in leafless winter trees. Otherwise, occasionally glimpsed in car headlights while hunting after dark, or located by tracking small birds mobbing a roosting bird in daytime.

SNOWY OWL *Bubo scandiacus* L 21–26 in

Huge and unmistakable species that lacks "ear" tufts. Often active during the day, and obliged to be diurnal in Arctic breeding grounds by perpetual summer daylight. Even if resting or roosting, open nature of its favored habitats, and sheer size, make it relatively conspicuous. Feeds on lemmings and voles during summer months; diet in winter range is often more varied. Sexes are dissimilar. **ADULT MALE** Has essentially pure white plumage with small black spots and bars; at close range, feathered feet, black bill, and yellow eyes can be seen. **ADULT FEMALE AND 1ST-WINTER MALE** Mainly white, but note more extensive blackish spots on upperparts and dark barring below. **1ST-WINTER FEMALE** Heavily marked with dark barring on all parts, except head. **VOICE** Mostly silent, although territorial male sometimes utters series of deep hoots. **STATUS AND HABITAT** Fairly common tundra breeding species within its high Arctic range, although numbers vary considerably from year to year, influenced by abundance or available selection of prey. Outside breeding season, most birds move south, the extent to which they travel influenced by severity of winter weather and availability of prey. **OBSERVATION TIPS** Relatively easy to see if you visit its high Arctic breeding grounds in summer. In winter, most observations are by chance. Can turn up almost anywhere in suitable habitat—often open grassland or coastal habitats. In such situations, white plumage makes it easy to spot.

JUVENILE

ADULT

GREAT HORNED OWL

ADULT

MALE

FEMALE

SNOWY OWL

Strigidae

GREAT GRAY OWL *Strix nebulosa* L 27–28 in

Huge and beautifully patterned owl with a proportionally long tail, large head, and rounded facial disc marked with dark concentric rings around eyes. Fluffed-up body feathers often accentuate bulky appearance. Feeds mainly on small rodents and typically scans for prey while perched over-looking forest clearing or grassland adjacent to trees. Mostly nocturnal in winter, but during breeding season, lengthy daylight hours oblige diurnal hunting too. Sexes are similar. **ADULT** Has mainly gray-brown plumage, upperparts with intricate darker markings; underparts are barred and streaked. Note staring yellow eyes and yellow bill. **JUVENILE** Fluffy at first, but by fall acquires adultlike plumage. **VOICE** Territorial male's "song" comprises a series of deep *hoo* notes, whose pitch rises at first then falls throughout the series. **STATUS AND HABITAT** Widespread, but nomadic, presence or absence dictated by availability of prey; territories widely spaced and so seldom common. Favors boreal forests across northern part of range, montane conifer forests further south. Mainly sedentary, but shortage of prey and adverse weather sometimes causes irruptive movements south of usual range in winter. **OBSERVATION TIPS** Male's song is clue to species' presence. Fiercely protective of nest, so do not approach closely.

ADULT

BARRED OWL *Strix varia* L 21–22 in

Our most familiar medium-sized woodland owl. Sometimes found perched on tree branch during daytime, when fluffed up body plumage, proportionally large head, and rounded facial disc are obvious. Feeds on small mammals, amphibians, and large invertebrates. Sexes are similar. **ADULT** Has brown plumage overall; upperparts are dark brown, but beautifully marked with white spots, flight feathers with dark bars, while underparts are buffy gray with bold dark streaks. Note short barred tail, brown concentric rings around eyes, and ruff of brown-barred feathers on throat. Eyes are dark and bill is yellow. **JUVENILE** Has fluffy plumage at first, but acquires adultlike plumage by fall. **VOICE** Utters a series of gruff hooting notes—typically *who-hu-ho-hoo*—mostly after dark, but sometimes during daytime. **STATUS AND HABITAT** Widespread and common, associated with mixed deciduous woods and coniferous forest, often near water. Nests in tree holes or abandoned crow's nests. **OBSERVATION TIPS** Easy to hear in wooded habitats and occasionally flushed from roost in daytime.

SPOTTED OWL *Strix occidentalis* L 17–18 in

Beautifully patterned owl with plump body, proportionally large head, and rounded facial disc. Sexes are similar. **ADULT** Has rich brown plumage overall, adorned with white spots on head, neck, back, and underparts. **JUVENILE** Has fluffy plumage at first, but acquires adultlike appearance by fall. **VOICE** Utters a series of sharp-sounding, abrupt hoots, typically *hu-hoo, hu-hoo-hoo*. **STATUS AND HABITAT** Uncommon and generally scarce resident of undisturbed wooded habitats. Northern population of Spotted Owl is particularly threatened in Pacific Northwest by loss of old-growth forest to which it is tied; it is a conservation icon and its demise a testament to man's short-sightedness. **OBSERVATION TIPS** At well known and regularly visited sites where disturbance is minimal (e.g. in some Arizona canyons), roosting birds are sometimes indifferent to human observers, affording superb views.

ADULT

GREAT
GRAY OWL

ADULT

SPOTTED
OWL

BARRED OWL

ADULT

ADULT

Strigidae

WESTERN SCREECH-OWL
Megascops kennicottii L 8.5–9 in

Compact and rather dumpy-looking owl with a proportionately large head, rounded facial disc, and short, but pronounced, "ear" tufts. Mainly nocturnal, but sometimes seen feeding at dusk. Particularly vocal in spring. Plumage markings create the impression of tree bark and afford roosting owl excellent camouflage when sitting adjacent to trunk.

ADULT

WHISKERED SCREECH-OWL

ADULT

Given plumage color variation, sexes are similar. **ADULT** Either brown overall or gray-brown; gray forms predominate in deserts in south. Upperparts are beautifully patterned with fine dark lines and white spots; feathers on underparts are marked with dark central streak and fine dark barring. Note the staring yellow eyes and pale-tipped dark bill. **JUVENILE** Similar to adult. **VOICE** Territorial birds utter an accelerating series of abrupt hooting calls; agitated birds utter a faster version and pairs often duet. **STATUS AND HABITAT** Common in a range of wooded and lightly wooded habitats, from native woodland to parks and deserts. **OBSERVATION TIPS** More easily heard than seen. Typically roosts during daytime hours in dense cover or a tree hole, but sometimes emerges to feed while there is a glimmer of light at sunset. Inquisitive birds will sometimes respond to imitations of their calls. **SIMILAR SPECIES Whiskered Screech-Owl** *M. trichopsis* (L 7.35–7.5 in) is marginally smaller, with a greenish yellow bill that is pale-tipped; neither feature is useful in field identification. Best distinguished by voice: "song" is a series of soft, piping calls that descend in pitch throughout sequence; lower pitched and with slower delivery than Western. Plumage is gray-brown overall, with similar patterning to Western, although barring on underparts is more striking. Favors mountain woodland (oaks and conifers), mainly in southern Arizona. Accessible canyons afford opportunities for observation, although species is strictly nocturnal.

EASTERN SCREECH-OWL *Megascops asio* L 8–9 in

Widespread owl of wooded habitats, whose predominantly eastern range abuts that of superficially very similar Western. The species are best separated in the field by voice. Bill color is different—pale-tipped and yellowish in Eastern, pale-tipped and blackish in Western—but this is not always easy to discern with typical brief, nocturnal views. Most birds seen in zone of overlap of Eastern and Western are gray overall or gray-brown and very similar to color range seen in Western. Rufous forms of Eastern are diagnostically different from Western, but are commonest east of geographical range of this book. Sexes are similar. **ADULT** Either brown overall or gray-brown. Upperparts are beautifully patterned with fine dark lines and white spots; feathers on underparts are marked with dark central streak and fine dark barring. Note the staring yellow eyes and pale-tipped yellowish bill. **JUVENILE** Similar to adult. **VOICE** Typical territorial call comprises a plaintive, descending whistle followed by a rapid series of tremulous, whinnying piping whistles. Other vocalizations include various screeching and hooting calls. **STATUS AND HABITAT** Favors a wide range of wooded and lightly wooded habitats from forests to mature, wooded gardens and parks. **OBSERVATION TIPS** More easily heard than seen, but sometimes tolerant of human observers in suburban settings where it is not disturbed.

WESTERN SCREECH-OWL

ADULT

EASTERN SCREECH-OWL

ADULT,
GRAY MORPH

ADULT,
RUFOUS MORPH

FLAMMULATED OWL *Otus flammeolus* L 6.5–7 in

Tiny, plump-bodied owl with a proportionately large head, rounded facial disc, and small "ear" tufts. Plumage markings resemble tree bark and afford bird superb camouflage when resting close to trunk. Nests and often roosts in tree holes, hence extremely hard to find during daytime. Sexes are similar. **ADULT** Has plumage color overall that varies from reddish brown in southeast of range to gray-brown in north. Upperparts have dark markings and gray and whitish spots and patches creating barklike appearance; note row of rufous-tipped or -flushed scapular feathers. Underparts have dark streaks and fine dark barring. Eyes are dark and grayish facial disc has subtly darker concentric rings and is variably flushed reddish brown. **JUVENILE** Similar to adult. **VOICE** Surprisingly loud and deep for so small a species; comprises a series of well-spaced, piping *poo-poo-poo* notes. **STATUS AND HABITAT** Fairly common, but easily overlooked summer visitor to mountain forests, mainly pine. Winters in Central American highlands. **OBSERVATION TIPS** Strictly nocturnal, unobtrusive habits, and retiring nature, make this a difficult species to find. Best chances come from learning the vocalizations and tracking down a calling bird after dark with the aid of a powerful flashlight; beware, however, Flammulateds are good ventriloquists, so this is not an easy task. Otherwise, befriend a birder who knows the species well. Almost impossible to find when not calling.

ELF OWL *Micrathene whitneyi* L 5.5–6 in

Tiny owl, the smallest of its kind in the world—most people are amazed at just how minute it is the first time they see one. Size, compact shape, short tail, and association with desert habitats make identification relatively straightforward, even though many sightings are of nocturnal silhouettes; note the extremely rounded head. Call is also distinctive. Feeds mainly on insects, which are often caught on the wing; flight is rather stiff-winged and birds will occasionally hover while feeding. Nests in cavities, typically former nest holes of woodpeckers excavated in saguaro cacti and trees. Sexes are similar. **ADULT** Has mainly reddish brown plumage overall; upperparts are adorned with buff spots, particularly on head and wings, while scapular feathers are tipped white; underparts are barred reddish buff and facial disc is flushed reddish brown. Note the yellow eyes and pale-tipped gray bill. **JUVENILE** Similar to adult. **VOICE** Male's territorial call is a series of shrill and rather raptorlike *wee-Ukk* notes. **STATUS AND HABITAT** Fairly common summer visitor to suitable arid habitats, particularly deserts with large, mature saguaro cacti and scrub-covered canyons; also riparian habitats. **OBSERVATION TIPS** Strictly nocturnal, but often peeps head out of nesting or roosting hole as dusk approaches. In breeding season, birds are extremely vocal at dusk, and on moonlit nights.

ADULT

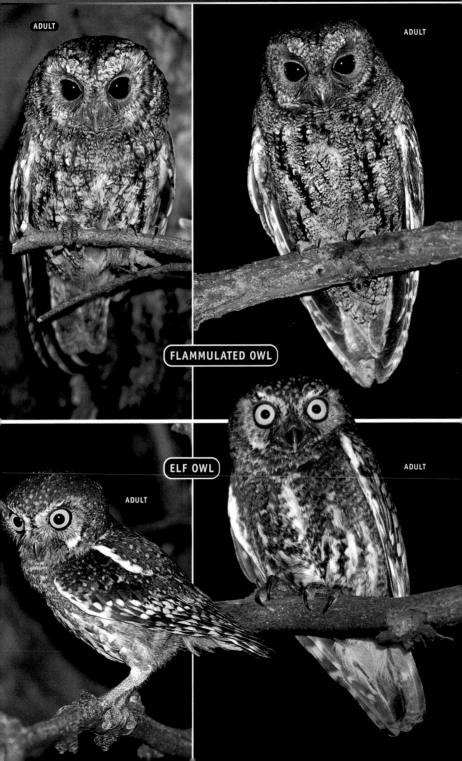

ADULT

ADULT

FLAMMULATED OWL

ELF OWL

ADULT

ADULT

Strigidae

NORTHERN PYGMY-OWL
Glaucidium gnoma L 6.5–7 in

Small, plump-bodied owl with proportionately large, rounded head and relatively long tail. Active during daytime, hunting small birds, reptiles, and large insects, mostly around dawn and dusk. Hunts mainly from a lookout perch and dives down on prey. Flight between perches is swooping and undulating. Sexes are similar, although within geographical variation, females are more rufous than males. **ADULT** Has brown to gray-brown plumage overall (interior birds are grayer than those on Pacific coast). Upperparts are marked with pale spots on wings, tiny white spots on head, and striking white-bordered black false "eyes" on nape; underparts are brown or gray-brown (depending on plumage color overall) on chest, whitish below, but with bold dark streaks. Tail is strikingly barred. Note yellow eyes and bill, and white, eyebrowlike margin to facial disc, between eyes. **JUVENILE** Similar to adult. **VOICE** Male's typical territorial call comprises a series of evenly spaced (1–2 second interval) piping calls—*poo-poo-poo...* (*poo'poo-poo'poo...* in southwestern montane birds). Call made by female is softer, higher pitched, and more rapid. **STATUS AND HABITAT** Widespread in coniferous forests. Territories are large, so individual birds are widely spaced, hence status is rather uncommon overall. Mainly resident, but some altitudinal movement seen in winter among mountain-dwelling birds. **OBSERVATION TIPS** Its mainly diurnal habits should make this a relatively easy owl species to see. However, its low density and unobtrusive nature work against the hopeful observer, so the best bet is to learn male's territorial call, identify an occupied territory and stealthily pinpoint caller's location.

ADULT

FERRUGINOUS PYGMY-OWL
Glaucidium brasilianum
L 6.5–7 in

Similar to Northern Pygmy-Owl, but much more rufous overall and with a different call. Mainly active during daylight hours. **ADULT** Has reddish brown upperparts and tail, with delicate pale streaks on head and nape, and spots on back and wings. Note the false "eyes" on the nape. Underparts are pale with bold rufous streaks. **JUVENILE** Similar to adult, but streaks and spots on upperparts are much less distinct. **VOICE** Male's typical territorial song is a rapid series of *pu-pu-pu* piping notes, recalling a frog or perhaps a smoke alarm. **STATUS AND HABITAT** A mainly Central and South American species whose resident range extends to southern Arizona and southern Texas. Favors desert scrub and riverside woodland. **OBSERVATION TIPS** Listen for the distinctive call.

BURROWING OWL *Athene cunicularia* L 9.5–10 in

Distinctive owl with a bold nature. Although hunting is mainly nocturnal, often sits or perches conspicuously during daytime, in vicinity of nest or roost burrow. Body is dumpy, head is rounded, and tail is proportionately short. Legs are relatively long, and often bobs up and down when curious or agitated. Sexes are similar. **ADULT** Gray-brown overall, but upperparts are beautifully patterned with pale spots (smallest on head), while dark breast is adorned with pale spots and underparts are otherwise pale with strong, brown barring. Facial disc is rounded and dark eyerings and white "eyebrows" frame yellow eyes. **JUVENILE** Similar to adult, but underparts are mainly pale and unmarked, except for darker chest. **VOICE** Male's typical song is a piping and repeated *cu-coo*, *cu-coo....* Birds utter soft, screeching calls when alarmed. **STATUS AND HABITAT** Fairly common in open habitats including grassland and deserts; has adapted well to modified landscapes such as golf courses. **OBSERVATION TIPS** Within its range, arguably the easiest owl to observe and typically tolerant of people.

NORTHERN
PYGMY-OWL

ADULT, ALARMED

ADULT

ADULT

ADULT

FERRUGINOUS
PYGMY-OWL

BURROWING OWL

Strigidae

NORTHERN HAWK-OWL *Surnia ulula* L 15–16 in

Long-tailed appearance is diagnostic. In silhouette, recalls a large falcon, but note large, rounded head and typical owl face. Active during daylight hours, typically perching on prominent lookout, scanning ground for small mammal prey. Nests in tree holes. Sexes are similar. **ADULT** Gray-brown overall. Upperparts are marked with pale spots, smallest and densest on head; underparts are barred, as is long, tapering tail. Eyes and bill are yellow and facial disc is pale and rounded with striking white "eyebrows." **JUVENILE** Similar to adult. **VOICE** Male's territorial call comprises series of trilling, piping notes that rise and fall in pitch throughout delivery. **STATUS AND HABITAT** Widespread in taiga forest, but never common. Precise distribution and breeding success dictated by numbers of small mammal prey. **OBSERVATION TIPS** Low density, nomadic habits, and fickle site faithfulness make it tricky to pin down. However, on the plus side, diurnal habits and fondness for perching on treetops allows superb views if you do find one.

NORTHERN SAW-WHET OWL
Aegolius acadicus L 7–8 in

Endearing, plump-bodied owl with a large head and short tail. Entirely nocturnal and roosts in dense cover during daytime. Nests in tree holes. Sexes are similar. **ADULT** Has reddish brown plumage overall. Upperparts are beautifully patterned with pale spots, largest on back and wings, and finest and densest on head; underparts are whitish, but heavily streaked rufous. Facial disc is more oblong than round, flushed buffy reddish around margins and with white "eyebrows" framing yellow eyes. **JUVENILE** Recalls adult, but has mainly reddish-brown upperparts and orange-buff underparts with white between the eyes. **VOICE** Male's territorial call (heard in spring) comprises an almost mechanical-sounding, repetitive series of piping whistles, fancifully recalling a saw being sharpened (whetted); a good 21st-century comparison might be an intruder alarm. **STATUS AND HABITAT** Fairly common, but low density breeding species in conifer and mixed forests. Interior northern populations migrate south for winter, and some altitudinal migration seen in otherwise rather sedentary populations. **OBSERVATION TIPS** Easiest to locate by imitating song (with practice, this is easy to whistle) and listening for response. Otherwise hard to locate, but usually indifferent to observers if discovered.

BOREAL OWL *Aegolius funereus* L 10–11 in

Plump-bodied owl with short tail and proportionately large head with oblong facial disc. Strictly nocturnal and roosts in dense cover.

ADULT

Sexes are similar. **ADULT** Has rich brown plumage overall. Upperparts are marked with bold white spots, smallest and densest on head; underparts are whitish, but heavily streaked with rufous brown. Facial disc is whitish with dark border; yellow eyes are framed by white "eyebrows." **JUVENILE** Mainly dark brown with white "eyebrows". **VOICE** Male's territorial call comprises a series of piping hoots that rise and fall in pitch during delivery. **STATUS AND HABITAT** Widespread, but present at low densities in boreal and mountain forests with mix of deciduous and coniferous trees. Mainly sedentary, but irruptive southward if prey numbers crash. **OBSERVATION TIPS** Hard to find because of unobtrusive habits and inclination to sit tight while roosting. Presence easiest to detect by call. Alternatively, befriend a birder who has installed nest boxes for the species.

NORTHERN HAWK-OWL

ADULT

NORTHERN SAW-WHET OWL

ADULT

ADULT

BOREAL OWL

Caprimulgidae

WHIP-POOR-WILL *Caprimulgus vociferus* L 9–10 in

Plump-bodied bird with relatively long wings and tail. Head is proportionately large and mouth and gape are huge, allowing flying
insects to be engulfed. Strictly nocturnal, feeding mainly on moths and beetles. Eyes are large, but typically hidden by partly closed eyelids in daylight.
Roosts unobtrusively in daytime, its beautifully patterned plumage providing
superb camouflage when resting on tree branch or among leaf litter on forest
floor. Sexes are separable with care. **ADULT MALE** Has gray-brown plumage
overall, but subtle and intricate patterns of black and buff create impression of
tree bark. Flight feathers and wing coverts are reddish brown. Note white half collar (sometimes hidden) separating blackish throat from dark brown chest band. Outer tail feathers are
extensively white toward tip. **ADULT FEMALE** Similar, but outer tail feathers are tipped buff (not extensively white). **JUVENILE** Similar to adult. **VOICE** Song (delivered after dark) in eastern population is a liquid *Whip-poo-weel*, the middle syllable slightly stuttering; that of southwestern population is lower
pitched, slower, and less onomatopoeic. Call of all birds is a liquid *quip*. **STATUS AND HABITAT** Common
summer visitor (mainly May–Sep), mostly in the east, to dry, typically mixed or deciduous forests with
clearings. Winters mainly in Central America, but also Florida. **OBSERVATION TIPS** Presence is easiest to
detect by listening for song. Roosting and nesting birds are hard to discover other than by chance. Territorial males will sometimes investigate observers after dark. **SIMILAR SPECIES Chuck-will's-widow**
C. carolinensis (L 12 in), a mainly eastern species whose range extends to Texas, Oklahoma, and Kansas,
is larger and more rufous overall, the reddish brown throat separated from the dark chest by a whitish half
collar. Plumage is patterned to resemble tree bark and tail is proportionately longer than that of Whip-
poor-will; female's tail is mostly reddish brown while male's has white inner webs to outer feathers.
Summer visitor, favoring mixed woodland. Song is *chuck-wee-whidow*.

CHUCK-WILL'S-WIDOW

ADULT

COMMON POORWILL
Phalaenoptilus nuttallii L 7.5–8.5 in

Western North America's smallest nightjar. Has a plump body, relatively short, rounded tail and wings, and proportionately large head. Mouth
and gape are huge, allowing bird to engulf flying nocturnal insects, such as
moths and beetles. In winter, metabolic rate slows down considerably and it
enters a torpid state akin to hibernation. Sexes are separable with care. **ADULT
MALE** Has grayish plumage overall, but close inspection reveals subtle and
intricate dark lines and bars, and rufous flush to wings and nape that create
superb cryptic pattern resembling tree bark. Dark chin and face are separated from
blackish chest band by white throat. Note dark crown and white tips to outer tail feathers. **ADULT FEMALE**
Similar, but tips to outer tail feathers are buff. **JUVENILE** Similar to adult. **VOICE** Song, uttered after dark,
is a liquid *poor-will* or *poor-weeup*. **STATUS AND HABITAT** Locally fairly common summer visitor (mainly
Apr–Sep) to north of range, birds wintering from southern U.S. to Mexico. Breeding birds from south of
range are probably mostly resident, or partial altitudinal migrants. Favors a range of dry habitats, but typically rocky ground with scrub and grass cover. **OBSERVATION TIPS** Presence is easiest to detect by
listening for song, after dark in spring. Sits tight when roosting and hard to spot in daytime.

FEMALE

WHIP-POOR-WILL

FEMALE

COMMON POORWILL

MALE

Caprimulgidae

COMMON NIGHTHAWK *Chordeiles minor* L 9–10 in

Our most widespread and familiar nighthawk. Feeds mostly after dark, using capacious mouth to capture flying insects, such as mosquitoes, moths, and beetles. However, not exclusively nocturnal and sometimes feeds in daylight, especially as dusk approaches. Often roosts or rests on tree branch or post. In flight, has a long-winged appearance (white wing patches are obvious), and note also the long, forked tail. Sexes are separable with care. **ADULT MALE** Has gray-brown plumage overall (birds from eastern North America are darker and browner). Upperparts are finely marked with fine black and whitish lines creating impression overall of tree bark; throat is white and underparts have dark brown barring on a pale background. White band across primaries is seen in resting birds and in flight (cf. Lesser Nighthawk). Tail has white subterminal band, only obvious in flight. **ADULT FEMALE** Similar, but throat patch is buff, not white, wing patch is less striking, and white tail band is typically absent. **JUVENILE** Similar to adult. **VOICE** Male's call is a slightly strangled, somewhat frog-like *we-ert* or *pe-ert*, uttered in flight. **STATUS AND HABITAT** Common summer visitor (mainly May–Sep) to much of the region, although range barely overlaps with that of Lesser, which favors more arid habitats. Common Nighthawk is associated with open areas such as forest clearings and cleared, disturbed ground, even towns and cities. Nests on bare ground, but in urban settings often uses flat-topped roofs. **OBSERVATION TIPS** As nighthawks and nightjars go, relatively easy to see because roosting birds often perch conspicuously, but also on account of species' part-diurnal feeding activity. Will sometimes hawk for insects around streetlights after dark. **SIMILAR SPECIES Common Pauraque** *Nyctidromus albicollis* (L 11–12 in) is a mainly tropical species (found throughout much of Central and South America), but with a small resident population in southern Texas. Plumage is gray-buff overall, but delicate and intricate patterning creates superb camouflage when resting among fallen leaves. Note extremely long tail that is round-tipped (not forked) and broad white band across primaries (broader than in nighthawks). Favors dry scrub and woodland and sometimes seen resting on roads after dark, detected by eyeshine.

COMMON NIGHTHAWK
MALE

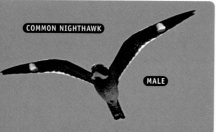
ADULT
COMMON PAURAQUE

LESSER NIGHTHAWK
Chordeiles acutipennis L 8–9.5 in

Recalls Common Nighthawk, but smaller and with relatively shorter wings and tail. Pale wing patch is relatively closer to wing tip than in Common. Also distinguished using voice. Plumage is more rufous overall; intricate patterning affords roosting bird superb camouflage on ground. More strictly nocturnal than Common Nighthawk and seldom seen in daylight, except when flushed by chance. Sexes are separable with care. **ADULT MALE** Has brown plumage overall, darkest on crown and palest and most finely marked on back and wing coverts. Primaries and secondaries are mainly dark, but with rows of buff spots and white band, the latter most obvious on underwing in flight. Tail is barred and appears square-ended or only slightly forked. Has white throat patch and underparts are otherwise buff with dark barring. **ADULT FEMALE** Similar, but throat and wing patches are buff. **JUVENILE** Similar to adult. **VOICE** Male's call is a trilling whistle. **STATUS AND HABITAT** Fairly common summer visitor (mainly Apr–Sep) to arid habitats in southwest. **OBSERVATION TIPS** Sometimes hawks insects around streetlights in desert towns.

MALE

COMMON
NIGHTHAWK

FEMALE

ADULT

FEMALE

LESSER NIGHTHAWK

MALE

MALE

Apopidae

VAUX'S SWIFT *Chaetura vauxi* L 4.75–5 in

Similar to Chimney Swift. Barely overlapping ranges aid species separation, but note subtle differences in plumage and flight pattern: Vaux's has paler underparts and rump and has speedier flight, with shorter glides between bouts of rapid wingbeats. Sexes are similar. **ADULT** Has mainly dark brown plumage, but contrastingly light brown on throat and chest, and on lower back and rump. **JUVENILE** Similar to adult. **VOICE** Utters chattering twitters. **STATUS AND HABITAT** Common summer visitor (mainly May–Sep), favoring mature forest with dead trees and branches that provide natural hollows for nesting. Nests in chimneys and often feeds over towns. Forms huge fall staging roosts in large chimneys in some Pacific Northwest cities. Winters mainly in South America, but small numbers linger on Californian coasts outside breeding season. **OBSERVATION TIPS** Easy to see within range in summer.

CHIMNEY SWIFT *Chaetura pelagica* L 5–5.5 in

Small swift with narrow, pointed wings and cigar-shaped body; fans tail when soaring and banking. Active flight is speedy, with frequent changes in direction and style; wingbeats are shallow and rapid. Catches flying insects on the wing. Sexes are similar, although males have slightly notched tail. **ADULT** Has dark brown plumage, palest on throat. Spinelike tips to tail feathers are only visible at close range. **JUVENILE** Similar to adult. **VOICE** Utters rapid, chattering twitters. **STATUS AND HABITAT** Common summer visitor (mainly May–Sep) to eastern North America, but range extends to Midwest, east of Rockies. Associated mostly with urban areas; nests in chimneys and cavities in tall buildings. **OBSERVATION TIPS** Easy to see within range in towns and cities, during summer months.

BLACK SWIFT *Cypseloides niger* L 7–7.5 in

Medium-sized, dark-looking swift with narrow, pointed wings. Rear body tapers; slightly forked tail looks square-ended when fanned. Catches insects on the wing and flight pattern varies from incredibly fast, with rapid maneuvers, to relatively slow and relaxed. Sexes are similar. **ADULT** Has mainly blackish plumage, but, seen from below, flight feathers are paler than rest of body. At very close range, white fringes to feathers on head and underparts may be noted. **JUVENILE** Similar, but pale feather margins are more striking on belly and undertail. **VOICE** Mostly silent, but chattering calls sometimes heard. **STATUS AND HABITAT** Local summer visitor (mainly May–Sep), favoring coastal and mountain cliffs, often in vicinity of waterfalls or damp gullies. **OBSERVATION TIPS** Visit suitable damp, shady cliff habitats within range to find this species.

WHITE-THROATED SWIFT
Aeronautes saxatalis L 6.25–6.5 in

Fast-flying swift with well-marked underparts. Wings are narrow and pointed, and forked tail is often held closed, adding to tapered appearance of rear body. Sexes are similar. **ADULT** Has mainly blackish upperparts. On underparts, note white throat extending as narrow line down center of chest to vent and white "thigh" patch, both framed by black on side of body; wing coverts are blackish and flight feathers mainly gray, except for white tips to tertials. **JUVENILE** Similar, but plumage is browner overall. **VOICE** Utters a rapid, chattering *je je je je je,* louder than Chimney and Vaux's Swifts. **STATUS AND HABITAT** Common near cliffs and canyons, increasingly in cities. Widespread in summer, restricted to southwest in winter. **OBSERVATION TIPS** Like other swifts, easiest to see well on drizzly days when insect prey is low in airspace.

VAUX'S SWIFT

ADULT

ADULT

CHIMNEY SWIFT

ADULT

BLACK SWIFT

ADULT

WHITE-THROATED SWIFT

ADULT

Trochilidae

CALLIOPE HUMMINGBIRD
Stellula calliope L 3–3.25 in

Adorable, tiny hummingbird; smallest of its kind in North America.
Body is dumpy, tail is short and square-ended, and needlelike bill is very

MALE

slightly downcurved. At rest, wings reach just beyond tip of tail. Sexes are dissimilar. **ADULT MALE** Has greenish upperparts and mainly whitish underparts with dull green spots on flanks and streaked throat "gorget"; in shade these look dark, but reveal pinkish purple iridescence at certain angles in direct sunlight. Note also, white eyering (thickest behind eye) and white stripe framing throat. **ADULT FEMALE** Has greenish upperparts; throat is gray-streaked and underparts are otherwise suffused buffy (in similar female Costa's, throat is less well marked and underparts are whitish). On fanned tail (seen when hovering), note white feather tips and black subterminal band. **JUVENILE** Similar to adult female; begins to acquire adult characteristics by first winter. **VOICE** Has a thin, whistling song, and call is a soft *chit*. **STATUS AND HABITAT** Locally common summer visitor (mainly Apr–Aug) to mountains, favoring meadows and forest clearings; winters in Mexico. **OBSERVATION TIPS** Regular visitor to feeders within breeding range; migrates mostly through the western mountains.

BROAD-TAILED HUMMINGBIRD
Selasphorus platycercus L 3.75–4 in

Tiny hummingbird with relatively long body; at rest, tail extends beyond wings. Bill is needlelike and almost straight. Beating wings of male create characteristic insectlike buzzing trill. Sexes are dissimilar. **ADULT MALE** Has metallic green upperparts. Underparts are mainly whitish, but with greenish patch on flanks; throat appears dark in most situations, but reveals rose-red iridescence at certain angles. Note also white eyering. **ADULT FEMALE** Has similarly green upperparts; throat is pale and gray-spotted and underparts are otherwise pale, suffused buff, mainly on flanks. On fanned tail note white feather tips, black subterminal band, and rufous bases to outer feathers. **JUVENILE** Similar to adult female; acquires adult characters in winter. **VOICE** Call is a metallic *chic*. **STATUS AND HABITAT** Common summer visitor to mountains, favoring meadows and open forest. Winters in Mexico. **OBSERVATION TIPS** Regular visitor to feeders.

RUBY-THROATED HUMMINGBIRD
Archilochus colubris L 3.5 in

Very similar to Black-chinned (*see* p.208), its southwestern counterpart, and separation is tricky: male's throat color is seen only occasionally and best features at rest are Ruby-throated's longer tail projection beyond wings and slightly tapering (not broad and blunt-ended) primary outline. Geographical range is best guideline for beginners. Needlelike bill is almost straight. Sexes are dissimilar. **ADULT MALE** Has metallic green upperparts. Throat usually appears black, but iridescent ruby gorget is seen at certain angles of direct sunlight. Underparts are whitish, with grubby green feathering on belly. Note white spot behind eye. **ADULT FEMALE** Has green upperparts and mainly whitish underparts, with fine gray streaks on throat and gray-green feathers on flanks. Fanned tail has white feather tips and black subterminal band. **JUVENILE** Similar to adult female. **VOICE** Call is a sharp *chip*. **STATUS AND HABITAT** Typical hummingbird in east, but summer range (mainly May–Aug) extends west, too. Favors gardens and open woodland. **OBSERVATION TIPS** Easy to see in summer range.

FEMALE

MALE

CALLIOPE HUMMINGBIRD

BROAD-TAILED HUMMINGBIRD

FEMALE

MALE

FEMALE

MALE

RUBY-THROATED HUMMINGBIRD

Trochilidae

BLACK-CHINNED HUMMINGBIRD
Archilochus alexandri L 3.75 in

Has a comparatively long bill by the standards of other similarly sized hummingbirds. Male is arguably the least colorful of North America's hummingbirds. Sexes are dissimilar. **ADULT MALE** Has metallic yellowish green upperparts. Hood usually appears uniformly dark, but in good light crown shows dark metallic green feathering while throat is sooty black; just occasionally, lower margin of throat catches the light and shines metallic violet. Underparts are pale, whitest on upper chest, and flushed with yellowish green feathering on flanks. Tail is uniformly dark. **ADULT FEMALE** Dull metallic yellowish green on upperparts except for cap, which is dull greenish gray. Underparts are grubby whitish and tail has striking white tips on outer two feathers (and small white tip to outer third). **JUVENILE** Similar to adult female; some immature males begin to acquire a darker crown and throat in fall. **VOICE** Utters a range of high-pitched squeaks and a soft *tchu* call. **STATUS AND HABITAT** Widespread and fairly common summer visitor to western U.S. Favors a wide range of habitats from well-vegetated desert areas, lower mountain slopes, orchards, and larger gardens. **OBSERVATION TIPS** Easiest to observe at feeders.

COSTA'S HUMMINGBIRD *Calypte costae* L 3.5 in

Males are stunningly attractive when true colors are revealed. Often indifferent to human observers, allowing superb views. Sexes are strikingly dissimilar. **ADULT MALE** Has a metallic greenish yellow back and nape. Cap, throat, and gorget usually appear dark (almost black in harsh light); once in a while, however,

FEMALE

feathers catch the light and sparkle metallic violet. Underparts are whitish, especially on breast, and flanks have greenish yellow feathering. **ADULT FEMALE** Has metallic greenish yellow upperparts. Underparts are whitish and clean looking. Tail has striking white tips on outer three feathers. **JUVENILE** Similar to adult female; immature male gradually acquires darker, iridescent feathers on throat and crown. **VOICE** Utters sharp, metallic call notes. **STATUS AND HABITAT** Fairly common summer visitor to southern Arizona and southern California; small numbers also winter in extreme south of its North American range. Favors vegetated desert areas and chaparral habitat. **OBSERVATION TIPS** Regular visitor to feeders within its range. In spring, males sometimes perch conspicuously, advertising territorial ownership and looking out for rivals.

ANNA'S HUMMINGBIRD *Calypte anna* L 4 in

Males are amazingly colorful when seen in the right light and are pugnacious when defending territory against rivals. Sexes are strikingly dissimilar. **ADULT MALE** Hood usually appears uniformly dark (almost black in harsh light), but when light catches it a metallic rose-red iridescence is revealed. **ADULT FEMALE** Has metallic greenish yellow upperparts. Underparts grayish white with yellowish green feathering on flanks and a few dark spots (iridescent in the right light) on throat. Tail has striking white tips on outer three feathers and a dark subterminal band. **IMMATURE** Similar to adult female; immature males gradually acquire adult's head coloration. **VOICE** Utters a sharp *tchik* call. **STATUS AND HABITAT** Common and widespread within its restricted west coast range. Resident year-round in many parts, especially in coastal districts, but often found at higher altitudes, and further inland, during breeding season than in winter. Favors deserts, scrub-covered slopes, urban parks, and gardens. **OBSERVATION TIPS** Easiest to observe at feeders throughout the year, and in city parks and ornamental gardens in winter.

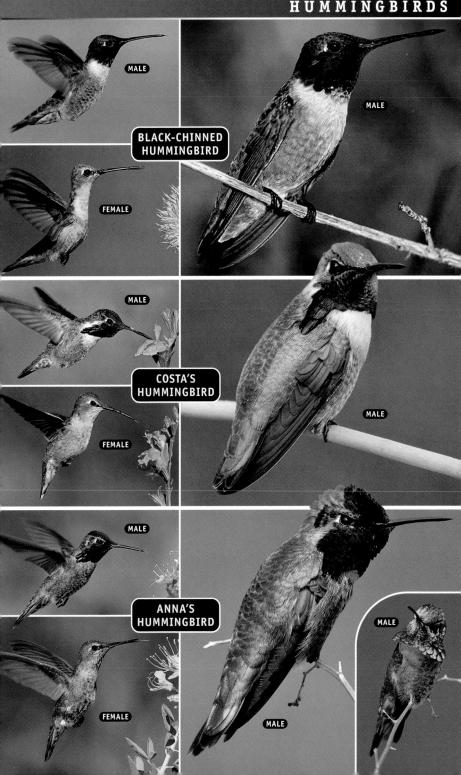

MALE

MALE

BLACK-CHINNED HUMMINGBIRD

FEMALE

MALE

MALE

COSTA'S HUMMINGBIRD

FEMALE

MALE

MALE

ANNA'S HUMMINGBIRD

MALE

FEMALE

MALE

Trochilidae

RUFOUS HUMMINGBIRD
Selasphorus rufus L 3.5–3.75 in
Colorful hummingbird. Extremely similar to Allen's, and separation
of juveniles and females is seldom possible in the field. Extremely well-
marked male Rufous (with rufous back) is more straightforward, but note
that many males have green backs, similar to male Allen's! Breeding range
(Mar–Jul) is a good guideline. Wings make a buzzing sound in direct flight.
Tail has pointed feather tips. Sexes are dissimilar. **ADULT MALE** Has main-

MALE

ly rufous upperparts, including
tail and tail coverts, but with
variable green feathering on back and green crown.
Underparts are flushed rufous, except for pale chest
band. Note shining orange-red gorget seen at certain
angles; in most light, throat looks dark. **ADULT
FEMALE** Has green upperparts and mainly pale underparts, with rufous on flanks and spots on throat
(central red spot seen at certain angles). Tail is mainly rufous with black band and white tips to outer feathers. **JUVENILE** Resembles adult female, but males soon
acquire adult characters. **VOICE** Call is a sharp *tik-tik*.
STATUS AND HABITAT Common breeding visitor (mainly Mar–Jul) to forest margins and clearings in northwest. Winters in Mexico. **OBSERVATION TIPS** Easy to see
within range. On migration, confusion possible with
Allen's; Rufous is most likely contender if encountered
east of California.

ALLEN'S HUMMINGBIRD *Selasphorus sasin* L 3.5–3.75 in
Hard to separate from Rufous in many plumages, although classic male is
distinctive. Breeding and winter ranges are useful guidelines in identification.
Tail has pointed feather tips. Sexes are dissimilar. **ADULT MALE** Has green crown
and back and rufous tail, tail coverts, and underparts, except for pale chest
band. Throat often looks dark, but iridescent red gorget may be seen at certain
angles in direct sunlight. **ADULT FEMALE** Has green upperparts and mainly pale
underparts, with rufous on flanks and spots on throat (central red spot seen at certain
angles). Tail is mainly rufous with black band and white tips to outer feathers. **JUVENILE**
Resembles adult female, but males soon acquire adult characters. **VOICE** Call is a sharp *tik-tik*. **STATUS
AND HABITAT** Common breeding visitor (mainly Feb–Jun) to coastal California, favoring chaparral, parks,
and meadows. Most winter in Mexico, but small resident population exists in southern California.
OBSERVATION TIPS Easy to see within range in spring, but beware confusion with migrant Rufous.
Any likely looking bird seen in southern California Nov–Jan is probably Allen's.

BROAD-BILLED HUMMINGBIRD
Cynanthus latirostris L 3.5–4in
Colorful hummingbird, males of which are particularly stunning. Sometimes
detected in dense foliage by hearing its chattering calls. Forked tail is often
obvious in perched birds. Sexes are dissimilar. **ADULT MALE** Has mainly metallic
green plumage with blue throat and clearly demarcated white undertail coverts. Bill
is long, mainly red, but dark-tipped. **ADULT FEMALE** Has greenish upperparts and dull
gray underparts; note the grayish supercilium behind the eye. **JUVENILE** Similar to adult
female. Male acquires adult characters in winter. **VOICE** Call is a chattering *chtt-chtt-chtt*. **STATUS AND
HABITAT** Mainly Mexican species that is a summer visitor (mainly Apr–Aug) to arid woodland in southeast Arizona; occasionally winters too. **OBSERVATION TIPS** Best looked for at garden feeding stations
within its range. Learn the call to improve your chances of observation.

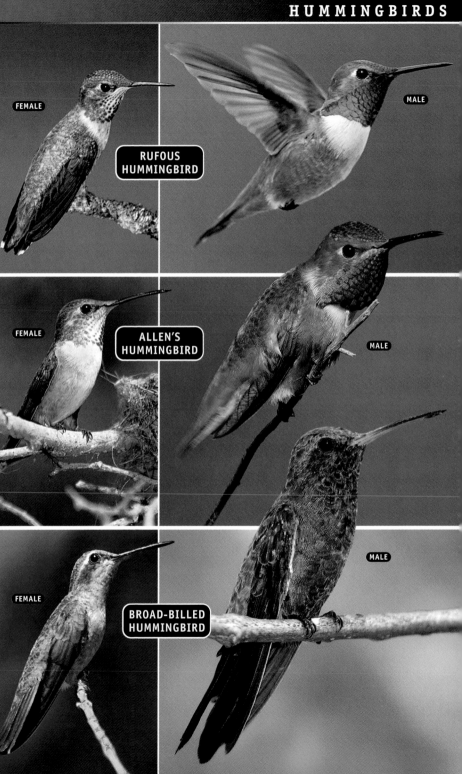

FEMALE

MALE

RUFOUS HUMMINGBIRD

FEMALE

MALE

ALLEN'S HUMMINGBIRD

MALE

FEMALE

BROAD-BILLED HUMMINGBIRD

Trochilidae

MAGNIFICENT HUMMINGBIRD
Eugenes fulgens L 5–5.25 in
In good light, males of this stunning hummingbird live up to their
name, but in harsh or dull light birds may look uniformly dark when seen from
below, making white vent and white spot behind eye appear obvious. Bill is
relatively long and tail is slightly forked. Sexes are dissimilar. **ADULT MALE**
Has green back, tail coverts, and tail. Head and underparts usually appear
blackish, but just occasionally iridescent violet crown and green gorget catch
the light, transforming appearance momentarily; these flashes are often so brief

MALE

that it is just a case of blinking and
you might miss it. **ADULT FEMALE** Has mainly green
upperparts with white tips and dark subterminal band on
outer feathers. Underparts are grayish overall, except for
pale vent, but streaked on the throat and mottled green
elsewhere. Note the dark stripe through the eye and white
spot behind it. **JUVENILE** Similar to adult female, but with
more extensive green marbling on underparts and more
obvious white malar stripe; soon begins to acquire adult
characters. **VOICE** Utters a sharp *chic*, in flight and while
perched. **STATUS AND HABITAT** Very locally common summer visitor (mainly Apr–Sep) to upland forests in southwest comprising pine and oak. Winters in Central America,
where populations are also resident. **OBSERVATION TIPS**
Visit known feeding stations in canyons of southeastern
Arizona or southwestern New Mexico to see this species.
Fortunately, it often perches in vicinity of feeders, allowing
prolonged (for a hummingbird) and good views.

BLUE-THROATED HUMMINGBIRD
Lampornis clemenciae L 5–5.4 in
A giant among North American hummingbirds and the largest of its kind in
North America. Plumage looks rather subdued overall in terms of color, but
just occasionally male is transformed when iridescent throat catches the light
at the right angle. Often seen at feeders alongside Magnificent when relatively
shorter bill is noticeable. When hovering, relatively long tail is often fanned and
looks rounded, and wingbeats are noticeably slower than with other, smaller hummingbirds. Sexes are dissimilar. **ADULT MALE** Has gray-green upperparts overall, darkest on tail (which

MALE

has white tips to outer feathers) and with paler, bronze
rump. Underparts appear gray for most of time, but stunning blue throat is revealed at certain angles. Note also
the white stripe behind the eye, and white malar stripe.
ADULT FEMALE Similar plumage overall, but gray throat
lacks male's iridescence. **JUVENILE** Similar to adult female,
but with buff fringes to many feathers; acquires adult
characters by winter. **VOICE** Utters a high-pitched *tseek*,
both in flight and when perched. **STATUS AND HABITAT**
Locally fairly common summer visitor (mainly May–Sep) to
a restricted area of southeastern Arizona, where it favors
shady wooded canyons comprising pine and oak; found in
similar locations to Elegant Trogon (*see* p.216) and Painted Redstart (*see* p.334). Winters in Central America.
OBSERVATION TIPS Views are typically brief when seen in
favored breeding habitat, but fortunately it frequently visits well-established canyon feeders and announces its
presence with sharp calls.

MALE

MAGNIFICENT
HUMMINGBIRD

FEMALE

MALE

MALE

FEMALE

MALE

BLUE-THROATED
HUMMINGBIRD

Alcedinidae

BELTED KINGFISHER *Ceryle alcyon* L 13–14 in

Powerfully built and magnificent waterside bird. This is the only widespread kingfisher in North America and the one that most birders will encounter. Feeds on fish, and all birds have a long, daggerlike dark gray bill with a pale base. Hovers, briefly and occasionally, but typically feeds by diving from perch overlooking water: dead branches and sometimes overhead power lines are favored. Alert to danger, and seldom tolerates close human approaches. Nests in riverbank burrows. Sexes are dissimilar. **ADULT MALE** Has blue-gray back, upper wings and tail, wings in particular adorned with small white spots.

JUVENILE

Head, which has shaggy crest, is also blue-gray (but note white spot in front of eye); separated from blue-gray breast band by broad white collar. Underparts are otherwise white. In flight, note contrast between the white coverts and dark flight feathers on the underwing, and white wing patch on the base of the outer flight feathers on upper wing. **ADULT FEMALE** Similar, but underparts are adorned with a prominent orange-red band on the belly; this extends along the flanks at the base of the wing, but is most obvious in flight. **JUVENILE** Similar to adult of respective sex, but with reddish mottling on otherwise blue breast band. **VOICE** Typical call is a distinctive, loud, harsh rattle. **STATUS AND HABITAT** Widespread and generally common in suitable habitats across southern half of North America; occurrence is more patchy further north. Extent to which migration occurs varies according to region; shift overall in numbers southward outside the breeding season throughout the region, but northern populations are entirely migratory summer visitors, moving south and to coasts for winter. Favors clear, fish-rich waters, typically rivers and lakes in summer, but also estuaries in winter. **OBSERVATION TIPS** Usually easy to find because it is tied to water and typically perches prominently. The rattling call often attracts attention.

RINGED KINGFISHER *Ceryle torquatus* L 16–17 in

A massive kingfisher and the largest of its kind in North America. Superficially similar to Belted, but larger size and reddish underparts enable easy recognition. Note also the proportionately massive, daggerlike bill with a yellow base and dark tip. Perches prominently, often on dead branches overhanging water, and dives for fish, which are carried back to perch to be eaten. Nests in riverbank burrows. Sexes are dissimilar. **ADULT MALE** Has blue back and upper wings, the latter marked with small white spots and dark streaks. Head is blue with a shaggy crest (and small white spot in front of eye); this is separated from back and reddish underparts by white collar. Tail is adorned with white spots above and below. **ADULT FEMALE** Similar, but note the broad blue breast band, separated from reddish underparts by a white chest band. **JUVENILE** Similar to respective adult, but female's chest band has some reddish feathering while male has hint of blue chest band. **VOICE** Utters a loud rattling call, lower pitched than that of Belted. **STATUS AND HABITAT** A mainly tropical species (widespread in South America), but with a foothold in southern Texas, mainly on the Rio Grande system. Local resident within its limited U.S. range and seldom wanders far from water. **OBSERVATION TIPS** Often perches prominently and so fairly easy to see if you visit the Lower Rio Grande.

MALE

FEMALE

BELTED KINGFISHER

MALE

RINGED KINGFISHER

FEMALE

GREEN KINGFISHER
Chloroceryle americana L 8.5–9 in

Distinctive and easily recognized bird: outline and habits clearly identify it as a kingfisher and relatively small size and coloration separate it from larger kingfisher species. All birds have a dark daggerlike bill and dive for fish, typically using branch or other perch over water as a lookout. Also catches insects and small lizards away from water. Flight is fast, direct, and usually low over water. When agitated, sometimes bobs body and pumps tail up and down. Sexes are dissimilar. **ADULT MALE** Has green back, wings, and upper tail; wings are adorned with white spots and outer tail feathers are white at base, white spotted toward tip and striking in flight. The head is mainly green and is separated from back and underparts by white collar. Has reddish orange chest band and otherwise white underparts with dark spots. From below, tail looks grayish with white spots. **ADULT FEMALE** Similar, but chest band is green, the

FEMALE

feathers having white margins and creating a mottled appearance. **JUVENILE** Similar to adult female, but many feathers are marked with buff. **VOICE** Utters an agitated, staccato series of *tchit-tchit-tchit-tcheirit* notes and a call resembling two stones being knocked together. **STATUS AND HABITAT** A mainly tropical species, widespread in Central and South America, whose range just extends into southern U.S., mainly southern Texas, but also very locally southern Arizona. Favors small streams and pools, but sometimes wanders away from water. As befits its smaller size, it favors smaller rivers and streams than Belted or Ringed kingfishers. **OBSERVATION TIPS** Easy to find and observe when perched on exposed dead branch. However, often sits unobtrusively in shady, dappled foliage in low waterside bushes when it is surprisingly hard to spot. Learn and listen for its distinctive calls.

ELEGANT TROGON *Trogon elegans* L 12–13 in

A stunning tropical species that provides birders visiting southern Arizona with a taste of the exotic. Appearance is so distinctive that it is almost unmis-

MALE

takable. However, it can be surprisingly hard to spot when sitting motionless in dappled foliage. Adopts an upright posture with tail hanging straight down when perched. Note proportionately large, rounded head and stout, curved yellow bill. Food, which is typically taken on the wing, includes flying insects and fruit plucked from branches. Nests in tree holes, typically those excavated by woodpeckers. Sexes are dissimilar. **ADULT MALE** Has a glossy green head, chest, and back. Wings are mainly blue-gray with white margins to flight feathers. White band separates chest from bright red underparts, including undertail coverts. From above, tail is coppery green, with a dark tip; from below it is gray with a black terminal band and otherwise pale feather tips. **ADULT FEMALE** Has green elements of male's plumage replaced by graybrown on head, chest, and upper back, and warmer brown on lower back and tail. Note striking white mark behind the eye. Diffuse white band borders chest and grades into buff belly; undertail coverts are red. **JUVENILE** Similar to adult female, but with bold pale spots on wings; undertail coverts are buffy. **VOICE** Call and song comprise various croaking *crrr* notes. **STATUS AND HABITAT** Fairly common within limited range in U.S. Restricted to streamside woodland where sycamores are common. **OBSERVATION TIPS** Reasonably easy to see, with patience, at Madera Canyon, Arizona.

FEMALE

MALE

GREEN KINGFISHER

FEMALE

MALE

ELEGANT TROGON

Picidae

NORTHERN FLICKER *Colaptes auratus* L 12–13 in

Familiar and well-marked medium-sized woodpecker. Variation exists in wing color and two forms are recognized and separated geographically, although hybrid intermediates occur in zone of overlap. So-called "Red-shafted" Flicker has reddish pink flight feather shafts and flush of same color on underwing coverts. In "Yellow-shafted," wing color is yellow. Excavates tree nest holes, and feeds on wood-boring insects and sometimes feeds on ground. Sexes are dissimilar. **ADULT MALE** Has golden brown back and upper wing coverts, both with black barring; rump is white and tail is black. Head is grayish overall with buffy forecrown in "Red-shafted", which has red malar stripe; "Yellow-shafted" has more extensive buff on face, black malar stripe and red nape patch. Note striking black crescent on chest, and dark-spotted whitish underparts. **ADULT FEMALE** Similar, but head lacks malar stripe; "Yellow-shafted" has red nape patch. **JUVENILE** Similar to respective sex adult. **VOICE** Utters a rapid, raptorlike *kew-kew-kew....* **STATUS AND HABITAT** Common in all kinds of wooded habitats. "Red-shafted" is widespread in west, while "Yellow-shafted" occurs east of Rocky Mountains, and across taiga. Northern populations of both forms are migratory, heading south in fall. **OBSERVATION TIPS** Easy to see. Presence often detected by rapid drumming.

FEMALE

GILDED FLICKER
Colaptes chrysoides
L 11–11.5 in

Desert counterpart of Northern Flicker (closest in appearance to "Yellow-shafted"), but paler overall, marginally smaller, and with subtle plumage differences. Sexes are dissimilar. **ADULT MALE** Has pale golden buff back and upper wing coverts, marked with narrow dark barring; rump is white and tail is black. Head is mainly gray, but with buffy brown crown and nape and with red malar stripe. Black chest patch is half-moon (not crescent-) shaped and whitish underparts are marked with black spots that grade to bars on undertail coverts. **ADULT FEMALE** Similar, but face lacks a malar stripe. **JUVENILE** Similar to respective sex adult. **VOICE** Utters a rapid, raptorlike *kew-kew-kew...*, almost identical to Northern Flicker. **STATUS AND HABITAT** Very locally common resident of arid woodland and saguaro cactus "forests" in southwest (mainly Arizona). **OBSERVATION TIPS** Easy to see in desert areas with large saguaro cacti.

FEMALE

GILA WOODPECKER
Melanerpes uropygialis L 9–9.5 in

Desert woodpecker whose range overlaps with that of larger Gilded Flicker. In flight, easily separated from Gilded by barred, not white, rump. Typically nests in holes excavated in saguaro cacti. Sexes are dissimilar. **ADULT MALE** Has striking black and white barring on back, much of upper-wing and upper-tail coverts. Head and underparts are mostly fairly uniform warm gray-buff, but note small, yet striking red crown. **ADULT FEMALE** Similar, but head lacks red crown. **JUVENILE** Similar to adult female. **VOICE** Utters a raucous *yeet-yeet-yeleet...* (vaguely reminiscent of distant gulls calling) and a rolling *churr* call. **STATUS AND HABITAT** Reasonably common in suitable desert habitats within its limited range, which extends from extreme southeastern California and southern Arizona, south through western Mexico. Favors desert woodlands where large saguaro cacti dominate. **OBSERVATION TIPS** Easy to see in suitable habitats in southern Arizona.

FEMALE YELLOW-SHAFTED

MALE

MALE YELLOW-SHAFTED

GILDED FLICKER

GILA WOODPECKER

NORTHERN FLICKER

FEMALE YELLOW-SHAFTED

FEMALE RED-SHAFTED

MALE RED-SHAFTED

MALE

FEMALE

GOLDEN-FRONTED WOODPECKER
Melanerpes aurifrons L 9 in

Well-marked woodpecker, with bold black and white barring on back and upper wings, white rump and golden yellow nape. Feeds on insects, seeds, and fruits, and will visit feeders. Nests in holes excavated in trees such as pecan. Drums loudly. Sexes are dissimilar. **ADULT MALE** Has grayish white underparts that show off dark eye and contrast with dark tail. Note the red crown and yellow above base of upper mandible. **ADULT FEMALE** Similar, but crown is gray, shows yellow on nape and feathers above base of bill are paler. **JUVENILE** Similar to respective sex adult, but yellow elements of plumage are absent. **VOICE** Calls include agitated, churring chatters and sharp series of *kek-kek-kek*... notes. **STATUS AND HABITAT** A mainly Central American species whose range extends to Texas and southern Oklahoma, where it is resident and locally common. Favors a wide range of wooded habitats. **OBSERVATION TIPS** Easy to see in Lower Rio Grande Valley.

RED-BELLIED WOODPECKER
Melanerpes carolinus L 9–9.5 in

Similar to Golden-fronted, except yellow elements of plumage on head are replaced by red, central tail feathers are barred (not black), and has red flush on belly. Drums loudly. Sexes are dissimilar. **ADULT MALE** Has finely barred black and white back and upper wings, white rump and mainly pale grayish white underparts with dark chevrons on flanks. Crown and nape are red. **ADULT FEMALE** Similar, but crown is grayish white (not red); red on loral and supraloral area typically less intense. **JUVENILE** Resembles adult, but nape is pale grayish orange. **VOICE** Utters a soft, almost disyllabic, but actually slurred, *chu-urrr, chu-urr, chu-urr*.... **STATUS AND HABITAT** Common in eastern North America, but range extends to Midwest. Found in a wide range of wooded habitats. Mainly resident, but some movements among northern birds occur in response to harsh winter weather. **OBSERVATION TIPS** Easy to see within range, and sometimes visits feeders in winter.

FEMALE

RED-HEADED WOODPECKER
Melanerpes erythrocephalus L 9–9.5 in

Extremely well-marked and distinctive woodpecker, recognized in flight from above by white rump and wing patches that contrast with otherwise black upper wings and tail. White on underwing is also striking in flight. Nests unobtrusively in excavated holes, mainly in dead trees. Drumming is rapid. Feeds on insects, seeds, and fruits, typically in trees, but will also feed on ground and "fly-catch" on the wing. Sexes are similar. **ADULT** Has mainly black back, tail, and upper wings, with white patch on tertials and rump. Head and neck are bright red and are separated from white underparts by narrow black border. Has a dark eye and rather pale gray and darker-tipped bill. **JUVENILE** Has red and black elements of adult's plumage replaced by brown. Underparts are whitish with dark streaks and pale tertials have brown barring. **VOICE** Call is a harsh *quee-erk*. **STATUS AND HABITAT** Common, mainly a resident species in eastern North America, but its range also extends west, across Great Plains, where it is a summer visitor. Favors a range of lightly wooded habitats, including orchards. **OBSERVATION TIPS** Easy to recognize in flight, but can be surprisingly hard to find when feeding unobtrusively. Sometimes visits feeders in winter.

GOLDEN-FRONTED
WOODPECKER

MALE

RED-BELLIED
WOODPECKER

MALE

JUVENILE

JUVENILE

RED-HEADED
WOODPECKER

ADULT

Picidae

ACORN WOODPECKER
Melanerpes formicivorus L 9–9.5 in
Boldly marked woodpecker, easily recognized by combination of striking white iris and red on the crown. Renowned and named for its acorn larders, neatly wedged in holes drilled in tree trunks. Often lives communally, with nonbreeding "helpers" aiding nest duties. Aerial sorties often employed to catch flying insects. Sexes are dissimilar. **ADULT MALE** Has mainly black upperparts, but note striking white lower back and rump. Underparts are mainly white, but with black chest and dark streaking on flanks. Head pattern comprises black at base of bill, and from eye surround to nape, red crown and white forehead, cheeks, and throat. In flight, note white patch at base of primaries. **ADULT FEMALE** Similar, but crown is black at front and red at rear. **JUVENILE** Similar, but has darker eye and entirely red crown in both sexes. **VOICE** Utters a screeching *wee-er, wee-er...* or a chattering *waka-waka-waka*. **STATUS AND HABITAT** Common resident in oak and oak-pine woodland. **OBSERVATION TIPS** Usually easy to find.

LEWIS'S WOODPECKER *Melanerpes lewis* L 10 in
A distinctive and easily recognized woodpecker. Feeds on nuts, seeds, and wood-boring insects, but also catches flying insects in aerial sorties, when flight looks relatively slow and controlled. Sexes are similar. **ADULT** Can look rather dark in dull light, but, seen well, upperparts, including upper tail, are mostly dark glossy green. Chest is pale gray and this extends as a narrow collar around neck; collar is striking in flight, particularly when seen from above. Breast and belly are pink while vent and undertail are dark. Face is deep red with dark surround on crown, nape, and throat. **JUVENILE** Resembles an extremely dull adult with rather scaly-looking underparts. **VOICE** Utters a range of agitated and rapid chattering calls. **STATUS AND HABITAT** Locally fairly common summer visitor (mainly Jun–Aug) to a range of forested habitats, including ponderosa pine woodland and pine-oak forests. In winter, also found in more dry, open woods with grassland and nomadic to a degree if food is in short supply. **OBSERVATION TIPS** Often perches in the open, on dead branch, making observation easy.

FEMALE

WILLIAMSON'S SAPSUCKER
Sphyrapicus thyroideus
L 9 in
Upland woodpecker, males of which are strikingly marked. Feeds on sap and insects. In flight, which is undulating, all birds look rather long-winged and show bold white rump. In other respects sexes are extremely dissimilar. **ADULT MALE** Has mainly black plumage overall, but note white stripe behind eye, white mustachial stripe and broad white bar on wing (seen as broad white patch in flight). Note red throat and yellow belly. **ADULT FEMALE** Has finely barred black and white back, wings, and tail. Head is brown, breast is black, and underparts are otherwise mostly yellowish, but barred on flanks and undertail. **JUVENILE** Similar to respective sex adult, but duller overall. **VOICE** Utters a raspy, trilling *que-e-e-e-rr*. Drums in short bursts. **STATUS AND HABITAT** Summer visitor (mainly Apr–Sep) to dry, open conifer forest (notably ponderosa pine) in mountains. Winters in similar habitat, and pine-oak woodland, from southwestern U.S. to Mexico. **OBSERVATION TIPS** Fairly easy to see in suitable habitats, but thinly scattered and seldom particularly common.

MALE

FEMALE

ACORN
WOODPECKER

ADULT

JUVENILE

LEWIS'S
WOODPECKER

MALE

WILLIAMSON'S
SAPSUCKER

Picidae

RED-NAPED SAPSUCKER
Sphyrapicus nuchalis L 8 in
Colorful and boldly marked woodpecker. Extremely similar to Yellow-bellied and best separated by studying head markings: has red (not white or black) nape, and red on throat in female (all-white in female Yellow-bellied). Simple, pragmatic approach for species separation is to use geographically distinct ranges. Sexes are separable with care. **ADULT MALE** Has mainly black and white body plumage with barring on back, wings, and tail, and white patch on wings; breast is black and underparts are otherwise grubby pale yellow with streaks and bars on flanks. Head is marked with red throat, nape, and crown, white stripe running below eye and curving around to breast, and white stripe behind eye. **ADULT FEMALE** Similar, but has white on chin and black ear coverts. **JUVENILE** Has barred brownish plumage overall, but with adult's bold, white wing patch. **VOICE** Utters a harsh, mewing *quee-err*, identical to that of Yellow-bellied. **STATUS AND HABITAT** Fairly common summer visitor (mainly Apr–Aug) to mixed montane forests in Rocky Mountains, favoring aspen groves. Winters in conifer forests in southwestern U.S. and Mexico. **OBSERVATION TIPS** Presence often easiest to detect by listening for call.

YELLOW-BELLIED SAPSUCKER
Sphyrapicus varius L 8–9 in
Northern and western counterpart of Red-naped. Feeds on sap (obtained by drilling holes) and insects. Sexes are separable with care. **ADULT MALE** Has mainly black and white body plumage, but note barring (more extensive than on Red-naped) on back, wings, and tail, and white patch on wings; breast is black and underparts are otherwise grubby pale yellow with streaks and bars on flanks. Head is well marked by a red throat (which is bordered black) and crown, white stripe running below eye and curving around to breast, and white stripe behind eye. **ADULT FEMALE** Similar, but throat is white. **JUVENILE** Has barred brownish plumage overall, but with adult's bold, white wing patch. **VOICE** Utters a harsh, mewing *quee-err*. **STATUS AND HABITAT** Common summer visitor (mainly May–Aug) to mixed and deciduous boreal forests. Winters in similar habitats in southeastern U.S. and Mexico. **OBSERVATION TIPS** Easy to see within range.

RED-BREASTED SAPSUCKER
Sphyrapicus ruber L 8–9 in
Colorful and distinctive woodpecker. Classic form is easy to identify, but hybrids with Red-naped and Yellow-bellied, in zones of species overlap,

ADULT, ssp. *ruber*

can be confusing. Sexes are similar. **ADULT** Has bright red head, neck, and breast, with white "mustache" at base of bill; this is longer in ssp. *daggetti* than ssp. *ruber*. Back is mainly black, but with pale barring on wings and back and large white wing patch. Underparts are yellow with dark streaks and chevrons on flanks. **JUVENILE** Has black and red elements of adult's plumage replaced by brown barring. **VOICE** Utters a rapid, dry, rasping rattle. Common call a squealed *quee-err*. **STATUS AND HABITAT** Fairly common in damp, mixed and coniferous forest; southern ssp. *daggetti* occurs at higher altitude than ssp. *ruber*. Mainly resident, but northern and high altitude birds move south or to lower elevations in winter. **OBSERVATION TIPS** Easy to see in suitable habitats.

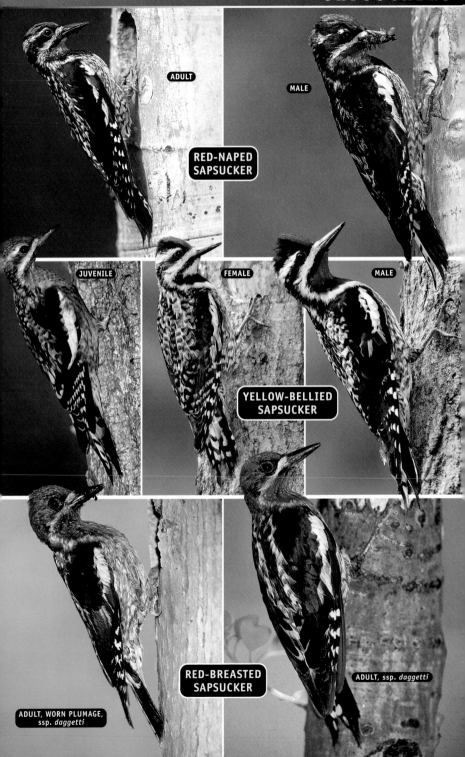

RED-NAPED
SAPSUCKER

ADULT

MALE

YELLOW-BELLIED
SAPSUCKER

JUVENILE

FEMALE

MALE

RED-BREASTED
SAPSUCKER

ADULT, WORN PLUMAGE,
ssp. *daggetti*

ADULT, ssp. *daggetti*

DOWNY WOODPECKER
Picoides pubescens L 6–7 in

Dainty woodpecker, the smallest of its kind in North America. As befits its size, often feeds on slender branches, males more so than females. Excavates cavities in trees for nesting. Sexes are separable with care. **ADULT MALE** Has mainly black upperparts, but with white spots and barring on wings, white stripe on back, and barred white outer tail feathers (birds from Pacific Northwest are tinged pale brownish). Head has black cap, ear coverts, mustache, and lower nape, with red patch on upper nape. Underparts and rest of head are otherwise white. **ADULT FEMALE** Similar, but nape is entirely black. **JUVENILE** Similar to adult female, but with dull red patch on crown. **VOICE** Utters an agitated, chattering *ki-ki-ki-ki* and a sharp *pic*. Drumming is rapid, but slower than that of Hairy. **STATUS AND HABITAT** Generally common and widespread resident of deciduous woodland, parks, and gardens, and to lesser extent of coniferous forest. **OBSERVATION TIPS** Typically indifferent to human observers, but unobtrusive and rather easy to overlook. Often visits feeders, when it is easy to observe.

HAIRY WOODPECKER *Picoides villosus* L 9–10 in

Similar to Downy, but appreciably larger. Our most widespread woodpecker. Variation exists in size and markings across North America, with many geographically distinct subspecies. Northern birds tend to be largest, with cleaner-looking white areas. Sexes are separable with care. **ADULT MALE** Has mainly black upperparts with a white back, and varying amounts of white barring and spots on wing depending on subspecies (birds from Pacific Northwest and Rockies have least amount of white on wings, while Alaskan birds have most). Head has black crown, ear coverts, mustache (linked to black shoulders), and lower nape; upper nape is red. Underparts and rest of face are whitish, grubbiest in Pacific Northwest birds and cleanest looking in birds from Alaska and Rockies. **ADULT FEMALE** Similar to respective subspecies male, but nape is entirely black. **JUVENILE** Similar to adult female, but crown has reddish patch. **VOICE** Utters a rasping *cheek* and a rattling whinny. Drumming is rapid. **STATUS AND HABITAT** Widespread and fairly common resident of all types of deciduous and coniferous woodland, as well as wooded parks and gardens. **OBSERVATION TIPS** Easy to see in suitable habitats.

WHITE-HEADED WOODPECKER *Picoides albolarvatus* L 9–9.5 in

Unmistakable woodpecker, with a largely white face and otherwise mainly black plumage. In flight, note the white patch at the base of the primaries and the proportionately long tail. Feeds on pine seeds, extracted from cones, and by probing for insects under bark and among needles. Nests in natural tree cavities and excavates fresh nest sites. Sexes are separable with care. **ADULT MALE** Has white head, red on rear of crown, and otherwise mainly black plumage, including nape. Note the white patch at base of primaries. **ADULT FEMALE** Similar, but rear of crown is black, not red. **JUVENILE** Similar, but pale red wash on crown. **VOICE** Utters a rapid, staccato *tik-er-tik*. **STATUS AND HABITAT** Local resident, restricted by precise habitat requirements and threatened by modern forestry. Needs undisturbed mature montane pine forest comprising several species and of mixed age so that feeding and nesting requirements are met; standing dead and dying trees provide suitable nest sites. **OBSERVATION TIPS** Reasonably easy to find in remaining suitable habitat in California and Oregon.

DOWNY
WOODPECKER

MALE

FEMALE

FEMALE

HAIRY
WOODPECKER

MALE

MALE

FEMALE

JUVENILE

WHITE-HEADED
WOODPECKER

MALE

Picidae

AMERICAN THREE-TOED WOODPECKER
Picoides dorsalis L 8–9 in

Medium-sized woodpecker with three toes—two forward-pointing, one pointing backward (apart from Black-backed, all other North American woodpeckers have four toes). Unobtrusive and easily overlooked. Feeds mainly on wood-boring beetles, located by drilling and bark-stripping. Northern subspecies *fasciatus* is described, unless otherwise stated. Sexes are separable with care. **ADULT MALE** Has mostly black upperparts with white barring on center of back, and subtle barring on flight feathers and outer tail feathers. Face is mainly black, but with yellow crown and white stripe behind eye (links to back) and white facial stripe. Throat and underparts are white, with dark barring on flanks. Rocky Mountain subspecies *dorsalis* is similar, but center of back is pure white. **ADULT FEMALE** Similar, but crown is speckled white (not yellow). **JUVENILE** Similar to adult female, but has some dull yellow on crown. **VOICE** Utters a sharp *wik* or *pik*. **STATUS AND HABITAT** Widespread, but scarce in old growth pine and spruce forest. Mostly resident, but partly nomadic outside breeding season in search of food; visits burned woodland with standing dead trees. **OBSERVATION TIPS** Listen for its call or look for fallen bark at base of tree.

BLACK-BACKED WOODPECKER
Picoides arcticus L 9–10 in

Similar to American Three-toed Woodpecker. Separable using plumage details and (with practice) call, although not especially vocal. Drumming is loud and far-carrying. Feeds mainly on wood-boring beetles, by drilling and bark-stripping. Sexes are separable with care. **ADULT MALE** Has mostly black upperparts, including tail, but note subtle pale barring on flight feathers. Head has yellow crown and bold white facial stripe. Throat and underparts are white, apart from dark barring on flanks. **ADULT FEMALE** Similar, but crown is black. **JUVENILE** Similar to respective sex adult, although duller, and female has a few yellow crown feathers. **VOICE** Utters a chattering *chik* call, sharper than that of American Three-toed. **STATUS AND HABITAT** Widespread, but never common, favoring old growth pine and spruce forests, but also visiting burned areas with standing trees to feed. **OBSERVATION TIPS** Unobtrusive and easily overlooked. Presence sometimes detected by drumming or discovery of stripped, fallen bark at base of tree.

LADDER-BACKED WOODPECKER
Picoides scalaris L 7–7.5 in

Well-marked, mainly black and white desert woodpecker. Similar to Nuttall's (*see* p.230), but ranges and habitats barely overlap, and separable on plumage details. Feeds on boring insects and cactus fruits. Excavates nest holes in trees and large cacti. Sexes are dissimilar. **ADULT MALE** Has barred black and white pattern on back and wings, and white barring on outer feathers of otherwise black tail. Head has red crown and nape, and black line around ear coverts on otherwise white face. Underparts are off-white, but with neat black spots on breast and bars on flanks. **ADULT FEMALE** Similar, but crown is black; nasal tufts are almost white. **JUVENILE** Resembles adult male. **VOICE** Utters a harsh, chattering call and a sharp *pik*. **STATUS AND HABITAT** Mainly Mexican species, but with an extensive resident range in southwestern U.S. Common in desert woodland. **OBSERVATION TIPS** Easy to see in suitable habitats.

AMERICAN
THREE-TOED
WOODPECKER

FEMALE

MALE

FEMALE

MALE

BLACK-BACKED
WOODPECKER

LADDER-BACKED
WOODPECKER

MALE

FEMALE

MALE

Picidae

NUTTALL'S WOODPECKER
Picoides nuttallii L 7–7.5 in

A California specialty. Similar to Ladder-backed (*see* p.228), but separable by differences in plumage, habitat preference, and range. Unobtrusive, and presence often first detected by calls. Sexes are dissimilar. **ADULT MALE** Has mainly black upperparts, including upper tail, but with neat white barring on back, wings, and outer tail feathers. Face is mainly black, but with broad, white stripe surrounding ear coverts and white nasal "tufts" and facial stripe; rear crown is red (red on crown is more extensive in male Ladder-backed). Throat and underparts are mostly white, but with neat black spots on flanks and black barring on flanks. **ADULT FEMALE** Similar, but crown is black. Nasal tufts are white (grubby in female Ladder-backed). **JUVENILE** Recalls adult male, but red on crown is more extensive. **VOICE** Calls include a sharp, upslurred *k'wik-k'wik*... and a trilling rattle. **STATUS AND HABITAT** Locally common resident of oak-dominated chaparral and woodland, often in vicinity of streams and rivers. World Population almost entirely restricted to California. **OBSERVATION TIPS** Easiest to locate by visiting suitable habitat and listening for call.

FEMALE

ARIZONA WOODPECKER
Picoides arizonae L 7–7.5 in

Distinctive and unique among North American *Picoides* woodpeckers in having a brown (not black) back. Excavates holes in dead branches for nesting and strips bark in search of insects. Rather shy. Sexes are separable with care. **ADULT MALE** Has mostly unmarked brown upperparts, but with subtle whitish barring on wings and outer tail feathers. Upper nape is red, but rest of nape and crown are dark brown. Dark ear coverts are surrounded by broad white stripe that links to white nasal "tufts" and are bordered below by black stripe. Throat and underparts are white with neat black spots. **ADULT FEMALE** Similar, but nape is uniformly brown. **JUVENILE** Similar to adult female, but with red crown. **VOICE** Utters a grating rattle and a sharp *pik*. **STATUS AND HABITAT** A mainly Mexican species that is a locally common resident of dry woodlands (usually pine/oak mixtures) on mountain slopes, mostly in southeastern Arizona. **OBSERVATION TIPS** Wary nature means it is hard to see well.

PILEATED WOODPECKER
Dryocopus pileatus L 16–17 in

Huge woodpecker, the largest in North America. Unmistakable with its mainly black plumage and white and red head markings. Bill is large, dark, and chisel-like. Feeds mainly on carpenter ants and beetle larvae excavated from timber (fallen and standing) via typically rectangular holes. Drumming is loud and far-carrying. Sexes are separable with care. **ADULT MALE** Has mainly black body plumage, except for small white patch at base of primaries on closed wing. In flight, patch is more obvious, and white underwing coverts are striking. Angular-looking head has white throat and white stripes behind eye and extending from base of bill down side of neck. Tufted crown is red; note red malar stripe and pale eye. **ADULT FEMALE** Similar, but only rear of crown is red and malar stripe is black. **JUVENILE** Resembles relevant sex adult, but has brownish eyes. **VOICE** Utters a harsh, agitated *ke-ke-ki-ki-ki*.... **STATUS AND HABITAT** Fairly common forest resident. Does best in undisturbed, old growth forest, but tolerates younger woodland if a few large trees are present for nesting. **OBSERVATION TIPS** Easy to find in suitable habitats.

FEMALE

MALE

NUTTALL'S WOODPECKER

MALE

ARIZONA WOODPECKER

PILEATED WOODPECKER

FEMALE

MALE

FEMALE

Tyrannidae

WESTERN KINGBIRD
Tyrannus verticalis L 8–9.5 in

The most widespread kingbird in the west. Typically perches on wires or dead branches and engages in flycatching sorties, repeatedly catching insects in flight and typically returning to the same perch. Male's tumbling aerial courtship display is interesting to watch. Sexes are similar. **ADULT** Has mainly pale gray head (darkest through eye and palest on cheek) and pale olive-gray back. Orange central crown patch is mostly concealed and seldom visible. Wings are dark, but with pale feather margins, and tail is mainly dark, but with pale margin to outer feathers. Chest is pale gray and underparts, including underwing coverts, are otherwise pale lemon yellow. **JUVENILE** Similar, but paler overall. **VOICE** Calls include a sharp *chip* and an agitated-sounding chatter; song comprises a series of *chip* notes. **STATUS AND HABITAT** Widespread and common summer visitor (mainly Apr–Aug) to farmland and a variety of mostly open-country habitats. Winters mainly in Central America. **OBSERVATION TIPS** Often perches in the open and easy to find beside roads through agricultural land.

ADULT

COUCH'S KINGBIRD

ADULT

TROPICAL KINGBIRD
Tyrannus melancholicus
L 9–9.5 in

Recalls Western, but separable with care: note in particular the stouter, longer bill, shorter wings, greenish yellow (not gray) breast, and forked (not straight-ended) tail. Sexes are similar. **ADULT** Has a darker gray head than Western, with a whitish throat and dark mask. Back is greenish, while wings and tail are brown with pale feather margins. Breast is greenish yellow and grades into bright yellow underparts; underwing coverts are also bright yellow. **JUVENILE** Similar, but wing feather margins are buffy. **VOICE** Utters a rapid chirruping trill. **STATUS AND HABITAT** A mainly tropical species, but a local summer visitor (mainly Apr–Aug) to open woodland in southern Arizona and scarce resident in Texas's Lower Rio Grande Valley. **OBSERVATION TIPS** Sometimes perches on roadside wires. **SIMILAR SPECIES Couch's Kingbird** *T. couchii* (L 8–9.5 in) is probably best separated by call, a rolling, slurred *pu-weeeer*; song is a series of twittering phrases including *tewit-tewit-tewichurr*. Adult has a gray head, dark mask, whitish throat, and greenish gray back. Wings are brown with pale fringes (buff in juvenile) and tail is forked. Greenish yellow chest grades into bright yellow underparts. Summer visitor and local resident in southern Texas, favoring woodland margins.

CASSIN'S KINGBIRD *Tyrannus vociferans* L 8.5–9 in

Well-marked kingbird. Told from similar Western (the only other widespread and common gray and yellow kingbird in west) by darker plumage overall, greater contrast between colors, different call and habitat preferences. Sexes are similar. **ADULT** Has dark gray head, back, and chest, with striking white malar patch below blackish lores. Orange-red crown patch is mostly concealed and seldom visible. Wings are brown with pale feather margins, and straight-tipped tail is dark brown, but with (often indistinct) pale terminal margin. Underparts are bright yellow, with a distinct demarcation from gray breast. **JUVENILE** Similar, but with buffy margins to wing feathers and less distinct pale tip to tail. **VOICE** Call is a sharp, strident *che-Beer*; song is a series of *chrr-chrr-chrr...* notes. **STATUS AND HABITAT** Locally common summer visitor (mainly Apr–Aug) to open woodland. Most birds winter in Mexico, but small numbers are found in southern California. **OBSERVATION TIPS** Reasonably easy to see in suitable habitats within range; often perches high in tree.

WESTERN KINGBIRD

ADULT

ADULT

TROPICAL KINGBIRD

CASSIN'S KINGBIRD

ADULT

ADULT

Tyrannidae

EASTERN KINGBIRD *Tyrannus tyrannus* L 8–9 in

Widespread and familiar kingbird, with essentially black and white plumage. Typically perches conspicuously, sometimes on roadside wires, and often indifferent to human observers. Reddish orange concealed crown stripe is seldom revealed. Feeds mainly by making aerial sorties after insects from an exposed perch. Sexes are similar. **ADULT** Has neatly defined black hood grading to dark gray back and dark wings, the latter having whitish feather margins. Tail is black with white terminal band. Underparts, including throat, are mostly white, but note subtle pale gray wash on chest. Feet and bill are dark. **JUVENILE** Similar, but cap, back, and wings are tinged brownish. **VOICE** Utters a metallic, rasping *k'dzee-k'dzee...*, sometimes more rapid and accelerating. **STATUS AND HABITAT** Common and widespread summer visitor across much of temperate North America east of Rockies. Favors a variety of open habitats and present mainly May–Aug. Winters in South America, mainly Amazonia. **OBSERVATION TIPS** Generally easy to find.

ADULT

SCISSOR-TAILED FLYCATCHER
Tyrannus forficatus
L 10–15 in

Striking flycatcher. Adults in particular are unmistakable with their long tails. Juveniles are shorter-tailed and could possibly be confused with other kingbirds; note, however, the relatively long, deeply forked tail and pale plumage overall. All birds feed on insects, typically caught in aerial sorties; often perches on overhead wires. Adult males perform spectacular courtship displays in flight. Sexes are similar, but male's tail streamers are longer than female's. **ADULT** Has very pale gray (nearly white) head, pale gray back, and breast. Wings are blackish with white feather margins and tail is deeply forked, the outer feather long and streamerlike. Underparts are whitish, but flushed pinkish orange on belly, undertail, and underwing coverts; note the deep red axillaries ("armpits"). **JUVENILE** Much paler than adult with only faint pinkish flush on underparts. Although tail is relatively long, outer feathers are not so long and streamerlike. **VOICE** Utters a sharp *wip* or more chattering *wip-k'prrr*. **STATUS AND HABITAT** Locally common summer visitor (mainly Apr–Aug) to Texas, Oklahoma, and adjacent states. Favors open country and farmland. Winters mainly in Central America. **OBSERVATION TIPS** Easy to see and tolerant of people.

GREAT KISKADEE *Pitangus sulphuratus* L 9.5–10 in

Colorful and exotic-looking Texas specialty. Has a proportionately bulky body and large head with a relatively long, powerful bill. Usually perches conspicuously and announces its presence with its onomatopoeic call. Feeds mainly on large insects; flying prey is caught on the wing, but occasionally drops on a variety of terrestrial prey in a shrikelike manner. Sexes are similar. **ADULT** Has a strikingly marked head with black stripe through eye and broad white supercilium bordering the black crown, which has a partially concealed orange-yellow central patch usually partly hidden, except when agitated or displaying. Throat is white and wings and tail are rufous. Back is brown and underparts are otherwise bright yellow. **JUVENILE** Similar, but with duller colors and no central crown patch. **VOICE** Utters a loud, piercing *kis-kadee*. **STATUS AND HABITAT** Fairly common resident in southern Texas, favoring a range of open to lightly wooded habitats, including parks and gardens. **OBSERVATION TIPS** Easy to see within range and often first detected by its call.

KINGBIRDS, FLYCATCHERS and KISKADEES

JUVENILE

EASTERN KINGBIRD

ADULT

SCISSOR-TAILED FLYCATCHER

ADULT

ADULT

GREAT KISKADEE

Tyrannidae

ASH-THROATED FLYCATCHER
Myiarchus cinerascens L 7.5–8.5 in

The typical *Myiarchus* flycatcher across much of the southwest. Adopts an upright posture when perched and looks rather slim-bodied with proportionately large head and long neck and tail. Flycatches, gleans insects from foliage, and drops to ground for prey. Sexes are similar. **ADULT** Has brown cap, gray-brown back, and paler nape. Wings are blackish with pale margins to coverts creating two wing bars; secondaries are pale-fringed, primaries are rufous-fringed. Tail feathers are mainly rufous, but note that, especially when seen from below, color does not extend to tip, which is dark grayish (rufous extends to tip in Great Crested). Throat and chest are pale gray, grading to otherwise very pale lemon underparts. Legs and bill are dark. **JUVENILE** Similar, but duller; secondaries are rufous- not pale-fringed. **VOICE** Call and song comprise series of *k'Brik* notes. **STATUS AND HABITAT** Common summer visitor (mainly Apr–Aug) to arid woodland and deserts. Winters mainly in Central America, but some remain in southern U.S. **OBSERVATION TIPS** Easy to see. **SIMILAR SPECIES Dusky-capped Flycatcher** *M. tuberculifer* (L 6.5–7.25 in) has grayer upperparts, duller and less distinct wing bars, brighter yellow underparts, and little rufous in adult's tail. Summer visitor (mainly Apr–Jul) to upland woodlands, mainly southeastern Arizona. Call is a drawn out *pe-ooo*, unlike Ash-throated.

GREAT CRESTED FLYCATCHER
Myiarchus crinitus L 8–9 in

Well-marked *Myiarchus* flycatcher. Perches upright and feeds in manner of Ash-throated. Useful identification pointers include more colorful appearance overall than other genus members, noticeably pale base to lower mandible, call, and range. Sexes are similar. **ADULT** Has dark gray-brown hood and nape grading to olive-brown back. Wings are mainly dark, but note rufous fringes to primaries and white fringes to other feathers, most noticeably on the tertials and coverts (wing bars). Face, throat, and breast are dark gray with clear separation from yellowish underparts, creating somewhat dark-hooded appearance. Gray wash extends onto flanks. Tail is mainly rufous. **JUVENILE** Similar, but with duller colors, and wing bars and most flight feather fringes rufous. **VOICE** Utters an upslurred *whu-eep* and a harsh *chrrrt*. **STATUS AND HABITAT** Widespread and common summer visitor (mainly Apr–Sep) across eastern North America; range extends to Midwest and breeds further north than other *Myiarchus* flycatchers. Favors wooded habitats. Winters mainly in Central and South America. **OBSERVATION TIPS** Easy to see.

BROWN-CRESTED FLYCATCHER
Myiarchus tyrannulus L 7.5–9 in

Similar to Great Crested, but slightly larger and paler on average. Bill is noticeably larger (particularly birds from Texas) and has only very limited amount of pale at base of lower mandible (cf. Great Crested). Sexes are similar. **ADULT** Has gray-brown hood, nape, and back. Wings are mainly blackish, but with rufous fringes to primaries and dull whitish fringes to other flight feathers and wing coverts (latter creating wing bars). Throat, face, and breast are gray and underparts are otherwise pale yellow. Tail is mainly rufous and, as with Great Crested, color extends to tip. **JUVENILE** Similar, but most flight feathers and wing coverts are fringed rufous. **VOICE** Utters a liquid *wrrt* or *wrrt-willado*. **STATUS AND HABITAT** Locally common summer visitor (mainly May–Aug) to deserts. Winters in Mexico. **OBSERVATION TIPS** Easy to find within range.

DUSKY-CAPPED
FLYCATCHER

ADULT

ASH-THROATED
FLYCATCHER

ADULT

ADULT

DUSKY-CAPPED FLYCATCHER

GREAT CRESTED
FLYCATCHER

ADULT

ADULT

BROWN-CRESTED
FLYCATCHER

Tyrannidae

OLIVE-SIDED FLYCATCHER
Contopus cooperi L 7–8 in

Plump-bodied, rather dark-looking flycatcher. Often perches on exposed dead branches, adopting an upright posture. Flying insects caught in aerial forays. Bill is dark and relatively large, and tail is short. Sexes are similar. **ADULT** Has mostly dark olive-brown upperparts, with indistinct pale eyering. Wings and tail are mostly blackish with faint pale wing bars; white feathers on side of rump sometimes overlap inner wing feathers at rest. Throat is white and color continues down center of breast to belly and undertail. Streaked dark olive-brown flanks look like an unbuttoned vest. **JUVENILE** Similar, but plumage, including wing bars, is warmer buff overall. **VOICE** Utters a liquid *quip-wee-ber* or a rapid *wip-wip-wip*. **STATUS AND HABITAT** Widespread and still a locally common summer visitor (mainly May–Aug) to boreal forests and damp, coniferous woodland. Has declined markedly in recent years and now on Audubon's Watchlist. Forest loss and degradation here, and in South American winter quarters, are probably to blame. **OBSERVATION TIPS** Easy to observe, but scarcer in recent years.

WESTERN WOOD-PEWEE
Contopus sordidulus L 6.25–6.5 in

Slimmer and longer-tailed than Olive-sided Flycatcher, with more pronounced wing bars and uniformly olive-brown breast (without central white line bordered by dark "vest"). Compared to Willow and Alder Flycatchers (*see* p.244), darker overall, with less striking wing bars and relatively longer wings (extending well beyond rump when perched). Legs are dark and bill is mostly dark, but with dull orange base to lower mandible. Makes aerial sorties after flying insects, from perch at mid-tree level (lower than Olive-sided Flycatcher). Sexes are similar.

EASTERN WOOD-PEWEE

ADULT

ADULT Has dark gray-brown upperparts overall. Wings and tail are mostly blackish, but note pale wing bars and pale fringes to secondaries and tertials. Underparts are gray-brown overall, palest on throat and grading to whitish on belly and vent. **JUVENILE** Similar, but brighter-looking with buffy wing bars and fringes to inner flight feathers. **VOICE** Utters a piercing, downslurred *psee-err*. **STATUS AND HABITAT** Widespread and common, but declining summer visitor (mainly May–Sep) to open woodland. Winters in northern South America. **OBSERVATION TIPS** Easy to see. **SIMILAR SPECIES Eastern Wood-pewee** *C. virens* (L 6–6.5 in) is almost identical; separate using summer range (much of eastern North America, barely overlapping with Western's range) and song (tri-syllabic *pee-err-wee*). Plumage is paler than Western, with more obvious wing bars, and orange on lower mandible.

GREATER PEWEE *Contopus pertinax* L 7.5–8 in

Larger and more uniform than related species; has a distinct crest. Perches near treetop, higher than Western Wood-pewee. Bill is relatively long with orange lower mandible. Sexes are similar. **ADULT** Has gray-brown upperparts and blackish wings and tail with pale gray-buff wing bars and whitish fringes to secondaries and tertials. Underparts are grayish, palest on throat, belly, and undertail. **JUVENILE** Similar, but wing bars are buffy. **VOICE** Utters a distinctive, upslurred *per-Wip* and a whistling song *per-pay-p'weeo* (José Maria). **STATUS AND HABITAT** Locally common summer visitor (mainly May–Aug) to wooded canyons, mainly Arizona. Winters in Central America. **OBSERVATION TIPS** Often first detected by hearing song.

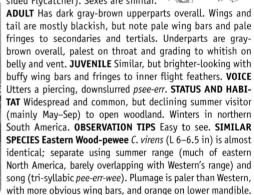

OLIVE-SIDED FLYCATCHER

ADULT

WESTERN WOOD-PEWEE

ADULT

ADULT

GREATER PEWEE

ADULT

ADULT

Tyrannidae

EASTERN PHOEBE *Sayornis phoebe* L 6–7 in

Dumpy-bodied flycatcher with understated plumage. Perched bird often pumps forked tail up and down, sometimes with a swaying motion. Flycatches in flight, usually from a low perch; sometimes hovers.

JUVENILE

Often associated with man-made habitats, nesting under bridges or on buildings. Sexes are similar. **ADULT** Has mainly gray-brown upperparts, darkest on head. Wings are blackish with two whitish wing bars and pale fringes to secondaries and tertials. Throat and rest of underparts are whitish, but with grayish flanks and variably yellow-buff suffusion on belly, most obvious in freshly molted fall plumage. **JUVENILE** Similar, but with buffy wing bars and subtly more intense yellow wash on belly. **VOICE** Utters a sharp *chip* call; song is a shrill *phee-werr, phee-eer-d'dip*. **STATUS AND HABITAT** Common and widespread summer visitor (mainly Apr–Sep) to woodland, parks, and gardens, across much of eastern North America; range extends to edge of Midwest U.S. and across much of southern Canada. Winters in southeastern U.S. and Mexico. **OBSERVATION TIPS** Easy to see, often near water, although frequently unobtrusive; listen for the distinctive song.

BLACK PHOEBE *Sayornis nigricans* L 6–7 in

Plump-bodied, essentially black and white flycatcher with a peaked rear crown, not rounded head. Tail is wagged up and down. Usually perches low, but in the open, and engages in aerial sorties to catch flying insects. Sexes are similar. **ADULT** Has a black head and chest, grading to a dark gray back. Wings are black with subtly pale wing bars and fringes to secondaries and tertials. Tail is rather long and mostly black, but with white outer feathers. Belly and undertail are white. **JUVENILE** Similar, but many wing and back feathers have brown fringes. **VOICE** Call is a sharp *tsii*; song is a squelchy, repeated *tch'wee, tch'we....* **STATUS AND HABITAT** Locally common resident in southwestern U.S., favoring open woodland, parks, and gardens, but invariably in the vicinity of water. **OBSERVATION TIPS** Easy to see and usually rather indifferent to observers, affording good views.

SAY'S PHOEBE *Sayornis saya* L 7–7.5 in

Subtly attractive flycatcher with a relatively long tail. Often perches conspicuously on wires or dead branches. Typically catches flying insects during aerial sorties from favored perch, and commonly feeds on insects caught on the ground; sometimes also feeds on berries. Often uses manmade structures for nesting. Sexes are similar. **ADULT** Has mainly gray-brown upperparts, darkest on head and particularly noticeable as mask through eye. Wings are dark, but with hint of subtle pale wing bars and pale fringes to inner flight feathers. Tail is blackish. Throat and breast are gray-buff, grading to orange-buff on belly and undertail; underwing coverts are flushed peachy orange. **JUVENILE** Similar, but plumage is browner overall and wing feather fringes are orange-buff. **VOICE** Song is a strident, whistling *pi'weer, pi'weep...*; call is a sharp *pe-eer*. **STATUS AND HABITAT** Widespread and common summer visitor (mainly Apr–Aug) to a wide range of open habitats, including deserts, grassland, and tundra, across much of western North America. Present year-round in southwestern U.S., but most birds winter further south, mainly Mexico. **OBSERVATION TIPS** Easy to see in open habitats.

EASTERN PHOEBE

ADULT

BLACK PHOEBE

ADULT

ADULT

ADULT

SAY'S PHOEBE

Tyrannidae

GRAY FLYCATCHER *Empidonax wrightii* L 5.25–6 in

Empidonax flycatchers (also known as "empids") seldom sit still for
long. When perched, wings appear rather short; head and eyes are
relatively large, and upright posture is adopted by most when sitting. Diagnostically (among empids), Gray habitually pumps tail when perched; down-
ward stroke is slow (as if pushing against pressure) while return stroke is rapid.
Flycatches insects and gleans prey from foliage while hovering. Sexes are
similar. **ADULT** Has plain gray head, neck, and back. Wings are dark with two
bold pale wing bars. Underparts are pale gray, palest on throat and belly. Has
pale eyering and narrow bill (seen side-on), whose lower mandible is orange-pink
with a dark tip. Postbreeding molt occurs after migration, so fall adults look worn. In winter, plumage
has a faint yellow wash. **JUVENILE** Similar, but plumage has a buffy wash. **VOICE** Song is a rapid, liquid
and repeated *chiowip*; call is a sharp *whit*. **STATUS AND HABITAT** Common summer visitor (mainly Apr–
Aug) to pinyon pine woodland, sagebrush, and other dry, brushy areas. Winters mainly in Mexico with
small numbers in southern Arizona. **OBSERVATION TIPS** Fairly easy to find in suitable habitats.

HAMMOND'S FLYCATCHER
Empidonax hammondii L 5.25–5.5 in

Often seems permanently agitated, flicking wings and cocking tail at
same time. Primary projection is relatively long when perched. Head and eye
are large, and bill is short and mainly dark in most adults. Sexes are similar.
ADULT Has gray head and neck grading to gray-olive back. Wings are dark, but
note bold pale wing bars. Has white eyering, most striking behind the eye.
Underparts are grayish, palest on throat and belly (the latter faintly washed
yellow). Postbreeding molt occurs on breeding grounds, hence fall plumage is
fresher looking than adults of other similar empids (which molt after migration).
Winter plumage is washed yellow-olive overall. **JUVENILE** Similar to fall adult, but with buffy wing bars
and orange base to lower mandible. **VOICE** Song is a squelchy *tch'wip*; call is a sharp *peek*. **STATUS
AND HABITAT** Fairly common summer visitor (mainly Apr–Aug) to mature coniferous forests in mountains,
and from sea level from the Pacific Northwest northwards. Winters mainly in Central America, with very
small numbers in southern Arizona. **OBSERVATION TIPS** Active and often hard to follow.

DUSKY FLYCATCHER
Empidonax oberholseri L 5.5–5.75 in

Similar to both Gray and Hammond's. Behavior, bill size and color,
and relative wing length are useful pointers: less active than Hammond's,
but flicks tail and wings (like that species, but unlike Gray, which pumps tail);
bill length is intermediate between Gray and Hammond's, with an orange-pink
base to dark-tipped lower mandible; primaries do not extend beyond rump
when perched. Sexes are similar. **ADULT** Has uniformly olive-gray upperparts
with pale eyering. Wings are dark with two whitish wing bars and tail is dark.
Underparts are pale gray, palest on throat and belly. Postbreeding molt occurs
after migration, so fall birds look worn (compared to Hammond's). Winter birds appear faintly washed
olive-yellow. **JUVENILE** Similar, but brighter than fall adult, with buffy wing bars. **VOICE** Song is a series
of repeated phrases *s'lit-chrrp, s'lit-cheep…*; call is a soft *whit*. **STATUS AND HABITAT** Common summer
visitor (mainly May–Aug) to mountain coniferous forests, chaparral, and brushy areas. Winters mainly
in Mexico; small numbers in southern Arizona. **OBSERVATION TIPS** A challenge to identify with certainty.

ADULT

GRAY
FLYCATCHER

ADULT

ADULT

ADULT

HAMMOND'S
FLYCATCHER

DUSKY
FLYCATCHER

ADULT

Tyrannidae

LEAST FLYCATCHER
Empidonax minimus L 5.25–5.5 in

Small, short-winged empid. Flycatches actively from low to mid-height perches; also gleans insects from foliage while hovering. Often perches upright and routinely flicks wings and tail in agitated manner. Head is relatively large and large eye is emphasized by whitish eyering. Lower mandible of rather dainty bill is pale orange-buff with a darker tip. Sexes are similar. **ADULT** Has dull olive-gray upperparts overall. Dark wings have pale fringes to inner flight feathers and two white wing bars; tail is dark. Underparts are whitish, palest on throat and belly, with diffuse gray band on chest and faint yellow wash on lower flanks. **JUVENILE** Similar, but in fall has buffy wing bars. **VOICE** Song is a repeated *ch'Wik, ch'Wik...*; call is a sharp *whit*. **STATUS AND HABITAT** Common summer visitor (mainly May–Aug) to open deciduous woodlands. Winters in Central America. **OBSERVATION TIPS** Although it can be very difficult, try using body proportions, voice, and habitat preference to aid separation from similar species. **SIMILAR SPECIES Northern Beardless-Tyrannulet** *Camptostoma imberbe* (L 4.25–4.5 in) is small, with pale olive-gray upperparts and whitish underparts; note dark eyestripe and faint white supercilium. Dark wings have two white wing bars and underparts are whitish. Forages in deliberate, hopping manner and call is a thin whistle. Summer visitor to arid woodland in southern Arizona and Texas.

NORTHERN BEARDLESS-TYRANNULET

ADULT

WILLOW FLYCATCHER *Empidonax traillii* L 5–6 in

Best separated from Alder using voice. Occurs as several subspecies: eastern birds are almost identical to Alder; western ones are subtly browner and darker. Feeding habits similar to those of Alder. Sexes are similar. **ADULT** Has olive-gray upperparts in eastern birds, olive-brown in western (Alder's upperparts are usually subtly greener). Has faint pale eyering (on average, less distinct than Alder) and pinkish orange lower mandible. Wings are dark with pale fringes to inner flight feathers and two white wing bars; tail is dark (wings and tail slightly longer in Alder's). Underparts are pale with pale wash on chest: olive in eastern birds, brown in western. **JUVENILE** Similar to respective regional adult, but with buffy wing bars. **VOICE** Song is a harsh, buzzing *fzz'Byew*; call is a sharp *whuit*. **STATUS AND HABITAT** Fairly common summer visitor (mainly May–Aug) to damp woodlands. Winters in Central and South America. **OBSERVATION TIPS** Fortunately, like Alder, sometimes sings on migration as well as on breeding grounds.

ALDER FLYCATCHER
Empidonax alnorum L 5.5–6 in

Confusingly similar to Willow, and both species favor damp woodland. Best identified by voice; silent birds are often not separable. *See* Willow's entry for discussion of subtle structural differences. Engages in aerial sorties from perches near top of tree after flying insects; also hovers and gleans insects from foliage. Sexes are similar. **ADULT** Has dull olive-green upperparts. Note narrow white eyering and broad-based bill with pinkish orange lower mandible. Wings are dark with pale inner flight feather fringes and two bold white wing bars. Underparts are pale with olive-gray wash on chest. **JUVENILE** Similar, but with buffy wing bars. **VOICE** Song is a harsh, repeated *rrr'BEE-eh*; call is a sharp *piip*. **STATUS AND HABITAT** Common and widespread summer visitor (mainly Jun–Aug) to damp, deciduous woodland with alders and willows. Winters in South America. **OBSERVATION TIPS** Hard to identify with certainty, unless song is heard; with practice, call is a good clue too.

LEAST FLYCATCHER

WILLOW FLYCATCHER

ADULT

ADULT

ADULT

ADULT

ALDER FLYCATCHER

Tyrannidae

PACIFIC-SLOPE FLYCATCHER
Empidonax difficilis L 5.5–5.75 in
Active "empid" that often adopts upright posture when perched.
Extremely similar to Cordilleran and often only reliably separable by voice and
breeding range; *see* that species' entry for discussion of subtle structural differences. Both species have distinctive-looking eye: relatively large and
oddly accentuated by white eyering that is incomplete above the eye, but
expands behind it. Rear of crown is slightly peaked, much like a phoebe. Sexes
are similar. **ADULT** Has olive-brown upperparts. Broad-based bill has pinkish
orange lower mandible. Wings are dark with pale fringes to inner flight feathers
and two buffy white wing bars; white elements on wing are less obvious through wear as summer progresses. Tail is dark. Underparts are pale, with olive or brownish wash on breast. Channel Islands
endemic subspecies *insulicola* is duller, with whiter wing bars, a longer bill, and lower-pitched song.
JUVENILE Similar, but wing feather fringes and wing bars are buffy brown. **VOICE** Song comprises
repeated phrases: a thin *tsi*, an explosive *sche-Wee*, and a thin, sharp *pik*; call is a slurred *tseweep*.
STATUS AND HABITAT Common summer visitor (mainly May–Aug) to damp, shady coniferous woodlands and often seen near streams. Winters in Mexico. **OBSERVATION TIPS** Outside breeding range,
silent birds are hard to separate from Cordilleran.

CORDILLERAN FLYCATCHER
Empidonax occidentalis L 5.5–5.75 in
Almost identical to Pacific-slope. Silent birds, outside breeding
range, can be impossible to identify with certainty. Breeding range is a good
pointer and call, once learned, is reasonably diagnostic. Behavior is similar
to that of Pacific-slope. Sexes are similar. **ADULT** Has subtly browner upperparts and marginally longer bill than Pacific-slope. Wings are dark with pale
fringes to inner flight feathers and two buffy white wing bars; white elements
on wing become less apparent through wear as summer progresses. Tail is dark
and subtly longer than Pacific-slope's. Underparts are pale, with olive or brown-
ish wash on breast. **JUVENILE** Similar, but wing feather fringes and wing bars are buffy brown. **VOICE**
Song typically comprises a thin *see*, a chirping *see-oo* and a thin, sharp *pik*; call is a thin, whistling
tsee-seet, often almost disyllabic. **STATUS AND HABITAT** Common summer visitor (mainly May–Aug) to
coniferous forests in Rocky Mountains. Winters in Mexico. **OBSERVATION TIPS** Learn the call as an aid
to identification.

YELLOW-BELLIED FLYCATCHER
Empidonax flaviventris L 5–5.5 in

Distinctive, but unobtrusive
"empid," which favors deep shade;
often first detected by its voice. Usually adopts an upright posture when
perched. Head looks proportionally
large and tail relatively short. Sexes are
similar. **ADULT** Has olive-green upperparts, whitish eyering, and pale pinkish
orange lower mandible. Wings are dark with pale fringes to inner
flight feathers and two striking white wing bars. Underparts are
yellowish, with darker olive wash across breast. **JUVENILE** Similar, but brighter, with buffy yellow wing bars. **VOICE** Song is a
sharp, chirping and disyllabic *ch'Week*; call is a whistling *ch'wee*.
STATUS AND HABITAT Widespread and common summer visitor
(mainly Jun–Aug) to northern forests, favoring areas of dense
spruce in particular. Winters in Central and South America.
OBSERVATION TIPS Easily overlooked and presence best detected
by recognizing voice.

ADULT

PACIFIC-SLOPE
FLYCATCHER

ADULT

ADULT

CORDILLERAN
FLYCATCHER

YELLOW-BELLIED
FLYCATCHER

ADULT

ADULT

Tyrannidae and Laniidae

VERMILION FLYCATCHER
Pyrocephalus rubinus L 4.5–6 in

Distinctive flycatcher, adult male of which is unmistakable. Females and immature are distinguished from similar-sized phoebes by streaked underparts. Often perches conspicuously. Sexes are dissimilar. **ADULT MALE** Has very dark brown mask, nape, back, wings, and tail; rest of plumage is bright red. **ADULT FEMALE** Has gray-brown upperparts, dark wings with two faint

JUVENILE

pale wing bars, and dark tail; note the pale supercilium. Underparts are pale, with dark streaking on breast and flanks and pinkish orange flush to belly and undertail. **JUVENILE** Similar to adult female, but with spots (not streaks) on breast and flanks and otherwise whitish underparts. In first-year, immature female acquires adultlike plumage, but with yellow flush to belly and vent; immature male acquires blotchy red patches on head and underparts. **VOICE** Song is a series of sharp *pit* notes, ending in a trill; call is a thin *psee*. **STATUS AND HABITAT** Summer visitor (mainly May–Sep) to parks and open, brushy woodland, seldom far from water. Most winter in Mexico, but occurs year-round in southernmost U.S. **OBSERVATION TIPS** Usually indifferent to people, allowing superb views.

LOGGERHEAD SHRIKE
Lanius ludovicianus L 8.5–9.5 in

Predatory passerine that perches on wires and dead branches. Prey ranges from insects to small birds and mammals, which it often impales on thorns or barbed wire fences before tearing the prey apart with its powerful, hooked bill. Can be confused with larger Northern, from which it is distinguished by its smaller body and bill, shorter wings and tail, and various subtle plumage differences. Sexes are similar. **ADULT** Has blue-gray upperparts, darkest in birds from southern California. Has a dark mask that extends around the forehead, above bill line, defined above by narrow white line above and white cheeks and throat below. Wings are mainly black, but with small white patch (obvious in flight) on base of primaries. Tail is long and wedge-shaped, mainly black, but with white outer tips. Underparts are pale, whitest on throat, darkest on breast. **JUVENILE** Similar, but has scaly-looking upperparts due to pale feather margins; underparts are faintly barred. **VOICE** Song is a series of repeated, harsh chirping *ch'Wee* phrases; call is a harsh *chakk*. **STATUS AND HABITAT** Widespread, but declining resident, across much of its range, favoring open country such as meadows and farmland with plenty of perches. Northernmost populations are migratory. **OBSERVATION TIPS** Seldom numerous, but usually conspicuously perched on fences or bushes along roadside.

NORTHERN SHRIKE *Lanius excubitor* L 9.5–10.5 in

Striking predatory passerine that captures small birds and mammals (also impales its prey on thorns and barbed wire fences). Similar to Loggerhead, but larger and bulkier; subtle plumage differences also aid separation. Sexes are similar. **ADULT** Has pale blue-gray upperparts. Black mask extends to bill, but does not continue around forehead. Wings are mainly black, but note white patch at base of primaries (striking in flight and a bit more extensive than in Loggerhead). Tail is long and wedge-shaped, mainly black, but with white outer tips. Underparts are pale gray. **JUVENILE** Has gray and white elements of adult's plumage replaced by light brown or tan; underparts are scaly and mask is absent or very faint. Some birds begin to acquire adult plumage during first winter. **VOICE** Song is a series of harsh phrases; calls include an insistent *kree, kree....* **STATUS AND HABITAT** Breeds across the Arctic; widespread but never numerous. Winters across central North America; favors open country with scattered trees. **OBSERVATION TIPS** Hard to find for such a striking bird.

VERMILION FLYCATCHER

FEMALE

MALE

LOGGERHEAD SHRIKE

JUVENILE

ADULT

NORTHERN SHRIKE

JUVENILE

ADULT

Vireonidae

BLACK-CAPPED VIREO *Vireo atricapillus* L 4.5–4.75 in

Distinctive vireo. Forages among foliage and gleans insects while hovering. Sexes are dissimilar. **ADULT MALE** Has a black hood, and white lores and mask

FEMALE

surrounding red eye. Back and rump are greenish, dark wings have two pale wing bars and pale fringes to inner flight feathers, and underparts are whitish, palest on throat with buff wash on flanks. **ADULT FEMALE** Similar, but hood is dark gray. **JUVENILE** Recalls adult female, but has browner plumage overall and dull eye. **VOICE** Song comprises warbling phrases such as *fzz-ch'ch'ch-chee* with pauses between; calls include a harsh *zrree*. **STATUS AND HABITAT** Local and endangered summer visitor (mainly Apr–Aug) to scrub-covered rocky ground with sumac, oaks, and juniper; dense, ungrazed new growth is ideal. Habitat destruction and nest parasitism by Brown-headed Cowbird have aided decline. Winters in Mexico. **OBSERVATION TIPS** Listen for the distinctive song.

WHITE-EYED VIREO *Vireo griseus* L 5–5.5 in

Pale-eyed, secretive vireo that is heard more often that it is seen. Sexes are similar. **ADULT** Has greenish cap, back, and rump. Face and sides of neck are gray. Eye has pale iris, with dark line in front and is surrounded by yellow "spectacle" and supercilium extending forward. Darkish wings have two white wing bars. Throat is white and underparts are otherwise pale with gray wash on chest and yellow wash on flanks. Bill is stout and legs are blue-gray. **JUVENILE** Similar, but paler, with dark iris and white eyering. Acquires adultlike plumage and pale iris in winter. **VOICE** Song is a series of loud phrases such as *chic, chip-ee-err-cheeo*; call is a harsh *shrrr*. **STATUS AND HABITAT** Common summer visitor (mainly Apr–Sep) to dense, brushy deciduous woodland; widespread in east, range extending to Texas. Winters from southeastern U.S. to Mexico. **OBSERVATION TIPS** Easier to hear than to see.

YELLOW-THROATED VIREO
Vireo flavifrons L 5–5.5 in

Colorful vireo, with disproportionately large head and stout bill. Sexes are similar. **ADULT** Has yellowish green upperparts and bright yellow lores, eyering, throat, and breast; underparts are otherwise white. Dark wings have pale fringes to inner flight feathers and two white wing bars. Legs are blue-gray. **JUVENILE** Similar to adult. **VOICE** Song is a repeated *zse'eret, tchu-et*; calls include harsh *tche* notes. **STATUS AND HABITAT** Common summer visitor (mainly Apr–Aug) to deciduous and mixed woodland in east, range extending to Texas and states northward. **OBSERVATION TIPS** Easy to identify.

BELL'S VIREO *Vireo bellii* L 4.5–4.75 in

Active, but very secretive, warblerlike vireo. Sexes are similar. **ADULT** Has plain grayish upperparts overall, palest and grayest in western birds, greenish in eastern birds; marginally darker wings have two pale wing bars, lower one brighter and more distinct than upper. Dark eye has white supercilium and white "eyelid" below, creating incomplete spectacled effect. Underparts are pale: grayish white in western birds; washed buffy yellow in eastern birds. **JUVENILE** Similar to respective regional adult. **VOICE** Song is a rapid, chattering *chewee-cheweed'de'de'der*; call is a thin *chee*. **STATUS AND HABITAT** Scarce and threatened summer visitor (mainly Apr–Aug); favors dense, riverine woodland and scrub. Winters in Mexico. **OBSERVATION TIPS** Listen for its distinctive song.

BLACK-CAPPED VIREO

ADULT

MALE

WHITE-EYED VIREO

ADULT

ADULT

YELLOW-THROATED VIREO

BELL'S VIREO

ADULT

Vireonidae

HUTTON'S VIREO *Vireo huttoni* L 4.75–5 in

Stocky, large-headed vireo. Recalls Ruby-crowned Kinglet (*see* p.292), but has stubby (not needlelike) bill and different voice. Forages for insects in foliage. Sexes are similar. **ADULT** Has olive-gray upperparts, grayest in interior subspecies, greenest in Pacific coast subspecies. Note dark eye, whitish eyering, and pale lores. Dark wings have pale fringes to inner flight feathers and two white wing bars. Underparts are pale olive-gray, palest on throat. Legs are blue-gray. **JUVENILE** Similar to adult. **VOICE** Song is a simple *tsu-Eee* or *tsi'U* phrase, repeated every second or so; call is a rasping *rrrh*. **STATUS AND HABITAT** Locally common resident of evergreen woodlands, favoring live oaks. **OBSERVATION TIPS** Search for it among nomadic flocks of small birds outside breeding season.

BLUE-HEADED VIREO *Vireo solitarius* L 5–5.5 in

Male is fairly easy to identify (if well-marked), but some dull-plumaged females are almost identical to Cassin's. Unobtrusive and easily overlooked. Sexes are similar. **ADULT** Has olive-green back and blue-gray hood with striking white "spectacles." Dark wings have yellowish fringes to inner flight feathers and two yellowish wing bars. Tail has white outer feathers. Throat is white and underparts are otherwise mostly white with buffy yellow wash on flanks. Male is usually brighter than female. **JUVENILE** Duller than female, but with clearer demarcation between dark hood and white throat than other similar vireos. **VOICE** Song is a series of spaced, thin whistling notes; call is a rasping *tche*. **STATUS AND HABITAT** Common summer visitor (mainly Apr–Sep) to woodland habitats; winters in southern U.S., Mexico, and Central America. **OBSERVATION TIPS** Easiest to locate by its song.

CASSIN'S VIREO *Vireo cassinii* L 5–5.5 in

Very similar to Hutton's and dull Blue-headeds. Breeding range and seasonal distribution are pointers. Sexes are similar, but males are usually brighter than females. **ADULT** Has greenish gray back and grayish hood with white "spectacles." Wings are dark with pale (often yellow) wing bars and fringes to inner flight feathers. Throat and underparts are mostly white with yellow-olive flush to flanks. Legs are blue-gray. **JUVENILE** Similar, but duller. **VOICE** Song comprises repeated, well-spaced whistling upslurred *tchee'Ooee* followed by a downslurred *tchewee*; call is a rasping *rrrh*. **STATUS AND HABITAT** Common summer visitor (mainly May–Aug) to open coniferous forests on mountain slopes. Winters from southern Arizona to Mexico. **OBSERVATION TIPS** Some birds are impossible to identify with certainty.

PLUMBEOUS VIREO *Vireo plumbeus* L 5.25–5.75 in

Robust vireo. Most individuals are grayer and stouter-billed than other similar species. Breeding range is also a pointer. Sexes are similar. **ADULT** Has mainly blue-gray upperparts, with white "spectacles." Dark wings have whitish fringes to inner flight feathers and two white wing bars. Underparts are whitish, with gray wash on flanks. **JUVENILE** Similar, but with hint of yellow wash on flanks. **VOICE** Song is very similar to Cassin's; call is similar to Blue-headed. **STATUS AND HABITAT** Locally common summer visitor (mainly May–Sep) to Rocky Mountain forests. Winters mainly in Mexico. **OBSERVATION TIPS** Fairly easy to find in suitable habitats.

ADULT

HUTTON'S VIREO

ADULT

BLUE-HEADED VIREO

ADULT

ADULT

CASSIN'S VIREO

ADULT

PLUMBEOUS VIREO

ADULT

Vireonidae

ADULT

GRAY VIREO *Vireo vicinior*
L 5.25–5.5 in
Unremarkable plumage (as vireos go), but absence of striking features is in itself a means of identification. Habits are unobtrusive; best detected by song. Flicks tail from side-to-side like a gnatcatcher. Sexes are similar. **ADULT** Has blue-gray upperparts, darkest on back. Dark eye is accentuated by faint pale eyering. Wings have faint pale margins to flight feathers and one faint pale wing bar. Tail is rather long and underparts are whitish, palest on throat and flanks. **JUVENILE** Similar to adult. **VOICE** Song is a repeated *tche'Woo*; call is a rasping *chrrr*. **STATUS AND HABITAT** Common summer visitor (mostly May–Aug) to arid scrub and chaparral. Winters mainly in Mexico. **OBSERVATION TIPS** Listen for the distinctive song.

RED-EYED VIREO *Vireo olivaceus* L 6–6.5 in
Well-marked, rather large vireo. Forages unobtrusively and gleans insects while hovering. Attracts attention with its incessant song. Sexes are similar. **ADULT** Has olive-gray back and neck. Head has striking pattern of dark gray crown and long, white supercilium, defined above and below by black lines. Note the red iris and rather long bill. Underparts are whitish, with dull yellow wash on flanks and undertail. **JUVENILE** Similar, but with dull iris. **VOICE** Song is a varied series of 2-, 3-, and 4-syllable phrases, including *tse-Oo-ee* and *tsee-Ooo*, sometimes sung in triplets; call is a nasal *zz'nrrr*. **STATUS AND HABITAT** Common summer visitor (mainly May–Aug) to temperate woodlands in west; range is more extensive in east. Winters in South America. **OBSERVATION TIPS** Easy to find.

WARBLING VIREO *Vireo gilvus* L 5.5–6 in
Unobtrusive warblerlike vireo with a distinctive song. Note the relatively large head and stout bill. Western subspecies are subtly smaller, greener, and have shorter bills than eastern counterparts and may be a separate species; all are treated similarly here. Sexes are similar. **ADULT** Has olive-green upperparts, marginally darkest on forecrown. Has whitish supercilium and lores. Wings lack obvious pale feather fringes or wing bars. Underparts are pale overall with drab yellow wash on flanks and undertail. **JUVENILE** Similar to respective subspecies adult, but with obvious yellow flush to flanks and undertail. **VOICE** Song comprises bursts of warbling phrases, with pauses between as if bird is catching its breath; call is a nasal *tchrrr*. **STATUS AND HABITAT** Common summer visitor (mainly Apr–Sep) to riverside deciduous woodland. Winters in Central America. **OBSERVATION TIPS** Listen for the distinctive song. Often feeds near top of tree, making observation tricky.

PHILADELPHIA VIREO
Vireo philadelphicus L 5.25–5.5 in
Short-billed, short-tailed, warblerlike vireo. Sexes are similar. **ADULT** Has an olive-green back and neck with a grayish crown, white supercilium, and a dark eyestripe with a white line below. Underparts, including throat, are variably flushed yellow with least amount of color on belly. **JUVENILE** Similar, but yellow on underparts is more obvious. **VOICE** Song comprises a series of short phrases with pauses in between, rather similar to that of Red-eyed; call is a nasal *tchrrr*. **STATUS AND HABITAT** Scarce summer visitor (mainly May–Sep) to new growth deciduous woodland; often in similar habitats to Red-eyed. **OBSERVATION TIPS** Easiest to detect by song.

GRAY VIREO

ADULT

ADULT

RED-EYED VIREO

ADULT

ADULT

WARBLING VIREO

ADULT

PHILADELPHIA
VIREO

ADULT

ADULT

ADULT

Corvidae

BLUE JAY *Cyanocitta cristata* L 11–12 in

Familiar and unmistakable, mainly blue bird with a distinct crest. Bold and inquisitive in gardens and parks where it is not persecuted, but otherwise it can be unobtrusive. Opportunistic feeder and varied diet includes birdfeeder food as well as eggs and young of songbirds. Sexes are similar. **ADULT** Has bright blue cap, nape, and back. Wings are blue overall with laddered black markings and bold white patches and wing bar. Tail is blue

ADULT

with laddered black, and white outer tips. Underparts are pale gray, face and throat with a dark border. **JUVENILE** Similar, but blue elements of plumage are grayer. **VOICE** Calls are varied and include a shrill *jay, jay, jay...* and a whistling *pee'de-de*. A good mimic, especially of raptors. **STATUS AND HABITAT** Common resident in a wide variety of wooded habitats, from forests to parks and gardens. Common in east, but range extends westward almost to Rockies. In some years, northern populations are irruptive, or migratory southward in fall in variable numbers; in some years there are widespread movements involving large flocks. **OBSERVATION TIPS** Easy to observe.

STELLER'S JAY *Cyanocitta stelleri* L 11.5–12 in

Western counterpart of Blue Jay that is darker and more uniformly colored overall. Note the conspicuous crest. Bold, inquisitive, with opportunistic feeding habits and eclectic diet, making it a familiar resident of most campgrounds. Typically lives in flocks of a dozen or so birds outside the breeding season. Sexes are similar. **ADULT** Has dark sooty gray back and nape, and mainly blackish head. Length of erectile crest varies and some subspecies have colored feathers at base: crest is longest in birds from southern Rockies, which also have basal whitish feathering; coastal birds have shorter crests, with some blue basal feathering. Plumage is otherwise dark blue, with variable extent of dark laddering on wings and tail according to subspecies. **JUVENILE** Similar, but duller and browner overall. **VOICE** Utters a range of calls including a chattering rattle and a harsh *sch'Eck*. **STATUS AND HABITAT** Common resident of coniferous forests and mixed woodland. In some years, birds are irruptive south and east in fall and winter. **OBSERVATION TIPS** Take a picnic to the forest and Steller's Jays will soon visit you.

GRAY JAY *Perisoreus canadensis* L 11.5–12 in

Distinctive, plump-bodied bird with a relatively large, rounded head, short bill, and "fluffy," soft-looking plumage. Usually unobtrusive, but sometimes bold and inquisitive, particularly around campsites and picnic areas. An opportunistic feeder that lives in small groups outside the breeding season. Sexes are similar. **ADULT** Has a dark gray back and rear of crown; extent and intensity of dark color varies according to subspecies and is palest in southern birds. In all birds, nape, forecrown, and underparts are pale gray. Wings are dark, with pale feather margins in some northern birds; tail is dark. **JUVENILE** Rather uniformly dark gray overall. **VOICE** Utters a soft, fluty *pheeoo* and a harsh, chattering *chakkk*. **STATUS AND HABITAT** Widespread and fairly common resident in taiga and mountain coniferous forests. **OBSERVATION TIPS** Listen for its distinctive calls. Often easy to see if you camp in an established and well-used site in northern or upland forests within the species' range.

JUVENILE

BLUE JAY

ADULT

STELLER'S
JAY

JUVENILE

ADULT

ADULT

JUVENILE

GRAY JAY

Corvidae

MEXICAN JAY
Aphelocoma ultramarina L 11.5–12 in

Subtly beautiful bird with a typical jay appearance: slim body, long tail, narrow bill, and bluish coloration overall. Usually seen in sizeable and noisy family groups that forage, methodically, at human walking pace, through foliage and undergrowth; engages in cooperative breeding. Sexes are similar. **ADULT** ssp. *arizonae* has pale gray back, mostly pale blue head, wings, and tail, and pale gray underparts. Bill and legs are dark. Adult ssp. *couchii* is much darker overall, particularly on upperparts. **JUVENILE** Dark gray overall, with a hint of blue on head. Bill is yellow in ssp. *arizonae*, dark in ssp. *couchii*. **VOICE** Utters a clipped *wiik, wiik...*, with members of family flock calling to one another. **STATUS AND HABITAT** A mainly Mexican species with two distinct populations in U.S.: ssp. *arizonae* in Arizona and southeastern New Mexico, and ssp. *couchii* in western Texas. **OBSERVATION TIPS** It may take a while to track down your first Mexican Jay, but once you see an individual bird you are likely to encounter a whole flock. Listen for their distinctive contact calls.

WESTERN SCRUB-JAY
Aphelocoma californica L 11–12 in

Distinctive bird with a typical jaylike appearance: slim body, long tail, and stout, and rather elongated bill. Occurs as two subspecies groups in U.S.: Pacific birds (comprising three subspecies found on the Pacific coast) are more colorful than interior birds (three subspecies that occur inland). Some individuals, particularly Pacific birds, are bold, tame, and inquisitive, and easy to see; birds from interior south and east of range are more retiring and unobtrusive. An opportunistic feeder with an omnivorous diet that includes berries, fruits, insects, and the eggs and young of songbirds. Sexes are similar. **ADULT** Pacific bird has a gray-brown back, but otherwise mostly dark blue upperparts; note, however, the dark cheeks and faint white supercilium. Throat is whitish and streaked, with discrete demarcation from otherwise grubby gray underparts. Adult interior bird is similar, but underparts are darker. **JUVENILE** Has mainly dull gray head, back, and wing coverts, with blue flight feathers and tail. Underparts and forehead are whitish gray. **VOICE** Utters a harsh, nasal *cheerp, cheerp, cheerp...* and other chattering calls. **STATUS AND HABITAT** Common and widespread resident of scrubby woodland and chaparral, especially with pinyon, juniper, and oak. **OBSERVATION TIPS** Easiest to see near the Pacific coast. **SIMILAR SPECIES Island Scrub-Jay** *A. insularis* (L 12–12.5 in) is an endemic resident of Santa Cruz Island, off Californian coast. Similar to Western, but larger and more colorful. Note particularly the adult's brighter blue upperparts, dark brown back, and black cheeks. Juvenile has mainly gray upperparts with blue flight feathers and tail; underparts are pale gray.

ISLAND SCRUB-JAY

ADULT

MEXICAN JAY

ADULT

ADULT, PACIFIC

ADULT, INTERIOR

WESTERN SCRUB-JAY

Corvidae

PINYON JAY *Gymnorhinus cyanocephalus* L 10.5 in

Subtly colorful corvid, with the body proportions and bill shape of Clark's Nutcracker. Social, typically living in large (often 100+ indi-

viduals) flocks, some individuals of which are always on lookout for danger. As name suggests, feeds primarily on seeds of pinyon pines, but omnivorous and opportunistic diet also includes other types of seeds, as well as fruits and insects. Nests colonially. Sexes are similar. **ADULT** Has blue plumage overall, darkest on crown, back, and wings, and palest on throat and belly; note streaking on throat. Bill is slender and dark and legs are blackish. **JUVENILE** Rather uniformly pale blue-gray. **VOICE** Call is an odd nasal, quail-like *woah-keeh-keeh*. **STATUS AND HABITAT** Widespread and fairly common resident of pinyon-juniper forests; declining, probably due to habitat loss and degradation, and on the Audubon Watchlist. **OBSERVATION TIPS** Listen for the distinctive call. If you find one Pinyon Jay, you are likely to find lots.

CLARK'S NUTCRACKER
Nucifraga columbiana L 11.5–12 in

Distinctive and subtly attractive corvid, with a relatively short tail, but long wings. Bill is slender and pointed. Main diet is pine seeds, which are stored and eaten throughout winter. Mostly rather unobtrusive, but individuals resident near campsites and picnic grounds within species' range are often bold and inquisitive, and opportunistic feeders. Sexes are similar. **ADULT** Has soft-looking pale purplish gray body plumage, palest around eye and on face, and on undertail coverts. Wings are mainly black except for white inner flight feathers (seen as white patch on closed wing) and tail has black central and white outer feathers (appears mostly white from below, in flight). Bill and legs are dark. **JUVENILE** Similar to adult, but a shade paler overall. **VOICE** Utters a range of harsh, rasping calls including *shrerr-shrerrr* and *craa-craa-craa*. **STATUS AND HABITAT** Widespread and common resident of mountain conifer forests. **OBSERVATION TIPS** Easy to see if you camp or picnic in suitable areas of pine forest; often the birds will find you.

GREEN JAY *Cyanocorax yncas* L 10.5–11 in

Colorful and exotic-looking corvid, with proportionately short wings and very long tail. Coloration blends in surprisingly well with foliage and stationary birds can be rather unobtrusive. Omnivorous and food includes insects, fruits, and seeds. Typically, lives in small, roving flocks. Sexes are similar. **ADULT** Has a rich green back and wings, grading to blue on the nape, above eye, and on cheeks; face is otherwise black, except for white patch in front of eye. From above, tail is blue-green with yellow outer feathers; from below, appears mainly yellow. Underparts are otherwise pale green, grading to yellowish on undertail coverts. Bill and legs are dark. **JUVENILE** Similar to adult, but duller. **VOICE** Calls are varied and include bell-like tones and a series of almost insectlike, chattering notes, oddly faint-sounding for such a sizeable bird. **STATUS AND HABITAT** A mainly Central and South American species whose range extends to southern Texas (mainly the Lower Rio Grande Valley), where it is resident. **OBSERVATION TIPS** Presence is easiest to detect by learning and listening for its distinctive calls.

PINYON JAY

ADULT

CLARK'S NUTCRACKER

ADULT

ADULT

GREEN JAY

Corvidae

BLACK-BILLED MAGPIE *Pica hudsonia* L 18–21 in

Striking and unmistakable black and white, long-tailed bird. Outside
breeding season, often seen in small flocks and roosts in large groups,
sometimes 100s strong. In flight, note the rounded black and white wings
and long tail, tapered toward the tip. On the ground, walks with a rolling
swagger or moves with long hops. An opportunistic feeder with an omnivorous diet including fruit, insects, animal road kills, and the eggs and young
of birds; it will also happily scavenge discarded leftover food scraps in towns.
Sometimes picks ticks from the backs of large, grazing animals. Nest is a large,
long-lasting structure of twigs, usually built among dense tree branches. Sexes
are similar. **ADULT** Has mainly black plumage with contrasting white belly and white patch on the closed
wing. At close range, and in good light, a bluish green sheen can be seen on wings and tail. In flight,
outer half of the short, rounded wings appears strikingly white. **JUVENILE** Similar to adult, but has pale
(not dark) iris, shorter tail, and duller (not iridescent), browner plumage. **VOICE** Utters a range of harsh,
screeching and chattering calls. **STATUS AND HABITAT** Widespread and common resident. Favors a range
of lightly wooded habitats including farmland and grassland; often in vicinity of water, the common
factors being a wide range of potential food sources to suit its omnivorous diet, and dense shrubs and
trees for nesting. Also seen in suburban areas. Formerly widely persecuted by shooting, trapping, and
poisoning. Now protected in U.S., but not in Canada. **OBSERVATION TIPS** You will have little difficulty
finding the species in most lowland areas within its range.

ADULT

YELLOW-BILLED MAGPIE *Pica nuttalli* L 16.5–18 in

A Californian endemic, superficially similar to Black-billed, but appreciably smaller
and with a striking yellow bill and variable yellow skin below eye. Gregarious, particularly outside breeding season, when it often forages and roosts in sizeable flocks.
An opportunistic feeder with an omnivorous diet that includes insects, seeds, fruits,
and eggs and nestlings of small birds. Sexes are similar. **ADULT** Has mainly black
plumage, with a contrasting white belly and white patch on the closed wing. At
close range, and in good light, a bluish green sheen can be seen on wings and tail.
Note the bright yellow bill and variable area of yellow skin below eye. In flight,
outer half of the short, rounded wings is strikingly white. **JUVENILE** Similar to
adult, but has pale (not dark) iris, blackish bill, shorter tail, and duller (not iridescent), browner plumage. It lacks the yellow patch below the eye. **VOICE** Calls are
varied, but often comprise a rapid series of harsh screeches, similar to those of Black-
billed. **STATUS AND HABITAT** Resident, restricted to wooded foothills centered on
California's Central Valley. Favors oak savanna and orchards, but also occurs on fringes of urban areas.
Threatened by habitat loss and poisoning; poisoned bait put out for ground squirrels is a particular
problem. **OBSERVATION TIPS** Not hard to find if you visit suitable habitats within its range.

BLACK-BILLED MAGPIE

ADULT

YELLOW-BILLED MAGPIE

ADULT

Corvidae

AMERICAN CROW
Corvus brachyrhynchos L 15–18 in

Archetypal crow and the yardstick by which to judge other dark-plumaged corvids. Sometimes bold, but becomes more wary where persecut-

ed. An opportunistic feeder with an omnivorous diet that includes carrion, scraps scavenged at garbage dumps and grain spills, and live prey. Variably gregarious outside breeding season. Sexes are similar. **ADULT** Has glossy, all-black plumage with a relatively long bill. In flight, note the rather long, fan-shaped tail. Shows subspecies variation across range, and western subspecies is rather small and essentially identical to Northwestern Crow (*see* below). **JUVENILE** Similar, but has pale iris and brownish tinge overall to plumage. **VOICE** Utters a familiar, raucous *caaw, caaw*. **STATUS AND HABITAT** Populations have declined markedly due to West Nile Virus in some areas, but still widespread and common, favoring a wide range of habitats, including

urban areas. Resident across much of its range, but northern birds migrate south in fall. **OBSERVATION TIPS** Easy to find. **SIMILAR SPECIES Northwestern Crow** *C. caurinus* (L 14–16 in), the coastal Northwest counterpart of American Crow, is indistinguishable in field from American in small zone of overlap in Washington (here both voice and appearance are almost identical). Elsewhere, unsatisfactorily, geographical location is best pointer to identification: coastal crows in British Columbia or Alaska will be Northwestern. **Fish Crow** *C. ossifragus* (L 15–17 in) is extremely similar to American and occurs in southeastern U.S. Has subtly shinier plumage and longer wings and tail, but best separated by voice: call is a weak nasal, downslurred *kee-ahh*.

COMMON RAVEN *Corvus corax* L 24–25 in

Large and impressive bird, and our largest corvid. Appreciably larger than American Crow or Chihuahuan Raven and easily recognized on the ground by its more massive bill and the shaggy throat that appears most ruffled when the bird is calling. In flight, recognized by the long, thick neck and wedge-shaped tail. Incredibly aerobatic, tumbling and rolling in mid-air; often seen in pairs. Sexes are similar. **ADULT** Has mainly black plumage but, in good light, an oily or metallic sheen is discernible. **JUVENILE** Similar, but has paler eye and brownish tinge to plumage. **VOICE** Utters a loud and deep *cronk* call. **STATUS AND HABITAT** Widespread and fairly common resident in a wide range of habitats from deserts to farmland and tundra. **OBSERVATION TIPS** Size, coloration, and long, wedge-shaped tail usually make identification in flight easy.

CHIHUAHUAN RAVEN *Corvus cryptoleucus* L 19–20 in

Arid-country corvid. Very similar to Common Raven. Smaller size is of little use in field identification. Overall, looks sleeker and with less shaggy throat than Common; bill is also subtly shorter, and its tail is more rounded and less wedge-shaped. Diagnostic white bases to neck feathers are sometimes revealed if feathers are wind-ruffled. Sexes are similar. **ADULT** Has glossy black plumage. **JUVENILE** Similar, but with brown wash to plumage. **VOICE** Utters a coarse, croaking *who-aak*; distinctly crowlike and lacking deep resonance of Common Raven. **STATUS AND HABITAT** Fairly common in deserts and dry grasslands of southwestern U.S. Mostly resident, but range expands north in summer and contracts south in winter. **OBSERVATION TIPS** Tail shape, neck feather-bases and call separate Chihuahuan and Common Ravens.

AMERICAN CROW

ADULT

ADULT

ADULT

COMMON RAVEN

ADULT

ADULT

ADULT

CHIHUAHUAN RAVEN

Alaudidae and Hirundinidae

HORNED LARK *Eremophila alpestris* L 7–8 in

Ground-dwelling and rather long-bodied songbird, recognized by striking black and yellowish facial markings and "horn"like head feathers, particularly striking in summer males. Many subspecies exist in North America, differing in size, intensity of yellow on face, and shade of brown on upperparts; ranges of some overlap in winter. Forms flocks outside breeding season, sometimes mixing with longspurs (*see* pp.360–2). In flight, all birds show pale underwings. Sexes are similar, but females are duller than respective subspecies male counterparts. **ADULT** Has black mask, breast band, forecrown, and "horns"; face is otherwise pale—white in Arctic breeders, but yellow in all others. Underparts are whitish overall. Upperparts are rufous overall in West Coast subspecies, but sandy brown in interior and Arctic subspecies. **JUVENILE** Speckled, with hint of adult's facial markings. **VOICE** Flight calls include a thin *tsee-titi*; song is a series of tinkling notes, preceded by a few rasping *chrrt* notes. **STATUS AND HABITAT** Common in open, barren habitats, including grassland and deserts; northern and tundra-breeding populations move south for winter. **OBSERVATION TIPS** Easy to find.

MALE, PALE SUBSPECIES

TREE SWALLOW *Tachycineta bicolor* L 5.5–6 in

Distinctive swallow with contrasting, bicolored plumage. Colourful blue-green sheen on adult's dark upperparts is not always obvious in poor light and birds can look distinctly black and white. Catches insects on the wing and sometimes gathers in flocks when feeding is good; will also eat berries in winter months. Nests in tree holes and manmade nest boxes. Adult sexes are similar. **ADULT** Has blackish upperparts, but blue sheen, in good light, on cap, back, rump, and wing coverts. Dark elements of plumage on head form a complete cap that extends below eye. Underparts, including throat, are white. First-year females have browner upperparts, reduced sheen (or none at all), and white tips to tertials. **JUVENILE** Similar to dull adult (i.e. no sheen); often shows faint gray-brown breast band. **VOICE** Call and song comprise a series of whistling chirps. **STATUS AND HABITAT** Common summer visitor (mainly Apr–Sep) to a range of open habitats, often over or near water. Winters in southern U.S. and Central America. **OBSERVATION TIPS** Easy to see.

VIOLET-GREEN SWALLOW
Tachycineta thalassina L 5.25–5.5 in

Separable from similar Tree Swallow by white-faced appearance (white above and behind eye) and white sides to rump; in good light, color sheen is different, and note longer wings that extend well beyond relatively short tail when perched. Catches insects on the wing and sometimes congregates where feeding is good. Nests in tree holes, and cliff and building crevices. **ADULT** Has greenish back and wing coverts, greenish brown cap, and violet sheen to wings and upper tail. Underparts are white. Females have browner, much less colorful upperparts with white tips to tertials. **JUVENILE** Similar to female, but even browner, with gray-brown (not white) face. **VOICE** Utters a range of twittering and whistling notes. **STATUS AND HABITAT** Widespread and common summer visitor (mainly Apr–Sep) to western North America. Favors a range of habitats including open, wooded mountain slopes, and cities and towns. Winters mainly in Central America. **OBSERVATION TIPS** Easy to find.

MALE

MALE

HORNED LARK

TREE SWALLOW

ADULT

FEMALE, 1ST-YEAR

ADULT

MALE

VIOLET-GREEN SWALLOW

FEMALE

MALE

Hirundinidae

PURPLE MARTIN *Progne subis* L 7–8 in

Well-loved, plump-bodied hirundine; largest of its kind in the region. Readily takes to manmade nest boxes, although trait is more typical of eastern populations. In flight, broad-based, triangular wings and relatively slow wingbeats create passing resemblance to European Starling. Sexes are dissimilar. **ADULT MALE** Can look all-dark in poor light, but at close range note glossy bluish purple sheen on body plumage. **ADULT FEMALE** Has gray-brown upperparts overall, with variable hint of bluish sheen on back and cap; note the pale gray collar and forehead. Underparts are mottled gray-brown, palest (forming distinct patch) on belly. Western

birds are paler overall than eastern birds, particularly on underparts, nape, and forehead. **JUVENILE** Similar to female, but with much paler underparts, clean and whitish on belly and undertail. First-summer male retains many juvenile characters. **VOICE** Song is a series of gurgling, churring notes; calls include whistles and a liquid *chrrr*. **STATUS AND HABITAT** Locally common summer visitor (mainly Apr–Aug) to open rural and suburban habitats. More widespread in eastern North America and much more attached to human settlement there. Winters in South America. **OBSERVATION TIPS** Easy to see.

BANK SWALLOW *Riparia riparia* L 5.25–5.5 in

Tiny hirundine and the smallest of its kind in the region. Often seen catching insects in rapid flight, with flicking wingbeats, low over water; often congregates where feeding is good. Typically nests colonially in burrows excavated in vertical sand or gravel banks and cliffs, beside rivers and in quarries and excavations. Sexes are similar. **ADULT** Has sandy gray-

brown upperparts and mainly white underparts, with a striking, well-defined brown breast band. Division between brown cap and white throat is well defined. Tail is relatively long and slightly forked. **JUVENILE** Similar to adult, but with more obvious pale buff fringes to many wing feathers. **VOICE** Utters a buzzing alarm call and song is a series of abrupt, twittering notes. **STATUS AND HABITAT** Widespread and common summer visitor (mainly Apr–Sep) to a wide range of habitats. Winters in South America. **OBSERVATION TIPS** Easy to see, especially near water.

NORTHERN ROUGH-WINGED SWALLOW
Stelgidopteryx serripennis L 5–6 in

Similar to, but slightly larger than, Bank Swallow, separable in all plumages by noting absence of dark breast band; underparts are also grubbier white overall. Nests in crevices and holes in rock faces; either solitarily or in small colonies (not the large colonies sometimes seen in Bank Swallow).

Catches insects on the wing, often feeding over water. Sexes are similar. **ADULT** Has rather uniform brown upperparts, with pale fringes to inner flight feathers and coverts sometimes visible. Brown on face grades to light brown on throat and breast; underparts are otherwise whitish. Tail appears almost square-ended when fanned in flight. **JUVENILE** Similar, but more rufous overall, with noticeably broad, rufous margins to inner flight feathers and wing coverts; throat is warm buff. **VOICE** Utters a range of buzzing call notes. **STATUS AND HABITAT** Widespread and common summer visitor (mainly Apr–Sep) to a wide range of open habitats. Winters mainly in Central America. **OBSERVATION TIPS** Easy to see. Absence of dark breast bands separates it from Bank Swallow.

FEMALE

FEMALE

PURPLE MARTIN

MALE

BANK SWALLOW

ADULT

ADULT

NORTHERN ROUGH-WINGED SWALLOW

JUVENILE

Hirundinidae

CLIFF SWALLOW
Petrochelidon pyrrhonota L 5.5–6 in

Compact swallow with broad-based, triangular, and relatively short
wings. Pale orange-buff rump, obvious in flight, is diagnostic across much of
western range, but beware of confusion with Cave Swallow (*see* below) within
that species' limited American range. Nests colonially, making mud nests on
cliffs and manmade structures. Catches flying insects on the wing. Sexes are
similar. **ADULT** Has bluish black cap and white-lined bluish black back. Note
the pale collar, reddish orange cheeks and dark throat; forehead is white in most
birds, but reddish orange in those from southwest. Rump is buffy and square-ended
tail is dark. Underparts are mostly pale with darker spots on undertail coverts. **JUVENILE** Duller than adult,
with unmarked back; lacks reddish elements of facial plumage and has paler rump. Throat is dark (cf. juvenile Cave). **VOICE** Utters various soft twittering notes. **STATUS AND HABITAT** Common summer visitor
(mainly Apr–Sep) to a wide range of habitats. Winters in South America. **OBSERVATION TIPS** Easy to find.

CAVE SWALLOW *Petrochelidon fulva* L 5.5–6 in

Similar to Cliff Swallow, but separable with care. Reddish orange forehead distinguishes adult from all but southwestern Cliffs, and note
paler throat and face generally, showing obvious contrast with dark cap. Juvenile Cave's pale face, throat, and nape are best features for separation from
juvenile Cliff. Nests colonially, making mud nests in caves or under bridges.
Sexes are similar. **ADULT** Has bluish black cap and white-lined bluish black
back. Has pale collar and pale reddish orange cheeks and throat; forehead is
reddish orange (more extensive than in southwestern Cliffs). Rump is reddish
buff and square-ended tail is dark. Underparts are mostly pale with darker spots

on undertail coverts. **JUVENILE** Duller and less colorful than
adult, with pale buff forehead and pale buff nape, throat,
and breast, grading to whitish underparts. **VOICE** Utters a
sharp *che-wiit* and various twittering notes. **STATUS AND
HABITAT** Locally common summer visitor (mainly Mar–Aug),
mostly to Texas, but range expanding; often feeds in vicinity of water. A few remain in southern Texas throughout
year, but most are presumed to winter in Central America.
OBSERVATION TIPS Beware confusion with Cliff Swallow.

ADULT

BARN SWALLOW *Hirundo rustica* L 6.5–7 in

Familiar and colorful swallow. Flight is dashing and varied as it pur-
sues flying insects; often feeds low over ground or water. Builds mud

JUVENILE

nest, sometimes in cave or on cliff
ledge, but frequently on ledge in barn
or outbuilding. Sexes are separable.
ADULT MALE Has blue cap, nape, and
back, with red forehead and throat.
Blue breast band separates throat from
buffy orange underparts, including under-
wing coverts. Note the long deeply forked tail. **ADULT FEMALE**
Similar, but may have a shorter tail and can have much paler,
buffy white underparts. **JUVENILE** Similar to adult female, but
with very short tail streamers and orange-buff (not red) throat
and forehead. **VOICE** Song is a series of twittering warbles; calls
include a sharp *che-viit*. **STATUS AND HABITAT** Common and
widespread summer visitor (mainly Mar–Sep) to open country,
including farmland and grassland. Winters mainly in South
America. **OBSERVATION TIPS** Easy to see.

ADULT

ADULT

CLIFF SWALLOW

JUVENILE

CAVE SWALLOW

ADULT

FEMALE

BARN SWALLOW

MALE

BLACK-CRESTED TITMOUSE
Baeolophus atricristatus L 6–6.5 in

Distinctive and endearing bird because of its indifference to observers and occasional inquisitiveness. Easily recognized as a titmouse, with black crest and orange wash to flanks allowing confident identification. Nests in tree holes in natural habitats, but readily uses nest boxes in wooded suburbs. Formerly treated as a subspecies of Tufted Titmouse (*see below*), but now assigned full species status. Note that, very locally, hybrids between the two occur with intermediate characters (notably intensity of crest color). Sexes are similar. **ADULT** Has mainly soft blue-gray upperparts, with a peaked, black crest and pale forehead. Dark eye is emphasized by otherwise pale face, and underparts are mainly very pale blue-gray, with orange-buff wash on flanks and whitish undertail coverts. Bill is dark and legs are blue-gray. **JUVENILE** Similar, but lacks black crest and then extremely similar to juvenile Tufted. Note, however, the pale (not dark gray) forehead. **VOICE** Song is a series of *chiu* phrases; call is a nasal *zree*. **STATUS AND HABITAT** Common resident of dry, open wood habitats including riverine woodland, mature gardens, and urban parks. **OBSERVATION TIPS** Easy to find. **SIMILAR SPECIES Tufted Titmouse** *B. bicolor* (L 6–6.5 in) is the eastern counterpart of Black-crested. It is marginally larger and adult has a gray crest, the color of which is the same as that of most of remaining upperparts, and a blackish forehead. Juvenile is similar, but has a grayish forehead (pale in juvenile Black-crested). Voice is similar to Black-crested's, although song is a more disyllabic *peet-oo, peet-oo....* Favors similar habitats to Black-crested and resident range extends west to line from central Texas northward.

TUFTED TITMOUSE

ADULT

BRIDLED TITMOUSE
Baeolophus wollweberi L 5.25–5.5 in

Dainty little titmouse with distinctive and diagnostic "bridled" facial markings and pronounced crest that can be raised to near vertical. Forages for insects among foliage and nests in tree holes. Often found in family groups outside breeding season, which sometimes consolidate and form part of mixed-species flocks. Sexes are similar. **ADULT** Has mainly soft gray upperparts, with striking markings on face: black border to rear and side of crest, continuing as black line framing edges of nape; face is pale overall, but with black line through eye, framing edge of ear coverts and linking with black throat. Underparts are soft, pale gray. **JUVENILE** Similar, but black elements of facial markings are paler and less distinct, and crest is shorter. **VOICE** Song is a series of whistled *peed* notes; calls include a chickadeelike *tsika-dee-deed*. **STATUS AND HABITAT** A mainly Mexican species whose resident range extends into Arizona and New Mexico where it is locally common in mountains. Favors oak woodland for much of year, but sometimes undertakes altitudinal migration to lower elevations in winter. **OBSERVATION TIPS** Fairly easy to find if you visit the right habitats, but since birds form roving flocks outside breeding season you may have to search for a while to find them. Learn the distinctive calls and listen for these to detect species' presence.

BLACK-CRESTED TITMOUSE

ADULT

ADULT

BRIDLED TITMOUSE

ADULT

Paridae

OAK TITMOUSE *Baeolophus inornatus* L 5–6 in

Charming little titmouse with rather nondescript plumage. Obvious titmouselike structure and absence of any striking plumage features are good clues to separate it from most other species, except Juniper Titmouse (*see* below), with which it was formerly considered conspecific. For separation from that species, note subtle differences in plumage and more distinct differences in habitat preference and geographical range. Sometimes seen in small parties outside the breeding season and occasionally joins roving mixed-species flocks. Sexes are similar. **ADULT** Has plain and unmarked warm gray-brown upperparts including tail; note the short but distinct crest. Underparts are pale gray, with a subtle or barely visible pinkish or warm buffy wash on flanks. Bill is pointed and gray, and legs are dark gray. Subtle plumage variation exists within the species' range and several subspecies are recognized. **JUVENILE** Similar to adult. **VOICE** Song comprises a varied range of whistling notes including *peechew*; calls include a sharp *tsi-chrr*. **STATUS AND HABITAT** Fairly common resident within its rather limited range on the Pacific slopes of California and Oregon; although by no means restricted to oak woodland, this is its favored habitat. **OBSERVATION TIPS** For beginners, geographical range is the best initial clue to separation from Juniper Titmouse, especially since both species are rather sedentary in their habits. Get to know this species first in areas where it does not overlap with Juniper.

JUNIPER TITMOUSE *Baeolophus ridgwayi* L 5.25–5.75 in

Extremely similar to Oak Titmouse, and formerly considered to be conspecific and called Plain Titmouse. Geographical range is the best initial clue to separation from Oak Titmouse, since there is little overlap. If you are already familiar with Oak then you will notice subtle differences in plumage and voice. Juniper is slightly larger than Oak and bill is subtly longer. Often found in small family groups outside the breeding season and sometimes mixes with other species in roving flocks in winter. Sexes are similar. **ADULT** Has soft gray upperparts, including the tail; these lack the warm brown hue seen in Oak Titmouse. Dark eye is emphasized by the rather pale face. Underparts are pale gray with a subtle pinkish or buffy wash sometimes visible on the flanks. Bill is pointed and gray, and legs are gray. **JUVENILE** Similar to adult. **VOICE** Song is varied and generally lower pitched than Oak Titmouse with phrases often delivered in threes, e.g. *whidlidli-whidlidli-whidlidli*; call is a sharp *tsi-chk-chk*. **STATUS AND HABITAT** Widespread and fairly common resident. Typically associated with open juniper woodland, often on mountain slopes, but sometimes also in other woodland habitats outside the breeding season. **OBSERVATION TIPS** Geographical range is the best pointer to identification in the first instance. In the few areas where both species might occur, concentrate on assessing the plumage hue (brownish in Oak and plain gray in Juniper).

ADULT

OAK TITMOUSE

ADULT

ADULT

JUNIPER TITMOUSE

ADULT

Paridae

BLACK-CAPPED CHICKADEE
Poecile atricapillus L 5.25–5.5 in

Our most widespread chickadee and a familiar garden bird. Regular visitor to bird feeders and typically indifferent to people, especially ones who provide food. In natural settings, nests in tree holes, but readily occupies nest boxes. Feeds on invertebrates and seeds, depending on seasonal availability, and often joins roving mixed-species flocks outside the breeding season. Sexes are similar. **ADULT** Has a gray-buff back and mostly dark wings, but with whitish edges to inner flight feathers and greater coverts, forming a pale panel. Head has prominent black cap, extending narrowly down nape, and neatly defined black throat and bib. White on face covers cheeks and extends to sides of nape. Underparts are otherwise pale with buffy pinkish wash to rear of flanks. Tail is dark with pale fringes to feathers. Subtle variation exists in plumage across western populations, with those from Pacific Northwest being more richly colorful on flanks than those from Rockies and interior. Legs are gray and short; stubby bill is dark. **JUVENILE** Similar to adult. **VOICE** Song is a whistled, disyllabic *fee-bee*; calls its name: *chika-dee-dee-dee*. **STATUS AND HABITAT** Widespread and common resident in a wide range of wooded habitats, including mixed and deciduous forests and wooded gardens and urban parks. **OBSERVATION TIPS** Usually extremely easy to see and in many instances you will not need binoculars to obtain superb close-up views. Possibility for confusion exists with slightly smaller Carolina Chickadee (*see* below for full description). Geographical range is the easiest pointer to identification, but in zone of overlap, concentrate on subtle plumage differences, notably paleness of wing feather fringes and color of flanks.

CAROLINA CHICKADEE
Poecile carolinensis L 4.75–5 in

Very similar to Black-capped. Fortunately, ranges barely overlap. Slightly smaller size is of little use in field identification. With experience, Carolina's subtly different proportions (smaller head and shorter tail) and voice can be useful pointers. Visits feeders, uses nest boxes, and joins roving mixed-species flocks of small birds outside breeding season. Sexes are similar. **ADULT** Has "cold" look to plumage compared to Black-capped. Has gray-buff back and darkish wings; pale margins to inner flight feathers, and greater coverts are duller and show less contrast than on Black-capped. Black cap, throat, and bib are similar in extent to Black-capped, but white on face grades subtly from white cheeks to pale gray on sides of nape (uniformly white in Black-capped). Underparts are grayish overall with faint buff wash on flanks in populations within this book's range (flanks are warmer buff in Black-capped). Tail is dark, but with pale (not white) fringes. Legs are gray and bill is dark. **JUVENILE** Similar to adult. **VOICE** Song is a four-note whistling *fee-bee fee-bay*; call is a rapid *chika-dee-dee*, higher pitched than that of Black-capped. **STATUS AND HABITAT** Resident of deciduous wooded habitats, but occurrence is limited in the geographical range covered by this book. **OBSERVATION TIPS** Easy to see. **SIMILAR SPECIES Mexican Chickadee** *P. sclateri* (L 5–5.25 in), a mainly Mexican species, has a small resident range in Arizona and New Mexico. Note the dark gray upperparts, more extensive black bib, and gray-washed flanks on otherwise whitish underparts. Found in high-altitude conifer forests.

MEXICAN CHICKADEE

ADULT

BLACK-CAPPED CHICKADEE

ADULT

CAROLINA CHICKADEE

ADULT

MOUNTAIN CHICKADEE
Poecile gambeli L 5.25–5.5 in
Structurally rather similar to Black-capped and Carolina Chickadees
(*see* previous pages), but separable by plumage differences, notably the striking white supercilium (although this is less obvious in summer when plumage
is worn). Favored habitat and altitudinal range are also useful pointers.
Joins roving mixed-species flocks outside breeding season and caches seeds
as a food store for winter. Sexes are similar. **ADULT** Has gray back and darkish
wings; pale fringes to inner flight feathers and coverts are less striking than
in Black-capped. Has a black cap marked with a white supercilium; note also
the black throat and bib. Underparts are pale with gray wash to flanks. Legs are gray and bill is dark.
JUVENILE Similar to adult. **VOICE** Song is typically a four-note *fee-bee, fee-bay*; call is a nasal *chika-tzi-
tzi*. **STATUS AND HABITAT** Common resident of mountain coniferous and mixed forests. Some altitudinal
migration sometimes occurs in winter. **OBSERVATION TIPS** Easy to see in suitable habitats at appropriate
altitudes.

CHESTNUT-BACKED CHICKADEE
Poecile rufescens L 4.75–5 in
Colorful chickadee, whose identification is relatively straightforward.
Looks rather plump-bodied and short-tailed. Sometimes joins roving mixed-
species flocks of small birds outside breeding season. Sexes are similar. **ADULT**
Has a chestnut back and neatly defined white cheeks (framed by the black cap
that extends narrowly down nape) and black throat. Darkish wings have pale
feather fringes and tail is dark; underparts are gray-buff overall, but heavily
flushed with chestnut on flanks in most birds found north of California. Legs are
gray and bill is dark in all birds. **JUVENILE** Similar to adult. **VOICE** No obvious song;
calls include a sharp *tsiti-tchee-tchee*. **STATUS AND HABITAT** Common resident within its restricted range;
favors conifer and mixed forests. **OBSERVATION TIPS** Easy to find in suitable habitats within its limited
range. Often forages high in treetops, but its inquisitive nature sometimes brings it nearer to eye level.

BOREAL CHICKADEE *Poecile hudsonica* L 5–5.5 in
Hardy Arctic and northern chickadee with "warm" look to plumage
overall. Caches seeds as a food resource for winter months. Sexes
are similar. **ADULT** Has brown cap, extending narrowly down nape, and gray-
brown back; back is warmer brown in eastern subspecies. Wings are dark with
very indistinct pale feather margins. Neatly defined black throat borders the
grayish face, which is whitish only toward the front. Pale underparts are
strongly washed orange-buff on flanks; precise hue of wash varies according
to subspecies. **JUVENILE** Similar to adult. **VOICE** Has a trilling song; calls include
a thin *dee* and a *tsika-chay-chay*.

GRAY-HEADED CHICKADEE

ADULT

STATUS AND HABITAT Widespread and fairly common
resident of northern and boreal conifer forests. Mostly
rather sedentary, but occasionally forced to undertake irruptive movements south in late fall and winter
if food supplies fail. **OBSERVATION TIPS** Easy to find,
except during breeding season, when it is unobtrusive
and easily overlooked. **SIMILAR SPECIES Gray-headed
Chickadee** *P. cincta* (L 5.5 in) is an Alaskan specialty
whose northern range barely overlaps that of Boreal.
Has much more striking pale fringes to wing feathers,
white (not gray) cheeks, and ill-defined lower margin
to black bib. Resident of stunted spruce, alder, and
willow woodland.

MOUNTAIN CHICKADEE

ADULT

CHESTNUT-BACKED CHICKADEE

ADULT

ADULT

ADULT

BOREAL CHICKADEE

ADULT

Remizidae, Aegithalidae, and Timaliidae

VERDIN *Auriparus flaviceps* L 4.5 in

Striking and distinctive little desert bird with a rather warblerlike appearance. Forages actively but unobtrusively among foliage for invertebrates, and frequently flicks tail. Sexes are similar, but female is duller than male. **ADULT** Has gray-buff back and nape. Wings are mainly gray-buff, but with darker flight feathers and small reddish patch on "shoulder" (often indistinct or partly hidden).

Face is mostly yellow, but with dark lores and eye. Underparts are pale gray, and legs and tiny, pointed bill are dark. **JUVENILE** Plain gray overall, lacking adult's color on face and "shoulders." Could be mistaken for immature Lucy's Warbler (*see* p.314), whose range and habitat preferences overlap in southwest. **VOICE** Has a whistling, tri-syllabic song; calls include a sharp *tseip*. **STATUS AND HABITAT** Widespread and fairly common resident of desert scrub and open mesquite woodland. **OBSERVATION TIPS** Its typically solitary nature outside breeding season can make it a tricky species to find. Persistence usually pays off.

BUSHTIT *Psaltriparus minimus* L 4.5–5 in

Endearing little short-winged, long-tailed bird, with a rounded head and stubby, pointed bill. Outside breeding season, often found in active, acrobatic flocks. Sexes are similar, but iris of male is dark, while that of female is whitish. Subspecies variation in plumage exists. **ADULT** Interior subspecies has mostly uniformly blue-gray upperparts, darkest on primaries and tail; subtly browner patch on ear coverts can usually be discerned. Under-

parts are pale gray. Legs and bill are dark. Pacific coast subspecies is similar, but with brown cap. Note that many adult Mexican birds have a black mask (so-called "Black-eared Bushtit"); this feature is sometimes seen in juve-nile males in southwestern U.S. **JUVENILE** Similar to respective adults, although initially female has dark eye. **VOICE** Utters a range of buzzing and thin chipping notes. **STATUS AND HABITAT** Fairly common and generally rather sedentary resident of chaparral, and various wood-ed and scrub habitats in southwest. **OBSERVATION TIPS** Presence often first detected by noting contact calls uttered by members of roving flocks.

WRENTIT *Chamaea fasciata* L 6–6.5 in

Charming little bird that is rather secretive and unobtrusive for much of the time. Rec-ognized by its squat body, proportionately large head and short wings, and relatively long tail that is often cocked. Pale iris is also distinctive. Sexes are similar, but color tone of plumage varies subtly throughout the species' range. **ADULT** From north of range typically has mostly brownish upperparts including tail, grading to grayish on crown and face; note the hint of a pale supercilium. Throat is pinkish buff and streaked, and underparts are otherwise streaked pinkish buff grading to gray-buff on flanks. Legs and short, pointed bill are dark. From south of range has plumage that is grayer overall, both above and below. **JUVENILE** Similar to adult. **VOICE** Song of male is an accelerating series of abrupt whistles, ending in a trill; that of female is more even and without the trill. All birds utter a rattling call. **STATUS AND HABITAT** Common and rather sedentary resident of chaparral woodland. **OBSERVATION TIPS** Skulking habits mean that patience is often needed to get a good, prolonged view.

VERDIN

MALE

BUSHTIT

MALE, INTERIOR

WRENTIT

ADULT

Sittidae

WHITE-BREASTED NUTHATCH
Sitta carolinensis L 5.75–6 in

Our largest nuthatch. Often joins roving mixed-species flocks outside breeding season; visits bird feeders. Like other nuthatches, often climbs down tree trunks headfirst. Several subspecies exist, and Pacific coast and interior populations have subtle differences in plumage and voice. Sexes are separable. **ADULT MALE** Has slate-gray back and wings; dark markings on tertials and wing coverts are more striking, and back is darker overall in interior birds, compared to Pacific ones. Nape and crown are black in all birds, contrasting with white face, throat, and breast; underparts are otherwise rather pale, with gray wash on flanks (darkest on interior birds) and rufous and white on vent and undertail. **ADULT FEMALE** Similar to respective regional male, but crown and nape are dark gray, not black, and flanks are paler. **JUVENILE** Similar to adult, but wing feathers have buff fringes. **VOICE** Song is a series of whistling notes. Pacific birds utter a nasal *eeerp* call; that of interior birds is a rapid series of high-pitched whistles. **STATUS AND HABITAT** Common resident of mixed and deciduous woodland. Some dispersal occurs outside breeding season, presumably related to food shortages. **OBSERVATION TIPS** Easy to see and identify.

RED-BREASTED NUTHATCH
Sitta canadensis L 4.5–5 in

Colorful and well-marked nuthatch with a compact, plump body and slender, pointed bill. Joins roving mixed-species flocks of small birds outside the breeding season. Sexes are separable with care. **ADULT MALE** Has blue-gray back, wings, and tail. Head is marked with black crown and eyestripe, and white supercilium, cheeks, and chin. Throat and rest of underparts are reddish buff. **ADULT FEMALE** Similar, but black elements of head plumage are paler and underparts are paler orange-buff. **JUVENILE** Similar to respective sex adult, but with brownish wing feathers. **VOICE** Song is a series of nasal *errn* notes, similar to its nasal call, which is reminiscent of a toy trumpet. **STATUS AND HABITAT** Widespread and common in coniferous forests. Mainly resident across much of range, but northern populations migrate south in fall and many others periodically undertake irruptive movements (some long distance), presumably in response to food shortages. **OBSERVATION TIPS** Often first detected by its distinctive call.

PYGMY NUTHATCH *Sitta pygmaea* L 4.25–4.5 in

Charming little nuthatch with an extremely compact body, and proportionately large head, long bill, and short tail. Cooperative behavior observed when breeding and social at other times too, foraging in extremely vocal flocks outside breeding season. Sexes are similar. **ADULT** Has blue-gray back and wing coverts, with darker flight feathers. Back color grades to brown on cap, but note pale nape patch and dark stripe through eye. Face and throat is whitish, grading to buff yellow on rest of underparts, apart from grayish wash on flanks. Legs and bill are dark. **JUVENILE** Similar to adult, but less colorful. Subspecies variation exists in contrast between cap and eyestripe, and intensity of buffy wash on underparts. **VOICE** Utters various sharp, rapid calls including *kip-kip-kip*. Song comprises disyllabic phrases, similar in tone to call. **STATUS AND HABITAT** Common resident of pine forests. **OBSERVATION TIPS** Easiest to detect by call.

ADULT

FEMALE

WHITE-BREASTED NUTHATCH

MALE

FEMALE

RED-BREASTED NUTHATCH

MALE

ADULT

PYGMY NUTHATCH

ADULT

Certhiidae and Cinclidae

BROWN CREEPER *Certhia americana* L 5–5.25 in

Distinctive and unmistakable woodland bird, whose well-marked brown plumage is a good match for tree bark. Feeds by climbing tree trunks in an almost mouselike manner, probing crevices for small invertebrates with its needlelike, downcurved bill. Spiky tail is used as support and bird typically works its way upward from base of tree in a spiral manner, then drops to base of adjacent trunk to repeat the process. Sometimes joins roving mixed-species flocks outside the breeding season. Not unduly wary, but unobtrusive habits mean it is easy to overlook. Nests in natural crevices under loose tree bark. Several subspecies exist: those in western North America are darker, smaller, and longer-billed overall than those from east. Mexican birds (found in southern Arizona and southern New Mexico) are rather dark overall, with contrasting pale spots on upperparts and gray underparts. Sexes are similar. **ADULT** Has brownish upperparts heavily marked with pale teardrop spots on crown, face, and back; note the bold whitish supercilium. Short wings have buffy barring, and rump and base of tail are rufous. Underparts are whitish overall, with buff wash on flanks and undertail. Variation exists in precise hue of upperparts (ranging from grayish to rufous), even within the same regional populations. **JUVENILE** Similar to adult, but with faint barring on chest. **VOICE** Song is a series of *tsee-see-see* notes; call is a thin *tsee*, recalling that of Golden-crowned Kinglet (*see* p.292). **STATUS AND HABITAT** Widespread and fairly common in forest habitats; resident across much of western range, but numbers are boosted and range extends into interior in winter due to influx of birds from north. **OBSERVATION TIPS** Outside breeding season, search roving mixed-species flocks and listen for its high, thin calls. Note, however, people who are hard of hearing may not be able to detect the notes.

AMERICAN DIPPER *Cinclus mexicanus* L 7–7.5 in

Stocky, short-tailed bird invariably associated with fast-flowing water. Despite its uniform and rather undistinguished plumage, unmistakable because of its body form, habitat preference, and habits. Typically seen perched on stones in midstream, often bobbing up and down; tail is often cocked. Feeds on submerged aquatic invertebrates—mostly insect larvae and nymphs—caught either by foraging in shallows or completely submerging itself and walking around the rocks underneath the water. White eyelids look striking and flash in direct sunlight when bird blinks. Flies on whirring wingbeats, usually low over water. Sexes are similar. **ADULT** Has dark blue-gray plumage overall, with brownish wash sometimes visible on head. Bill is dark and relatively stout and long legs are pale. **JUVENILE** Similar to adult, but pale feather margins on underparts create scaly appearance, wing feathers have pale margins, and bill is dull yellow. **VOICE** Song comprises a series of whistled phrases, each repeated a few times; call is a sharp *tzeet*. **STATUS AND HABITAT** Widespread and fairly common, but almost entirely restricted to rocky streams and rivers. Mostly resident and rather sedentary, although birds from high altitudes are often obliged to descend to lower stretches of river by winter ice. **OBSERVATION TIPS** Easy to see on suitable rivers and streams within range.

ADULT

BROWN CREEPER

ADULT

AMERICAN DIPPER

ADULT

Troglodytidae

HOUSE WREN *Troglodytes aedon* L 4.75–5 in

Tiny bird with typical wren proportions: rounded body and short wings. Tail is often cocked. Has a needlelike bill and relatively short legs. Forages in vegetation for insects and spiders. Nests in tree holes, but readily uses nest boxes and cavities and crevices in buildings. Sexes are similar, but regional subspecies variation exists. **ADULT** Has brown plumage overall, darkest on upperparts with barring on wings and tail. Western ssp. *parkmanii* (main representative in region covered by this book) has gray face and throat and otherwise mostly pale buff underparts with rufous wash and barring on flanks. Eastern ssp. *aedon* is similar, but face, throat, and underparts are more rufous. Birds from southern Arizona are more buff overall. **JUVENILE** Similar to respective subspecies adult, but averages more rufous above with scaly appearance to paler face and throat. **VOICE** Song is an accelerating series of sweet, raspy trilling notes, ending in a flourish; call is a raspy *tche-tche*. **STATUS AND HABITAT** Widespread and common summer visitor (mainly May–Aug), favoring gardens, woodland, and scrub. Winters mainly in Mexico, but birds are found year-round in parts of southwest. **OBSERVATION TIPS** Unobtrusive, often first detected by song.

WINTER WREN *Troglodytes troglodytes* L 4–4.5 in

Smaller than House Wren; much shorter tail is often cocked. Unobtrusive; looks mouselike as it creeps through low vegetation after insects. Flies on whirring wingbeats, usually from one patch of cover to another. Extremely vocal, and unseen birds often detected by their distinctive call. Sexes are similar, but subtle regional variation exists. **ADULT** Has reddish brown upperparts, with barring on wings and tail; note the pale buff supercilium. Underparts are buffy brown, with barring on the flanks. Western ssp. *pacificus* is more rufous overall than eastern ssp. *hiemalis*. (It is likely that these two subspecies will be given full species status in the near future.) Birds from Aleutians are larger and darker than mainland counterparts. Bill is needlelike and legs are reddish in all birds. **JUVENILE** Similar to adult, but with subtly less distinct barring. **VOICE** Song is variable and warbling, often ending in a trill; call is a sharp *chip-chip*. **STATUS AND HABITAT** Locally common in dense woodland with tangled undergrowth. Resident in many areas, but northern, interior birds are summer visitors (mainly Apr–Aug), migrating mainly to southeastern U.S. for winter. **OBSERVATION TIPS** Easy to overlook. Listen for the call.

BEWICK'S WREN *Thryomanes bewickii* L 5.25–5.5 in

Well-marked wren with a striking pale supercilium. Rather long tail has white outer tips and is often cocked. Forages for insects and spiders among foliage and on ground, as well as in dense cover. Regional variation exists in plumage (palest and grayest in southwestern birds), but variation also seen within populations in same area. Sexes are similar, given this variability. **ADULT** Has brown upperparts overall, unmarked except on tail, which is barred. Underparts are grayish white, palest on throat and with rufous wash on rear of flanks in all but southwestern birds. **JUVENILE** Similar to adult. **VOICE** Song comprises a series of wheezy, rasping notes, ending in a trill; calls include various harsh, raspy notes. **STATUS AND HABITAT** Mostly a fairly common resident of woods with clearings and thickets, and mature gardens; eastern birds move south in winter. **OBSERVATION TIPS** Listen for the song.

HOUSE WREN

ADULT

WINTER WREN

ADULT

BEWICK'S WREN

ADULT

Troglodytidae

CAROLINA WREN
Thryothorus ludovicianus L 5.25–5.5 in

Vocal and familiar garden bird and a colorful, well-marked wren. Where range overlaps with similar Bewick's, separated by warmer colors overall, uniformly barred, brown tail (without white outer tips) and delicate white-spotted wing bars. Indifferent to, or sometimes curious about, human observers. Sexes are similar. **ADULT** Has rich brown upperparts, with faint dark barring on wings and tail, and striking white supercilium. Face is speckled grayish buff and underparts are warm buff. Bill is downcurved, and legs are orangish. **JUVENILE** Similar to adult. **VOICE** Song is a rapid series of fluty whistles; call is a harsh, agitated *tchee-tchee-tchee....* **STATUS AND HABITAT** Widespread and common in gardens, scrub, and dense woodland; mainly sedentary. Northern populations suffer badly in harsh winters. **OBSERVATION TIPS** Easy to see and hear around houses and in gardens.

MARSH WREN *Cistothorus palustris* L 5–5.25 in

Vocal, but secretive wren that is easier to hear than see. In flight (between one patch of cover and another), note the whirring, rounded wings and rounded tail. Perched birds often cock tail. Subtle geographic plumage variation exists (with several subspecies), and western populations have more subdued plumage colors than eastern counterparts; experienced ears can also detect differences in song. Sexes are similar, given subspecies variation. **ADULT** From west has reddish brown upperparts overall, with subtle barring on wings and tail, white streaks on back and striking, pale supercilium. Face is gray-buff, palest on throat, warmest on flanks and with speckling on face. Eastern birds have richer brown colors. **JUVENILE** Similar to respective adult, but with grayer face and less distinct supercilium. **VOICE** Song is extremely variable; typical western bird sings a rattling trill of fluty notes preceded by a rather hesitant, fluty warble; song of eastern bird is more musical and less rattling. Calls of all birds include an agitated *tchut*. **STATUS AND HABITAT** Locally common in cattail marshes. Resident in parts of southwest and Pacific U.S.; elsewhere mostly a summer visitor (present mainly May–Aug), wintering in southern U.S. and Mexico. **OBSERVATION TIPS** Easy to hear, but a challenge to see. Patient watching usually pays off.

SEDGE WREN *Cistothorus platensis* L 4.5–4.75 in

Superficially similar to Marsh Wren, but separated by voice, habitat preference, and subtle plumage differences: Sedge has paler, warmer buff plumage overall, with more conspicuous barring on wings and more extensively streaked back. Like many other wrens (including Marsh), male builds several "dummy" nests that are not used. Sexes are similar. **ADULT** Has reddish buff upperparts overall, with subtle dark barring on tail, more striking dark and pale barring on wings, bold dark and pale streaks on back, and a streaked crown; supercilium is buffy. Underparts are buffy brown overall, but palest and whitish on throat. **JUVENILE** Similar to adult, but colors and markings are duller overall. **VOICE** Song is a dry rattle preceded by a couple of sharp *chip, chip* notes; call is a sharp *chip*. **STATUS AND HABITAT** Locally common summer visitor (mainly May–Sep) to wet meadows and marshes where sedges predominate. Winters in similar habitats (plus coastal marshes) in southeastern U.S. **OBSERVATION TIPS** Easiest to find when vocal on breeding grounds.

CAROLINA WREN

ADULT

MARSH WREN

ADULT

ADULT

SEDGE WREN

ADULT

Troglodytidae

CANYON WREN *Catherpes mexicanus* L 5.5–6 in

Well-marked and distinctive wren, with a long bill and rather long tail, rounded when fanned. Forages unobtrusively, with a creeping manner, in rock crevices for insects and spiders. Inaccessibility of its favored habitats (such as steep-sided rocky canyons) means that views are often distant and that silent birds are hard to locate. Sexes are similar. **ADULT** Has rufous-brown upperparts overall, with dark barring on wings and tail and tiny black and white spots on back and rump. Crown is speckled gray, face, throat, and chest are white, and underparts are otherwise rufous, with spots and bars. **JUVENILE** Similar to adult, but with less distinct bars and spots. **VOICE** Song is a descending series of whistling notes ending with 3–4 rasping, wheezy notes; call is a piercing *jeet*. **STATUS AND HABITAT** Locally common resident, restricted to dry, steep-sided rocky canyons and cliffs. **OBSERVATION TIPS** Easiest to detect by listening for call and song. Prolonged scanning of rock face may be needed to locate bird itself.

ROCK WREN *Salpinctes obsoletus* L 6–6.5 in

Dumpy-bodied wren that forages among rocks for insects and spiders, often with a bouncing gait. Pairs create pathway of flattened pebbles leading to nest entrance. Sexes are similar. **ADULT** Has mostly dark gray-brown upperparts (slightly rufous on rump), speckled on crown, back, and rump with tiny black and white spots. Tail is mostly brown and barred, but note the pale buff tips to the outer feathers, appearing as a pale terminal band in flight. Face is speckled gray with a pale supercilium. Throat and chest are grayish white and streaked and underparts are otherwise pale orange-buff. **JUVENILE** Similar to adult, but speckling on upperparts is less distinct. **VOICE** Renowned and varied songster. Song is typically a series of trilling whistles, many phrases repeated 2–6 times, but also including a prolonged rattle; calls include a shrill *ch'tzee*. **STATUS AND HABITAT** Locally common summer visitor (mainly May–Sep) to dry habitats where areas of loose stones, pebbles, and boulders predominate; range of favored habitats include scree slopes, boulder fields above the treeline, and stony desert washes. Winters from southwestern U.S. to Mexico. **OBSERVATION TIPS** Reasonably easy to find in suitable habitats.

CACTUS WREN
Campylorhynchus brunneicapillus L 8.5–9 in

Large and distinctive desert wren that recalls a miniature thrasher; has a proportionately large, downcurved bill. Often perches on, or forages

ADULT

among, cacti for insects and spiders. Builds decoy and real nests among dense cholla cacti. Sexes are similar. **ADULT** Has brown or gray-brown upperparts overall, with dark barring on wings and tail and white streaks on back; in flight, note white tips and barred white outer edge to tail. Crown is rufous brown, and note the striking white supercilium. Face is streaked gray-brown and underparts are whitish overall, but heavily spotted on the throat and breast. Belly and flanks are flushed orange-buff in interior birds, but white and more heavily spotted in birds from coastal California. **JUVENILE** Similar to adult, but with less distinct markings. **VOICE** Song is a rapid series of dry, chattering notes; calls include various harsh notes. **STATUS AND HABITAT** Fairly common resident of dry brushy and desert habitats. **OBSERVATION TIPS** Easy to see in suitable locations.

CANYON WREN

ADULT

ROCK WREN

ADULT

ADULT

CACTUS WREN

ADULT

Regulidae

GOLDEN-CROWNED KINGLET
Regulus satrapa L 3.75–4 in

Tiny and extremely active songbird with a thin, needlelike bill. Superficially warblerlike overall, but recognized by rather dumpy proportions and extremely small size. Distinctive head markings allow separation from similarly sized Ruby-crowned. Forages continuously for small insects and spiders, searching along twigs, buds, and among needles, and sometimes hovering to glean prey from otherwise inaccessible spots. Sometimes found in small flocks, and joins roving mixed-species flocks of other small birds outside breeding season. People with good hearing often locate hidden feeding birds by their thin calls.

Sexes are dissimilar. **ADULT MALE** Has mostly gray olive-green upperparts, but note the striking markings on the wings with two white wing bars, the lower and bolder of the two emphasized by black at the base of the secondaries. Face is adorned with long, white supercilium, emphasized below by dark eyestripe and above by black margin to golden yellow crown; bright orange center to crown is revealed only when bird is displaying. Face is otherwise olive-gray and underparts are pale gray-buff. Legs are black and feet are

MALE, DISPLAYING

yellowish. **ADULT FEMALE** Similar to male, but with a more yellow crown that lacks the orange center. **JUVENILE** Similar to adult female, but lacks yellow on crown. **VOICE** Song is a sweet *tswee, tswee, tswoo, tswit-tswit-tswit*; call is a thin *twsee*. **STATUS AND HABITAT** Widespread and common summer visitor (mainly Apr–Sep) to northern coniferous forests. Found year-round in conifer and mixed forests further south, including increasingly in spruce plantations (less frequently in deciduous woodland); winter migrants favor similar habitats. **OBSERVATION TIPS** Can be hard to follow when foraging actively high in foliage. However, migrants in particular, will often forage much lower and are typically indifferent to human observers.

RUBY-CROWNED KINGLET
Regulus calendula L 4–4.25 in

Marginally larger than Golden-crowned, from which it is readily distinguished by its relatively plain face, unmarked except for the broken white patch that surrounds and emphasizes the beady black eye. Forages actively and tirelessly for insects and spiders, caught with its needlelike bill. Often hovers to glean insects in manner of Golden-crowned and also flicks wings in agitated manner. Female in particular is extremely similar to Hutton's Vireo (*see* p.252), with which it sometimes associates in winter on Pacific slope and in southwestern U.S.: note 1. Hutton's relative inactivity compared to Ruby-crowned; 2. Hutton's thicker, stubbier bill; 3. Hutton's bluish legs (black with yellow feet in Ruby-crowned); and 4. Hutton's pale lores, as well as eye surround. **ADULT MALE** Has mainly grayish olive-green upperparts, but note the dark wings and two white wing bars; lower one is more pronounced than upper one. Ruby crown patch is only visible in

MALE, DISPLAYING

displaying or agitated birds. Underparts are pale olive-gray. **ADULT FEMALE** Similar to male, but lacks ruby crown patch. **JUVENILE** Similar to adult female. **VOICE** Song comprises chattering and warbling notes, preceded by thin *tsee-tsee-tsee* notes; call is a raspy *d'dit*. **STATUS AND HABITAT** Widespread and common summer visitor (mainly May–Sep) to northern and upland coniferous forests. Winters from southern U.S. to Central America, favoring a range of wooded habitats. **OBSERVATION TIPS** Easy to see in suitable habitats.

FEMALE

GOLDEN-CROWNED KINGLET

MALE

RUBY-CROWNED KINGLET

ADULT

Sylviidae

BLUE-GRAY GNATCATCHER
Polioptila caerulea L 4.25–4.5 in
Our most widespread gnatcatcher and the one by which to judge others; often seen in pairs. Has a thin bill and slim body; long tail is often cocked. Tail pattern and voice are the features to concentrate on. Forages actively in foliage for insects and sometimes hovers. Sexes are dissimilar. **ADULT MALE** When breeding, has blue-gray upperparts, except for blackish wings with contrasting white tertial edges. Tail, from above, is mainly black, but with contrasting and striking white outer feathers; from below, tail is

mostly white. Note the white eyering and black on forehead extending to above eye. Underparts are pale gray. Nonbreeding male has gray, not black, forehead. **ADULT FEMALE** Similar to nonbreeding male. **JUVENILE** Similar to adult female, but sometimes with subtle brownish wash on back. **VOICE** Song is a series of thin notes, often with some mimicry; call is a soft, grating *zwe'oe*. **STATUS AND HABITAT** Widespread and common summer visitor (mainly Apr–Aug) to deciduous wooded habitats. Winters from southern U.S. to Central America. Present year-round in some southern parts. **OBSERVATION TIPS** Easy to see.

BLACK-TAILED GNATCATCHER
Polioptila melanura L 4–4.5 in
Desert counterpart of Blue-gray and California Gnatcatchers. Separated from former by smaller size and virtual absence of white (except for tips to outer feathers) in otherwise black tail when seen from above; tail is mostly black (not white) from below, but with broader white tips to feathers than in California. Vocal differences can be detected. Separated from California by geographical range, habitat preference, voice, and subtle plumage differences (*see* California for details). Sexes are dissimilar. **ADULT MALE** When breeding, has blue-gray upperparts, except for blackish wings with contrasting white tertial edges. Tail, from above, is mainly black, but with white tips to outer feathers; from below, tail is mostly black, except for white tips. Note black cap and white eyering. Underparts are pale gray. Nonbreeding male has gray cap. **ADULT FEMALE** Similar to nonbreeding male. **JUVENILE** Similar to adult female. **VOICE** Calls include *tch'tch'tch* and *tchee-tchee* notes; song comprises similar phrases. **STATUS AND HABITAT** Locally common resident of desert habitats. **OBSERVATION TIPS** Fairly easy to find in suitable habitats.

CALIFORNIA GNATCATCHER
Polioptila californica L 4.25–4.5 in
Similar to, but duller overall than, Black-tailed, with which, formerly, it was treated as conspecific; also separated geographically and by habitat. Sexes are dissimilar. **ADULT MALE** When breeding, has blue-gray upperparts; blackish wings have gray-white tertial edges (white in our other gnatcatchers). Tail, from above, is mainly black, but with white tips to outer feathers; from below, tail is mostly black, and white feather tips are much less striking than in Black-tailed. Note black cap and indistinct pale eyering. Underparts are gray. Nonbreeding male has gray, not black, cap. **ADULT FEMALE** Similar to nonbreeding male. **JUVENILE** Similar to adult female. **VOICE** Calls include a sequence of rather plaintive, kittenlike mewing notes that rise and fall; song comprises similar phrases. **STATUS AND HABITAT** Rather scarce, with entire World population restricted to Baja California and southern California, where it favors coastal chaparral with sagebrush. **OBSERVATION TIPS** Learn to recognize its preferred habitat to find this species.

BLUE-GRAY GNATCATCHER

MALE, BREEDING

BLACK-TAILED GNATCATCHER

MALE, NONBREEDING

MALE

FEMALE

MALE

CALIFORNIA GNATCATCHER

Turdidae

WESTERN BLUEBIRD *Sialia mexicana* L 7–7.25 in

Colorful bird that perches on wires and branches, scanning for insect prey; also eats berries. Nests in tree holes and uses nest boxes. Sexes are dissimilar. **ADULT MALE** Has mostly deep blue upperparts including head and neck, with clear demarcation from orange-red breast and flanks; note orange-brown scapulars. Underparts are whitish with bluish wash on center of belly and undertail. **ADULT FEMALE** Recalls drab version of male,

with gray-brown head, neck, and back, palest on throat. Has bluish flight feathers and tail and orange wash to breast and flanks; underparts are otherwise pale gray-buff. **JUVENILE** Brown overall with pale spots on upperparts and scaly-looking underparts. **VOICE** Song, heard mainly at dawn, is a series of call notes *chut't* and *chew*. **STATUS AND HABITAT** Scarce summer visitor (mainly Apr–Aug) across much of the north of its range; resident or winter visitor further south. Favors open woodland. Numbers reduced by habitat loss and nest competition with European Starling and House Sparrow. Nest-box schemes help restore numbers. **OBSERVATION TIPS** Visit an area with nest boxes.

EASTERN BLUEBIRD *Sialia sialis* L 7–7.25 in

Similar to Western, but separable using ranges (barely overlap, except slightly in winter in southwest) and plumage differences. Females are very similar, so focus on colors on face and underparts. Nesting and feeding habits are similar to those of Western. Forms flocks outside breeding season, sometimes mixing with other species. Sexes are dissimilar. **ADULT MALE** Has mainly deep blue upperparts, including scapulars, but on head color forms a cap (hood in male Western). Throat, sides of neck, breast, and flanks are orange-red, while belly and undertail are white. **ADULT FEMALE** Has mostly gray-brown upperparts, with blue flight feathers and tail, and orange wash on underparts. Compared to female Western, note that orange wash extends to side of neck, and belly and undertail are cleaner white. **JUVENILE** Similar to juvenile West-

ern. **VOICE** Song is a rapid series of twittering warbling notes; call is a sharp *tch'ree*. **STATUS AND HABITAT** Fairly common in west of range. Summer visitor in north (mainly Apr–Sep), but present year-round or just in winter further south. Favors lightly wooded terrain including secondary woodland and large gardens. Has declined, in part due to nest competition with European Starlings and House Sparrows. Nest-box schemes help restore many local populations. **OBSERVATION TIPS** Easy to see within range.

MOUNTAIN BLUEBIRD
Sialia currucoides L 7.25–7.5 in

Stunning bird with longer wings and tail than other bluebirds. Often hovers while scanning ground for insect prey. Nests in tree holes and readily uses nest boxes. Forms flocks outside breeding season. Sexes are dissimilar.

ADULT MALE Has mostly sky-blue plumage, darkest on wings and tail, palest on belly and undertail. **ADULT FEMALE** Gray-buff overall, but with blue on wings and tail and variable orange wash to breast; brightly marked birds told from other female bluebirds by longer wings and tail, paler upperparts, and hovering habits. **JUVENILE** Recalls adult female, but underparts are pale-spotted. **VOICE** Song is a series of call notes, including a whistling *tche'ew*. **STATUS AND HABITAT** Common summer visitor (Apr–Aug) to woodland; winters at lower altitudes. **OBSERVATION TIPS** Easy to see.

FEMALE

WESTERN
BLUEBIRD

MALE

FEMALE

EASTERN
BLUEBIRD

MALE

FEMALE

MOUNTAIN
BLUEBIRD

MALE

Turdidae

TOWNSEND'S SOLITAIRE
Myadestes townsendi L 8.25–8.5 in

Slim-bodied and long-tailed bird. Voice is evocative of wilderness forests. Often sits on exposed perch for long periods, adopting upright pos-

JUVENILE

ture. Varied diet includes insects and berries. Nests in crevices on steep slopes. Sexes are similar. **ADULT** Has gray, mostly un-marked, plumage overall, palest on underparts; note the white eye-ring. Wings, however, are rather dark and contrastingly marked with orange-buff patches and whitish tips to ter-tials and greater coverts; in flight, dark median line to pale underwing coverts is striking, as is pale wing bar seen above. Tail is mostly black, but with white edges and broad tips to outer feathers. **JUVENILE** Shares wing and tail markings with adult, but body is brown overall with pale spots above and scaly appearance below. **VOICE** Song is a rich, chattering warble, with a finchlike quality; call is a whistled, sonar-bliplike *tu, tu*.... **STATUS AND HABITAT** Common summer visitor (mainly May–Aug) to montane coniferous forests. Moves south and to lower altitudes in winter, and present year-round in parts of south. **OBSERVATION TIPS** Easy to see.

VEERY *Catharus fuscescens* L 7–7.25 in

Secretive thrush. Forages among leaf litter for invertebrates. Plumage markings are understated; ironically, this helps with separation from other *Catharus* species (it is the least spotted). Sexes are similar. **ADULT** Has mainly reddish brown upperparts; western birds are subtly darker and duller than eastern ones. Face is gray-brown and faintly marked, and pale buff throat is bordered by brown line. Breast is yellow-buff with brown spots, grading to grayish white on rest of underparts with gray-washed flanks and faint gray spots on lower breast and flanks. **JUVENILE** Brown and spotted, but first-fall bird resembles adult, but with buff tips to wing coverts. **VOICE** Song is a whistled *vee, v'didi, v'didi, veer, veer*, descending stepwise in tone; call is a sharp *veer*. **STATUS AND HABITAT** Common summer visitor (mainly May–Aug) to damp, deciduous woodland, especially thickets of willow. Winters in South America. **OBSERVATION TIPS** Easiest to detect by song.

HERMIT THRUSH *Catharus guttatus* L 6.75–7 in

Well-marked, by *Catharus* thrush standards. The only genus member that winters in our region. Considerable subspecies variation, but three main groups recognizable: Pacific coast, Western Interior, and Eastern and Northern. All show some contrast between back (gray-brown or brown depending on subspecies) and more rufous tail. Forages on forest floor for invertebrates; flicks wings and cocks tail. Sexes are similar. **ADULT** Has brown upperparts overall, grayest in Western Interior birds, reddish brown in Eastern and Northern birds; note rufous panel on primaries, most striking in Eastern and Northern birds. Has a white eyering; white throat is bordered by black lateral line. Whitish underparts are washed yellow on breast (most noticeably in Eastern and Northern birds, which also have buffy undertail) and heavily dark-spotted on breast. **JUVENILE** Spotted, but first-fall bird resembles adult of respective subspecies, but with pale tips to coverts. **VOICE** Song is a series of fluty whistles, with a pause between each phrase; call is a muted *tchuck-tchuck*. **STATUS AND HABITAT** Common summer visitor (mainly May–Aug) to coniferous forests; winters from southern and southwestern U.S. to Central America. **OBSERVATION TIPS** Easy to see.

ADULT

ADULT

TOWNSEND'S SOLITAIRE

ADULT

ADULT

VEERY

JUVENILE

ADULT

HERMIT THRUSH

Turdidae

SWAINSON'S THRUSH *Catharus ustulatus* L 7 in

Similar to other *Catharus* thrushes, but separable. Pale buff "spectacles" (eyering and line to base of bill) are reliable features, but geographical variation causes confusion: warmer colored Pacific birds recall Hermit Thrush, but note lack of contrast between back color and tail (tail is contrastingly reddish in Hermit Thrush); dark line bordering side of throat and more distinct breast spotting are useful when considering Veery; with interior birds (olive-brown above), "spectacles" and buff (not gray) cheeks allow separation from Gray-cheeked. Sexes are similar. **ADULT** Has olive-brown upperparts overall although Pacific coast birds are a warmer hue. Pale buff throat is bordered by dark line and face and ear coverts are also buff. Underparts are pale with yellow-buff wash and dark spots on breast, subtle gray spots on lower breast and olive-gray flanks. **JUVENILE** Olive-brown and spotted, but first-fall bird resembles adult, with buff tips to wing coverts. **VOICE** Song is a series of fluty whistles, with tone rising and intensity diminishing throughout sequence; call is a sharp *quiirp*. **STATUS AND HABITAT** Common summer visitor (mainly May–Sep) to coniferous forests. Winters in South America. **OBSERVATION TIPS** Learn and listen for its song.

GRAY-CHEEKED THRUSH

Catharus minimus L 7.25–7.5 in

Similar to Swainson's: features to focus on include grayish upperparts, gray (not buff) cheeks, and absence of buff "spectacles." Forages in leaf litter for invertebrates. Sexes are similar. **ADULT** Has mostly gray-brown upperparts, with tail concolorous with back. Has grayish eye surround, with subtle pale gray eyering; cheeks are grayish. Whitish throat is bordered by dark line that defines pale malar stripe. Breast is washed yellow-buff and heavily marked with dark spots; underparts are otherwise pale, except for pale gray spots on lower breast and gray flanks. **JUVENILE** Gray-brown and spotted, but first-winter plumage is similar to adult, but with pale tips to wing coverts. **VOICE** Song is a series of fluty, whistling notes, often ending in a downslurred, trilling flourish; call is a rather nasal *piuup*. **STATUS AND HABITAT** Common summer visitor (mainly May–Aug) to wet, northern forests (coniferous and deciduous). Winters in northern South America. **OBSERVATION TIPS** Easiest to detect by listening for song and call.

VARIED THRUSH *Ixoreus naevius* L 9.5–10 in

Unmistakable thrush whose song is evocative of northwestern forests. Forages on forest floor for invertebrates and also eats berries. Sexes are dissimilar. **ADULT MALE** Has rich blue-gray crown, back, and rump. Dark wings are marked with orange-buff bars on flight feathers and two orange-buff wing bars. Face is marked with dark patch through eye, linking to dark breast band. Broad super-cilium, and throat and underparts, are orange-

FEMALE

buff, with bluish scaling and wash on flanks. **ADULT FEMALE** Similar to male, but bluish elements of plumage are brown, as are patch through eye and breast band. **JUVENILE** Similar to adult female, but with more scaly-looking underparts. **VOICE** Song is a series of weird, mechanical-sounding, grating whistles, each note well-spaced; calls includes whistles and a sharp *tchuup*. **STATUS AND HABITAT** Locally common summer visitor (mainly May–Sep) to damp, shady coniferous forests. Winters south to California. **OBSERVATION TIPS** Easiest to detect by voice.

ADULT

SWAINSON'S THRUSH

ADULT

ADULT

GRAY-CHEEKED
THRUSH

VARIED THRUSH

MALE

AMERICAN ROBIN *Turdus migratorius* L 10–11 in

Iconic and most familiar of all thrushes. Tolerance of people makes it commonly encountered foraging on lawns in gardens and urban parks. Feeds mainly on invertebrates, particularly earthworms. Forms flocks during the winter months. Sexes are separable with care in most cases, especially if seen side by side. **ADULT MALE** Has gray-brown back, rump, and wings, grading to almost black on head and neck. Note, however, the striking white "eyelids" and throat that is variably streaked black and white. Tail is dark brown and underparts are mostly brick-red to orange-red, but contrastingly white on belly and undertail. In flight, note the reddish underwing coverts. Legs are dark, and bill is yellowish. **ADULT FEMALE** Similar to male, but with paler gray-brown upperparts, more obviously pale throat, and less colorful underparts with pale feather fringes creating slightly scaly look. **JUVENILE** Recalls pale adult female, but has bold white teardrop spots on back and dark spots on otherwise washed-out underparts. **VOICE** Song consists of rich, whistling phrases, with pauses between each phrase; calls include a sharp *puup*; flight call is a high, sibilant *wee-wheep*. **STATUS AND HABITAT** Widespread and common summer visitor (mainly Apr–Sep) to Canada and northern U.S., favoring a wide range of habitats, from wilderness to gardens and parks. Present year-round (with numbers boosted in winter) across much of southern U.S., but essentially just a winter visitor to extreme south of range. **OBSERVATION TIPS** Easy to see, especially in suburban areas with mature gardens. **SIMILAR SPECIES Clay-colored Thrush** *T. grayi* (L 10 in), a mainly Central American species that now breeds regularly in southern Texas. All birds have mainly gray-brown plumage, warmest and palest on underparts; throat is pale with dark streaks. Song recalls that of American Robin; calls include a slurred whistle. Favors wooded parks and gardens.

AMERICAN ROBIN

JUVENILE

CLAY-COLORED THRUSH

ADULT

GRAY CATBIRD *Dumetella carolinensis* L 8.5–9 in

Distinctive and unmistakable bird if seen well, but retiring habits mean it is easily overlooked. Fortunately, however, its distinctive meowing call, after which species is named, often alerts observers to its otherwise hidden presence in deep cover. Tail is relatively long and often cocked. Forages for insects and other invertebrates on the ground among leaf litter, and also among foliage; also feeds, seasonally, on berries. Sexes are similar. **ADULT** Has mainly deep blue-gray body plumage, but with a striking black cap, dark eye, and brick-red undertail coverts. Tail is blackish and legs and bill are dark. **JUVENILE** Similar to adult. **VOICE** Song is series of harsh, abrupt and rather chattering whistles and squeaks, often with elements of mimicry; unlike songs of Northern Mockingbird and Brown Thrasher, with which it could perhaps be confused, each phrase of Catbird's song is not repeated (typically repeated several times in those other species). Song is usually delivered from dense cover. Call is a loud *mew*. **STATUS AND HABITAT** Widespread and common summer visitor (mainly May–Aug) to a wide range of densely vegetated wooded habitats, including mature parks and gardens as well as thickets of secondary growth in woodland. Winters from southeastern U.S. to Mexico and Caribbean islands in similar habitats. **OBSERVATION TIPS** Much easier to hear than to see, but patient and persistent observation usually pays off.

AMERICAN ROBIN

FEMALE

MALE

GRAY CATBIRD

ADULT

Mimidae

NORTHERN MOCKINGBIRD
Mimus polyglottos L 10–10.5 in

Familiar, long-tailed bird and accomplished songster. Often perches conspicuously. Varied diet includes insects and berries. White flashes are striking when wings are spread in display. Sexes are similar. **ADULT** Has mainly gray upperparts, but note the blackish wings with striking white wing bars and white patch (larger in males) at base of primaries. Tail is mainly black, but with contrasting white outer feathers. Dark line emphasizes the beady yellow eye. Underparts are pale

JUVENILE

gray-buff, palest on throat and undertail. Bill is dark and slightly downcurved and legs are dark. **JUVENILE** Recalls adult, but has paler upperparts, while underparts are warmer buff and heavily spotted on throat and breast. **VOICE** Song consists of rich, warbling phrases, each repeated several times; often sings after dark, especially in artificially lit suburban areas. Call is a sharp *tchek*. **STATUS AND HABITAT** Common in a wide range of habitats with scattered trees and scrub, including suburban gardens and parks. **OBSERVATION TIPS** Easy to see and hear.

SAGE THRASHER
Oreoscoptes montanus L 8.25–8.5 in

Slim-bodied, dry-country bird. Tail is long, although by thrasher standards, both it and bill are relatively short. Often perches on wires or on top of bush. Searches for insects on ground, often with tail cocked, and also feeds, seasonally, on berries. Sexes are similar. **ADULT** Has mainly gray-brown upperparts, back and head with faint, dark streaking; note the two white wing bars (upper one black-bordered) and pale supercilium linking to pale ear surround. Has a beady yellowish eye. White throat is bordered by black malar stripe and underparts are pale, but with bold, dark streaking on all areas except undertail, and orange-buff wash to flanks and undertail. **JUVENILE** Similar to adult, but with bolder streaking on upperparts and less distinct streaking on underparts. **VOICE** Song is a rolling series of rich, warbling and whistling phrases, with some repetition; call is a sharp *tchup*. **STATUS AND HABITAT** Locally common summer visitor (mainly Mar–Sep) to sagebrush habitats; winters from southwestern U.S. to Mexico in similar habitats. **OBSERVATION TIPS** Reasonably easy to see, by the standards of some thrashers, since it sometimes perches conspicuously.

BROWN THRASHER *Toxostoma rufum* L 11–11.5 in

Well-marked, long-tailed, slim-bodied bird with a longish, down-curved bill. Forages mainly on the ground for insects and other invertebrates, but also feeds on berries and seeds. Rather skulking generally, but retiring habits abandoned by territorial singing birds. Sexes are similar. **ADULT** Has mainly rich reddish brown upperparts including tail. Wings have two black and white wing bars, face is grayish, and note the beady yellow eye. Underparts are creamy white, but with bold dark streaks on all parts except undertail. **JUVENILE** Similar to adult, but with dark eyes. **VOICE** Song is a series of rich, fluty, whistling phrases, each typically repeated a couple of times; calls include a tongue-smacking *stutt* and a softer *chrrr*. **STATUS AND HABITAT** Fairly common summer visitor (mainly May–Aug) to northern U.S. and Canada; much more widespread in eastern North America. Favors dense thickets and scrub. Present year-round in southeastern U.S. and winter visitor to parts of Texas. **OBSERVATION TIPS** Easiest to see when singing.

NORTHERN MOCKINGBIRD

ADULT

SAGE THRASHER

ADULT

BROWN THRASHER

ADULT

Mimidae

CURVE-BILLED THRASHER
Toxostoma curvirostre L 11–11.5 in

Our most widespread long-billed, desert thrasher and the yardstick by which to judge other thrashers. Fortunately, compared to most others, it is not unduly shy, even outside breeding season. Searches for invertebrates on the ground and also feeds on berries. Sexes are similar. **ADULT** Has gray-brown upperparts overall that are plain and unmarked, except for the two whitish wing bars. Note the fiery orange iris and subtle pale supercilium. Pale throat is bordered by dark brown malar stripe and underparts are otherwise rather pale, with subtle brown spots that are most intense on breast. Tail has white tips, broadest on outer feathers. Bill is curved and dark. **JUVENILE** Similar to adult, but with yellow iris, shorter bill, and less obvious spotting on underparts. Can be confused with Bendire's. **VOICE** Song is an attractive series of abrupt, chattering whistles and chirping trills; calls include a sharp, whistled *wi'Weet*. **STATUS AND HABITAT** Common resident of cactus deserts, especially where chollas are common. Often lives close to human habitation (where desert survives) as in Tucson. **OBSERVATION TIPS** Particularly easy to see in spring.

BENDIRE'S THRASHER *Toxostoma bendirei* L 9.5–10 in

Similar to juvenile Curve-billed, which has straighter shorter bill than adult; possibility for confusion exists, May–Aug, in limited zone of overlap. Habitat preferences and calls are useful pointers for separation. Mostly secretive, bordering on furtive, but in late winter and early spring males often sing from exposed perch. Sexes are similar. **ADULT** Has sandy brown plumage overall with unmarked upperparts, except for two subtle, buff wing bars. Note the faint, buff supercilium and yellowish iris. Bill is only very slightly downcurved. Throat is pale

ADULT

with a buffy malar stripe and underparts are marked with subtle arrowhead spots, concentrated mainly on breast; toward end of breeding season, birds with worn plumage show reduced spotting. Undertail coverts are warm orange-buff and tail is mostly dark, but with white tips, most noticeable on outer feathers. **JUVENILE** Similar to adult, but with less distinct spots on underparts. **VOICE** Song is a series of musical, but slightly grating warbling phrases, several delivered without pause for breath; call is a soft *tchuk*. **STATUS AND HABITAT** Locally common in deserts where yuccas, scrub, and grassland predominate. Present year-round in south of range, but summer visitor to north. **OBSERVATION TIPS** Look for it in late winter.

LONG-BILLED THRASHER
Toxostoma longirostre L 11.25–11.5 in

Structurally similar to Brown Thrasher (with which range overlaps slightly in winter), but lacks that species' reddish brown coloration overall; instead, plumage is grayer and cleaner-looking. Bill is also appreciably longer than Brown's and behavior is even more secretive, except when males are singing in early spring. Sexes are similar. **ADULT** Has mostly brown upperparts, including tail, but with bold white wing bars. Face is gray, iris is reddish orange, and bill is downcurved. Underparts are whitish, but with bold, black teardrop streaks. **JUVENILE** Similar to adult. **VOICE** Song is a series of rapid, chirping and fluty whistles, given with gusto; call is a sharp *tsuup*. **STATUS AND HABITAT** Resident of dense, woodland thickets; Lower Rio Grande Valley is a hotspot. **OBSERVATION TIPS** Singing males are fairly easy to see in spring.

CURVE-BILLED THRASHER

ADULT

BENDIRE'S THRASHER

ADULT

LONG-BILLED THRASHER

ADULT

Mimidae

CRISSAL THRASHER *Toxostoma crissale* L 11.5–11.75 in
Plain-colored desert thrasher with a strikingly long and downcurved bill, used to probe ground for invertebrates. Extremely secretive and positively furtive when people are around; typical view will be of a bird glimpsed dashing, tail cocked, from one patch of cover to another. In spring, however, male sometimes sings from exposed branch. Sexes are similar. **ADULT** Has rich gray-brown plumage overall, mostly plain and unmarked and subtly paler below than above; note, however, the chestnut undertail coverts. Has a yellow iris and striking throat markings: white throat, bordered by black malar stripe and white "mustache." **JUVENILE** Similar to adult. **VOICE** Song is a series of musical, whistling notes, with some duplication of phrases or pairs of phrases; call is a repeated *chiralee, chiralee....* **STATUS AND HABITAT** Rather scarce resident associated with dense streamside thickets in desert habitats. **OBSERVATION TIPS** Easiest to see in spring, but still a challenge.

CALIFORNIA THRASHER
Toxostoma redivivum L 11.75–12 in
Similar to Crissal, but ranges do not overlap and habitat preferences differ. Note also California's dark iris (yellow in Crissal), hint of a supercilium, lack of white "mustache" bordering dark malar stripe, and marginally shorter bill. Mostly secretive and keeps to dense cover, but sometimes seen running, tail cocked, from one thicket to another. Male sings from exposed perch, mostly in late winter and early spring, but occasionally at other seasons. Sexes are similar. **ADULT** Has mostly plain and unmarked, rich brown upperparts with subtly paler underparts flushed orange-buff on belly, flanks, and undertail coverts. Head pattern comprises subtle buff supercilium and pale throat bordered by dark malar stripe. **JUVENILE** Similar to adult. **VOICE** An accomplished mimic, but typical song comprises chirping, whistling, and chattering phrases, each typically repeated 2–3 times; call is a soft *tchak*. **STATUS AND HABITAT** Fairly common resident of chaparral-covered slopes. **OBSERVATION TIPS** Easiest to see in spring.

ADULT

LE CONTE'S THRASHER *Toxostoma lecontei* L 11–11.25 in
Recalls Crissal, with which geographical range overlaps, but appreciably paler and marginally smaller, with shorter tail, more slender bill, and daintier proportions overall. Habitat preferences are subtly different too: Le Conte's favors rather open, sandy deserts, while Crissal occurs in dense thickets near desert streams. Secretive, but sometimes seen running for cover, tail cocked. Male sings from exposed perch in early spring, but typically briefly and at dawn and dusk. Sexes are similar. **ADULT** Has pale and unmarked, sandy gray-brown plumage overall, subtly darker above than below. Note the orange-buff undertail coverts and dark tail. Has a whitish throat with discrete dark malar stripe; lores and iris are dark. **JUVENILE** Similar to adult. **VOICE** Song is a series of whistling phrases, with some repetition; calls include a whistled *sweeip*. **STATUS AND HABITAT** Scarce resident of barren desert areas with scattered cholla cacti and bushes. Declining due to habitat degradation and disturbance; features on the Audubon Watchlist. **OBSERVATION TIPS** A challenge to find; a dawn visit to suitable habitat in early spring offers your best chance for observation.

CRISSAL THRASHER

ADULT

CALIFORNIA THRASHER

ADULT

LE CONTE'S THRASHER

ADULT

Sturnidae and Motacillidae

ADULT, WINTER

JUVENILE

EUROPEAN STARLING
Sturnus vulgaris L 8.5–9 in
Introduced, but now familiar bird
of urban and rural areas. Forms sizeable
flocks outside breeding season. Walks with
a characteristic swagger. Flight is rather
undulating and wings look pointed and
triangular in outline. Sexes are separable
with care in summer. **ADULT MALE SUMMER**
Has mostly dark plumage with green and violet
iridescence. Legs are reddish orange and bill is yellow with bluish base
to lower mandible. **ADULT FEMALE SUMMER** Similar, but has a few pale
spots on underparts; base of lower mandible is pale yellow. **WINTER
ADULT (BOTH SEXES)** Has numerous white spots adorning dark
plumage. Bill is dark. **JUVENILE** Gray-brown, palest on throat, and with
dark bill. First-winter similar to adult but often retains gray-brown
head and neck into fall. **VOICE** Highly vocal and an accomplished
mimic. Song includes repertoire of clicks, whistles, and elements of
mimicking other birds and manmade sounds, such as car alarms; calls
include chatters and drawn-out whistles. **STATUS AND HABITAT**
Abundant; all birds are descendents of 100 individuals released in
Central Park New York City in 1890s. Found in a wide range of habitats; northern populations move south in winter. **OBSERVATION TIPS**
Hard to miss.

AMERICAN PIPIT *Anthus rubescens* L 6.25–6.5 in
Slim-looking pipit that forms large flocks in winter. Often bobs tail.
Plumage varies throughout year and across geographical range; given
this variation, sexes are similar. **ADULT SUMMER** Has grayish upperparts
with faint streaking on back; darkish wings show two whitish wing bars and
pale margins to tertials. Arctic breeders have heavily streaked, buffy underparts, buffy throat with dark malar stripe, and buff supercilium. Rocky Mountain breeders have unstreaked buffy orange underparts and face. Legs are dark
in all birds. **ADULT WINTER** Has more heavily streaked gray back. Arctic birds
have paler throat and supercilium; heavily streaked underparts have buff wash
confined mostly to flanks. Rocky Mountain birds are similar, but warmer buff overall and with less distinct
streaking on underparts. **JUVENILE** More heavily marked than respective adult. **VOICE** Song (often
given in flight) is a slightly accelerating series of tinkling *tlee-tlee-tlee...* notes; call is a thin *p'peet*.
STATUS AND HABITAT Common summer visitor (mainly May–Aug) to tundra and bare mountaintops.
Winters in southern U.S. and Mexico, favoring arable fields and open country. **OBSERVATION TIPS** Easiest
to see in winter.

SPRAGUE'S PIPIT *Anthus spragueii* L 6.5–6.75 in
Prairie specialist. Secretive and far easier to hear (in spring at least)
than to see: male performs aerial song display for long periods.
Otherwise, skulks in short grasses and hard to flush. Does not bob tail. Sexes
are similar. **ADULT** Has heavily streaked brown upperparts and two white
wing bars. Dark eye is emphasized by pale buffy face; note the whitish throat,
lores, and supercilium. Underparts are pale, flushed buff on flanks and breast
and mostly unmarked, except for streaking on breast. Legs are pale pinkish.
JUVENILE Similar to adult, but with more striking wing bars and scaly-looking
back. **VOICE** Song is a descending series of breezy whistles; call is a thin *squeet*.
STATUS AND HABITAT Rare and declining species, favoring short grass prairies for nesting (mainly May–
Sep) and rough grassland with more bare ground in winter. **OBSERVATION TIPS** Striking white outer tail
feathers (seen in flight) aid identification.

ADULT, SUMMER

ADULT, WINTER

EUROPEAN STARLING

ADULT, BREEDING

ADULT, NONBREEDING

AMERICAN PIPIT

ADULT

ADULT

SPRAGUE'S PIPIT

Bombycillidae and Ptilogonatidae

BOHEMIAN WAXWING
Bombycilla garrulus L 8–8.25 in

Distinctive bird. Winter flocks are often tame, allowing superb views. In flight, silhouette is Starlinglike. Sexes are separable with care. **ADULT MALE** Has mainly pinkish buff plumage, palest on belly. Has a crest, black throat, and black mask through eye. Rump is gray, undertail is chestnut, and dark tail has a broad yellow terminal band. Primaries have white and yellow margins; wings also show red, waxlike projections and white bar at base of primary coverts. **ADULT FEMALE** Similar, but has narrower yellow tip to tail, shorter waxy wing projections, and narrower dark throat. **JUVENILE** Gray-buff, streaked, and blotchy-looking overall; first-winter is similar to adult, but white margins to primaries are absent, as are red, waxlike projections. **VOICE** Utters a trilling call and does not sing. **STATUS AND HABITAT** Locally common summer visitor (mainly Apr–Sep) to boreal coniferous forests. Present year-round further south, but elsewhere a winter visitor (variable numbers and range), with flocks roving after berry-laden bushes. **OBSERVATION TIPS** Easiest to see in winter, but occurrence is unpredictable.

CEDAR WAXWING
Bombycilla cedrorum L 7.25–7.5 in

Similar to Bohemian Waxwing, but separable using differences in plumage details and color: overall, Cedar's plumage is warmer-looking, undertail coverts are white (not chestnut), and its dark wings are almost unmarked. Forms roving flocks outside breeding season, searching for berry trees and bushes. Sexes are similar. **ADULT** Has orange-buff plumage overall, palest on underparts and white on undertail. Wings are dark, except for white inner edge to tertials and red, waxlike feather projections. Rump is gray and dark tail has a broad yellow terminal band. Note the prominent crest; dark mask through eye is defined above and below by white line (more striking above than in Bohemian). **JUVENILE** Gray-buff overall; differs from juvenile Bohemian in having unmarked dark wings, except for pale inner margin to tertials. First-winter is similar to adult, but lacks red, waxy wing projections. **VOICE** Song comprises a series of piercing *tzeee* call notes. **STATUS AND HABITAT** Common in open woodland. Present year-round in much of northern U.S.; summer visitor further north and winter visitor south to Mexico. **OBSERVATION TIPS** Easiest to find outside breeding season.

JUVENILE

PHAINOPEPLA *Phainopepla nitens* L 7.5–8 in

Distinctive bird, recognized by its slim body, long tail, and shaggy crest. Intriguingly, habitat and habits vary throughout year, reflecting seasonal availability of food: diet includes insects in summer, berries (particularly mistletoe) in winter. Usually rather solitary in winter desert haunts, but more gregarious in wooded habitat favored in summer. Sexes are dissimilar. **ADULT MALE** Unmistakable, with its glossy black plumage. Note the beady red eye. White wing flash (on primaries) is obvious only in flight. **ADULT FEMALE** Structurally similar to male, but plumage is buff-gray overall, with white margins to wing feathers and bluish gray tone to head; iris is red. **JUVENILE** Similar to adult female, but with warmer buff tone to plumage. **VOICE** Song includes warbles and some mimicry; call is an upslurred, liquid *wu'ip*. **STATUS AND HABITAT** Common in desert habitats in winter, riverside woodland in summer. **OBSERVATION TIPS** Easy to see and identify.

FEMALE

MALE

BOHEMIAN WAXWING

1ST-WINTER

CEDAR WAXWING

FEMALE

ADULT

PHAINOPEPLA

MALE

Parulidae

WOOD-WARBLERS can often daunt the novice birder, with many species exhibiting striking plumage differences between the sexes, and at different times of year. Becoming familiar with their songs and calls (by listening to recordings) can be a great aid. In the field, concentrate on features such as the presence or absence of wingbars, and throat and rump color. Behavior and habitat preference are also important.

TENNESSEE WARBLER
Vermivora peregrina L 4.5–4.75 in
Active wood-warbler with plain, clean-looking plumage and dull legs.
Probes flowers for nectar and insects, and searches among foliage for other
invertebrates, notably Spruce Budworm. Sexes are dissimilar. **MALE** In spring,
has olive-green back and tail and subtly darker wings with very faint pale wing
bars. Head is grayish, with dark line through eye and whitish supercilium and
throat; underparts are otherwise whitish, with gray wash on flanks. **FEMALE** In
spring, recalls male, but is duller with yellowish wash to head and neck. **FALL ADULT**

IMMATURE

Similar to respective sex in spring, but with less colorful upperparts.
IMMATURE Yellowish green overall, with discrete pale wing bars and
pale supercilium; undertail coverts are usually whitish, but even when
washed faint yellow are much paler than rest of underparts. **VOICE**
Song is a three-part series of short notes, the last part the fastest:
sip-sip-sip-sip, si-si-si-si, si'si'si'si'si; call is a tongue-smacking *tchht*.
STATUS AND HABITAT Fairly common summer visitor (mainly May–Jul)
to boreal coniferous forests, particularly wet spruce woods. Winters in
Central and South America. **OBSERVATION TIPS** Easy to see.

ORANGE-CROWNED WARBLER
Vermivora celata L 5–5.25 in
Widespread and relatively long-tailed wood-warbler whose plumage
varies across range, and represented by different subspecies, all with dark
legs. Immature northern birds resemble Tennessee Warbler while immature
Pacific birds recall immature Yellow Warbler (*see* p.326), which has pinkish
legs. Orange crown is usually indistinct and not useful in field identification.
Sexes are dissimilar. **ADULT MALE** From Pacific, is dull yellow-green overall,
palest and faintly streaked below, with broken pale eyering and indistinct pale
supercilium; northern male has much grayer face, underparts, and back, but note
the yellow-buff undertail (whitish in Tennessee). **ADULT FEMALE** Similar to respective subspecies male,
but grayer overall and duller. **IMMATURE** Similar to adult female of respective subspecies; yellow undertail coverts are striking in northern birds (cf. immature Tennessee). **VOICE** Song is a vibrating trill whose pitch drops from start to finish; call is a sparrowlike *tik*. **STATUS AND HABITAT** Common summer visitor (mainly May–Sep) to deciduous woodland edges and weedy clearings. Winters in southern U.S. and Mexico. **OBSERVATION TIPS** Voice, color of underparts, and face pattern are clues to identification. First impressions of face are useful in immature birds: if pale broken eyering is the most obvious feature, then Orange-crowned is likely; if pale supercilium strikes you, then Tennessee is the best contender.

LUCY'S WARBLER *Vermivora luciae* L 4–4.25 in
Dainty little wood-warbler with plain but distinctive plumage and dark legs.
Nests in tree holes and cavities. Sexes are separable with care. **ADULT MALE**
Has mostly pale blue-gray upperparts, except for chestnut rump and dark gray
wings and tail. Dark eye is emphasized by pale surround and lores, and note
chestnut crown (often partly concealed). Underparts are mostly pale gray, except
for white undertail. **ADULT FEMALE** Similar to male, but with smaller crown patch and
paler face. **JUVENILE** Similar to adult female, but crown patch is absent and has pale buff
wing bars. **VOICE** Song is a short, sweet and rapid trill; call is a sharp *sheenk*. **STATUS AND HABITAT**
Locally common summer visitor (mainly Apr–Jul) to brushy riparian and mesquite woodland; threatened
due to habitat loss. Winters in Mexico. **OBSERVATION TIPS** Easy to see in suitable habitats.

WOOD-WARBLERS

FEMALE

TENNESSEE WARBLER

ADULT, FALL

MALE

ADULT

ORANGE-CROWNED
WARBLER

IMMATURE

ADULT

LUCY'S WARBLER

ADULT

NASHVILLE WARBLER
Vermivora ruficapilla L 4.5–4.75 in

Active wood-warbler. Western subspecies is more colorful than eastern and often bobs tail. Sexes are separable. **ADULT MALE** Has mainly olive-
green back, with darker flight feathers and tail. Head and neck are mostly
blue-gray, but note rufous crown patch and white eyering; throat and underparts are bright yellow. Legs are dull. **ADULT FEMALE** Similar to male, but
less colorful, with dull underparts, browner head, and reduced crown patch.
IMMATURE Similar to adult female, but even paler, with whitish throat and belly
and no crown patch. **VOICE** Song is in two parts, first bouncy and whistling,
second rapid and trilling: *t'se-t'se-t'se-t'se, se'se'se'se'se*; call is a thin *tsip*. **STATUS AND HABITAT** Common
summer visitor (mainly May–Aug) to deciduous and mixed, brushy woods; often in secondary growth.
Winters in Central America. **OBSERVATION TIPS** Easy to see.

VIRGINIA'S WARBLER
Vermivora virginiae L 4.5–4.75 in

Separated from Nashville by plumage differences (back and wings
blue-gray in Virginia's, olive-green in Nashville) and song; breeding ranges
barely overlap. Sexes are separable. **SPRING MALE** Has mostly blue-gray
upperparts, with darker flight feathers and tail; note yellowish rump, white
eyering, and chestnut crown patch. Underparts are pale overall, whitish on
throat and yellow on breast and undertail. Legs are dark. **SPRING FEMALE**
Similar to male, but with reduced yellow on breast and smaller crown patch.
FALL ADULT Similar to spring adult, but duller and browner. **IMMATURE** Recalls
spring female, but lacks crown patch and has only a hint of yellow on breast. **VOICE** Song is two-part
and rattling: *swee-swee-swee-swee, swit-swit-swit-swit*; call is a sharp *shink*. **STATUS AND HABITAT**
Locally common summer visitor (Apr–Aug) to scrubby oak woodland. Winters in Mexico. **OBSERVATION
TIPS** Easy to see.

NORTHERN PARULA
Parula americana L 4.25–4.5 in

Colorful wood-warbler. Often forages high in treetops. Sexes are
separable. **ADULT MALE** Has mainly blue upperparts with greenish patch
on back; note the bold white wing bars and white "eyelids." Underparts are
mostly yellow, with blue and orange breast band, and grading to white on
undertail. Lower mandible is yellow and legs are dull orange. **ADULT FEMALE**
Similar to male, but less colorful and without breast band. **IMMATURE** Similar
to female, but less colorful. **VOICE** Song is a buzzing, squeaky trill; call is a
sharp *tzip*. **STATUS AND HABITAT** Common summer visitor (mainly Apr–Aug) to
woodlands; main range is east of that covered by this book. Winters in West Indies, Mexico, and Central
America. **OBSERVATION TIPS** Easy to see.

BLACK-AND-WHITE WARBLER
Mniotilta varia L 5–5.25 in

Striking, pied wood-warbler with dark legs; bill is slightly downcurved. Forages for insects on tree trunks. Sexes are separable. **ADULT MALE**
Striped black and white overall, palest on underparts, with two white wing
bars. Throat is black in spring, white in fall; ear coverts black in spring, gray
in fall. **ADULT FEMALE** In spring is similar to fall male; often has buff-
washed underparts in fall. **IMMATURE** Recalls fall adult of respective sex, male
with white cheeks. **VOICE** Song is a thin *seesa-seesa...*; call is a sharp *tchak*.
STATUS AND HABITAT Common summer visitor (May–Aug) to woodland. Winters
mainly in Central America. **OBSERVATION TIPS** Easy to see.

MALE

FEMALE

MALE

NASHVILLE WARBLER

IMMATURE

MALE

VIRGINIA'S WARBLER

NORTHERN PARULA

FEMALE, IMMATURE

MALE, IMMATURE

FEMALE

MALE

BLACK-AND-WHITE WARBLER

FEMALE

MALE

Parulidae

CAPE MAY WARBLER
Dendroica tigrina L 4.75–5 in

Well-marked wood-warbler. Often feeds high in foliage. Pale yellow patch on side of neck is a useful field mark (combined with other plumage features); least obvious in immatures. Sexes are dissimilar. **SPRING MALE** Has olive-yellow upperparts (except side of neck), palest on rump; note the white wing patch (greater coverts). Face is yellowish overall, but with chestnut ear coverts and yellow supercilium. Underparts are mostly yellowish, with bold dark streaks; grades to white on undertail. **SPRING FEMALE** Recalls adult male, but yellow elements of plumage are less intense, ear coverts are olive, and wings have two white wing bars. **FALL ADULTS** Duller than spring counterparts, male typically without chestnut ear coverts. **IMMATURES** Recall fall adults of respective sex, but with yellow elements of plumage even less colorful; female is grayish overall. **VOICE** Song is a series of piping notes: *peeoo-peeoo-peeoo...*; call is a sharp *tzip*. **STATUS AND HABITAT** Common summer visitor (mainly May–Aug) to boreal forests. Winters in Caribbean. **OBSERVATION TIPS** Easy to see.

MAGNOLIA WARBLER
Dendroica magnolia L 4.75–5 in

Colorful wood-warbler with diagnostic tail underside: white with broad, dark tip. Often feeds at low levels. Sexes are dissimilar. **SPRING MALE** Has blackish back and wings, except for broad, white wing panel. Rump is yellow and dark tail has white marginal band toward middle. Blackish nape links to mask through eye, above which is white supercilium and blue-gray crown. Underparts are mostly bright yellow with black chest band and streaks from chest band to flanks; undertail coverts are white. **SPRING FEMALE** Similar, but black elements of body plumage are gray or much duller black. **FALL ADULT** Recalls spring female, but lacks white supercilium; white on wings is confined to two wing bars. **IMMATURE** Less colorful than fall adult and with little or no streaking below. **VOICE** Song is a whistled *swee-swee-swee-sweep*; call is a thin *tzic*. **STATUS AND HABITAT** Fairly common summer visitor (mainly Jun–Aug) to northern mixed coniferous forests. Winters in Central America. **OBSERVATION TIPS** Easy to see.

YELLOW-RUMPED WARBLER
Dendroica coronata L 5.25–5.5 in

Widespread wood-warbler. Plumage varies across range: "Audubon's Warbler" is subspecies in west, "Myrtle Warbler" is subspecies in north and east. Yellow rump and yellow flank patch are seen in all birds (Magnolia has yellow rump *and* underparts). Sexes are dissimilar. **SPRING MALE** "Audubon's" has dark gray upperparts, streaked on back, with broad white wing patch and yellow crown stripe. Throat is yellow, breast is blackish, and underparts are white with dark streaks and yellow flank patch. "Myrtle" is similar, but has white throat (extending to frame ear coverts), white supercilium, and two white wing bars. **SPRING FEMALE** Similar to respective male, but paler; has indistinct crown patch. **FALL ADULT** Duller than spring counterpart. **IMMATURE** Recalls dull, buffy fall female without crown patch; note yellow rump and flank patch, and white wing bars. "Audubon's" has buff throat, extending to frame ear coverts; "Myrtle" has white throat and narrow supercilium. **VOICE** Song is a trilling series of whistles. "Audubon's" call is an abrupt *tchip*, "Myrtle's" is a flatter *chep*. **STATUS AND HABITAT** Common summer visitor (mainly May–Aug) to a variety of mixed woods and open, brushy areas, as well as coniferous forests. Winters in southern U.S. and Central America. **OBSERVATION TIPS** Hard to miss.

MALE MYRTLE

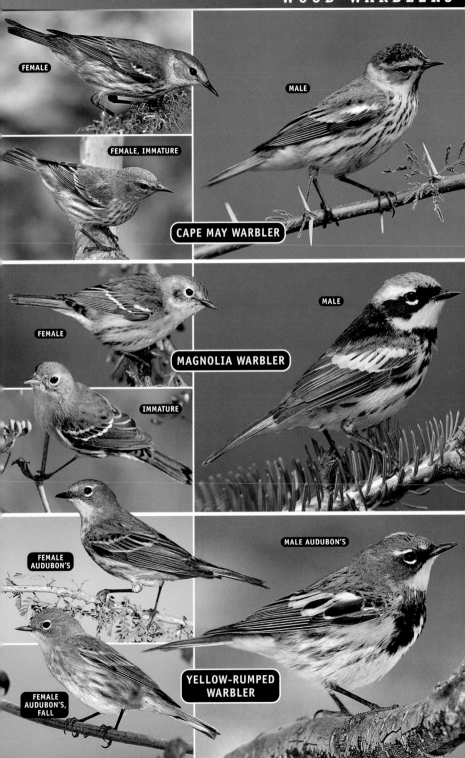

FEMALE

MALE

FEMALE, IMMATURE

CAPE MAY WARBLER

FEMALE

MALE

IMMATURE

MAGNOLIA WARBLER

FEMALE
AUDUBON'S

MALE AUDUBON'S

FEMALE
AUDUBON'S,
FALL

YELLOW-RUMPED
WARBLER

Parulidae

BLACK-THROATED GRAY WARBLER
Dendroica nigrescens L 5 in

Strikingly marked wood-warbler. Tiny yellow spot in front of eye can be obvious. Sometimes forages at low levels. Sexes are dissimilar. **ADULT MALE** Has mostly dark gray back and wings with two striking white wing bars. Head is marked with broad white supercilium and malar stripe, contrasting with black crown, eye stripe, and throat. Underparts are otherwise white, with bold black streaks on flanks. Tail is mostly white below, dark with white outer feathers above. **ADULT FEMALE** Similar, but throat is mostly white with some black streaking; black elements of head pattern are grayer. **IMMATURE** Similar to adult female, but grayer overall, with less distinct breast band, and buff wash to underparts. **VOICE** Song is a rapid *whzz-whzz-wheez-wheez-Tzee'Tsoo*; call is a thin *tsip*. **STATUS AND HABITAT** Common summer visitor (mainly May–Aug) to open, mixed, dry oak, juniper, and coniferous woodland. Winters mainly in Mexico. **OBSERVATION TIPS** Easy to see in suitable habitats.

TOWNSEND'S WARBLER
Dendroica townsendi L 5–5.25 in

Stunning Pacific Northwest breeding species. Often forages high in treetops and sometimes joins mixed species flocks outside breeding season. Sexes are dissimilar. **ADULT MALE** Has streaked olive-yellow back and rump, darkish tail with white outer feathers, and blackish wings with two broad,

white wing bars. Head markings are striking, with dark crown, dark "mask" (ear coverts) bordered entirely by yellow and with small yellow patch below eye, and black throat and chest. Underparts are yellow on breast and flanks, grading to white on belly and undertail coverts, with black streaks on flanks. **ADULT FEMALE** Similar, but paler overall; black elements of head pattern are olive-gray. **IMMATURE** Similar to adult female, but duller and less colorful; dark on breast is much reduced. **VOICE** Song is a breezy *wee-wee-wee-weez-we'Che*; call is a sharp *tsic*. **STATUS AND HABITAT** Locally common summer visitor (May–Aug) to coniferous forests. Winters mainly California to Mexico. **OBSERVATION TIPS** Fairly easy to see in suitable habitats. **SIMILAR SPECIES Blackburnian Warbler** *D. fusca* (L 4.75–5 in) has a mainly eastern range, extending west only in Canada. Male has striking orange throat and surround to dark ear coverts, and broad white wing patch; female and immature are much less colorful with two white wing bars replacing male's white wing patch.

HERMIT WARBLER
Dendroica occidentalis L 5–5.25 in

Pacific specialty. Breeding range overlaps with Townsend's in Oregon and Washington; hybrids are often noted. Secretive and often feeds high in treetops. Sexes are separable. **ADULT MALE** Has mostly blackish gray upperparts with two bold white wing bars on blackish wings. Tail is white from below, but mostly dark from above, with white outer feathers. Face is bright yellow, framed by black nape, throat, and chest. Underparts are mostly white, with only faint streaking. **ADULT FEMALE** Similar, but black elements on upperparts are grayer and has grayish ear coverts and crown. **IMMATURE** Similar to adult female, but gray elements on upperparts are dull olive-brown. **HYBRIDS** Usually recall Hermit, but with yellow on underparts, streaked sides, and olive-yellow on back and rump. **VOICE** Song is a wheezy rattle; call is a thin *tsip*. **STATUS AND HABITAT** Locally common summer visitor (May–Aug) to mature coniferous forests. Winters in Central America. **OBSERVATION TIPS** A challenge to see.

FEMALE

BLACK-THROATED GRAY WARBLER

MALE

MALE

FEMALE

FEMALE

TOWNSEND'S WARBLER

FEMALE

IMMATURE

MALE

HERMIT WARBLER

Parulidae

BLACK-THROATED GREEN WARBLER
Dendroica virens L 4.75–5 in
Well-marked, black-throated wood-warbler. Forages actively among
vegetation and sometimes gleans insects while hovering. Sexes are separable.
ADULT MALE Has olive-green back, extending up nape to crown. Tail is white
from below and dark, with white outer feathers, from above. Wings are blackish with two striking white wing bars. Face is bright yellow, with olive ear
coverts. Throat and chest are black, while underparts are otherwise mostly
white, with black streaks on flanks and yellow wash on lower chest and rear of
flanks. **ADULT FEMALE** Similar, but

FEMALE

throat is whitish or mottled pale yellow. **IMMATURE** Similar to
adult female, but black elements of plumage on underparts are
greatly reduced, consisting mainly of grayish streaks on flanks.
VOICE Song is a buzzing *tzur-zee-tzur-tzur-zee* or *zee-zee-zee-tzur-
zee*; call is a soft *t'sip*. **STATUS AND HABITAT** Summer visitor
(mainly May–Jul), mostly to coniferous woodland; widespread in
eastern North America, but range extends west across central
Canada. Winters around Caribbean. **OBSERVATION TIPS** Within
the range of this book, easily found only in northern forests.

GOLDEN-CHEEKED WARBLER
Dendroica chrysoparia L 5–5.25 in
Stunning and distinctive wood-warbler whose habitat preference and
restricted range are good pointers for separation from other black-throated
warblers. Sexes are separable. **ADULT MALE** Has a bright yellow face (with
dark eyestripe) framed by black on crown, neck, throat, and breast, this color
extending to back. Wings are black with two white wing bars and tail is white
below and dark above, with white outer feathers. Underparts are white, with bold
black streaks on flanks. **ADULT FEMALE** Similar, but throat is yellowish and black
elements of upperpart plumage are dark gray. **IMMATURE** Similar to adult female, but lacks
black chest band and has indistinct streaks on flanks and eye stripe. **VOICE** Song is a buzzing *d'd'd'd*
drrr-drruz-zee; call is a soft *t'sip*. **STATUS AND HABITAT** Rare and endangered summer visitor (mainly
Apr–Jun) to undisturbed oak- and juniper-covered slopes in Edwards Plateau, Lampasas Cut Plain and
Central Mineral Region in Texas. Winters in Central America. **OBSERVATION TIPS** Specific trip to known
breeding areas is needed to see this species.

GRACE'S WARBLER *Dendroica graciae* L 4.75–5 in
Attractive wood-warbler that often feeds high in pine trees. Sexes
are separable. **ADULT MALE** Has mostly blue-gray upperparts, with
dark streaking on crown and back and two bold white wing bars on blackish
wings. Face is marked with yellow supercilium and spot below eye; throat
and breast are also yellow, grading to white on rest of underparts, with dark
streaks on flanks. **ADULT FEMALE** Similar, but paler and less colorful overall,
with unstreaked upperparts. **IMMATURE** Similar to adult female, but paler still,
with browner upperparts and yellowish wash on flanks. **VOICE** Song is an accelerating series of chattering trills;

MALE

YELLOW-THROATED
WARBLER

call is a soft *tchip*. **STATUS AND HABITAT** Local summer
visitor (mainly May–Aug) to open montane coniferous forest, especially where Ponderosa Pines are common. Winters in Central America. **OBSERVATION TIPS** Visit suitable
habitats in Arizona and New Mexico at the right time
and you will surely see this species. **SIMILAR SPECIES**
Yellow-throated Warbler *D. dominica* (L 5.25–5.5 in)
has white supercilium and patch on side of neck.
Range extends into eastern Texas; favors cypress swamps.

IMMATURE

BLACK-THROATED GREEN WARBLER

MALE

FEMALE

MALE

GOLDEN-CHEEKED WARBLER

GRACE'S WARBLER

FEMALE

MALE

Parulidae

BAY-BREASTED WARBLER
Dendroica castanea L 5.25–5.5 in

Adult male is colorful and striking. Sexes are dissimilar. **SPRING MALE**
Has streaked, dark gray back and nape, and blackish wings with two white
wing bars. Side of head is creamy white toward the rear, face is mainly black,
while crown, throat, chest, and flanks are chestnut; underparts are oth-

erwise creamy white. Upperside to
mostly dark tail has only limited white
tips. Legs are dark. **SPRING FEMALE**
Recalls male, except that back, head, neck,
and breast are yellowish green, heavily streaked above. **FALL ADULT**
Similar to spring female, but less heavily streaked. **IMMATURE** Dull
olive-yellow overall with only subtle streaking on back and buff
wash on underparts, including undertail coverts; dark wings have
two white wing bars. Very similar to immature Blackpoll; note the
dark (not orange) legs. *See* that species' description for further distinctions. **VOICE** Song is a rapid series of five or so piercing whistles; call is a thin *tssip*. **STATUS AND HABITAT** Common summer
visitor (mainly May–Aug) to mature spruce forests; breeding success
influenced by Spruce Budworm numbers. Winters mainly in Central
America. **OBSERVATION TIPS** Easy to see. **SIMILAR SPECIES Chest-
nut-sided Warbler** *D. pensylvanica* (L 4.75–5 in) is a summer
visitor to northern deciduous woods; adults have chestnut flanks
and white cheeks and underparts; immatures are bright yellow-green
above with two white wing bars, and pale gray below. Mainly
eastern breeding range; extends west into central Canada.

BLACKPOLL WARBLER
Dendroica striata L 5.25–5.5 in

Striking wood-warbler in spring (especially male), more tricky to
identify in fall: immature is similar to other warbler species, notably Bay-
breasted. Sexes are dissimilar. **SPRING MALE** Has olive-gray, dark-streaked
back and nape, with black cap and white cheek, defined below by black malar
stripe. Underparts are white, with bold black streaks on flanks. Legs and feet
are orange-yellow. **SPRING FEMALE** Recalls male, but head is mostly streaked
olive-gray, except for whitish throat and dark malar stripe. **FALL ADULT** Similar
to spring female. **IMMATURE** Recalls fall adult, but has olive-yellow wash to upperparts and brighter yellow face and underparts. Compared to immature Bay-breasted, note orange legs
and feet and white (not buff) undertail coverts. **VOICE** Song is a short series of high-pitched, thin notes;
call is a sharp *chip*. **STATUS AND HABITAT** Common summer visitor (Jun–Aug) to boreal, particularly
spruce, forests; winters in northern South America. **OBSERVATION TIPS** Easy to see.

PALM WARBLER *Dendroica palmarum* L 5.5–5.75 in

Feeds in conifer foliage and on ground. Often pumps tail. Sexes are
similar, although male is subtly more colorful than female. Western
birds are duller and less yellow than their eastern counterparts (mostly
extralimital to this book). **SPRING ADULT** From west, has gray-brown, dark-
streaked back and grayish wings with two very faint pale wing bars. Note
the chestnut crown, pale supercilium, otherwise gray face, and yellow throat
bordered by dark malar stripe; underparts are otherwise pale gray with streaked
flanks and yellow undertail coverts. Eastern male has yellower underparts with
rufous streaks. **FALL ADULT AND IMMATURE** Gray-brown overall, only lightly
streaked above and with faint buff wing bars and pale supercilium; undertail coverts are yellow. **VOICE**
Song is a buzzing trill; call is a sharp *tchik*. **STATUS AND HABITAT** Common summer visitor (May–Aug)
to boreal forests, particularly spruce bogs. Winters around Caribbean. **OBSERVATION TIPS** Easy to see.

WOOD-WARBLERS

MALE, IMMATURE

BAY-BREASTED WARBLER

MALE

FEMALE

MALE

BLACKPOLL WARBLER

MALE, NONBREEDING

FEMALE

IMMATURE

IMMATURE

ADULT, BREEDING

ADULT, NONBREEDING

PALM WARBLER

Parulidae

YELLOW WARBLER *Dendroica petechia* L 4.75–5 in

Colorful and familiar wood-warbler showing subtle regional plumage variation. Often forages at relatively low levels, hence easy to observe. Sexes are separable. Fall adults are slightly duller than in spring. **ADULT MALE** From southwest, is bright yellow overall, darkest on back and with two subtle pale wing bars. Breast has reddish streaks. Legs are pinkish. Eastern male is similar, but with bolder brick-red streaks below. Northwestern male is similar to eastern, but with darker, greenish yellow upperparts and even bolder red streaks below.

MALE, SOUTHWESTERN

ADULT FEMALE Recalls respective regional male, but is more uniformly yellow overall and with little or no streaking below. **IMMATURE** Recalls adult female with washed out colors; many individuals are olive-gray overall. **VOICE** Song is a whistling *swee' swee'swee'swee-swit-su-su*; call is a sharp *tchup*. **STATUS AND HABITAT** Common summer visitor (mainly Apr–Aug) to wet thickets (especially willow) and secondary woodland edges. Winters in Central and South America. **OBSERVATION TIPS** Easy to see.

MOURNING WARBLER
Oporornis philadelphia L 5–5.25 in

Shy and rather secretive, plump-bodied wood-warbler that usually feeds on, or near, the ground. Sexes are separable. **ADULT MALE** Has olive-green back, wings, and tail. Has a blue-gray hood (head and neck), lower margin of which is defined by black, scaled-looking bib. Lores are often darkish. Note virtual absence of pale eyering (cf. MacGillivray's and Connecticut). Underparts are otherwise bright yellow, with olive wash on flanks, and legs are pinkish. **ADULT FEMALE** Similar, but hood is uniformly pale gray (without black

FEMALE, 1ST-FALL

bib and lores). **IMMATURE** Recalls adult female, but has mostly olive-gray head and neck, with indistinct pale eyering, yellowish throat, and darker, incomplete breast band (corresponding to lower margin of adult's hood). **VOICE** Song is a rich *chrr-chrr-chrr-chrr chu'chu*; call is a thin *tchit*. **STATUS AND HABITAT** Fairly common summer visitor (mainly Jun–Aug) to scrub thickets and dense, secondary woodland. Winters in Central and South America. **OBSERVATION TIPS** Presence easiest to detect by sound. Patient observation is needed to obtain good, prolonged views.

MACGILLIVRAY'S WARBLER
Oporornis tolmiei L 5–5.25 in

Western counterpart of Mourning Warbler. Separable on subtle plumage differences, and range and habitat preferences barely overlap. Secretive and mainly terrestrial. Sexes are separable. **ADULT MALE** Has olive-green back, wings, and tail. Has a blue-gray hood (head and neck); lower margin grades into indistinct darker bib. Broken white eyering is emphasized by dark lores. Underparts are otherwise bright yellow, with olive wash on flanks. Legs are pinkish. **ADULT FEMALE** Similar, but hood is uniformly pale gray (without dark bib and lores); broken white eyering is striking. **IMMATURE** Recalls adult female, but has mostly olive-brown head and neck, with pale throat and darker, incomplete breast band (corresponding to lower margin of adult's hood). **VOICE** Song is a rich, chirpy *swe'et-swe'et-swe'et-swe'et choo-ee-oo*; call is a sharp *tzik*. **STATUS AND HABITAT** Common summer visitor (mainly Jun–Aug) to dense thickets and secondary woodland, usually within coniferous forests and typically in vicinity of water. Winters in Central America. **OBSERVATION TIPS** A challenge to see well. Listen for its distinctive song.

FEMALE

IMMATURE

MALE

YELLOW WARBLER

MALE

MALE

MOURNING WARBLER

FEMALE

MALE

MacGILLIVRAY'S WARBLER

Parulidae

CONNECTICUT WARBLER
Oporornis agilis L 5.5–5.75 in

Relatively large, but sleek-looking, terrestrial wood-warbler. Furtive behavior and largely inaccessible breeding habitat make it a challenge to see. Complete white eyering is a reliable feature in all birds (cf. *Oporornis* species on previous pages). Sexes are separable. **ADULT MALE** Has olive-green back, wings, and tail. Has a gray hood, palest on throat and darkest on lower margin. Note the striking white eyering. Underparts are otherwise bright yellow, with olive wash on flanks. Legs are pinkish. **ADULT FEMALE** Similar, but with duller, browner hood. **IMMATURE** Recalls adult female, but hood and upperparts are warmer buffy brown. **VOICE** Song is a rich, chirpy *wee-chup'chup, wee-chup'chup, wee-chup'chup, wee-chup'chup, wee*; buzzing call is seldom heard. **STATUS AND HABITAT** Scarce summer visitor (mainly May–Aug) to boggy terrain with thick brush in boreal forests. Winters in South America. **OBSERVATION TIPS** To find this elusive species, learn the song and call, and visit suitable habitats in spring.

CANADA WARBLER *Wilsonia canadensis* L 5–5.25 in

Colorful, well-marked, relatively long-tailed wood-warbler. Searches for insects among foliage, but also flycatches. Sexes are separable. **ADULT MALE** Has deep blue-gray upperparts, darkest on wings, forehead, and ear coverts. Note the spectacled effect (top, front of white eyering continuing as curved yellow line to base of bill). Underparts, including throat, are mostly bright yellow, but with blackish streaked breast band forming a characteristic "necklace." Legs are pinkish. **ADULT FEMALE** Recalls adult male,

IMMATURE

but upperparts are paler and "necklace" is paler and much less distinct. **IMMATURE** Similar to adult female, but with paler forehead and even less distinct "necklace." **VOICE** Song is short, sweet *chut'tti, chuwee, tchwee-sheree*; call is a sharp *ti'up*. **STATUS AND HABITAT** Common, but declining summer visitor (mainly Jun–Jul) to damp conifer and mixed forest with a dense shrub layer; often found near water. Winters in northern South America. **OBSERVATION TIPS** Fairly easy to see within range, but present only briefly in our region.

WILSON'S WARBLER *Wilsonia pusilla* L 4.75–5 in

Small, plump-bodied wood-warbler with a dainty bill. Forages actively for insects and spiders, and sometimes flycatches. Subtle geographical plumage variations exist, mainly in tone of yellow: northern and eastern nesters appear lemon-yellow overall, while yellow tone of Pacific birds is more akin to egg yolk. Given this variation, sexes are separable. **ADULT MALE** Has mostly olive-yellow upperparts, darkest on wings. Black eye and middle crown are emphasized by mostly yellow face, including forehead. Underparts, including throat, are bright yellow. Legs are pinkish. **ADULT FEMALE** Similar to adult male, but crown is variably dark olive, mottled black at the front (i.e. not entirely black). **IMMATURE** Similar to adult female, but crown is entirely olive-brown (no black). **VOICE** Song is a sweet, whistling rattle *wee che'che'che'che'che'che*; call is a tongue-smacking *tchep*. **STATUS AND HABITAT** Common summer visitor (mainly May–Aug) to damp woodland with a dense understory of shrubs. Winters mainly in Central America. **OBSERVATION TIPS** Easy to see, although hard to follow, given its activity levels.

CONNECTICUT WARBLER

FEMALE, IMMATURE

MALE

CANADA WARBLER

FEMALE

MALE

FEMALE

WILSON'S WARBLER

FEMALE

MALE

Parulidae

OVENBIRD *Seiurus aurocapilla* L 5.5–6 in

Plump, mainly terrestrial wood-warbler. Appearance and some of its habits recall those of thrushes. Forages among leaf litter on forest floor for invertebrates. Combination of crown pattern and proportionately large eye (emphasized by striking white eyering) are diagnostic. Species is named after its domed nest, which is sited on the ground. Sexes are similar. **ADULT** Has mostly olive-brown upperparts and wings, and a striking black-bordered, orange crown. Face is olive-brown, with white eyering surrounding the dark eye. Throat is white with black malar stripe; underparts are otherwise mostly white with bold black spots and streaks, concentrated mainly on the breast and flanks. Legs are pinkish. **IMMATURE** Similar to adult, but has two subtly pale wing bars; crown color is marginally less intense. **VOICE** Song is a vibrant, whistling *ke'Chee ke'Chee ke'Chee ke'Chee*; call is a sharp *tsik*. **STATUS AND HABITAT** Common summer visitor (mainly May–Aug) to mature deciduous and mixed forests; least numerous in west of range. Winters mainly in Central America, but to limited extent also in southern U.S. **OBSERVATION TIPS** Listen for the distinctive song and look for birds foraging unobtrusively on forest floor.

NORTHERN WATERTHRUSH

Seiurus noveboracensis L 5.75–6 in

Well-marked, rather atypical warbler. Often found near water, usually foraging along muddy margins, constantly pumping tail up and down. Similar to Louisiana, but *see* that species' description for separation details. Sexes are similar. **ADULT AND IMMATURE** Have mostly dark olive-brown upperparts, including wings and tail. Note the long, bold supercilium, which is an even width and buffy along its entire length. Underparts are whitish overall, with a yellow wash (variable in intensity); has bold dark streaks on throat and all areas of underparts, except undertail coverts. Legs are stout and dull pink. **VOICE** Song is a rich *tu'et-tu'et-tu'et-tu'et tchu-tchu-tchu-tchu*; call is a thin, sharp *tzip*. **STATUS AND HABITAT** Common summer visitor (mainly May–Aug) to wet habitats (bogs, streams, and rivers) in wooded regions. Winters in Central and northern South America. **OBSERVATION TIPS** Unobtrusive, but fairly easy to see. Found in waterside habitats even during migration.

LOUISIANA WATERTHRUSH *Seiurus motacilla* L 5.75–6 in

Similar to Northern Waterthrush, but marginally larger and longer-billed. Voice and subtle plumage differences (mainly supercilium and throat) are best features for separating the species during migration; breeding ranges barely overlap in region covered by this book. Habits and habitat preferences are similar to those of Northern, although Louisiana has affinity for streams and Northern prefers still water. Sexes are similar. **ADULT AND IMMATURE** Have mostly dark olive-brown

ADULT

upperparts, including wings and tail. Note the long, bold supercilium that becomes wider above and behind the eye and is more buff in front of eye, white behind (even width and uniformly buffy in Northern). Underparts are whitish overall, with a buff wash on rear of flanks and bold dark streaks on all areas except throat and undertail coverts (throat is streaked in Northern). Legs are stout and bright pink. **VOICE** Song is a resonant, whistling *ti' tsiu tsiu tchew tchew*; call is a grating *tchtt*. **STATUS AND HABITAT** Common summer visitor (mainly Apr–Aug) to wet wooded habitats in southeastern U.S.; breeding range barely extends to range covered by this book. **OBSERVATION TIPS** Presence easiest to detect by song.

OVENBIRD and WATERTHRUSHES

OVENBIRD

ADULT

1ST-FALL

NORTHERN WATERTHRUSH

ADULT

LOUISIANA WATERTHRUSH

ADULT

Parulidae

COMMON YELLOWTHROAT
Geothlypis trichas L 5–5.25 in
Secretive wood-warbler, easier to hear than to see. Black mask makes male unmistakable. Sexes are dissimilar. **ADULT MALE** Has olive-brown nape, back, wings, and tail. Head has broad, black mask, bordered above by a broad, grayish band, and below by bright yellow throat. All birds have bright yellow undertail coverts; those from southwest have entirely bright yellow underparts; those from Pacific coasts and east have flanks washed olive-brown; birds from interior have grayish flanks. Legs are pink in all birds. **ADULT FEMALE** Lacks male's striking head markings (face is olive-brown), but is otherwise similar, given regional variation; yellow throat and undertail coverts are striking in all birds. **IMMATURE** Similar to adult female, but throat is less colorful. **VOICE** Song is a vibrant, whistled *wee-ter, wee-chertee, wee-chertee, wee*; call is a tongue-smacking *tchet*. **STATUS AND HABITAT** Common summer visitor (mainly Apr–Aug) to grassy and brushy marsh habitats, often near water. Winters from southern U.S. through Central America. **OBSERVATION TIPS** Learn song and call.

YELLOW-BREASTED CHAT
Icteria virens L 7.25–7.5 in
Another secretive and furtive wood-warbler, easier to hear than to see. Distinctive on account of striking plumage, relatively large size, thick bill, and long tail (western birds have subtly longer tails than eastern ones). Sexes are separable. **ADULT MALE** Has gray-olive back, wings, and tail (with a warmer brownish tint in western birds than eastern ones). Face is grayish overall, but dark eye is emphasized by broken white eyering and upper part leading to base of upper mandible; has black lores. White malar stripe defines margin of yellow throat; yellow breast and flanks; belly and undertail coverts are white. Legs are dark. **ADULT FEMALE** Similar, but markings on head show less contrast. **IMMATURE** Similar to adult female, but duller overall. **VOICE** Song is varied and includes wide range of harsh chatters and fluty notes (sometimes repeated three or so times) and shrill whistles; call is a harsh *chew*. **STATUS AND HABITAT** Local summer visitor (mainly May–Aug) to dense shrubby habitats. Winters mainly in Central America. **OBSERVATION TIPS** Learn to recognize its song.

AMERICAN REDSTART *Setophaga ruticilla* L 5–5.25 in
Familiar and well-marked wood-warbler. Forages actively, often fanning tail to reveal colorful patches at base (orange in adult male, yellow in other plumages); behavior may startle insect prey. Sexes are dissimilar. **ADULT MALE** Has mostly black upperparts, but with striking orange patches on wings and base of tail. Head, neck, and chest are black, with orange on sides of breast and flanks, and otherwise white underparts. **ADULT FEMALE** Has greenish gray back, wings, and tail, grayish head, and grayish white underparts; orange elements of male's plumage are yellow. **IMMATURE** Similar to adult female, although some (probably females) have some indistinct yellow color on wings and some males show orange tone to color on flanks and side of breast. First-spring females like adult females. First-spring males show some adult feather details; full adult plumage is acquired with subsequent molt. **VOICE** Song is a thin, sweet *see-see-see-see-shweer*; call is a thin *chip*. **STATUS AND HABITAT** Very common summer visitor (mainly May–Aug) to a wide range of wooded habitats. Winters mainly in Central and South America. **OBSERVATION TIPS** Easy to see.

FEMALE

MALE, 1ST-SUMMER

YELLOWTHROAT, CHATS, and REDSTARTS

FEMALE, IMMATURE, FALL

FEMALE

MALE

COMMON YELLOWTHROAT

YELLOW-BREASTED CHAT

ADULT

MALE

AMERICAN REDSTART

Parulidae and Peucedramidae

PAINTED REDSTART *Myioborus pictus* L 5.5–5.75 in

Stunning southwestern specialty. Male is particularly striking, but all
plumages are recognized by combination of broad, white wing patches and
white outer feathers on the relatively long tail; features are obvious when
perched bird fans tail and flicks its wings. Sexes are dissimilar. **ADULT MALE**
Has mostly black plumage, except for white on wings and tail (detailed above)
and bright red belly. Note also the white lower "eyelid." **ADULT FEMALE** Similar
to male, but underparts may be more orange. **IMMATURE** Similar to adult female at
first but underparts are smoky gray; adult plumage is acquired in fall. **VOICE** Song is a rapid
weeper weeper weeper wee-pee-pee; call is a thin, whistled *schreeu*. **STATUS AND HABITAT** Very locally common summer visitor (mainly Mar–Sep) to oak and pine woodland in canyons and mountain
foothills; restricted in U.S. to Arizona and New Mexico, but range extends south into Mexico where
the species is also resident. Winters in Central America. **OBSERVATION TIPS** Usually easy to find in
suitable canyon habitats in southern Arizona.

RED-FACED WARBLER *Cardellina rubrifrons* L 5.25–5.5 in

Stunning and keenly-sought southwestern specialty, whose range overlaps
that of Painted Redstart. Among wood-warblers, unmistakable in all plumages
on account of the red face. Feeds mainly on insects, caught by gleaning and
flycatching. Sexes are separable. **ADULT MALE** Has a gray back, with contrasting white rump (seen in flight). Wings are gray with a white wing bar (on median

FEMALE

coverts) and darker flight
feathers; tail is uniformly dark
gray. Head is colorful and predominantly
red, but with bonnetlike dark patch from crown to
ear coverts, and white nape patch. Underparts are
whitish. **ADULT FEMALE** Similar, but color on face is
less intense. **IMMATURE** Similar to adult female, but
back has a buffy wash. **VOICE** Song is a sprightly,
whistled *wi'si'wi, wi'si'wi, wi'si'weeoo*; call is a sharp
tchuk. **STATUS AND HABITAT** Locally common summer visitor (mainly May–Aug) to montane pine, fir,
maple, and oak forest canyons. Winters in Central
America. **OBSERVATION TIPS** Fairly easy to find
in some southern Arizona canyons; usually found
at higher elevations (7,000–9,000 ft) than Painted
Redstart.

OLIVE WARBLER *Peucedramus taeniatus* L 5–5.25 in

Third in the trio of southwestern specialties. Similar to some *Dendroica*
warblers, but not classified in the wood-warbler family, but in its own
family, the Peucedramidae. Feeds actively and often flicks its wings, in the
manner of a kinglet. Sexes are dissimilar. **ADULT MALE** Has a gray back and
darkish wings overall with two bold white wing bars and a white patch at base
of primaries; inner flight feathers have white margins. From above, slightly forked
tail is mostly dark, with white outer feathers; from below, looks white with dark outer
tips. Head, neck, and chest are reddish orange, but note the dark mask. Underparts are otherwise mostly grayish, but with white undertail coverts. **ADULT FEMALE** Similar, but orange elements of plumage
are yellow and mask is much less distinct. **IMMATURE** Similar to respective sex adult, but duller and
with less obvious white on wings. **VOICE** Song is a rapid, trilling whistle *tu'e-tu'e-tu'e-tu'e-tu*; call is a soft
tuip. **STATUS AND HABITAT** Locally common in southwestern montane coniferous forests; occurs year-
round in south of range (and in Mexico), but a summer visitor further north. **OBSERVATION TIPS**
Fairly easy to find if you trek to suitable habitats.

RED-FACED WARBLER

MALE

ADULT

PAINTED
REDSTART

MALE

OLIVE WARBLER

FEMALE

Thraupidae

WESTERN TANAGER
Piranga ludoviciana L 7.25–7.5 in

Colorful, plump-bodied songbird. Male in particular is stunning. However, species' unobtrusive habits make it easily overlooked. Diet includes insects during breeding season (sometimes flycatches), but otherwise mainly fruit and berries. Sexes are dissimilar. **ADULT MALE** Has black back and tail and contrasting yellow rump. Wings are black with two wing bars, upper yellow, lower white. Neck and underparts are yellow and head is flushed red. Nonbreeding male loses most of red color, retaining hint around base of bill. **ADULT FEMALE** Recalls nonbreeding male, but black elements of plumage are greenish gray, yellow elements are duller, red color is absent, and wing bars are thinner. **JUVENILE** Recalls respective sex nonbreeding adult, but is paler and less colorful overall. **VOICE** Song is a series of short, chirpy phrases; call is a rattling *prrt't't.* **STATUS AND HABITAT** Common summer visitor (mainly May–Aug) to variety of coniferous forests and mixed woodland. Winters in Central America. **OBSERVATION TIPS** Easy to find.

SUMMER TANAGER *Piranga rubra* L 7.5–7.75 in

Male is stunningly colorful, but surprisingly easy to overlook when perched unobtrusively in dappled foliage. Diet includes berries and fruit, but also insects including bees and wasps; stingers are removed by rubbing prey on bark. All birds have a slightly peaked crown. Distinguished from Hepatic Tanager by yellowish not gray bill. Sexes are dissimilar. **ADULT MALE** Has bright red plumage overall, darkest on wings and tail. **ADULT FEMALE** Usually rather uniformly buff-yellow overall, darkest on wings, back, and tail. Some individuals (especially east of range of this book) are mottled with red. **IMMATURE** Recalls adult female at first, but by first spring male has acquired blotchy red elements to plumage on head, neck, and back. **VOICE** Song is a series of fluty, whistling phrases, mostly disyllabic and with a robinlike quality; call is a rattling *pik-tuk'tuk.* **STATUS AND HABITAT** Common summer visitor (mainly May–Aug) to mixed woodland, but in southwest (the part of its range covered by this book) associated primarily with riparian woodland. Winters in Central America. **OBSERVATION TIPS** Fairly easy to see in suitable habitats.

HEPATIC TANAGER *Piranga flava* L 8–8.5 in

Rather large tanager, with a flatter-capped appearance than Summer. Also note gray not yellowish bill. Male is colorful, but slightly subdued in comparison with male Summer. Diet includes insects during breeding season, but berries and fruit at other times. Sexes are dissimilar. **ADULT MALE** Red overall, brightest on crown, throat, and undertail coverts; gray wash to back and on ear coverts. **ADULT FEMALE** Yellow-olive overall, with grayish wash to back and flanks, but brighter yellow forecrown and throat; latter features are best guide to separation from plain yellowish form of female Summer.

FEMALE

IMMATURE Recalls adult female, but is duller overall. **VOICE** Song is a series of short, vibrant whistling phrases, most slurred, disyllabic, and robinlike; call is a soft *tchup.* **STATUS AND HABITAT** Locally common summer visitor (mainly May–Aug) to montane pine and pine-oak forests in southwest; range extends into Mexico. Winters mainly in Mexico. **OBSERVATION TIPS** Fairly easy to see in suitable habitats and sometimes can be seen singing from an exposed perch.

FEMALE

WESTERN TANAGER

MALE

SUMMER TANAGER

MALE

MALE, 1ST-SUMMER

FEMALE

MALE

MALE

HEPATIC TANAGER

Emberizidae

GREEN-TAILED TOWHEE
Pipilo chlorurus L 7–7.25 in

Long-tailed bird. Not unduly wary, but remains within cover of scrub much of the time. Mainly terrestrial; scratches through leaf litter with both feet, feeding on insects and fallen seeds. Sexes are similar. **ADULT** Has olive-green back, wings, and tail; yellow edges to wing feathers form a striking patch. Head, neck, and underparts are largely gray, grading to pale buff on belly and undertail coverts, but note the striking head markings: chestnut crown, white patch in front of eye, and well-defined white throat and malar stripe separated by dark line. **JUVENILE** Brown overall, darker above than below, and heavily streaked on upperparts, head, neck, and breast. Throat markings recall those of adult. **VOICE** Song comprises a series of abrupt *tchup* notes followed by burst of chatters and whistles; call is a rather plaintive, upslurred mew. **STATUS AND HABITAT** Locally common summer visitor (mainly Apr–Sep) to dense chaparral- and scrub-covered slopes. Winters mainly in Mexico, but also in southwestern U.S. **OBSERVATION TIPS** Relative impenetrability of favored habitat makes observation challenging, but singing males are sometimes obvious in spring.

SPOTTED TOWHEE *Pipilo maculatus* L 7.5–8.5 in

Colorful bird. Scratches ground with both feet together, to expose seeds and insects. Sexes are separable, but note subtle regional plumage variation. **ADULT MALE** Has blackish hood, upperparts, and tail, with variable amounts of white on wings and back according to subspecies: interior birds have white spots on back, two white wing bars, and white on tertials and scapulars; Pacific

MALE

EASTERN TOWHEE

FEMALE

Northwest birds have reduced white markings, with almost uniformly dark back; Southwest birds are intermediate. All birds have beady red eyes, reddish orange flanks, buff undertail coverts, and otherwise white underparts. **ADULT FEMALE** Recalls respective regional male, but black elements of plumage are brown. **JUVENILE** Brown and heavily streaked with two buff wing bars. **VOICE** Song is usually a buzzing trill preceded (or not) by variable number of sweet, whistling *tuup* notes. **STATUS AND HABITAT** Favors dense chaparral and brush. Found year-round in much of range, but northern and interior birds are migratory; winter range extends south and east. **OBSERVATION TIPS** Listen for rustle of feeding birds scratching through leaf litter. Singing males are often conspicuous. **SIMILAR SPECIES Eastern Towhee** *P. erythropthalmus* (L 7.5 in) has mainly unmarked blackish upperparts, apart from white at base of primaries. An eastern species, whose range barely overlaps that of Spotted.

ABERT'S TOWHEE *Pipilo aberti* L 9–9.5 in

Rather secretive, arid-country towhee. Usually feeds in dense cover by scratching ground for insects and seeds. Plumage is unremarkable and plain overall, except for striking dark face and contrasting pale bill. Sexes are similar. **ADULT** Has mostly sandy brown plumage with warm, pinkish flush to underparts and pinkish orange undertail coverts. **JUVENILE** Similar, but has subtle streaks on underparts and faint pinkish wing bars. **VOICE** Song is an accelerating series of squeaky *pik* notes, ending in a chattering trill; call is a thin, but grating *peek*. **STATUS AND HABITAT** Common resident of dense cover in desert woodlands, particularly those that fringe rivers, but range is extremely restricted, hence vulnerable to habitat loss and destruction. **OBSERVATION TIPS** Listen for feeding birds.

GREEN-TAILED TOWHEE

ADULT

SPOTTED TOWHEE

FEMALE

MALE

ABERT'S TOWHEE

ADULT

Emberizidae

CALIFORNIA TOWHEE *Pipilo crissalis* L 9 in

Plump-bodied, long-tailed and perky bird with plain, rather nonde-script plumage. Generally unobtrusive, but sometimes bold in gardens and parks. Sexes are similar. **ADULT** Brown overall, marginally darker above than below. Throat is yellow-buff and lightly streaked, its lower margin defined by "necklace" of streaklike dark spots. Undertail coverts are warm pinkish orange. Bill is dark gray. **JUVENILE** Similar to adult, but with subtle streaking on breast as well as throat, and faint buffy wing bars. **VOICE** Song is an accel-erating series of squeaky notes; call is a thin *peenk* note. **STATUS AND HABITAT** Common resident of scrub and chaparral woodland with dense cover on ground. Has adapted to human presence within its range, and now also commonly found in parks and rural gar-dens that offer suitable cover. Some individuals undertake altitudinal movements (hardly migration), moving uphill in late summer, but to lower elevations in harsh winter weather. **OBSERVATION TIPS** Easiest to see in parks and gardens.

CANYON TOWHEE *Pipilo fuscus* L 8–9 in

Formerly considered conspecific with California Towhee, but slimmer and paler. Ranges of two species do not overlap and subtle plumage differences also help with identification. Mainly terrestrial and usually feeds unobtru-sively in dense cover. Sexes are similar. **ADULT** Has sandy brown plumage over-all, darker above than below. Note the reddish brown cap and largely yellow-buff face, with throat defined by dark lateral line and "necklace" of dark streaklike spots on lower margin; below this, note the dark central spot on upper breast. Under-tail coverts are pinkish orange. **JUVENILE** Recalls adult, but has subtle streaking on underparts and faint buff wing bars; crown is sandy brown. **VOICE** Song is a vibrant series of whistles, some with a fluty quality; each note is typically repeated several times; call is a nasal *ch'lup*. **STATUS AND HABITAT** Common resident of arid canyons with dense cover of scrub and brush. **OBSER-VATION TIPS** Not unduly shy, but dense nature of favored habitat makes observation tricky. Wait for birds to emerge from cover rather than attempt to track them in brush.

OLIVE SPARROW *Arremonops rufivirgatus* L 6.25–6.5 in

Secretive, arid-country sparrow. Combination of distinctive crown stripes and olive-yellow back and wings are useful in identification. Feeds mainly in dense cover, making it hard to observe well. Sexes are similar. **ADULT** Has

ADULT

olive-green back, wings, and tail. Head is marked with dark brown eyestripe, broad pale supercilium, and brown crown with pale central stripe. Face is otherwise grayish and throat is white. Underparts are otherwise mostly pale gray, but whitish on belly and buffy on undertail coverts. Bill and legs are pinkish. **JUVENILE** Recalls adult, but is warmer brown overall and streaked above and below, with buffy wing bars. **VOICE** Song is delightful, accelerating series of rather soft *tsip* notes; call is a sharp *tship*. **STATUS AND HABITAT** Fairly common resident of dense thorny scrub and desert woodland. **OBSERVATION TIPS** A challenge to find. Learn the species' song and call to detect its presence in an area. Will sometimes respond and emerge from cover if you use a bird "squeaker", a device used by birders to imitate bird calls.

CALIFORNIA TOWHEE

ADULT

CANYON TOWHEE

ADULT

OLIVE SPARROW

ADULT

Emberizidae

GRASSHOPPER SPARROW
Ammodramus savannarum L 5–5.25 in

Secretive, grassland sparrow; seldom willingly leaves cover of its
favored meadow habitats. Feeds mainly on insects, but seeds are also eaten.
Like other *Ammodramus* spp., has relatively large head, long bill, and short
tail. Sexes are similar, but subtle subspecies differences are recognized across
range. **ADULT** Has dark brown upperparts overall, but feathers on back and
tertials in particular have rufous margins. Dark crown has white central stripe
and note broad, pale supercilium, grayish behind eye, but buffy in front, with
color extending onto lores. Has a white eyering and buffy face with a dark spot
on ear coverts. Underparts are pale and unmarked, with buff wash on breast and flanks that is more
pronounced in fall than spring. **JUVENILE** Recalls adult, but is heavily streaked on breast and flanks.
VOICE Song is a high-pitched, insectlike buzzing trill preceded by a short *tik* or *tik-tok* notes; call is
a sharp *tsip*. **STATUS AND HABITAT** Locally common summer visitor (mainly Apr–Sep) to tall grassy
habitats, from prairies to hay meadows. **OBSERVATION TIPS** Easiest to see well in spring when males
sing from relatively exposed position.

BAIRD'S SPARROW
Ammodramus bairdii L 5.25–5.5 in

Well-marked, secretive sparrow with typical *Ammodramus* proportions: large, flat-capped head and short tail and wings. Bill is relatively
large. Sexes are similar. **ADULT** Has well-patterned upperparts, feathers on
back and wings having dark centers and buffy margins. Nape and side of
neck have fine, dark streaks. Head is buff yellow overall, with dark crown
and buffy central stripe, and one or two dark spots behind ear coverts.
Lateral margins of pale throat are defined by dark stripe and spaced dark
streaks form a breast band that is flushed buff. Underparts are otherwise
whitish with rufous streaks on flanks. **JUVENILE** Similar, but pale feather edges create scaly appearance to back. **VOICE** Song is usually a sweet, rapid trill preceded by two or three thin *tsip* notes, and
followed by a subdued warble; call is a thin *tsee*. **STATUS AND HABITAT** Local and scarce summer visitor (mainly May–Sep), restricted to short-grass prairies when breeding; threatened by habitat loss
and degradation. Winters mainly in Mexico. **OBSERVATION TIPS** Furtive behavior (actively avoids being
seen) means it is a challenge to see; does not flush until you are almost on top of it. Easiest to observe
when males are singing in spring.

LE CONTE'S SPARROW
Ammodramus leconteii L 5–5.25 in

Secretive sparrow that prefers to scurry from danger rather than fly,
often through and under flattened grass tussocks. Color and pattern on face
are distinctive. Sexes are similar. **ADULT** Has warm buffy brown upperparts
overall, but alignment of dark-centered, buff-edged back feathers creates
lengthways lines. Face looks buff-orange overall, but note dark crown with
white central stripe, and blue-gray ear coverts with two dark spots. Pale throat
is defined laterally by thin dark stripes and lightly streaked breast is flushed
buffy yellow; underparts are otherwise whitish, with dark streaks and buffy wash
on flanks. **JUVENILE** Similar, but patterns and colors on head are muted. **VOICE** Song is a strangled-
sounding buzzing trill; call is a thin *tzeet*. **STATUS AND HABITAT** Locally common summer visitor (mainly May–Sep) to marshes and wet grassland. Winters in southeastern U.S. **OBSERVATION TIPS** Easiest to
see in spring.

GRASSHOPPER SPARROW

ADULT

ADULT

BAIRD'S SPARROW

ADULT

ADULT

ADULT

ADULT

LE CONTE'S SPARROW

NELSON'S SHARP-TAILED SPARROW
Ammodramus nelsoni L 4.75–5 in

Extremely secretive sparrow; prefers to run or scurry from danger, rather than fly. Very hard to flush. Well-marked plumage is a good match for favored marshy habitats. Feeds on invertebrates and seeds. Sexes are similar; interior-breeding birds are brighter than those from Arctic and east. **ADULT** Has rich brown back and wings; pale margins to back feathers align to form lines (white in interior birds, duller gray in birds from elsewhere in species' range). Head has dark-bordered gray crown and yellowish buff face, with dark line behind eye and blue-gray ear coverts; nape is also blue-gray. Throat is pale and unmarked, breast and flanks are streaked and flushed yellow-buff; underparts are otherwise white. **JUVENILE** Recalls adult, but is bright yellow-buff overall with little streaking on underparts. **VOICE** Song is a vibrating, hissing trill; call is a sharp *tssic*. **STATUS AND HABITAT** Locally common summer visitor (mainly Jun–Sep) to wet grassland and freshwater marsh margins in interior; Arctic and eastern birds favor salt marshes. Winters on coastal Atlantic salt marshes. **OBSERVATION TIPS** Least tricky to find in spring.

VESPER SPARROW
Pooecetes gramineus L 6.25–6.5 in

Not unduly shy and often feeds on ground in the open. Uses poles and isolated trees as song posts. Sometimes mixes in small flocks with other sparrow species. Sexes are similar. **ADULT** Has brown, streaked back; mostly dark tail has white outer feathers (striking in flight). Wing feathers have mostly dark centers and pale margins, but note chestnut lesser coverts (often hidden by body feathers) and two subtle pale wing bars. Dark-streaked crown has pale central stripe. Has a white eyering, dark line behind eye and dark margins to ear coverts. Whitish throat is bordered by dark stripe and pale underparts are streaked on breast and flanks. **JUVENILE** Similar, but warmer buff overall. **VOICE** Song (sometimes sung at dusk) comprises two or three drawn-out whistles, followed by a chattering trill; call is a sharp *tchip*. **STATUS AND HABITAT** Fairly common summer visitor (mainly Apr–Sep) to arid grassland and sagebrush; declining due to changes in farming. Winters in southern U.S. and Mexico. **OBSERVATION TIPS** Sometimes feeds beside roads.

SAVANNAH SPARROW
Passerculus sandwichensis L 5.5–5.75 in

Well-marked sparrow. Feeds unobtrusively, but sometimes perches in bush if flushed. Shows geographical variation in size, color, and bill size. "Belding's" from southern California is darkest, while tundra and interior birds are palest; Mexican "Large-billed" (occasional in southwestern U.S.) has largest bill. Given this variation,

ADULT, "LARGE-BILLED"

sexes are similar. **ADULT** Brown overall with bold dark streaking on back. Inner flight feathers and greater coverts look reddish brown in most birds; note also two subtle pale wing bars. Tail is brownish in most birds, but some have subtly paler outer feathers. Darkish crown has indistinct pale central stripe and note dark line behind eye and yellowish supercilium; pale "mustache" and throat are separated by dark malar stripe. Underparts are pale, but with reddish streaks on breast and flanks. **JUVENILE** Similar to respective subspecies adult. **VOICE** Song is a two-part, buzzing trill (*bzzzrt-tzeee*) preceded by two or three *chip* notes; call is a thin *stip*. **STATUS AND HABITAT** Summer visitor (mainly Apr–Sep), favoring a range of grassy habitats, including tundra and salt marsh. Winters south from southern U.S. **OBSERVATION TIPS** Easy to see.

NELSON'S
SHARP-TAILED
SPARROW

VESPER
SPARROW

ADULT

ADULT

SAVANNAH SPARROW

ADULT

ADULT

ADULT

ADULT, "BELDING'S"

Emberizidae

SONG SPARROW *Melospiza melodia* L 6–7 in

Long-tailed sparrow and a familiar songster. Considerable plumage
and size variation exists across its range, with numerous subspecies
present. Central breast spot (not always obvious) is a useful field mark, but
not exclusive to this species. Mixes in small flocks with other sparrows in
winter and visits feeders. Given subspecies variation, sexes are similar. **ADULT**
Has streaked brown back, reddish brown wings and tail, and two pale wing
bars. Crown is brown with pale central stripe. Face is gray overall; dark eyeline
emphasizes gray supercilium. Has pale malar stripe and dark border to whitish
throat. Breast and flanks are brown and streaked. Underparts are otherwise
mostly whitish, but undertail coverts are streaked. Pacific Northwest and Alaskan island birds
are largest and darkest (sooty overall); southwestern birds are most rufous; Californian birds are mostly strikingly streaked below. **JUVENILE** Similar to regional adult, but more buff overall. **VOICE** Song
comprises 3–4 whistles followed by a trill and variable rich, fluty notes; call is a flat *cheerp*. **STATUS
AND HABITAT** Common in a wide range of open habitats; widespread resident, but summer visitor to
interior north. **OBSERVATION TIPS** Easy to see.

LINCOLN'S SPARROW
Melospiza lincolnii L 5.75–6 in

Plump-bodied sparrow with understated, but subtly attractive
plumage. Smaller and shorter-tailed overall than Song Sparrow. Peaked crown
is often raised when agitated. Sexes are similar. **ADULT** Has streaked brown
back and reddish brown wings, with two indistinct pale wing bars, and reddish brown tail. Head is marked with brown crown and pale central stripe,
and broad, gray supercilium, defined below by dark line through eye. Cheeks
are grayish and has buff malar stripe and dark line bordering faintly streaked
whitish throat. Breast and flanks are washed buff and heavily streaked; under-
parts are otherwise whitish. **JUVENILE** Similar, but more buff overall and with more distinct wing bars.
VOICE Song starts with a breezy *zee-err*, followed by a delightful series of jingling trills, each on a different pitch; call is a soft *tchup*. **STATUS AND HABITAT** Common summer visitor (mainly Apr–Sep) to
weedy, brushy fields and other open habitats, often close to water; winters from southern U.S. to Central
America. **OBSERVATION TIPS** Easy to see.

SWAMP SPARROW *Melospiza georgiana* L 5.75–6 in

Dumpy-looking sparrow, similar to Lincoln's, but with much more
rufous wings, tail, and (when breeding) crown. Calls of two species
are also different. Sexes are similar. **ADULT SUMMER** Has streaked brown back
and rufous wings and tail. Crown is rufous and face is gray overall, with dark
eyestripe, and dark lower edge to ear coverts bordering the buffy malar
stripe. Dark line borders unstreaked white throat and underparts are otherwise
mostly unmarked gray, but with rufous wash on flanks. **ADULT WINTER AND
IMMATURE** Similar, but crown is dull brown with pale central stripe, and breast
and flanks are streaked.
JUVENILE Similar to winter adult, but browner
overall and more heavily streaked. **VOICE** Song
is a sweet, musical rattle, about 2–3 seconds
in duration; call is a sharp *tchip*. **STATUS AND
HABITAT** Common summer visitor (mainly Apr–
Sep) to shrubby wetlands; winters from southeastern U.S. to Central America. **OBSERVATION
TIPS** Fairly easy to see. Like many other
sparrows, responds to "pishing."

ADULT, WINTER

ADULT, ALASKA

ADULT, CALIFORNIA

SONG SPARROW

LINCOLN'S SPARROW

ADULT

SWAMP SPARROW

ADULT

Emberizidae

LARK SPARROW
Chondestes grammacus L 6.25–6.5 in

Large, well-marked sparrow. Often feeds on relatively open ground, hence easy to see. Forms small flocks outside breeding season. In flight, note the long, rounded, and mostly dark tail with striking white edges; pattern also used in display. Sexes are similar. **ADULT** Has streaked, gray-brown back, and brown wings with faint pale wing bars. Head is boldly patterned: chestnut crown with pale central stripe, white supercilium, dark-framed chestnut ear coverts, and black malar stripe bordering white "mustache" and throat. Underparts are otherwise whitish, with striking dark central breast spot. **JUVENILE** Similar, but duller and much more streaked. **VOICE** Song is a series of musical trills, buzzing phrases, and whistling notes; call is a thin *tsit*. **STATUS AND HABITAT** Fairly common summer visitor (mainly Apr–Aug) to bare, grassy ground, open woodland and prairies with scattered bushes and trees. Winters in southern U.S. and Mexico. **OBSERVATION TIPS** Easy to see in suitable habitats, but usually fairly thinly scattered.

SAGE SPARROW *Amphispiza belli* L 6–6.25 in

Dry-country sparrow with understated plumage. Often cocks tail when running or feeding and flicks tail in agitated manner at other times. Forms small flocks outside breeding season. Sexes are similar, but two reasonably distinct subspecies occur. **ADULT** Pacific ssp. *belli* ("Bell's") has

ADULT, "BELL'S"

gray-brown back, rump, and tail, brown wings with buff feather margins, and mostly dark gray nape and crown; note the white eyering and spot in front of eye. Cheeks are gray, and note white "mustache," black malar stripe, and mostly white throat and underparts, except for black central breast spot and light streaks on flanks. Interior ssp. *nevadensis* is similar, but paler overall; in particular, dark gray elements of head pattern are pale gray. **JUVENILE** Similar, but duller overall and heavily streaked. **VOICE** Song is a short burst (2 secs or so) of tuneful tinkly notes, with longer pause between phrases; call is a thin, sharp *tsip, tsip*.... **STATUS AND HABITAT** Fairly common in scrubby habitats; *belli* is resident in coastal chaparral while *nevadensis* is a summer visitor (mainly May–Aug) to sagebrush habitats in north of range, moving south and into Mexico in winter. **OBSERVATION TIPS** Easy to see in suitable habitats.

BLACK-THROATED SPARROW
Amphispiza bilineata L 5.5–5.75 in

Striking and distinctive sparrow, easily recognized by its extensive black throat and chest. Sometimes forms small flocks outside breeding season. Sexes are similar. **ADULT** Has mostly unmarked borwnish gray upperparts; flight feathers and tail are darkest. In flight, note white tips to outer tail feathers. Striking head pattern comprises dark crown, white supercilium, dark cheeks, white "mustache," and black throat and chest. Underparts are otherwise grayish white and clean-looking. **JUVENILE** Recalls adult, but is paler overall, particularly on head; throat is white and chest is streaked. **VOICE** Song is a short burst of sweet whistles, ending in a trill; call is a thin, high *teep*. **STATUS AND HABITAT** Fairly common summer visitor (mainly May–Aug) to a range of desert habitats with limited vegetation and some bare, open ground. **OBSERVATION TIPS** Easy to see in suitable habitats and sometimes rather indifferent to people.

LARK SPARROW

ADULT

SAGE SPARROW

ADULT, INTERIOR FORM

ADULT, INTERIOR FORM

JUVENILE

ADULT

BLACK-THROATED SPARROW

Emberizidae

CASSIN'S SPARROW *Aimophila cassinii* L 6–6.5 in

Secretive sparrow with unremarkable plumage. Scurries through dense vegetation and hard to flush. Only realistic opportunity for observation comes in spring, when males are vocal; sometimes seen in parachuting song flight. Sexes are similar. **ADULT** Has gray-brown upperparts overall; back feathers have pale margins with rufous centers and dark subterminal mark. Gray-brown crown has pale central stripe; note the indistinct pale supercilium and face markings. Pale throat is bordered by indistinct dark line. Underparts are gray-buff with indistinct streaks on breast and flanks. **JUVENILE** Similar, but

with bolder head pattern and more pronounced streaking below. **VOICE** Song is a brief, sweet trill preceded by, and ending with, a couple of whistling notes; call is a thin *tseep*. **STATUS AND HABITAT** Summer visitor (mainly May–Aug) to arid, dense, tall grassland with scattered bushes; winters in southern U.S. and Mexico, where also present year-round. **OBSERVATION TIPS** Fairly easy to see when singing, but otherwise a real challenge. **SIMILAR SPECIES Botteri's Sparrow** *A. botterii* (L 5.75–6 in) has more rufous back, grayer face, and yellow-buff wash to underparts; very local summer visitor (Apr–Sep) to southeastern Arizona and southern Texas grassland.

RUFOUS-CROWNED SPARROW
Aimophila ruficeps L 5.75–6 in

Unobtrusive sparrow, invariably associated with rocky or stony ground. Sometimes sings and surveys territory from prominent boulder. Subtle subspecies variation exists. Sexes are similar. **ADULT** Has grayish plumage overall, but back is streaked rufous brown and has rufous edges to inner flight feathers. Crown is rufous with pale central stripe, and gray face is marked with white eyering; supercilium is very pale in front of eye. Pacific birds have dark eyestripe and buffy "mustache"; Interior birds have rufous eyestripe and

whitish "mustache." All birds have dark malar stripe and otherwise gray underparts. **JUVENILE** Similar, but more streaked. **VOICE** Song comprises a couple of nasal cheeps followed by a rattling *chip-chip-chip chip-chit*; call is a sharp, nasal *d'neer*. **STATUS AND HABITAT** Locally common resident of stony, grassy slopes. **OBSERVATION TIPS** Easiest to see when singing in spring. **SIMILAR SPECIES Rufous-winged Sparrow** *A. carpalis* (L 5.75–6 in) has rufous lesser coverts (most obvious in flight) and stubbier, yellowish (not dark) bill; very local resident in arid grassland in southern Arizona.

AMERICAN TREE SPARROW
Spizella arborea L 6–6.25 in

Distinctive sparrow. Combination of bicolored bill (dark upper mandible, yellowish lower one), subtle rufous eyestripe, and dark breast spot, are good identification features. Forms flocks outside breeding season. Birds are brightest in breeding season and sexes are similar. **ADULT** Has dark-streaked rufous back and rufous wings with two pale wing bars. Face is gray overall, but with rufous crown and stripe behind eye, and subtle dark stripe bordering gray throat. Underparts are otherwise pale gray, with rufous wash on flanks and dark breast spot. **JUVENILE** Recalls adult, but is heavily streaked. **VOICE** Song is a descending series of rather piercing notes, ending with a trilling flourish; call is a thin *tseeup*. **STATUS AND HABITAT** Locally common summer visitor (mainly Apr–Sep) to shrubs and trees at northern edge of boreal forest; winters in weedy, grassy habitats adjacent to trees and shrubs across much of U.S. except in south. **OBSERVATION TIPS** Easy to see in suitable habitats.

CASSIN'S SPARROW

ADULT

RUFOUS-CROWNED SPARROW

ADULT

AMERICAN
TREE SPARROW

JUVENILE

ADULT

Emberizidae

FIELD SPARROW *Spizella pusilla* L 5.75–6 in
Superficially similar to American Tree Sparrow (*see* p.350), but distinguished by its uniformly pinkish (not bicolored) bill and absence of breast spot. Chipping has a dark eyestripe and white supercilium. Forms flocks outside breeding season. Western birds (those covered by this book) are grayer overall than eastern birds. Sexes are similar. **ADULT** Western bird has a dark-streaked reddish brown back and wings with two white wing bars. Plumage is otherwise mainly gray, but note rufous crown, white eyering, and faint rufous wash on flanks. Eastern birds are more extensively rufous on underparts and have reddish brown ear coverts and eyestripe. **JUVENILE** Similar to respective regional adult, but heavily streaked below. **VOICE** Song is a series of rich, whistling, disyllabic *tee-oo* phrases, ending in an accelerating trill; call is a sharp *tik*. **STATUS AND HABITAT** Common summer visitor (mainly Apr–Aug) to grassy, weedy fields with nearby scrub; found year-round in much of southeastern U.S. and winter range extends to Mexico. **OBSERVATION TIPS** Easy to see. Sometimes perches in bushes when disturbed.

CHIPPING SPARROW
Spizella passerina L 5.5–5.75 in
Familiar, well-marked sparrow. Forms flocks outside breeding season and often rather tame in suburban parks and gardens. Sexes are similar, but plumage varies seasonally. **ADULT BREEDING** Has dark-streaked buffy brown back and buffy brown wings with two whitish wing bars. Paler, grayer rump is sometimes observed in flight. Plumage is otherwise mostly gray, but note the chestnut crown, white supercilium, and dark eyestripe. Also has whitish throat. **ADULT NONBREEDING** Similar, but has brown crown with pale central stripe and buffy supercilium. **JUVENILE** Recalls nonbreeding adult, but is heavily streaked. First-winter recalls nonbreeding adult, but brown elements of plumage are buffy. It is the only sparrow to migrate in its juvenile plumage. **VOICE** Song is a rapid, rattling trill with a rather inanimate quality; call is a thin *tzip*. **STATUS AND HABITAT** Common summer visitor (mainly May–Sep) to a range of open wooded habitats, including parks and mature gardens. **OBSERVATION TIPS** Easy to see.

CLAY-COLORED SPARROW
Spizella pallida L 5.5–5.75 in
Fairly distinctive when breeding, but nonbreeding birds are similar to Chipping and Brewer's. At that time, Chipping has richer brown upperparts with more contrasting face pattern: darker eyestripe, paler supercilium, and more rufous crown. Brewer's is grayer overall (particularly on face and underparts), with less intense streaking. Forms flocks outside breeding season. Sexes are similar. **ADULT BREEDING** Has heavily dark-streaked brown back and brown wings with two white wing bars; note the buffy brown rump. Nape is gray, crown is brown, and has whitish supercilium; brown ear coverts are defined above by dark eyestripe and below by dark malar stripe, and note white "mustache" and throat. Underparts are otherwise gray-buff. **ADULT NONBREEDING** Paler overall and more buff, most noticeably on underparts and supercilium. **JUVENILE** Similar to nonbreeding adult, but heavily streaked below. **VOICE** Song is a series of breezy, vibrating, buzzing trills, vaguely cricketlike; call is a thin *tzip*. **STATUS AND HABITAT** Fairly common summer visitor (mainly May–Aug) to grassland and prairies; winters in similar habitats in Mexico. **OBSERVATION TIPS** Fairly easy to see on breeding grounds.

FIELD SPARROW

ADULT, RUFOUS

ADULT, GRAY

ADULT, NONBREEDING

CHIPPING SPARROW

ADULT, BREEDING

JUVENILE

CLAY-COLORED SPARROW

ADULT, BREEDING

ADULT, NONBREEDING

Emberizidae

BREWER'S SPARROW *Spizella breweri* L 5–5.5 in

Small sparrow with a dainty, pointed bill and unremarkable plumage. Forms flocks outside breeding season. Ssp. *taverneri* (so-called Timberline Sparrow) from northwest is isolated in breeding season from southern ssp. *breweri*, and possibly a separate species. Sexes are similar. **ADULT BREEDING** Has streaked gray-brown back and brown wings with two buff wing bars. Nape is gray in *taverneri*, gray-buff in *breweri*, and all birds have gray-brown crown and pale-centered brown ear coverts, with pale gray supercilium and lores, and pale throat bordered by dark malar stripe. Underparts are otherwise almost unmarked pale gray-buff. **ADULT NONBREEDING** Similar, but paler overall and with less contrast in streaking and face markings. **JUVENILE** More heavily streaked (especially *taverneri*) than respective adult. **VOICE** Song is a series of buzzing trills, sometimes preceded by wheezy whistles; call is a thin *tzik*. **STATUS AND HABITAT** Common summer visitor (mainly Apr–Aug) to dense brush and sagebrush habitats; winters in arid sagebrush and brushy desert habitats in southwestern U.S. and Mexico. **OBSERVATION TIPS** Easiest to see on breeding grounds.

BLACK-CHINNED SPARROW
Spizella atrogularis L 5.5–5.75 in

Distinctive, but unobtrusive pink-billed sparrow that is often a challenge to see. Sexes are separable when breeding. **ADULT MALE BREEDING** Has a streaked reddish brown back and reddish brown wings with two faint wing bars; rump and tail are gray. Plumage is otherwise mostly gray, except for black face

ADULT WINTER

and white undertail coverts. **ADULT FEMALE BREEDING** Similar, but without black face. **ALL WINTER BIRDS** Similar to breeding female. **JUVENILE** Similar to winter adult, but with faintly streaked underparts. **VOICE** Song starts with a slurred, whistling *tsee'ooerr-tsee* and ends in a rapid trill; call is a thin *tzik*. **STATUS AND HABITAT** Locally common summer visitor (mainly May–Aug) to rocky slopes with impenetrable scrub or (in California) dense chaparral; threatened by habitat loss and degradation. Winters in similar habitats from southwestern U.S. to Mexico. **OBSERVATION TIPS** Easily overlooked when not singing.

HARRIS'S SPARROW
Zonotrichia querula L 7.5–8 in

Large, plump and distinctive sparrow. All birds have a pink bill. Endemic to Canada as a breeding species. Forms flocks outside the breeding season and mixes with other sparrow species. Sexes are similar, although typically male has larger bib than female and bib increases in size with age. **ADULT BREEDING** Has streaked reddish brown back and reddish brown wings with two white wing bars. Head has largely gray cheeks with black crown, face, throat, bib, and ear covert margins. Underparts are whitish gray, with dark streaks on flanks. **ADULT NONBREEDING** Similar, but gray elements of head plumage are buffy brown and dark crown is speckled. **JUVENILE** Lacks black on face and has streaked breast and flanks. First-winter has hint of adult's black face markings, but a white throat and dark streaking on breast. **VOICE** Song comprises long, drawn-out and penetrating whistles; call is a sharp *tchink*. **STATUS AND HABITAT** Locally common summer visitor (mainly May–Sep) to stunted boreal forests on brushy fringes of tundra; in winter, favors open woodland and scrub in central Great Plains. **OBSERVATION TIPS** Note species' restricted breeding and winter ranges.

BREWER'S SPARROW

ADULT

BLACK-CHINNED SPARROW

MALE, BREEDING

ADULT, BREEDING

HARRIS'S SPARROW

ADULT, NONBREEDING

Emberizidae

WHITE-THROATED SPARROW
Zonotrichia albicollis L 6.5–6.75 in

Woodland sparrow. Forms flocks outside breeding season. Sexes are similar, but two colour morphs occur. **ADULT** Has dark-streaked brown back and reddish brown wings with two white wing bars; rump and tail are gray-brown. Has dark crown; White-striped form has pale central stripe and broad supercilium (white behind eye, yellow-buff in front); Tan-striped form has yellow-buff central stripe and supercilium. All birds have white throat and gray cheeks and underparts, palest on belly and undertail coverts. **JUVENILE** Recalls adult, but is heavily streaked below; head markings are indistinct. First-winter recalls "Tan-striped" adult, but duller overall. **VOICE** Song is a piercing, whistling *see-tsee-chrr-ch'd'd-ch'd'd*; call is a sharp *cheenk*. **STATUS AND HABITAT** Common summer visitor (mainly Apr–Aug) to northern mixed and deciduous forests; winters in dense wooded and brushy habitats, mainly south and southeastern U.S. **OBSERVATION TIPS** Often visits feeders.

WHITE-CROWNED SPARROW
Zonotrichia leucophrys L 7–7.5 in

Distinctive sparrow, widespread and familiar in winter. Forms large flocks outside breeding season. Subtle subspecies variation exists across range. Sexes are similar. **ADULT** Has dark-streaked brown back and reddish brown wings with two white wing bars; tail and rump are gray-brown and has black crown and eyestripe. Pacific breeders have dull white central crown stripe and supercilium behind eye; bill is dull pink and plumage is otherwise gray, with buff wash on nape and flanks. Northwest taiga breeders have bright white crown stripe and supercilium behind eye, gray lores, bright pink bill, and

ADULT, PACIFIC

otherwise mostly gray plumage, with limited brown on flanks. Interior and eastern birds are similar to northwest taiga birds, but have black lores and darker bill. **JUVENILE** Recalls adult, but is heavily streaked above and below. First-winter recalls adult, but black elements of head pattern are brown. **VOICE** Song comprises a couple of piercing whistles followed by several birdsqueakerlike grating chirps; call is a sharp *pink*. **STATUS AND HABITAT** Generally common and associated with a range of brushy to lightly wooded habitats, from taiga to chaparral in the breeding season; northern populations are present within their breeding ranges mainly May–Aug, but some western populations are sedentary. Winters from southern U.S. to Mexico. **OBSERVATION TIPS** Easy to see.

GOLDEN-CROWNED SPARROW
Zonotrichia atricapilla L 7–7.25 in

Pacific specialty. Forms flocks outside the breeding season, sometimes mixing with other species; often visits feeders, but prefers to keep near cover. Sexes are similar. **ADULT BREEDING** Has dark-streaked brown back and reddish brown wings with two white wing bars; rump and tail are gray-brown. Face and neck are gray and has a black crown with a yellow central stripe. Underparts are mostly grayish, but with brown wash on breast and flanks, and whitish undertail coverts. **ADULT NONBREEDING** Similar, but dark crown is mottled and less extensive, and central stripe is less colorful. **JUVENILE** Recalls nonbreeding adult, but head pattern is indistinct and plumage is heavily streaked. First-winter recalls nonbreeding adult, but with even fainter head markings. **VOICE** Song is a delightful, piercingly whistled *see'er-duu-see*; call is a chattering *cheep*. **STATUS AND HABITAT** Locally common summer visitor (mainly May–Aug) to wet boreal woodland; winters in dense woodland and chaparral. **OBSERVATION TIPS** Easiest to see at feeders.

JUVENILE
TAN-STRIPED FORM

ADULT, WHITE-STRIPED

**WHITE-THROATED
SPARROW**

ADULT, WHITE-STRIPED

ADULT, ROCKY MOUNTAIN

ADULT, TAIGA

**WHITE-CROWNED
SPARROW**

IMMATURE

ADULT, BREEDING

**GOLDEN-CROWNED
SPARROW**

ADULT, WINTER

Emberizidae

FOX SPARROW *Passerella iliaca* L 7–7.25 in

Large, plump-bodied sparrow whose plumage markings and bill size vary considerably across its vast geographical range. Several sub-species are recognized; although intergrades exists, four main groups (Thick-billed, Slate-colored, Sooty, and Red) are reasonably easy to discern, each with fairly discrete breeding ranges. In all birds, streaks and spots on breast often coalesce to form a central spot or patch of dense spots. Given the subspecies variation, sexes are similar. **ADULT** "Thick-billed" has reddish brown wings, rump, and tail, and lead-gray back and head, except for streaked whitish throat. Underparts are otherwise white, with bold dark spots on breast and flanks and gray-buff wash on flanks. Bill is large, conical and gray. "Slate-colored" is similar, but bill is smaller and yellowish, and it has two faint buff wing bars. "Sooty" has rather uniform sooty brown upperparts, and underparts that are heavily spotted dark brown; bill is smallish and pinkish. "Red" has gray and reddish brown upperparts (face pattern is striking), underparts boldly streaked reddish brown, and two pale wing bars; bill is pinkish. **JUVENILE** Similar to respective subspecies adult. **VOICE** Experienced ears can discern subspecies differences in song, but typical form is a sweet, whistled *swee too-wee, see tchet-tchu-tchu ee*; call is a sharp *tch'tup* in most subspecies; that of "Thick-billed" is a sharp *tcheenk*. **STATUS AND HABITAT** Common and often associated with willow and alder woodland. "Thick-billed" breeds on California's chaparral-covered Pacific slope; "Slate-colored" breeds across much of interior west; "Sooty" breeds in Pacific Northwest; and "Red" breeds in taiga across whole of northern North America. All birds winter south of their breeding ranges, from southern U.S. to Mexico. **OBSERVATION TIPS** Often visits feeding stations, collecting food from the ground. Otherwise usually keeps to cover and can be unobtrusive.

LARK BUNTING
Calamospiza melanocorys L 7–7.25 in

Large and well-marked, sparrowlike grassland bird, males of which are striking and unmistakable in breeding plumage. All birds have a stout, conical, blue-gray bill, and a white tip to the tail. Often perches on fences and forms large flocks outside the breeding season. Sexes are dissimilar. **ADULT BREEDING MALE** Has mostly black plumage, but with striking white patch (mostly the greater coverts) on wings (obvious when perched and in flight). **ADULT NONBREEDING MALE** Has black elements of plumage replaced by streaked gray-brown on upperparts; underparts are whitish with bold dark streaks. **ADULT FEMALE** Recalls nonbreeding male, but plumage is paler overall and white on wing is restricted to less distinct patch formed by white edges to greater covert feathers. Note also the bold dark line bordering the pale throat. **JUVENILE** Similar to adult female, but with less distinct markings. **VOICE** Song is a delightful and varied mixture of trills and shrill and liquid whistles; call is a soft *hu-eee*. **STATUS AND HABITAT** Common summer visitor (mainly May–Aug) to prairies; winters from southern U.S. to Mexico in grassland habitats. **OBSERVATION TIPS** Easy to see within range, in suitable habitats.

MALE, NONBREEDING

FEMALE

ADULT, "RED"

FOX SPARROW

ADULT, "THICK-BILLED"

LARK BUNTING

MALE, BREEDING

Emberizidae

DARK-EYED JUNCO *Junco hyemalis* L 6.25–6.5 in

Confusingly variable, with five recognizably distinct, named groups, separated on plumage differences and with fairly distinct breeding ranges. All birds form flocks outside breeding season and have white outer tail feathers and a dark eye. Females are duller and browner than respective group males; for reasons of space, the following adult descriptions relate to males. **ADULT** "Slate-colored" has mostly slate-gray plumage, except for white belly and undertail coverts; bill is pink. "White-winged" is similar, but slightly paler overall, with darker mask and two white wing bars. "Oregon" has black hood, reddish brown back, reddish brown flanks, and otherwise white under-

ADULT, "PINK-SIDED"

parts. "Pink-sided" has gray hood and dark mask, brown back and wings, pinkish flanks, and otherwise white underparts. "Gray-headed" has reddish back and otherwise mostly gray plumage, except for dark mask and white belly and undertail coverts. **JUVENILE** Recalls adult of respective group, but plumage is much browner and heavily streaked. **VOICE** Song is a rapid, trilling *tu'-tu'tu'tu'tu*; call is a tongue-smacking *tchht*. **STATUS AND HABITAT** Common, favoring coniferous forests for breeding. "Slate-colored" is widespread in boreal forests; "White-winged" breeds in Black Hills of South Dakota and Wyoming; "Oregon" is a West Coast bird; "Pink-sided" breeds in the northern Rockies; and "Gray-headed" breeds mainly in the southern Rockies. All birds move south of breeding ranges in winter to scrub and woodland. **OBSERVATION TIPS** Easy to see.

> **!** There is a lot of overlap and intergrading among Dark-eyed Junco "races" and subspecies; assignment to subspecies is probably best done on the basis of "balance of probability" rather than "beyond reasonable doubt," and absolute certainty is not always possible.

YELLOW-EYED JUNCO *Junco phaeonotus* L 6–6.25 in

Recalls "Gray-headed" form of Dark-eyed, but eye has yellow iris and rufous on upperparts is more extensive, extending onto wings. Bill is bicolored (dark upper mandible, pale lower one); Dark-eyeds have uniform bills, except for "Red-backed" form whose range overlaps that of Yellow-eyed. Sexes are similar. **ADULT** Has reddish back and reddish on tertials and greater coverts. Upperparts are otherwise gray, with dark mask surrounding pale eye. Underparts are pale gray, palest on belly and undertail coverts. **JUVENILE** Recalls adult, but is browner overall and heavily streaked. **VOICE** Song is a sweet *tsiu'tsiu'tsiu'tsiu* followed by a trill; call is a sharp *tchht*. **STATUS AND HABITAT** Mainly Mexican species with limited resident range in open coniferous and mixed forests in southern Arizona and New Mexico. **OBSERVATION TIPS** Fairly easy to see, but has restricted range.

SMITH'S LONGSPUR *Calcarius pictus* L 6–6.25 in

Breeding male is distinctive. All birds have noticeably "warm" buff plumage. Forms flocks outside breeding season when easy to overlook in favored grassland habitats. Bill is narrower than in other longspurs (*see* p.362). Sexes are dissimilar. **ADULT BREEDING MALE** Has streaked brown back and brown wings with two white wing bars and white "shoulder" patch. Head has dark cap with white supercilium and eye surround, and white spot on ear coverts. Underparts and neck are orange buff. **ALL OTHER PLUMAGES** Recall breeding male, but are duller overall, lack white "shoulder" patch, but have streaked back and nape; black elements of head pattern are replaced by streaked brown, white elements are replaced by buff. **VOICE** Song is a sweet whistling trill; call is a dry rattle. **STATUS AND HABITAT** Local summer visitor (mainly Jun–Aug) to northern tundra; winters in grassland. **OBSERVATION TIPS** Note its limited range.

ADULT, "SLATE-COLORED"

ADULT, "GRAY-HEADED"

ADULT, "OREGON"

DARK-EYED JUNCO

ADULT

YELLOW-EYED JUNCO

SMITH'S LONGSPUR

NONBREEDING

MALE, BREEDING

Emberizidae

McCOWN'S LONGSPUR
Calcarius mccownii L 6–6.25 in

Male is distinctive. All birds have mostly white tail with black inverted "T" (central stripe and terminal band); courting male uses this in aerial display. Forms flocks outside breeding season. Conical bill is dark in breeding male, but pinkish in all other birds. Sexes are separable. **ADULT BREEDING MALE** Has buff and black streaks on back and gray-brown wings with a striking chestnut band (median coverts). Grayish white head has black cap and malar stripe, and very pale throat and eye surround. Has black crescentlike patch on breast and otherwise mostly pale gray underparts, palest on undertail coverts. **ADULT NONBREEDING MALE** Recalls breeding male, but black elements of plumage have pale feather fringes. **ADULT FEMALE** Recalls nonbreeding male, but has streaked brown crown and brown breast; palest in winter. **JUVENILE** Recalls winter female, but is streaked below and scaly-looking above. **VOICE** Song is a varied jumble of scratchy warbles; call is a rattling *ch't't*. **STATUS AND HABITAT** Local summer visitor (mainly Apr–Aug) to short-grass prairies and more barren open ground, such as pastures; winters in similar habitats. **OBSERVATION TIPS** Worth visiting on breeding grounds.

CHESTNUT-COLLARED LONGSPUR
Calcarius ornatus L 5.75–6 in

Well-marked longspur. Forms flocks outside breeding season. All birds have a mostly white tail with a black terminal triangle. Sexes are separable. **ADULT BREEDING MALE** Has black, brown, and buff stripes on back and brownish wings with two pale wing bars and white shoulder patch. Nape is chestnut, crown and ear covert margins are black, and otherwise whitish head is yellowish on face. Underparts are mostly black (some have chestnut on chest), except for white belly and undertail coverts. **ADULT NONBREEDING MALE** Like bleached version of breeding male with muted colors and pale feather fringes obscuring black elements of plumage. **ADULT FEMALE** Recalls a plain nonbreeding male, without white shoulder patch. **JUVENILE** Heavily streaked; first-winter recalls plain, washed out adult female. **VOICE** Song is a descending, chirpy *tsi, sidididi zer'de*; call is a rattling *ch'd'd*. **STATUS AND HABITAT** Local summer visitor (mainly Apr–Sep) to short-grass prairies; winters in short, dense grassland. **OBSERVATION TIPS** Rewarding in spring—singing, breeding plumage males are a delight.

LAPLAND LONGSPUR
Calcarius lapponicus L 6–6.25 in

Colorful longspur. All birds have striking reddish brown greater coverts. Forms flocks outside breeding season. Sexes are separable. **ADULT BREEDING MALE** Has buff, brown, and black streaks on back, and brown wings with reddish brown greater coverts and tertial edges. Broad pale stripe (mostly white, but yellowish behind eye) runs from base of wings, framing the ear coverts to the eye; breast, face, and crown are black and nape is reddish brown. Underparts are otherwise mostly white, but streaked black on flanks. **ADULT NONBREEDING MALE** Similar, but paler overall and black ele-

1ST-WINTER

ments of plumage are mostly brown, but with dark-framed buff ear patch, white throat, and dark breast. **ADULT FEMALE** Recalls nonbreeding male, but is paler overall. **JUVENILE** Recalls adult female, but is heavily streaked. **VOICE** Song is a short series of scratchy whistles; call is a rattle. **STATUS AND HABITAT** Common summer visitor (mainly Apr–Aug) to northern tundra; winters in bare, grassy habitats. **OBSERVATION TIPS** Easy to see in suitable habitats.

McCOWN'S LONGSPUR

FEMALE

MALE, BREEDING

FEMALE

MALE, BREEDING

CHESTNUT-COLLARED LONGSPUR

ADULT, NONBREEDING

MALE, NONBREEDING

LAPLAND LONGSPUR

MALE, BREEDING

Emberizidae and Cardinalidae

SNOW BUNTING *Plectrophenax nivalis* L 6.75–7 in

Plump-bodied bunting. In flight, note extensive white on inner wing. Forms flocks outside breeding season. Sexes are separable. **ADULT BREEDING MALE** Has mainly white plumage, except for black back, outer flight feathers, patch on leading edge of wing and tail center. Legs and bill are black. **ADULT NONBREEDING MALE** Recalls breeding male, but back has orange-buff feather fringes, and similar color is seen on tertial margins and to fringes of feathers on crown, nape, ear coverts, and flanks. Orange-buff fringes wear during winter, revealing black and white plumage by spring. Bill is yellow during winter months. **ADULT FEMALE** Recalls dull male in seasonal plumages, but in summer white elements of plumage are grubby while black feathers are fringed brown. **JUVENILE** Streaked, and by first winter recalls respective sex winter adult, but with more extensive orange-buff on face and underparts. **VOICE** Song is a tinkling series of twittering whistles; calls include a soft *tiu*. **STATUS AND HABITAT** Common summer visitor (May–Sep) to tundra; winters in grassy fields. **OBSERVATION TIPS** Fairly easy to find, but precise winter occurrence is unpredictable.

BLACK-HEADED GROSBEAK
Pheucticus melanocephalus L 8.25–8.5 in

Plump songbird. Immature and female birds are similar to Rose-breasted counterparts; warmer orange-buff underparts and light streaking

FEMALE

are good identification features and breeding range is also a clue. Bill is usually darker above than below (uniformly pale in Rose-breasted) and underwing coverts are yellowish in all birds. Sexes are dissimilar. **ADULT MALE** Has streaked dark brown back and dark wings with white "shoulders" and wing bars. Rump is orange-buff (white in Rose-breasted). Has a mostly dark hood with orange-buff neck and underparts. **ADULT FEMALE** Has mostly streaked brown upperparts with two white wing bars and white supercilium. Margin of throat is pale, but underparts are otherwise pale orange-buff with faint streaking. **JUVENILE** Streaked; first-winter birds recall adult female, but male has richer underparts. **VOICE** Song is rich and warbling, with some wolf-whistlelike phrases; call is a sharp *eek*. **STATUS AND HABITAT** Common summer visitor (Jun–Aug) to hardwood stands and coniferous forests; winters in Mexico. **OBSERVATION TIPS** Easy to see.

ROSE-BREASTED GROSBEAK
Pheucticus ludovicianus L 8–8.25 in

Large-billed songbird. Often feeds unobtrusively in cover. Feasts on fruit prior to fall migration. Sexes are dissimilar. **ADULT BREEDING MALE** Has black hood and back (with white rump), and black wings with white "shoulder" patch, wing bar, and base to primaries; latter seen as broad patch in flight when bright red underwing coverts are also noticed. Breast is bright red and underparts otherwise mostly white. First-summer male like adult male, but some femalelike elements in plumage. **ADULT NONBREEDING MALE** (plumage acquired before fall migration) Similar, but black elements of plumage are mottled brown. **ADULT FEMALE** Has mostly streaked brown upperparts with two white wing bars and white base to primaries. Has broad, pale supercilium, and underparts are pale overall, but with bold dark streaking. Underwing coverts are yellowish and bill is pink. **JUVENILE** Like heavily streaked female; by first fall, male has hint of red breast. **VOICE** Song is a series of rich, fluty whistles, recalling that of American Robin; call is a sharp *piik*. **STATUS AND HABITAT** Common summer visitor (mainly May–Aug) to deciduous woodland; winters in Central America. **OBSERVATION TIPS** Easy to see.

1ST-WINTER

SNOW BUNTING

MALE, BREEDING

MALE, NONBREEDING

MALE, 1ST-FALL

MALE, BREEDING

BLACK-HEADED GROSBEAK

ROSE-BREASTED GROSBEAK

MALE, 1ST-FALL

FEMALE

MALE, BREEDING

Cardinalidae

NORTHERN CARDINAL
Cardinalis cardinalis L 8.75–9 in

Distinctive bird, whose shape alone makes it arguably North America's most instantly recognizable bird. Combination of erectile peaked crest, long tail, and stout bill, can only be confused with Pyrrhuloxia, from which it differs in plumage and habitat preferences. Male is extraordinarily colorful, but surprisingly unobtrusive when sitting in foliage. A frequent visitor to bird feeders and feeding stations and particularly noticeable during the winter months. Western birds have a slightly longer crest, slightly thicker bill, and less black around the face. Sexes are dissimilar. **ADULT MALE** Mostly bright red, except for well-defined black face. Bill is bright red. **ADULT FEMALE** Has mostly gray-buff body plumage with red tail, red tinge on wings, and red tip to crest. Has a limited amount of black on face and subdued red bill. In flight, note the red underwing coverts (underwing is entirely red in male). **JUVENILE** Recalls adult female, but is dull brown overall, with reddish flush to breast and tail in particular. Bill is dark. **VOICE** Song is an insistent series of rich, fluty whistles typically either *tiu-tiu-tiu-tiu* or *p'dee-p'dee-p'dee-p'dee*; call is a sharp *tik*. **STATUS AND HABITAT** Common resident of wooded habitats, parks, and gardens. Widespread in eastern North America, but range is restricted in southwest by predominance there of arid habitats: here, Northern Cardinals are typically found near water. Range in eastern half of North America has expanded northwards over the last century, the expansion generally attributed to the creation of more suitable habitats (parks and gardens) by man. By contrast, species has fared less well in southwest. **OBSERVATION TIPS** Easy to see in most parks and gardens within its range.

MALE, ARIZONA

PYRRHULOXIA *Cardinalis sinuatus* L 8.75–9 in

Similar to Northern Cardinal and in many ways its southwestern, arid-country counterpart. Distinguished by its largely gray upperparts with contrasting red crest, red (not black) face, and its proportionately large, rounded, stubby, and yellowish bill. Forms nomadic flocks outside the breeding season. Sometimes visits bird feeders. Sexes are separable. **ADULT MALE** Has grayish back and gray wings with red leading edge; tail is mainly red. Plumage is otherwise mostly buff-gray, but note the largely red crest and red face with color continuing down center of breast and belly. In flight, note the red underwing coverts. **ADULT FEMALE** Mainly buffy gray with red outer tail feathers and red leading edge to wings; tip of crest is red. **JUVENILE** Similar to adult female, but duller overall, and red elements of plumage are subdued or absent; bill is dark. **VOICE** Song is a series of liquid, upslurred whistles: *wee-p'wee-p'wee-p'wee*; call is a sharp, chattering *chit't't't*. **STATUS AND HABITAT** Locally common resident of desert scrub and mesquite thickets in southern Arizona, New Mexico, and Texas. **OBSERVATION TIPS** Easy to see in suitable habitats, often particularly visible in winter.

NORTHERN CARDINAL

FEMALE

MALE, EASTERN

FEMALE

MALE

PYRRHULOXIA

Cardinalidae

DICKCISSEL *Spiza americana* L 6.25–6.5 in

Sparrowlike grassland bird with a proportionately large bill. Forms huge flocks outside breeding season and prior to migration. Sexes are dissimilar. **ADULT MALE** Has a dark-striped, gray-brown back, reddish brown wings, and gray tail and nape. Head is gray overall, but with striking yellow supercilium and eye surround, yellow malar stripe, and black bib surrounding white throat patch. Underparts are flushed yellow on breast, grading to grayish white on belly; undertail coverts are white. Colors are subdued in nonbreeding plumage and black bib is obscured by pale feather fringes. **ADULT FEMALE** Recalls a dull, washed-out male with no black bib and more extensive white throat. **JUVENILE** Recalls plain adult female with hint of adult's face pattern. **VOICE** Song is a repeated, vaguely onomatopoeic *dik-dik-dik, ciss-sess-sel*; call is a buzzing *fzzppt*. **STATUS AND HABITAT** Common summer visitor (mainly May–Aug) to Midwest prairies and farmland; numbers and breeding locations affected by factors such as rainfall. Winters mainly in Venezuelan llanos, where subject to persecution in agricultural areas. **OBSERVATION TIPS** Easy to see in Midwest.

BLUE GROSBEAK *Passerina caerulea* L 6.75 in

Plump-bodied bird with a large, conical bill. Bill size allows separation of colorful male from other blue bunting species; female's plain, unstreaked plumage allows separation from other grosbeak species' females with similar-sized bills. Feeds unobtrusively in brush, but sometimes sings from exposed perch. Sexes are dissimilar. **ADULT MALE** Stunning, with mainly blue plumage; note the two reddish brown wing bars, buffy tertial edges, and black face. **ADULT FEMALE** Has brown plumage overall, darker above than below and with two reddish brown wing bars and pale throat. **JUVENILE** Recalls adult female, and by first winter has warmer reddish brown plumage overall. By first spring, male acquires blue color on head, rump, and tail. **VOICE** Song is a burst of bright, chirping whistles; call is a sharp *pink*. **STATUS AND HABITAT** Common summer visitor (mainly May–Aug) to brushy areas and neglected, overgrown grassland; winters in Central America. **OBSERVATION TIPS** Easy to see.

INDIGO BUNTING *Passerina cyanea* L 5.5–5.75 in

Familiar roadside bird in many areas and stunning male sometimes perches on fence wires, twitching tail in an agitated manner. Forms flocks outside breeding season. Sexes are dissimilar. **ADULT BREEDING MALE** Has mostly uniformly bright blue plumage, darkest and grayest on flight feathers; bill is silvery gray and conical. **ADULT NONBREEDING MALE** Has blotchy brown and blue plumage (caused by brown feather edges); resplendent again by spring. **ADULT FEMALE** Has brown plumage overall, darker above than below and with two faint wing bars and faint streaking on underparts. **JUVENILE** Recalls adult female; by first spring male acquires some blue elements of adult's plumage, but still looks blotchy. **VOICE** Song is a slightly descending series of chirpy, slurred whistles, ending in a trilling flourish; call is a sharp *stik*. **STATUS AND HABITAT** Common summer visitor (mainly May–Sep) to weedy fields, scrubby margins to deciduous woods, and similar habitats; widespread in east, but more restricted in west and often found in vicinity of water. Winters mainly in Central America. **OBSERVATION TIPS** Easy to see.

DICKCISSEL, GROSBEAKS, and BUNTINGS

DICKCISSEL

FEMALE

MALE

FEMALE

BLUE GROSBEAK

MALE, 1ST-SPRING

MALE

FEMALE

INDIGO BUNTING

MALE

MALE, 1ST-SPRING

Cardinalidae

LAZULI BUNTING *Passerina amoena* L 5.5–5.75 in

Colorful bunting that replaces Indigo in western North America. Sometimes perches on roadside fence wires and twitches tail in an agitated manner. Forms large flocks outside breeding season; these concentrate at migration hotspots (e.g. in southern Arizona), where partial molt occurs. Sexes are dissimilar. **ADULT BREEDING MALE** Has blue hood and back and darker blue-gray wings with two white wing bars. Breast is orange-buff with faint wash on flanks; underparts are otherwise white. **ADULT NONBREEDING MALE** Similar, but colors are less intense and blue elements of plumage are blotched brown (brown feather edges). **ADULT FEMALE** Has mostly gray-buff upperparts with bluish rump, darker tail, and two pale wing bars. Has buff wash on breast (brightest in nonbreeding birds) grading to otherwise whitish underparts. **JUVENILE** Recalls adult female, but warmer buff; by first spring, male has acquired some of adult's blue coloration. **VOICE** Song is a varied mix of sweet, whistling phrases; call is a sharp *tchht*. **STATUS AND HABITAT** Locally common summer visitor (mainly May–Aug) to brushy deciduous woodland margins, often near water; winters in Mexico. **OBSERVATION TIPS** Easy to see. Flocks seen prior to migration are impressive.

FEMALE

PAINTED BUNTING *Passerina ciris* L 5.5–5.75 in

Male is flamboyantly colorful and color combination might be considered vulgar if employed in fashion! Rather secretive nature and unobtrusive habits (often feeds in deep cover) can make it hard to spot. Sexes are dissimilar. **ADULT MALE** Has mostly blue hood, with narrow bright red center to throat; underparts and rump are also bright red. Back is bright yellowish green and wings are brown with green feather margins. **ADULT FEMALE** Has mostly bright yellowish green upperparts including tail and hood, and mostly paler yellow underparts including narrow throat. **JUVENILE** Recalls plain, gray-buff version of adult female, with only hint of green on upperparts; by first spring, male has acquired some of adult's blue and red feathering. **VOICE** Song is a sweet series of warbling whistles; call is a sharp *tchip*. **STATUS AND HABITAT** Locally common summer visitor (mainly May–Sep) to dense undergrowth and thickets bordering woods and streams; winters mainly in Central America, but also southern Florida. **OBSERVATION TIPS** Often a challenge to find, despite its bright colors.

FEMALE

VARIED BUNTING *Passerina versicolor* L 5.25–5.5 in

Southwestern, arid-country bunting, male of which is highly colorful (although it can look rather dark in poor light). Usually keeps to cover and can be tricky to see, except when male is singing. Close view reveals slightly downcurved culmen. Sexes are dissimilar. **ADULT MALE** Has a mostly blue tail, rump, and head, except for the red nape and black face. Plumage is otherwise purplish. **ADULT FEMALE** Extremely uniform, with unstreaked gray-buff plumage, darker above than below; plumage hue is warmest buff in winter months. **JUVENILE** Similar to adult female; by first spring, male acquires variable amount of adult's blue and purple coloration. **VOICE** Song is a series of sweet, whistling phrases, similar to Painted Bunting; call is a sharp *tchip*. **STATUS AND HABITAT** Locally common summer visitor (mainly Jun–Sep) to mesquite thickets and desert washes; winters in Mexico. **OBSERVATION TIPS** Easiest to find when male is singing.

LAZULI BUNTING

PAINTED BUNTING

MALE, BREEDING

MALE, NONBREEDING

MALE

VARIED BUNTING

FEMALE

MALE

Icteridae

BOBOLINK *Dolichonyx oryzivorus* L 7–7.25 in

Well-marked grassland bird. Often perches conspicuously and forms flocks outside breeding season. Male performs song flight in spring. Sexes are dissimilar. **ADULT BREEDING MALE** Has mostly black plumage, but with buff nape, white rump, and white "shoulder" patch (scapulars); edges of tertials and greater coverts are edged white. **ADULT BREEDING FEMALE** Has buffy brown plumage overall, with dark streaking on back, and with dark

FALL BIRD

centers and buff margins to covert feathers and tertials. Head has dark stripe behind eye and dark crown with pale central stripe. Throat is pale and underparts are otherwise pale buff, with dark streaking on flanks. **ALL OTHER PLUMAGES** Similar to breeding female, but warmer buff overall. **VOICE** Song (given in flight) is a fluty and vaguely onomatopoeic *b'bob-o-lii'ink* followed by various chattering notes; call is a melodious *pink*. **STATUS AND HABITAT** Common summer visitor (mainly May–Aug) to tall-grass prairies and weedy meadows. Winters in central South American grassland. **OBSERVATION TIPS** Easy to see.

WESTERN MEADOWLARK
Sturnella neglecta L 9.5–10 in

Long-billed grassland bird. Often sings from roadside posts. Easily recognized as a meadowlark, but specific identification is tricky where range overlaps with Eastern. Note differences in voice, Western's full yellow throat (Eastern has white malar stripe) and extent of white in tail—outer two feathers are white, third-in having limited white (Eastern has three white outer tail feathers, fourth-in having limited white). Northern birds are darker than southern ones; given this variation, sexes are similar. **ADULT** Has marbled brown upperparts including wings. Head has buff cheeks, dark stripe behind eye, and dark crown. Pale supercilium is yellow in front of eye and yellow throat is defined below by "V"-shaped black chest band. Underparts are flushed yellow on breast, grading to white on belly and with dark spots on flanks. In winter, black "V" is obscured by pale feather tips. **JUVENILE** Similar to winter adult. **VOICE** Song is a short burst of fluty whistles *tu'lu Tee te'oo tliu'oo-tu*; call is a dull *tchuup*. **STATUS AND HABITAT** Common in grassland and farmland; resident in south of range, but northern birds migrate south in fall. **OBSERVATION TIPS** Easy to see.

EASTERN MEADOWLARK
Sturnella magna L 9.5–10 in

Very similar to Western and shares similar habits; in areas of overlap, usually found in damper habitats. Note Eastern's white malar stripe bordering yellow throat and greater extent of white in outer tail. Also, flank markings tend to look streaky in Eastern, but spotty in Western. Subspecies plumage variation exists across range; Southwestern "Lilian's" (*lilianae*) is palest and most similar to sympatric Westerns. Sexes are similar. **ADULT** Has marbled brown upperparts. Head has buff cheeks, dark stripe behind eye, and dark crown. Pale supercilium is yellow in front of eye and yellow throat is bordered by white malar stripe and defined below by "V"-shaped black chest band. Underparts are flushed yellow on breast, grading to white on belly and with dark spots on flanks. In winter, "V" is obscured by pale feather tips. **JUVENILE** Similar to winter adult. **VOICE** Song is a whistled *tsee'oo'ee tseeuu*; call is a rattle. **STATUS AND HABITAT** Common in grassland; largely resident, but northern birds migrate south in fall. **OBSERVATION TIPS** Easy to see.

BOBOLINK

FEMALE

MALE, BREEDING

MALE, BREEDING

ADULT, BREEDING

ADULT, BREEDING

WESTERN
MEADOWLARK

EASTERN
MEADOWLARK

ADULT, NONBREEDING

ADULT, NONBREEDING

ADULT, NONBREEDING

Icteridae

YELLOW-HEADED BLACKBIRD
Xanthocephalus xanthocephalus L 9.5–9.75 in
Stocky wetland bird. Male is unmistakable. Forms flocks outside
breeding season. Sexes are dissimilar and male is larger than female. **ADULT
MALE** Has bright yellow hood and breast (with black eye surround), and otherwise mostly black plumage, except for striking white wing patch (primary
coverts). **ADULT FEMALE** Has a yellowish buff face and breast (palest on
throat, malar stripe, and supercilium) and otherwise rather uniform and
unstreaked dark brown plumage. **JUVENILE** Yellow-buff overall, darker above
than below, with two white wing bars; first-winter female is similar to adult
female; first-winter male is similar to adult female, but has hint of adult male's white wing patch, plus
dark lores and more intense yellow suffusion on head. **VOICE** Song comprises harsh, grating and chattering screeches; call is a dry *k'duk*. **STATUS AND HABITAT** Common summer visitor (mainly May–Aug) to
marshy habitats; winters mainly in Mexico. **OBSERVATION TIPS** Easy to see.

RED-WINGED BLACKBIRD
Agelaius phoeniceus L 8.75–9 in
Widespread and familiar bird. Forms huge foraging and roosting
flocks outside breeding season. Male is easily separable from male Tricolored where ranges overlap in California. Female is hard to separate from
female Tricolored (only a problem where ranges overlap). *See* that species'
entry for discussion. Sexes are dissimilar. **ADULT MALE** Has mostly black
plumage with colorful "shoulder"—either entirely red (as in so-called
"Bicolored") or red, bordered with yellow. In winter, black elements of
plumage have subtle brown edges.

MALE, "BICOLORED"

ADULT FEMALE Brown overall, and heavily streaked on back
and underparts; plumage is palest on throat (sometimes
washed pinkish buff) and has a pale supercilium. "Bicolored" female is darker than typical female and can look
almost blackish in poor light. **IMMATURE MALE** Similar to
winter adult, but with more extensive brown edging to
feathers. **IMMATURE FEMALE** Recalls adult female, but lacks
pinkish buff wash to throat. **VOICE** Song is harsh, grating
and screechy; call is a sharp *tchik*. **STATUS AND HABITAT**
Contender for North America's most abundant bird; favors
farmland and wetlands. Summer range extends to fringe of
Arctic, but occurs year-round in much of U.S. Winter range
extends to Central America. "Bicolored" occurs in California.
OBSERVATION TIPS Hard to miss.

TRICOLORED BLACKBIRD
Agelaius tricolor L 8.75–9 in
Flock-forming, colonial bird. Bill is more slender than Red-winged's. Male is separated from typical form of Red-winged Blackbird by bright white (not yellow) edge
to red "shoulder." Female is very similar to female Red-winged; some birds may
not be identifiable with certainty in the field, but plumage is usually darker overall, without "warm" brown tones; throat is always whitish (some Red-winged
females have a pinkish buff throat). Sexes are dissimilar. **ADULT MALE** Has mostly
black plumage; red shoulder patch has bright white border. In winter, black feathers have gray-buff edges. **IMMATURE AND ADULT FEMALE** Dark gray-brown with heavy
streaking on back and underparts; plumage is least dark on throat, malar stripe, and supercilium. **IMMATURE MALE** Similar to winter male, but buff feather edges are more obvious.
VOICE Song is harsh, grating and screechy; call is a dull *chuk*. **STATUS AND HABITAT** Wetland
and farmland resident, almost entirely restricted to California. **OBSERVATION TIPS** Easy to see
within range.

YELLOW-HEADED BLACKBIRD

FEMALE

MALE

FEMALE

MALE

RED-WINGED BLACKBIRD

TRICOLORED BLACKBIRD

FEMALE

MALE

Icteridae

RUSTY BLACKBIRD *Euphagus carolinus* L 9–9.25 in

Pale-eyed blackbird with a slender bill. Named after rusty feather margins seen in fall and early winter. Sexes are dissimilar. **ADULT BREEDING MALE** Has blackish plumage overall with a green sheen in good light. **ADULT NONBREEDING MALE** Has rusty brown feather edges over much of body, which slowly wear away so that the plumage is usually pristine black by late winter. **ADULT BREEDING FEMALE** Dark gray-brown overall, darkest on wings and tail. **ADULT NONBREEDING FEMALE** Has rusty brown edges to many feathers; color is particularly striking on head (where supercilium contrasts with darker eyestripe), back, and tertials. **IMMATURES** Similar to

FEMALE, BREEDING

respective sex winter adults. **VOICE** Song is series of gurgling chatters (recalling a distant flock of European Starlings) followed by a breezy whistle; call is a soft *tchuk*. **STATUS AND HABITAT** A wet woodland species. Favors northern and taiga forests for breeding (present there mainly May–Sep). Winters in southeastern U.S. Formerly common, but now threatened: numbers have declined catastrophically in recent decades. **OBSERVATION TIPS** Breeding grounds are hard to access, so easiest to see in winter, but restricted in the West.

BREWER'S BLACKBIRD

Euphagus cyanocephalus L 9–9.25 in

Widespread and familiar colonially nesting bird. Often bold in suburban locations. Sexes are dissimilar. **ADULT BREEDING MALE** Has black plumage overall; in good light, has purple sheen on head and blue-green sheen to back, wings, and breast. Note the pale iris. **ADULT NONBREEDING MALE** Duller due to brownish feather edges, which gradually wear off. **ADULT FEMALE** Rather uniform dark gray-brown, darkest on wings and tail. Iris is dark in most birds. **IMMATURES** Similar to respective sex winter adults. **VOICE** Song is a piercing, squeaky whistle, sometimes followed by call-like *tchak* notes. **STATUS AND HABITAT** Common in suburban areas and on farmland. Resident in west of range and range extends north in summer; contraction of range south in winter is influenced by food availability and weather. Overall, range has expanded due to human alteration of natural environment. **OBSERVATION TIPS** Easy to see, and often tame in suburban parks and gardens.

BROWN-HEADED COWBIRD

Molothrus ater L 7.5–7.75 in

Widespread and familiar open-country bird, reviled in some quarters because of the impact its nest-parasitizing lifestyle has on songbirds. Effect on certain endangered species is undeniable, but, as with most things in natural world, the story behind many species' decline is seldom clear-cut. Sexes are dissimilar. **ADULT MALE** Has a dark brown hood and otherwise blackish plumage with a green sheen in good light. **ADULT FEMALE** Plain brown overall, darkest on wings and tail; note the subtly pale throat, malar stripe, and eye surround and supercilium. **JUVENILE** Similar to adult female, but with

JUVENILE

pale feather margins on back, faint pale wing bars, and streaked underparts. **VOICE** Song is a couple of quacking gurgles followed by a thin, upslurred whistle; call is a rattling *krrr'k*. **STATUS AND HABITAT** Common and widespread in farmland and open habitats. Resident in south of range and on Pacific slope, but migrant summer visitor (present mainly Apr–Aug) to north and interior regions. Range and population expanded greatly during 19th century: benefited from forest clearance and creation of farmland. **OBSERVATION TIPS** Hard to miss.

BLACKBIRDS and COWBIRDS

MALE, BREEDING

FEMALE, NONBREEDING

RUSTY BLACKBIRD

FEMALE

MALE

BREWER'S BLACKBIRD

FEMALE

MALE

BROWN-HEADED COWBIRD

Icteridae

BRONZED COWBIRD *Molothrus aeneus* L 8.75–9 in

Rather plump, thick-billed cowbird. Relative head size changes
according to whether generous nape feathers are raised and ruffled

FEMALE

or not. All adult birds have beady red eyes.
Nest parasite of other songbirds. Sexes are
dissimilar. **ADULT MALE** Has black plumage
overall, with bronze sheen to hood and
back and blue sheen to wings and tail.
ADULT FEMALE Has dark blackish brown
plumage overall in eastern ssp. *aeneus*; western
females (ssp. *loyei*) are gray-brown, darkest on wings and tail. **JUVE-
NILE** Similar to respective subspecies female, but iris is dark. **VOICE**
Song is series of weird gulping gurgles and upslurred squeaks; call is
a harsh *tchak*. **STATUS AND HABITAT** A mainly Central American species
with a toehold in southern states; locally common summer visitor
(mainly May–Aug) to farmland; winters mainly in Central America.
OBSERVATION TIPS Fairly easy to see, but U.S. range is restricted.

COMMON GRACKLE *Quiscalus quiscula* L 12–12.5 in

Western North America's most widespread grackle, recognized as such
(and separated from blackbirds) by its long bill and long, graduated
tail, which male holds keeled in cross-section. Male performs elaborate displays, including tail-fanning and body-arching. All adult birds have a pale iris.
Male is larger than female and sexes are separable by subtle plumage differences. **ADULT MALE** Looks all black in poor light, but in good light has a blue
sheen to hood and chest, bronzed sheen to much of body plumage, and bluish
purple tinge to wings and tail. Southeastern U.S. birds have purple, not bronzed,
back. **ADULT FEMALE** Similar to male, but duller overall and with less noticeable
sheen. **JUVENILE** Recalls adult female, but plumage is uniform brown overall, darkest on wings and tail,
and iris is dark. **VOICE** Song is harsh and grating; call is a sharp *tchuk*. **STATUS AND HABITAT** Common
and widespread in open and lightly wooded habitats, including farmland, parks, and gardens. Occurs year
round in southeastern U.S., but, further north and west, is a summer visitor (mainly May–Sep) with birds
moving south and east in fall. **OBSERVATION TIPS** Easy to see and often bold in parks and gardens.

GREAT-TAILED GRACKLE
Quiscalus mexicanus L 15–18 in

Large and raucous, slim-bodied grackle with a long, daggerlike bill.
Forms flocks outside breeding season. All birds have relatively long, narrow
wings and all adults have a pale iris. Male is larger than female and has a
bizarrely long, diamond-shaped tail (appreciably longer than female's
tail). Sexes are separable on plumage differences too. **ADULT MALE** Has
blackish plumage overall, but in good light note the bluish violet sheen on
much of the body. **ADULT FEMALE**

FEMALE

Brown plumage overall, darkest on
wings and tail, and warmest and palest on throat, chest, and
supercilium. Western birds are paler overall than eastern counterparts, especially on underparts. **JUVENILE** Similar to adult
female, but with streaking on underparts and dark eye. **VOICE**
Song is a strange mix of slurred whistles and electrical static-
type sounds, usually ending in a staccato, mechanical rattle; call
is a soft *tchut*. **STATUS AND HABITAT** Formerly primarily a Mexican species that is now very common in southwestern U.S.,
favoring open habitats from farmland to parks and gardens;
year-round resident in most parts, but range extends north in
summer. **OBSERVATION TIPS** Noisy and conspicuous.

COWBIRDS and GRACKLES

BRONZED COWBIRD

MALE

FEMALE

COMMON GRACKLE

MALE, PURPLE

MALE, BRONZED

GREAT-TAILED GRACKLE

MALE

Icteridae

SCOTT'S ORIOLE *Icterus parisorum* L 9 in

Dry-country oriole, with a slender and pointed bill. Sexes are dissimilar. **ADULT MALE** Has a black back, hood, and breast, and otherwise yellow underparts. From below, tail is yellow and dark-tipped; from above it is black with yellow sides to base of outer feathers. Wings are black overall, but with a yellow "shoulder," white wing bar, and white edges to flight feathers. **ADULT FEMALE** Black elements of male plumage on head and back are replaced with mottled olive-gray; some birds have more intense black on face, and on breast. "Shoulder" patch is less extensive than in male. **IMMATURE** Recalls dull version of respective sex adult with two pale wing bars (not wing bar and "shoulder" patch); male has dark breast, but mottled head and back, and female is dull olive-yellow overall, darkest on head and streaked on back. **VOICE** Song is a jaunty series of dancing, fluty whistles; call is a harsh *tchek*. **STATUS AND HABITAT** Locally common summer visitor (mainly Apr–Aug) to desert hillsides where yuccas grade into oak and juniper woodland; winters in Mexico. **OBSERVATION TIPS** Easy to see. **SIMILAR SPECIES Audubon's Oriole** *I. graduacauda* (L 9.5–10 in) adult has black hood and chest, olive-yellow back, and yellow underparts, and black wings with white wing bar and edges to flight feathers; head is olive-yellow in immature. Resident in waterside woodland in Rio Grande valley; range does not overlap with that of Scott's. **OBSERVATION TIPS** Secretive and tricky to see.

MALE

AUDUBON'S ORIOLE

FEMALE

ORCHARD ORIOLE *Icterus spurius* L 7.25–7.5 in

Our smallest oriole; has a slender, pointed, and slightly downcurved bill. Sexes are dissimilar. **ADULT MALE** Has a black hood, chest, and back, and brick-red underparts and "shoulder." Wings are black, with a white wing bar and white edges to flight feathers. Rump is brick-red and tail is black. **ADULT AND IMMATURE FEMALE** Have mostly yellow plumage, grading to olive-yellow on back. Dark wings have two white wing bars and white edges to flight feathers. Rump is yellow and tail is grayish. **IMMATURE MALE** Has a black face and throat, but otherwise mostly yellow plumage, grading to olive-yellow on back. Dark wings have two white wing bars and white edges to flight feathers. **VOICE** Song is a jaunty series of fluty whistles; call is a harsh chatter. **STATUS AND HABITAT** Locally common summer visitor (mainly May–Aug) to open wooded habitats, including orchards, parks, and waterside woodlands. Winters mainly in Central America. **OBSERVATION TIPS** Fairly easy to see in suitable habitats.

BALTIMORE ORIOLE *Icterus galbula* L 8.5–8.75 in

Colorful woodland bird. Bill is slender, pointed, and gray with a dark culmen. Sexes are dissimilar. **ADULT MALE** Has black hood and back, and orange "shoulder" and underparts. Dark wings have white wing bar and white edges to flight feathers. Rump is orange and tail is orange with dark base and midline. **ADULT FEMALE** Similar, but hood and back are variably mottled dark olive-brown, and "shoulder" stripe is white; rump and tail are dull orange-buff. **IMMATURES** Recall adult female, but male is richer orange on breast and undertail coverts; female is much paler overall, especially on belly. **VOICE** Song is a whistling *chewdi-chewdi-chew-chew-che*, uttered as though bird is losing enthusiasm; call is a rattle. **STATUS AND HABITAT** Common summer visitor (mainly May–Aug) to woodlands. Winters mainly in Central and South America; a few in southeastern U.S. **OBSERVATION TIPS** Easy to see.

MALE, 1ST-SUMMER

SCOTT'S ORIOLE

MALE

FEMALE

MALE

ORCHARD ORIOLE

FEMALE

MALE

MALE,
1ST-SUMMER

FEMALE

BALTIMORE
ORIOLE

FEMALE

MALE

Icteridae

BULLOCK'S ORIOLE *Icterus bullockii* L 8.75–9 in

Colorful oriole that is the western counterpart of Baltimore; formerly, both were lumped together as single species, Northern Oriole. Male
is unmistakable; confusion is possible between females and immatures of
both species, although ranges barely overlap. Identification of dull individuals
requires experience and may not be possible in some cases. But overall, immature Bullock's in fall has a brighter yellow face and neck than Baltimore and
back is plain gray (Baltimore's back has faint dark streaks). To add to the
confusion, hybridization occurs in narrow zone of overlap on Great Plains.
Sexes are dissimilar. **ADULT MALE** Has mainly orange face and underparts with
black back, nape, crown, eyestripe, and narrow line on throat. Black wings have white edges to flight
feathers and broad white patch on coverts. Rump is orange and orange tail is marked with an inverted
black "T." **ADULT AND IMMATURE FEMALES** Have an olive-gray back, pale yellow hood and breast, and
otherwise mostly whitish underparts. Wings are blackish with white edges to flight feathers and two
white wing bars. Rump and tail are yellowish. **IMMATURE MALE** Recalls adult male in terms of plumage
pattern overall, but orange elements of plumage are yellow (very pale on belly), back is streaked olive-
gray, and crown is grayish yellow. **VOICE** Song is a brisk, whistled *tch-t'tch-pe'wee-tu-wee-weep*; call
is a dry *tchup*. **STATUS AND HABITAT** Common and widespread summer visitor (mainly May–Aug) to
open woodland, especially waterside habitats where cottonwoods and willows flourish; winters
mostly in Mexico. **OBSERVATION TIPS** Although not unduly shy, surprisingly easy to overlook when
foraging unobtrusively in dappled foliage.

HOODED ORIOLE *Icterus cucullatus* L 8–8.25 in

As colorful as Bullock's Oriole, but slimmer-bodied and proportionately longer-tailed. Bill is slender and downcurved. Sexes are dissimilar. **ADULT MALE** Has mostly either rich yellow body plumage (western
birds) or orange body plumage (eastern birds). All birds have black face and
throat and black back. Wings are black with two white wing bars and white
edges to flight feathers. Tail is dark. In winter, pale feathers can be seen
on back. **ADULT AND IMMATURE FEMALES** Have mostly dull yellow face and
underparts, palest on flanks. Crown, nape, and back are olive-gray and dark
wings have two white wing bars and white edges to flight feathers. Rump and

ALTAMIRA ORIOLE

ADULT

tail are olive-gray. **IMMATURE MALE** Recalls
female, but by first spring has acquired incomplete
version of adult's black face and throat. **VOICE**
Song is a rapid series of chattering, warbling
phrases; call is a harsh *tchet* or *tchew*. **STATUS AND
HABITAT** Locally common summer visitor (mainly
Apr–Aug) to open woodland in southwest, often
near water and sometimes in suburban areas;
winters in Mexico. **OBSERVATION TIPS** Usually
easy to see and sometimes quite bold. **SIMILAR
SPECIES Altamira Oriole** *I. gularis* (L 10–10.5 in)
is appreciably larger with a stouter bill. Sexes are
similar and, compared to male Hooded, adult
Altamira has less extensive black throat and
orange (not white) "shoulder." Immature is similar to adult, but black elements of plumage are
less intense and orange elements are duller. A
mainly Mexican species with a resident toehold in
Lower Rio Grande valley in southern Texas;
favors open, riverside woodlands.

MALE, BREEDING

BULLOCK'S ORIOLE

FEMALE

MALE, 1ST-SPRING

FEMALE

HOODED ORIOLE

MALE

Fringillidae

AMERICAN GOLDFINCH
Carduelis tristis L 5–5.25 in

Familiar bird of weedy fields. Forms flocks outside breeding season and often feeds on thistle seeds. Breeding male is stunning. Sexes are dissimilar. **ADULT BREEDING MALE** Has largely bright yellow plumage with contrasting black cap and forehead; mostly black wings have a faint yellow wing bar. Rump and undertail coverts are white and contrast with black tail. **ADULT NONBREEDING MALE** Recalls breeding male, but yellow elements of plumage are yellow-buff above (brightest on face), grading to

ADULT, NONBREEDING

grayish white on belly; black on crown and forehead are usually absent. Wing bar on greater coverts is more apparent and pale lesser coverts (bright yellow in breeding male) are whitish and form a second wing bar. **ADULT FEMALE** Similar to winter male, but brighter yellow overall in summer (with white upper wing bar, buff lower one) and grayer overall in winter (when both wing bars are buff). **JUVENILE** Recalls nonbreeding female, but duller. **VOICE** Song is a series of chattering whistles and squeaks; calls include a tinkling whistle. **STATUS AND HABITAT** Common in open woodland and forest edge; resident across much of range, but a summer visitor in north. **OBSERVATION TIPS** Easy to see.

LESSER GOLDFINCH
Carduelis psaltria L 4.5–4.75 in

Striking southwestern specialty. Forms flocks outside breeding season and then often seen on roadside thistles. Sexes are dissimilar. **ADULT MALE** Has bright yellow underparts. Eastern ssp. *psaltria* has mostly black upperparts, but with white wing bar and wing patch, and white on tertials; mostly black tail has striking white patches on sides. Western ssp. *hesperophila* has black cap, olive nape and back, and black wings with similar white markings. **ADULT FEMALE** Has yellowish underparts and olive-green upperparts with dark wings showing two faint wing bars, small white patch (base of primaries), and white edges to tertials. Some individuals are much brighter than others. **JUVENILE** Similar to female; immature male soon acquires hint of adult's black cap and forehead. **VOICE** Song is a varied, rambling series of short, chirpy whistles and squeaks; call is a sharp, whistled *tee-oo*. **STATUS AND HABITAT** Favors dry, open woodland; resident in much of range, but interior birds move south in fall. **OBSERVATION TIPS** Easy to see.

LAWRENCE'S GOLDFINCH
Carduelis lawrencei L 4.75–5 in

Attractive California specialty. Forms flocks outside breeding season and often feeds on thistle seeds. Sexes are dissimilar. **ADULT BREEDING MALE** Has a black face, throat, and forecrown, pale gray cheeks, and gray nape and back. Blackish wings have two broad, yellow wing bars and yellow edges to flight feathers. Center of breast and belly are yellow, but underparts are otherwise gray. In flight, yellowish rump contrasts with dark tail. **ADULT NONBREEDING MALE** Similar, but gray elements of upperparts are olive-brown. **ADULT BREEDING FEMALE** Recalls adult breeding male, but is much paler overall, without black on face and only hint of yellow in plumage. **ADULT NONBREEDING FEMALE** Recalls breeding female, but upperparts are browner. **JUVENILE** Recalls nonbreeding female, but is streaked. **VOICE** Song is series of tinkling, whistling notes; call is tinkling and belllike. **STATUS AND HABITAT** Favors dry, weedy areas, woodland edges and sometimes gardens. Local, but precise occurrence is unpredictable: mostly resident, sometimes present locally in good numbers, but nomadic or migratory in winter. **OBSERVATION TIPS** Easiest to find in winter.

FEMALE, BREEDING

MALE, BREEDING

AMERICAN GOLDFINCH

LESSER GOLDFINCH

FEMALE

MALE, EASTERN

MALE, WESTERN

LAWRENCE'S GOLDFINCH

FEMALE

MALE

Fringillidae

RED CROSSBILL *Loxia curvirostra* L 6–6.25 in

Plump-bodied finch, whose bill has cross-tipped mandibles (feature shared only with White-winged); used to extract seeds from between scales of conifer cones. Precise size and shape of bill varies subtly across region and several forms (possibly even species) occur, each adapted to feed on different conifer species. Forms nomadic flocks outside breeding season. Sexes are dissimilar. **ADULT MALE** Has mostly deep red plumage overall, darkest and brownest on wings and tail. Note, some birds show indistinct pale wing bars (cf. White-winged). **ADULT FEMALE** Has dull yellow-green

plumage overall, darkest and brownest on wings and tail. **JUVENILE** Brown and heavily streaked, paler below than above. First-year male recalls adult female, but plumage is yellow-orange. First-year female is similar to adult female. **VOICE** Song begins with, and includes, several flight-call-like *kip-kip* notes, and often ends in a buzzing trill. Experts can discern differences in calls among separate populations. **STATUS AND HABITAT** Locally common resident of mature coniferous forests. Irruptive and wandering behavior make precise occurrence hard to predict. **OBSERVATION TIPS** Listen for its distinctive call.

WHITE-WINGED CROSSBILL
Loxia leucoptera L 6.5–6.75 in

Cross-tipped mandibles and bold white wing bars make for easy recognition (wing bars are much more striking than on variant Red Crossbill). Forms roving flocks outside breeding season. Sexes are dissimilar. **ADULT MALE** Has bright pinkish red plumage overall, palest and grayest on belly and flanks. Dark wings have two broad white wing bars; tail is blackish. **ADULT FEMALE** Has streaked, dull olive-yellow plumage overall, but dark wings show similar pattern to male. **JUVENILE** Brownish and heavily streaked, paler below than above; wing bars are less distinct than on adult. First-year male recalls adult male, but red elements of plumage are bright pinkish yellow. First-year female is similar to adult female. **VOICE** Song is a series of vibrating trills and whistles; flight call is a sharp *chip-chip*. **STATUS AND HABITAT** Fairly common resident of northern coniferous forests, especially favoring larch and spruce. Occurrence is hard to predict: wanders in search of ripe cones. **OBSERVATION TIPS** Feeding flocks can be hard to find.

PINE GROSBEAK *Pinicola enucleator* L 9–9.25 in

Plump-bodied finch with a stout, stubby bill. Sometimes forms small flocks outside breeding season, but often seen in ones and twos. Feeds on buds, seeds, and fruits. Typically, indifferent to observers, allowing great views. In all birds, eye is emphasized by dark eyeline and subtle pale, elongate "eyelids." Sexes are dissimilar. **ADULT MALE** Has pinkish red plumage overall with varying amounts of gray on flanks and belly.

Tail is dark and blackish wings have two striking white wing bars. **ADULT FEMALE** Shares male's dark tail and blackish wings with two white wing bars, but plumage is otherwise mostly grayish with varying amounts of olive-yellow on head, back, and rump. **JUVENILE** Brown overall, with pale wing bars. First-year birds are similar to adult female. **VOICE** Song comprises far-carrying, whistled phrases, such as *p'wee-wee, p'wee-wee, p'wee-wee...*; call is a whistled *piew*. **STATUS AND HABITAT** Local in coniferous forests; wanders and partly migratory outside breeding season. **OBSERVATION TIPS** Usually found in small numbers.

JUVENILE

MALE

RED
CROSSBILL

MALE, MOLTING

JUVENILE

WHITE-WINGED
CROSSBILL

FEMALE

MALE

PINE GROSBEAK

MALE

Fringillidae

PINE SISKIN *Carduelis pinus* L 5–5.25 in

Small finch with a slender, dainty bill. Feeds primarily on seeds; those of birch, alder, and spruce are favored. Forms roving flocks in winter and visits bird feeders. Sexes are dissimilar. **ADULT MALE** Brown overall, and heavily streaked above, its whitish underparts also heavily streaked; some birds have yellow-washed underparts. Wings have two wing bars, upper one narrow and white, lower one broad and tinged yellow; edges of flight feathers are variably yellow (obvious in flight and when perched). **ADULT FEMALE** Similar to plain-colored male; yellow elements of wing feathering are much less intense than the brighter males. **JUVENILE** Similar to adult female, but plumage is washed buff-yellow overall. **VOICE** Song is a mix of chattering trills and wheezy whistles; call is a buzzing *zhreee*. **STATUS AND HABITAT** Common in coniferous and deciduous forests; found year-round in parts of range, but northern breeders move south for winter and wander, often visiting parks and gardens. **OBSERVATION TIPS** Attract it to your garden using seed feeders.

COMMON REDPOLL *Carduelis flammea* L 5–5.25 in

Compact, well-marked little finch. Pointed bill has curved culmen (Hoary's bill is stubby and culmen is straight). Feeds mainly on seeds, especially in winter, notably those of alder and birch. Forms roving flocks outside breeding season. Sexes are dissimilar. **ADULT MALE** Has heavily streaked gray-brown upperparts, the wings with two white wing bars and white edges to flight feathers. Head is streaked gray with a red forecrown ("poll") and black face. Underparts are whitish overall, but heavily streaked on flanks. Breeding male has breast and flanks flushed pinkish red; this character is usually lost in winter although flanks are often flushed buff. **ADULT FEMALE** Similar to seasonal male, but always lacks red flush on breast. **JUVENILE** Buffy brown, heavily streaked and lacks adult's red forecrown (acquired by fall). **VOICE** Song comprises rattling twitters and vibrating trills; call is a rattling *ji'ji'ji....* **STATUS AND HABITAT** Common breeder in northern forests; present year-round in parts of range, but northern breeders move south in fall and winter range extends to northern U.S. **OBSERVATION TIPS** Flocks are best located by call.

HOARY REDPOLL *Carduelis hornemanni* L 5–5.5 in

Similar to Common Redpoll, but much paler, with a smaller, stubbier bill and white, unstreaked (or nearly so) rump. Underparts are much less streaked than Common Redpoll counterparts. Forms flocks outside breeding season and sometimes mixes with Common. Sexes are dissimilar. **ADULT MALE** Has buffy white upperparts with streaking on back and nape.

FEMALE

Head has pale gray face, red forecrown, and limited black at base of bill and on throat. Underparts are white, with faint dark streaks on flanks; in breeding season, breast is flushed pale pink, but this character is usually absent in winter. **ADULT FEMALE** Similar to winter adult male, but with subtly more noticeable streaking on flanks. **JUVENILE** Similar to adult female, but more heavily streaked on flanks and with buff wash to face and flanks. **VOICE** Song and calls are similar to Common Redpoll. **STATUS AND HABITAT** Breeds in tundra scrub; wanders south in fall and winter range extends across Canada. **OBSERVATION TIPS** Visit the high Arctic in summer or search for individuals among Common Redpoll flocks in winter.

ADULT

MALE

PINE SISKIN

COMMON REDPOLL

ADULT

ADULT

FEMALE

MALE

MALE

HOARY REDPOLL

Fringillidae

GRAY-CROWNED ROSY-FINCH
Leucosticte tephrocotis L 6–6.5 in

Hardy finch that favors Arctic or alpine habitats. Forms flocks outside breeding season and often searches for seeds at edge of snowfields. In flight, all birds show very pale flight feathers on underwing. All birds have black bills in summer, yellow in winter. Several subspecies exist, separable on plumage differences, range, and habitat. Sexes are separable. **ADULT MALE** Has black forecrown and throat, rosy wing coverts, rosy edges to flight feathers, and rosy rump and belly. Interior breeders (ssp. *tephrocotis*) have gray rear crown and warm brown cheeks, breast, and streaked back. Coastal breeders (ssp. *littoralis* aka "Hepburn's") are similar, but cheeks, as well as rear crown, are gray. Bering Sea island breeders also have gray cheeks, but back and breast, are blackish brown. **ADULT FEMALE** Similar to respective

ADULT, WINTER, INTERIOR

subspecies male, but paler overall; pink elements of plumage are less intense. **JUVENILE** Brown overall, with pale edges to wing feathers. **VOICE** Song is a descending series of call-like whistles; call is a harsh *chew*. **STATUS AND HABITAT** Locally common in suitable open ground habitats, particularly tundra. Interior breeders nest above treeline from central Alaska to northern Rockies, while coastal breeders nest from northwestern Alaska to Oregon; both subspecies move south for winter, typically found at high elevations. Bering Sea island birds are resident. **OBSERVATION TIPS** Fairly easy to find in summer at edges of melting snow.

BROWN-CAPPED ROSY-FINCH
Leucosticte australis L 6–6.25 in

High-altitude finch. Forms flocks outside breeding season and often feeds at edge of melting snow. All birds have black bill in summer, yellow in winter. Sexes are dissimilar in plumage terms. **ADULT MALE** Has warm brown plumage overall with dark crown and rosy pink wing coverts, rump, and belly; flight feathers are edged pale pink. **ADULT FEMALE** Recalls adult male, but plumage is more uniform brown overall, with very little pink. **JUVENILE** Recalls adult female, but plumage is grayer overall. **VOICE** Song comprises a series of harsh *chew* call notes. **STATUS AND HABITAT** Specialty of eastern Rockies, found mostly in Colorado, but also in southern Wyoming. Breeds in tundralike habitat above treeline and descends to lower elevations in winter; precise winter distribution is influenced by snow depth. **OBSERVATION TIPS** Mt. Evans Scenic Byway in the Rockies is a likely spot in summer.

BLACK ROSY-FINCH *Leucosticte atrata* L 6–6.25 in

Rocky Mountain specialty with smart plumage. Confusion is possible with interior Gray-crowned (winter ranges overlap), but plumage lacks that species' warm brown tone and is blacker overall. Forms flocks outside breeding season and feeds at edges of snowfields.

FEMALE

Sometimes nests and roosts in manmade structures. Sexes are dissimilar. **ADULT MALE** Has largely blackish plumage with some gray feather edging on back and breast; rear of crown is gray and has rosy pink wing coverts, edges to flight feathers, and flush on belly. **ADULT FEMALE** Similar, but plumage shows much less color and contrast, black elements of plumage being grayish. **JUVENILE** Gray overall, with two pink wing bars and pale flight feather edges. **VOICE** Song is a series of *chuup* call notes. **STATUS AND HABITAT** Breeds above treeline; snow cover forces dispersal and descent to lower elevations in winter. **OBSERVATION TIPS** Make use of ski facilities to visit this species' inhospitable home.

GRAY-CROWNED ROSY-FINCH

ADULT, WINTER, INTERIOR

ADULT, WINTER, HEPBURN'S

BROWN-CAPPED ROSY-FINCH

ADULT, WINTER

BLACK ROSY-FINCH

MALE, WINTER

Fringillidae

HOUSE FINCH *Carpodacus mexicanus* L 5.75–6 in

Aptly-named because of its association with people; often visits garden bird feeders. Confusion is possible with related species; habitat is a good pointer, but note House's stubby bill with curved culmen (straightish in Purple and Cassin's), male's brown cheeks and streaked flanks, and female's gray-brown plumage overall (including underparts) and rather plain face. Sexes are dissimilar. **ADULT MALE** Typically has bright red breast, rump, forehead, and supercilium; center of crown, nape, and back are brown and dark wing has two white wing bars and pale edges to flight feathers. Belly and rest of underparts are mostly white, with clear demarcation from red breast, and bold streaks on flanks. Birds in east of range in particular have orange tone to breast. **ADULT FEMALE** Has gray-brown plumage, streaked above and below, with two pale wing bars and pale edges to flight feathers. **JUVENILE** Similar to adult female. **VOICE** Song is a series of rich, chattering phrases; call is a shrill *whee'ert*. **STATUS AND HABITAT** Formerly a western species, now widespread due to introductions elsewhere, and an abundant resident of lightly wooded habitats, parks, and gardens. Has benefited from man's alteration of environment. **OBSERVATION TIPS** Hard to miss.

FEMALE

PURPLE FINCH *Carpodacus purpureus* L 5.75–6 in

Plump, relatively large-headed finch. Culmen of conical bill is only very slightly curved. Forms small flocks outside breeding season. Sexes are dissimilar. **ADULT MALE** Has mostly reddish pink head and breast, color grading into reddish brown wash and indistinct streaks on flanks; underparts are otherwise whitish in eastern birds, but mucky gray in western birds, all with unstreaked undertail coverts. Back is streaked pinkish brown and dark wings have two pinkish buff wing bars and buffy edges to flight feathers. **ADULT FEMALE** Has mostly streaked gray-brown upperparts; contrast between pale supercilium, submustachial stripe and throat, and darker ear coverts and malar stripe is greater in eastern birds than western ones. Underparts are whitish with dark streaks (except on undertail coverts), markings more distinct in eastern birds than western ones. **JUVENILE** Similar to adult female. Males remain brown in their first year but become sexually mature, sing, and attempt to breed. **VOICE** Song is a burst of rich, warbling notes; call is a sharp *pik*. **STATUS AND HABITAT** Common in coniferous forests. Western birds are resident or altitudinal migrants, with some dispersal; northern breeders move south and east in fall, wintering in southeastern U.S. **OBSERVATION TIPS** Easy to see.

CASSIN'S FINCH *Carpodacus cassinii* L 6.25–6.5 in

Similar to Purple, but slightly larger and ranges of two species barely overlap. Bill is conical, with straight culmen. Forms small flocks outside breeding season. Sexes are dissimilar. **ADULT MALE** Has a bright reddish pink crown and reddish pink throat, breast, and rump. Nape and back are streaked brown, and dark wings have two pinkish wing bars and pale edges to flight feathers. Breast color grades into pinkish flush on flanks; underparts are otherwise whitish, with faint streaks toward rear of flanks and on undertail coverts (these are unstreaked in Purple). **ADULT FEMALE** Has streaked brown upperparts, two pale wing bars, and whitish underparts with bold, distinct streaks (including on undertail coverts). **JUVENILE** Similar to adult female. Males remain brown in their first year but become sexually mature, sing, and attempt to breed. **VOICE** Song is a rapid, chirpy warble; calls include a slurred *tch'wu*. **STATUS AND HABITAT** Locally common in montane coniferous forests; moves to lower elevations in bad winter weather. **OBSERVATION TIPS** Fairly easy to see within range.

MALE

MALE

HOUSE
FINCH

MALE, ORANGE FORM

FEMALE

PURPLE
FINCH

MALE

FEMALE

CASSIN'S
FINCH

MALE

Fringillidae and Passeridae

EVENING GROSBEAK
Coccothraustes vespertinus L 8–8.25 in

A giant among finches, with a plump body, relatively large head, and massive, conical bill. Unobtrusive when breeding, but forms large, noisy, and conspicuous flocks in winter; these are regular visitors to bird feeders. In some years, food shortages cause irruptive movements beyond usual winter range. Sexes are dissimilar. **ADULT MALE** Strikingly marked and unmistakable. Has a bright yellow forehead, supercilium, and flanks. Lower back is bright yellow, grading through golden yellow to dull brown on neck and crown. Underparts are golden yellow, flushed bright yellow on flanks. Tail is black and mostly black wings have white secondaries and tertials; these appear as a striking panel when perched and in flight. Bill is grayish. **ADULT FEMALE** Plumage is mostly gray-buff with hint of yellow wash on underparts. Mostly black tail has a white tip and mostly black wings have white bases to inner primaries and edges to tertials. Bill is grayish. **JUVENILE** Recalls similar sex adult in terms of

FEMALE

patterns; female coloration is like adult female, while in male yellow elements of adult plumage are buffy brown. First-year males look like adult males except white wing patches have brown markings. **VOICE** Song is presumed to be a series of *pee-irp* call notes. **STATUS AND HABITAT** Widespread and common in mixed and coniferous forests. Resident across much of its range in many years, although some altitudinal movements and dispersal occur outside breeding season. More significant irruptive movements south of usual range occur in some winters. **OBSERVATION TIPS** Easy to see at feeders within range.

HOUSE SPARROW *Passer domesticus* L 6–6.25 in

Introduced from the Old World, but now a familiar bird across much of North America, mainly because of its affinity for human habitation and easy tolerance of manmade habitats. Seldom seen far from houses and farms; frequently dust-bathes and small groups are often seen sitting on roofs, uttering familiar sparrow chirps. Where it is fed in urban parks, it can become remarkably tame, sometimes even taking food from the hand. Sexes are dissimilar. **ADULT MALE** Has a gray crown, cheeks, and rump. Nape, sides of crown, back, and wings are chestnut-brown, underparts are pale gray, and throat and breast are black. Bill is dark and legs are reddish. In winter, chestnut and black elements of plumage are less intense (due to pale feather fringes) and bill is paler. **ADULT FEMALE** Has mainly brown upperparts, including crown; back is streaked with buff. Underparts are pale gray and note the pale buff supercilium behind eye. **JUVENILE** Similar to adult female, but plumage pattern is less distinct. **VOICE** Utters a range of chirping calls; in combination, these comprise the song. **STATUS AND HABITAT** Has flourished since its introduction to North America, first to New York City in mid-19th century; it is now common and widespread in a wide range of manmade and man-manipulated environments, namely town parks, gardens, and farms. Species is faring better in the New World than in many parts of its native Europe. **OBSERVATION TIPS** Hard to miss.

EVENING GROSBEAK

MALE

HOUSE SPARROW

MALE, SUMMER

FEMALE

MALE, WINTER

EMPEROR GOOSE *Chen canagica* L 25–27 in

Recalls blue morph Ross's or Snow Goose (*see* p.24), but plumage is much smarter, adult having well-defined white head and hindneck, black throat and foreneck, and blue-gray body plumage with scalloped pattern created by feathers' black subterminal bands and white edges. Bering Sea specialty; breeds in eastern Siberia and western Alaska, winters on coasts of Aleutian Islands. Casual south to California.

EUROPEAN TEAL *Anas crecca crecca* L 14–14.5 in

Eurasian counterpart of Green-winged Teal (*see* p.32), with identical behavior and habitat preferences. Adult male has almost identical plumage to male Green-winged, but vertical white line on flanks is missing; instead, shows horizontal white line where wings meet flanks. Female is not separable from female Green-winged in the field. Regular in Alaska and south to Washington.

TUFTED DUCK *Aythya fuligula* L 17–17.5 in

Eurasian counterpart of similar Ring-necked (*see* p.38). Head is rounded (not peaked) and has tuft at rear of crown (most pronounced in male). Male has mainly glossy black plumage, with white flanks; bill is mainly gray, becoming pale toward the black tip. Female has mostly brown plumage, palest on flanks, often with white feathering at base of dark-tipped bill; lacks female Ring-necked's "spectacle." Regular in Alaska and south to Washington.

SPECTACLED EIDER *Somateria fischeri* L 20–21 in

Bulky seaduck. Recalls Common Eider (*see* p.48), but all birds have a dark-framed, pale "spectacle" surrounding eye. In male it is white on an otherwise mostly lime-green head; the bill is pink. In female, it is pale gray-buff and contrasts with the otherwise brown, finely patterned plumage; the bill is gray. High Arctic, Alaskan specialty, wintering in Bering Sea.

STELLER'S EIDER *Polysticta stelleri* L 17 in

Compact seaduck with a dainty bill. Male has white head, with black eye patch and chin, lime green topknot, black stern, and black flight feathers; upperparts are otherwise white with black lines and underparts are tinged orange-buff with black spot on flanks. Female is rather uniformly brown. High Arctic Alaskan breeder, winters around Aleutians.

GRAYLAG GOOSE *Anser anser* L 34–35 in

Ancestor of domesticated goose, often seen in its ancestral wild-type plumage, but also as pure white. Wild-type bird has gray-brown plumage overall with white stern and pale panels on wing, seen in flight. Bill is stout and pink. Widespread in Eurasia, both wild and domesticated, and in North America widely kept in captivity from which it regularly escapes.

GRAYLAG GOOSE

ADULTS

BAR-HEADED GOOSE *Anser indicus* L 30–31 in

Distinctive Asian waterfowl species that is widely kept in captivity and which occasionally escapes. Adult has mainly gray body plumage with white stern. Neck is gray overall, but with dark nape and white stripe on side. White head is marked with two black bars. Bill is pinkish yellow and legs are orange-yellow.

EMPEROR GOOSE

ADULT

MALE

EUROPEAN TEAL

MALE

FEMALE

TUFTED DUCK

MALE

SPECTACLED EIDER

FEMALE

MALE

MALE

STELLER'S EIDER

GRAYLAG GOOSE

BAR-HEADED GOOSE

ADULT

ADULT

COMMON SHELDUCK *Tadorna tadorna* L 25–26 in

Goose-sized duck. Common on coasts and wetlands in Europe and Asia. In North America, occasionally escapes from captivity. Adult has green-glossed head and neck (often looks black), black back and flight feathers, and otherwise white plumage, except for orange breast band and flush on undertail coverts. Legs are pink and bill is red, male with a large basal knob. Juvenile shows less plumage contrast than adult.

RUDDY SHELDUCK *Tadorna ferruginea* L 25–26 in

Attractive, goose-sized duck. Widespread Asian wetland species, often kept in captivity. Adult has mostly orange-brown body plumage, with black flight feathers and white wing coverts, above and below. Neck is orange-buff grading to whitish on face; demarcation between neck and body plumage is clearly defined and marked with narrow black collar in male. Juvenile is paler overall than adult.

EGYPTIAN GOOSE
Alopochen aegyptiacus L 26–27 in

Distinctive African goose that is often kept in captivity and sometimes escapes. Adult has buff plumage overall, grayest on breast (which has dark central spot) and palest on head and neck (eye is dark-masked). Wings have black flight feathers and white coverts, bill is pink, and legs are red. Juvenile is paler overall than adult.

MANDARIN DUCK *Aix galericulata* L 16–18 in

Exotic duck that recalls Wood Duck (*see* p.28). Sadly, probably commoner in captivity today than in the wild, in its native China. Male has a striking orange mane with a broad, white supercilium, and orange "sails" near stern. Flanks are finely marked buff and separated from darker breast by vertical black and white lines. Female is similar to female Wood Duck, but has a white eyering, not large white eye surround, and is grayer overall, with more striking pale spots on flanks.

MALE

ANHINGA

ANHINGA *Anhinga anhinga* L 34–35 in

Unmistakable slim waterbird. Swims low in water often with just slender head and neck visible. Perches on branches with wings outstretched to dry. Found in fish-rich swamps and lakes. Easy to see on Gulf Coast.

RED-FACED CORMORANT
Phalacrocorax urile L 29–32 in

Has mainly glossy black plumage, with brownish wings and white thigh patch when breeding. Compared to similar but smaller Pelagic Cormorant (*see* p.80), has larger, blue-based bill and brighter, more extensive red facial skin, particularly when breeding. Restricted mainly to Pribilof and Aleutian Islands, where resident. Easy to see on St. Paul Island, Pribilofs.

CALIFORNIA CONDOR *Gymnogyps californianus* L 44–46; W 109–110 in

Unmistakable on account of immense size and silhouette in flight (the typical view). Recalls an oversized Black Vulture (*see* p.88), with proportionately longer, broader-based wings. Plumage is mostly black, but adult has white underwing coverts and white inner flight feathers on upper wing. Bald, red head is seen only at close range. Juvenile plumage shows less contrast than adult. Formerly extinct in wild; captive-bred birds now fly free in the Grand Canyon and at Big Sur, California.

ADULT

COMMON SHELDUCK
MALE

RUDDY SHELDUCK
MALE

EGYPTIAN GOOSE
ADULT

MANDARIN DUCK
MALE

FEMALE

RED-FACED CORMORANT
ADULT

CALIFORNIA CONDOR
ADULT

BAR-TAILED GODWIT *Limosa lapponica* L 15.5–16 in

Long-billed shorebird. Breeds in Arctic Eurasia and western Alaska and winters mainly in New Zealand and on Pacific coasts. Breeding male recalls Hudsonian, with variably orange-red body plumage, spangled brown and black on back; note that tail is barred (not black and white) and wings are uniform, without Hudsonian's striking white wing bar. In winter, recalls Marbled (*see* p.126), but bill is shorter and plumage is gray-buff overall, with whitish underwings (lacks Marbled's warm buff tone). The juvenile, the plumage most often seen south of Alaska, has a warm buff tone, while Marbled is reddish brown.

ADULT

ROSS'S GULL *Rhodostethia rosea* L 13–14 in

Stunning Arctic gull. Breeds mainly in Siberia (sometimes Churchill, Manitoba) and winters mostly in Arctic seas. Adult has pale gray back and upper wing, gray underwings, and otherwise mostly white plumage, including wedge-shaped tail and trailing edge to wing; in summer, underparts are faintly flushed pink. Hood is defined by neat black collar; feature reduced or absent in winter birds, which have a dark ear spot. Juvenile recalls winter adult, but has dark wing bar.

RED-LEGGED KITTIWAKE *Rissa brevirostris* L 15–17 in

Distinctive Bering Sea speciality. Breeds on island seacliffs and winters mainly at sea; easy to see on St. Paul Island, Pribilofs. Adult recalls Black-legged Kittiwake (*see* p.158), but has bright red legs. Compared to Black-legged, adult's yellow bill is shorter and gray back and upper wings are darker. Juvenile is similar to juvenile Black-legged, but black bill is shorter and lacks that species' black bar on inner wing.

ADULT

IVORY GULL *Pagophila eburnea* L 17–19 in

Beautiful Arctic gull. Breeds on Canadian high-Arctic islands and Greenland, winters mainly in Arctic seas. Vagrants occur further south in winter. Adult has pure white plumage, with black legs and eye, and yellow-tipped blue bill. First-winter is similar, but with grubby black face markings and black spots on upperparts and wingtips. Feeds on carrion and vagrants are sometimes attracted to tide-line cetacean corpses.

ALEUTIAN TERN *Sterna aleutica* L 12–12.5 in

Aleutian Island and western Alaskan specialty; presumed to winter in Pacific. Adult recalls much more numerous Arctic (*see* p.162), but back and upper wings are uniformly darker gray (without translucent areas on wing), and breast and belly are gray (not white). Bill is black (not red) and has white forehead (not entirely black cap). Juvenile recalls juvenile Arctic, but has bright orange-buff wash on back, wing coverts, and side of breast.

LONG-BILLED MURRELET *Brachyramphus perdix* L 10–12 in

Recalls Marbled Murrelet (*see* p.170), but with longer bill and subtle plumage differences: breeding adult is similarly marbled brown, but with a paler throat; winter adult is more distinctive with clear separation of blackish brown upperparts from white underparts. Note the broad white wing patch (scapulars). Breeds in northern Japan and Siberia; winters mainly in seas around Japan, but also wanders widely and vagrant in North America.

BAR-TAILED GODWIT

ADULT, WINTER

ADULT, SUMMER

ROSS'S GULL

RED-LEGGED KITTIWAKE

ADULT, WINTER

ADULT

IVORY GULL

ADULT

ALEUTIAN TERN

ADULT

LONG-BILLED MURRELET

1ST-WINTER

RED-CROWNED PARROT *Amazona viridigenalis* L 12–13 in
Endangered Mexican native, but a popular cagebird. Feral populations now thrive, locally, in California and Texas. Adult has green plumage overall, with black tips to primaries, red flash on secondaries, and red forecrown and bluish hindcrown; extent of red is greatest in male.

ROSE-RINGED PARAKEET *Psittacula krameri* L 16–16.5 in
Asian species with feral populations in California. Recognized in flight by long-tailed outline; often announces itself with loud, raucous shrieks. Plumage is mostly green, palest on head and underparts. Bill is red and male has head defined by dark collar, bordered on nape with rose-pink.

ADULT

GREEN PARAKEET *Aratinga holochlora* L 13 in
A mainly Mexican species with a limited, but expanding, range in southern Texas. Adult plumage is green overall, palest and most yellow below. Close inspection often reveals a few reddish feathers. Bill is stout and pinkish, and eyes are orange. Juvenile is similar, but with dull eyes. Usually found on margins of towns and suburbs.

NOTE: Many parrot family members—from Budgerigars to Macaws—are kept captive as pets. Inevitably, birds escape to freedom and feral populations become established from time to time, a few of which persist. The trade in captive-bred birds fuels, and to a degree, masks, the vile trade in wild-caught birds.

VIOLET-CROWNED HUMMINGBIRD *Amazilia violiceps* L 4–5 in
Rare breeding visitor (mainly Apr–Aug) to mountain scrub, mainly in southeastern Arizona, and also regularly seen at feeders in Arizona; winters in Mexico, where it is widespread. Adult has violet crown, otherwise greenish upperparts and tail, and white underparts (latter feature unique among our hummingbirds); bill is dark-tipped and red. Juvenile is like adult, but with brownish underparts.

BUFF-BELLIED HUMMINGBIRD *Amazilia yucatanensis* L 4–4.25 in
Mainly Mexican hummingbird with a toehold in southern Texas, where it breeds and occurs year-round in small numbers; most Texan birds migrate south in fall. Adult has a green head, neck, breast, and upper back, and a pale buff belly; lower back, rump, wings, and tail are reddish brown and bill is long, downcurved, dark-tipped, and reddish. Juvenile is similar, but duller.

LUCIFER HUMMINGBIRD *Calothorax lucifer* L 3.5–4 in
Tiny hummingbird with a long, downcurved bill. Male has green upperparts, purple-sheened throat, and otherwise whitish underparts, with gray-green flanks; tail is forked. Female has green upperparts and white throat; breast and flanks are washed orange-buff. Favors arid mountains and rare summer visitor (mainly Apr–Sep) to southern Arizona and southwest Texas.

ROSE-THROATED BECARD *Pachyramphus aglaiae* L 7–7.5 in
Widespread Central American species, with toehold in North America; present May–Sep in riverside woodland in southern Arizona and southern Texas. Adult male has mostly gray upperparts with dark cap, and paler gray underparts, but with a bright rose-pink throat patch. Female has similar black cap, but upperparts are warm brown and underparts are yellow-buff, without the throat patch.

THICK-BILLED KINGBIRD *Tyrannus crassirostris* L 9–9.5 in
Recalls Cassin's Kingbird (*see* p.232), but with a massive bill and much darker upperparts, particularly in adult bird. Throat is white and underparts are pale, flushed yellow on belly and undertail coverts, particularly in immature birds. Rare summer visitor (Jun–Sep) to cottonwood woodland in southern Arizona.

RED-CROWNED PARROT

ADULT

ROSE-RINGED PARAKEET

MALE

MALE

BUFF-BELLIED HUMMINGBIRD

MALE

VIOLET-CROWNED HUMMINGBIRD

MALE

LUCIFER HUMMINGBIRD

MALE

MALE

ROSE-THROATED BECARD

ADULT

THICK-BILLED KINGBIRD

SULPHUR-BELLIED FLYCATCHER *Myiodynastes luteiventris* L 8–8.5 in
Mainly Mexican species; scarce visitor to southeastern Arizona woodlands (Jun–Sep). Adult has streaked gray-brown upperparts, faint white supercilium, and bolder white "mustache"; ear coverts and malar stripe are dark. Underparts are pale, heavily streaked on breast, with yellow flush on belly and undertail coverts. Tail is reddish. Juvenile is similar, but duller.

BUFF-BREASTED FLYCATCHER *Empidonax fulvifrons* L 5–5.25 in
Large-headed flycatcher, with upright perched posture. A mainly Mexican species; occasional visitor to mountain coniferous forests in southeastern Arizona (May–Sep). Adult is gray-buff above; dark wings have two white wing bars. Eye is relatively large, with white surround and underparts are flushed rich buff, palest on throat and undertail coverts. Juvenile is similar, but duller.

BLUETHROAT *Luscinia svecica* L 5.5–5.75 in
Mainly Eurasian species that breeds (May–Aug) in western Alaska. Adults are gray-brown above, with pale supercilium and red sides to dark-tipped tail. Breeding male has blue throat with red central spot; underparts are white. Female and nonbreeding male are similar, but blue on throat is reduced or absent. Juvenile recalls female, but is warmer brown above; has dark-bordered white throat.

1ST-FALL

NORTHERN WHEATEAR
Oenanthe oenanthe L 5.5–6 in
Mainly Eurasian species that breeds (May–Aug) on tundra in Alaska and Canadian Arctic; vagrant throughout North America; winters in Africa. Plump-bodied and adopts upright posture when standing. All birds have white rump and upper tail. Call is like two stones being hit together. Adult male has blue-gray crown, nape, and back, dark wings and dark eye mask with white supercilium above. Underparts are pale, but neck and breast are variably flushed orange-buff. Female is similar, but plumage has less color and contrast. Juvenile is warm buff, darker above than below.

EASTERN YELLOW WAGTAIL *Motacilla tschutshcensis* L 6–6.5 in
Mainly Asian species that breeds in tundra scrub in western Alaska (May–Aug). Long tail and yellow underparts make male easily recognizable; note also the olive-green back, two pale wing bars on dark wings, and blue-gray crown, white supercilium, and dark cheeks. Female is similar, but less colorful. Juvenile recalls adult, but has gray upperparts and whitish underparts; note two pale wing bars and dark-bordered white throat.

1ST-WINTER

RED-THROATED PIPIT
Anthus cervinus L 6 in
Breeds in Siberia and occurs as scarce migrant in western Alaska in spring and fall; rare vagrant further south on West coast, mainly in fall, favoring short grassland. Breeding birds are striking (male especially) with brick-red face, throat, and breast. Fall birds lack this color, but have striking streaking. Call is thin and high-pitched.

ARCTIC WARBLER *Phylloscopus borealis* L 5–5.25 in
Mainly Asian species that breeds in Arctic scrub in Alaska (May–Aug). Adult has a stout, rather pale bill, mostly olive-green upperparts and grayish white underparts; note the dark eyestripe and bold white supercilium, and single white wing bar. Juvenile is similar, but brighter and more colorful.

SULPHUR-BELLIED
FLYCATCHER

ADULT

BUFF-BREASTED
FLYCATCHER

ADULT

NORTHERN
WHEATEAR

BLUETHROAT

MALE

MALE, FALL

EASTERN YELLOW
WAGTAIL

ADULT

ARCTIC
WARBLER

ADULT

GENERAL BIRDING INFORMATION

Alderfer, Jonathan, and Jon L. Dunn. (eds). 2006. *Complete Birds of North America*. National Geographic Books.

Alderfer, Jonathan, and Jon L. Dunn. 2007. *Birding Essentials*. National Geographic Books.

American Birding Association. 2002. *ABA Checklist: Birds of the Continental United States and Canada*, 6th ed. American Birding Association.

American Ornithologists' Union (AOU). 1998. *Check-list of North American Birds*, 7th ed.

Barrow, M.V. 1998. *A Passion for Birds: American Ornithology After Audubon*. Princeton University Press.

Baughman, Mel (ed). 2003. *Reference Atlas to the Birds of North America*. National Geographic Books.

Dunn, Jon L., and Jonathan Alderfer (eds). 2006. *Field Guide to the Birds of North America*, 5th ed. National Geographic Books.

Ehrlich, Paul R., Dobkin, David S., and Wheye, Darryl. 1988. *The Birder's Handbook*. Simon & Schuster/Fireside.

Elphick, Chris, John B. Dunning, Jr., and David Allen Sibley. 2001. *The Sibley Guide to Bird Life and Behavior*. Alfred A. Knopf.

Gill, Frank B. 2007. *Ornithology*, 3rd ed. W.H. Freeman.

Kaufman, Kenn. 1996. *Lives of North American Birds*. Houghton Mifflin Company.

Kerlinger, Paul. 1995. *How Birds Migrate*. Stackpole Books.

Poole, A., and F. Gill (eds). 1992–2002. *The Birds of North America*. The Academy of Natural Sciences and The American Ornithologists' Union.

Pyle, Peter, with Steve N.G. Howell, David F. DeSante, Robert P. Yunick, and Mary Gustafason. 1997. *Identification Guide to North American Birds, Part I*. Slate Creek Press.

Sibley, David A. 2000. *The Sibley Guide to Birds*. Alfred A. Knopf.

Sibley, David A. 2002. *Sibley's Birding Basics*. Alfred A. Knopf.

WEB RESOURCES

American Birding Association
www.americanbirding.org

American Ornithologists' Union
www.aou.org

Birding on the Net
www.birdingonthe.net

Brian E. Small – Bird and Nature Photography
www.briansmallphoto.com

Cornell Laboratory of Ornithology
www.birds.cornell.edu

eBird
www.ebird.org

The Birds of North America Online
www.bna.birds.cornell.edu/bna

All photographs taken by **Brian E. Small** with the exception of the following:

Nature Photographers Ltd.

Mark Bolton 387(m); Laurie Campbell 66(b), 93(bl); Kevin Carlson 95(ml), 183(b); Andrew Cleave 71(m inset), 400(b), 401(upper bl); Barry Hughes 51(tl), 52(t); Ernie Janes 51(upper mr), 95(mr), 134(b); David Osborn 35(br), 79(ml), 81(bl), 87(tr), 89(ml), 105(bl), 127(upper ml), 129(t), 131(t), 161(m), 163(lower tl), 165(upper ml & mr), 166(b); Bill Paton 51(tr), 189(br); Richard Revels 169(tr); Peter Roberts 144(b), 159(m center); Paul Sterry 8(b), 11(t & b), 13(b), 14(bl), 15(t), 17(br), 18(bl), 19(t), 22(t inset), 25(t & t inset), 26(t & b), 27(m & b), 30(t), 31(all pictures), 33(tr, upper & lower bl, & br), 35(tl & upper bl), 38(t), 39(m & m inset), 42(m), 43(m & m inset), 45(t & t inset, m & m inset, & b inset), 46(t & b), 47(m & m inset, & b & b inset), 48, 49(m & b), 51(lower mr & b), 55(br), 57(tl, tr, ml, & mr), 66(t & m), 67(t, upper ml, Red-throated Diver ad. summer, & br), 68, 69(b), 71(t, t inset, & m), 77(tl, ml, b, & b inset), 84(t), 85(tl & ml), 87(tr inset, m, & b), 100(b), 106, 107(m), 111(mr), 113(tl), 118(t), 123(b), 125(b), 131(t inset), 132(b), 133(upper bl), 134(t), 135 (upper & lower tl), 137(lower tl, upper br, & b center), 139(lower ml & br), 140, 141(tl, mr, bl, & br), 145(lower tl), 145(mr), 147(tr, b, & b inset), 149(bl), 153(tr & m), 155(m), 156(t), 157(tl), 159(ml, mr, mr inset, bl, & br), 161(t inset), 163(m & m inset), 169(tl & b), 170(t), 173(ml, mr, bl, & br), 175(t & t inset), 176, 177(all pictures), 178, 181(bl), 182, 183(t), 186(b), 187(tr), 188, 209(tr), 210, 215(m & b), 249(br), 265(ml), 269(bl), 310(t), 311 (tl & tr), 313(tl & tr), 325(m center), 331(tl), 362, 363(bl), 365(tl & tr), 395(m & b), 396, 397(upper tr, lower tr, ml, upper mr, bl, & br), 399(t, upper mr, & lower mr), 399(t & m), 400(t), 401(tr, ml, mr, & bl), 403(tr), 404(t & b), 405(ml & mr); Roger Tidman 30(bl), 44(t), 57(m center & lower mr), 67(bl), 75(tl), 92(t & b), 93(tr, upper br, & lower br), 101(t center), 104(b), 107(upper bl), 117(tl & m), 145(b & b inset), 146(t & b), 160(t), 165(tl & tr), 169(mr), 189(bl), 190, 268(t & b), 269(tl inset), 397(lower mr).

Individual photographers

Glenn Bartley 217(tr), 224; Len Blumin 374; Mike Danzenbaker 28(b), 33(tl), 36(m), 40(t, m, & b), 42(t & b), 74(t & b), 75(tr, bl, & br), 76(t), 77(tr & upper mr), 91(tr inset),

103(upper m center), 112, 114(m & b), 117(tr), 127(upper bl), 128(t), 130(b), 131(bl), 135(bl), 137(Western Sandpiper juv. flight & White-rumped Sandpiper ad. summer flight), 139(tl inset), 142(t), 145(tl), 149(lower ml), 156(m), 157(bl & br), 168, 170(b), 171(tl, tr, upper ml, upper mr, & lower m), 175(b), 179(tr), 205(tl & tr), 232(t), 267(bl), 271(tl); Stuart Healy 53(t); ©Steve Holt/VIREO 54; Phil Jeffrey 298, 323(tl); Kevin Karlson 22(t), 23(tl), 38(t & b), 41(t), 94(t), 95(bl), 101(upper ml), 114(t), 122(b), 130(t), 132(t), 138(t), 142(m & b), 151(tl), 152(b), 154(t), 158(t & b), 159(tr inset), 162(t), 170(Kittlitz's Murrelet t), 191(bl), 249(ml), 256, 264(b inset), 267(ml), 315(lower ml), 325(upper tl), 328, 333(upper tl), 338(b), 357(upper tl & b inset), 359(t), 377(tl); Russ Kerr 32, 34, 36(t), 65(t), 88(t), 94(m), 96(t), 107(tl & tr), 163(Forster's Tern r inset), 165(bl), 186(t), 189(tr inset), 262, 398(b); Greg Lasley 91(Mississippi Kite juv.), 137(br), 271(ml); Peter LaTourrette 124, 129(b inset), 137(bl), 173(t), 176, 336, 356; Wayne Lynch 107(br), 193(br); Garth McElroy 144(tl), 163(tl), 387(lower ml & lower mr); ©Philip D Moylan/VIREO 240; EJ Peiker 230; Robert Royse 49(t), 52(b); William Schmoker 79(tl); ©Robert Shantz/VIREO 180; Lloyd Spitalnik 163(tr), 221(bl), 314, 315(lower tl), 317(Northern Parula both imms), 319(lower tl), 329(tl), 353(bl), 376(t); Bob Steele 23(m), 24(b), 25(ml & br), 55(bl), 73(bl & br), 78, 82(t & b), 95(tr), 97(t inset), 98(b), 105(ml), 120(b), 121(ml & br), 122(t), 133(lower tl & lower ml), 143(br), 147(tl inset), 153(upper ml), 162(b), 171(lower tr), 174(b), 185(tl), 187(tl, bl, & br), 223(bl adult), 249(bl), 268(b), 269(br), 270(b), 280(b), 293(t inset), 299(bl), 312, 325(upper mr), 326(b), 351(bl & br), 354, 357(lower ml), 393(lower tl); Brian Sullivan 36(b), 80(br), 119(bl inset), 156(b), 270(t), 363(lower ml); ©Glen Tepke/VIREO 205(mr); U.S. Fish and Wildlife Service 172, 174(t); Gerrit Vyn 60(b), 139(bl), 278; Brian Wheeler 94(b), 95(br), 96(b), 97(Broad-winged Hawk × 3), 99(tl, t center, tr, lower ml, & lower m center), 101(tl & br inset), 103(lower ml), 105, 107(t center); Christopher Wood 27(tr), 55(tl), 76(b); Jim Zipp 136, 171(b), 185(b), 197(tl); ©T Zurkowski/VIREO 170(Kittlitz's Murrelet b).

Abbreviations: t = top, m = middle, b = bottom, l = left, r = right.